One America?

Political Leadership,

National Identity, and the

Dilemmas of Diversity

Stanley A. Renshon, Editor

GEORGETOWN UNIVERSITY PRESS / WASHINGTON, D.C.

g

Georgetown University Press, Washington, D.C.
© 2001 by Stanley A. Renshon. All rights reserved.
Printed in the United States of America

10 9 8 7 6 5 4 3 2 1   2001

This volume is printed on acid-free offset book paper.

Library of Congress Cataloging-in-Publication Data
One America? : political leadership, national identity, and the dilemmas
of diversity /
Stanley A. Renshon, editor.
       p.   cm.
Includes bibliographical references and index.
ISBN 0-87840-869-X (alk. paper) — ISBN 0-87840-870-3 (pbk. : alk. paper)
    1. National characteristics, American.   2. Group identity—United States.
3. Pluralism (Social sciences)—United States.   4. Multiculturalism—United States.
5. United States—Politics and government—1989-   6. Political leadership—United States.
7. United States—Race relations—Political aspects. 8. United States—Ethnic relations—Political Aspects.
I. Renshon, Stanley Allen.
E169.12 .049   2001
306.2—dc21   2001023259

Contents

Preface

Fueled in part by enormous and, in this century, unprecedented numbers of new immigrants, the United States is becoming dramatically more diverse—racially, ethnically, and culturally. As a result, this country now faces a number of political and cultural questions with the most profound consequences for its future. What does it mean to be an American? Is there developing a "new American identity," and if so, what is it?

At the same time, the stability of American national culture has been challenged in recent decades by an assertive expansion of individual and group rights, acerbic debates regarding the legitimacy and limits of these claims, and a preference on the part of national political leaders to finesse rather than engage these controversies. Advocates of diversity have given more attention to expanding their claims than to the requirements necessary to build a consensus that would support and sustain them. Critics of diversity have yet to explain how to accommodate the promise and reality of diversity satisfactorily without recourse to traditional forms of uniformity.

Many of the basic cultural and political frameworks on which this country was founded, and from which it developed, have become matters of intense, often angry, debate. In a country built on the ideal of merit and driven by the imperative of opportunity, how do we encourage individualism even as we attempt to recover a deeper sense of community? What is fair? Is it possible to be simultaneously a fully engaged American citizen and a citizen of another country as well? With a citizenry characterized by enormous diversity, what, if anything, binds Americans together? Are we U.S. citizens first or primarily members of our own racial, ethnic, gender, class, and religious groups?

The role of political leadership in addressing and resolving these pressing questions remains an open but critical question. Traditionally, our political leaders have defined their task as articulating their views of what is best and mobilizing others to accept it. Leadership so defined might well be appropriate when the public shares a frame of reference. It might be appropriate when the implications of alternative views and policies have been openly and honestly discussed. And it might be appropriate when common understandings have been reached.

Yet not one of these three conditions exists in contemporary American politics. A country that faces questions about whether cultural, ethnic, and psychological diversity will lead to a fragmented and dysfunctional national identity must surely ask if its traditional views of political leadership might not need to be revised. Is there a need for new forms of political leadership in countries where the basic frames of cultural and political assumption can no long be taken for granted? Do we need more heroic leadership? Or do we need leadership of a different kind altogether?

Whether diversity can be reconciled with the need for a core set of cultural, social, and political tenets able to provide the basis of a coherent and integrated national identity is one central question of this book. Assuming it is possible, then, a second question is how it might be done.

The first part of the book's title, *One America?*, minus the question mark, is borrowed from the hopeful name that Bill Clinton gave to his Initiative on Race. In those highly scripted public forums, with handpicked participants, the promise of a frank discussion rarely got much beyond bland platitudes. We hope to do better here.

Given that the issues addressed in this book are tendentious, a natural question arises as to how this book and its contributors are situated. The answer is that I have tried to place the book's center of gravity in the range of informed reflection that embraces both the thoughtful left and right of center. Some contributors are on one side of that spectrum, some are on the other, and many are squarely positioned between them. My primary purpose though, was not to achieve a book of perfectly balanced political views; rather, it was to provide a meeting place for well-articulated and thoughtful considerations of the core problems that frame its central concerns. It is my hope that the merits of the arguments advanced herein, the quality of the questions they raise, and the extent to which they stimulate our understanding of these critical issues will provide informed voices in a dialogue this country badly needs but has difficulty developing.

All books represent collaboration, and this one especially is no exception. I first want to express my appreciation to the contributors for agreeing to lend their considerable talents and knowledge to this effort. I appreciate their patience and willingness to respond to the questions and thoughts their work stimulated as I read them. I learned much from those exchanges and am thankful for having had the chance to do so.

I am also very fortunate to have Andrew Blauner as my literary representative. From the morning we met over a long coffee, it was clear that we were a good match. I truly appreciate his support and efforts on behalf of my work.

John Samples, formerly director of Georgetown University Press and now at the Cato Institute, saw merit in this book and gave us all the strong feeling that it had found a good home. All of the Georgetown University Press staff were equally enthusiastic and helpful.

In the past few years, I benefited from the support of several institutions while working on the ideas that shaped this book. A research fellowship from the Center for Immigration Studies in Washington, D.C. helped me in my thinking about the impact of immigration on American national identity and culture. A research fellowship at The Institute on Race and Social Division at Boston University helped me to reflect on racial and ethnic relationships in America. Grants from the City University Faculty Research Award Program and the Irving Louis Horowitz Foundation for Social Policy helped support my research on presidential leadership and the dilemmas of diversity. And, finally, a research fellowship from The Joan Shorenstein Center on the Press, Politics, and Public Policy at Harvard University allowed me to examine the role of political leadership in divided societies.

Finally, I owe much to my family. My conversations about American history and politics with my son Jonathan, my discussions of postmodern theory and its challenges with my son David, and my discussions about everything with my wonderful wife, partner, and friend Judith have always been enjoyable as well as helpful.

One America: Contemporary and Historical Settings

ONE

America at a Crossroads

Political Leadership,
National Identity, and the
Decline of Common Culture*

Stanley A. Renshon

U ntil recently, with one historical exception, America was able
to take a coherent national culture and identity for granted.
Successive waves of immigrants entered a country in which their ultimate
assimilation was considered a desirable, not a divisive, outcome. The country did not prove equally hospitable to everyone, and some groups endured
enormous hardships on their way to a fuller realization of America's vision of opportunity and freedom. Yet throughout, that common dream
propelled the collective desire to live up to it (Myrdal 1944 [1964]) and
provided the framework within which progress was understood and made.

Only the Civil War really tested the cultural and civic bonds that united
the country's disparate interests. That crisis confronted America's leadership, but especially its president, with a very profound but basic question:
Could Americans share a common future without a common culture? The
answer—over which the war was fought, and the recognition of which is
the starting point of Lincoln's greatness—was that we could not.

Now, for the second time in the nation's history, there is a real question of how to maintain a stable and effective relationship between
America's *unum* and *pluribus*. Unlike the Civil War, our contemporary conflicts do not pit commerce against agriculture, urban centers against rural
traditions, or North against South. Rather, the new danger lies in conflicts between people of different racial, cultural, and ethnic heritages, and
between those who view themselves as socially, culturally, politically, and
economically disadvantaged and those who are viewed as privileged. Unlike the Civil War, this conflict's primary focus is not being waged between

3

one section of the country and another, but rather in *every* section of the country. Moreover, today's antagonists cannot take the primary institutions in their part of the country—familial, religious, social, cultural, or political—for granted. These are precisely the places where the wars are being fought.

The consequences of these conflicts are not to be found in the number of killed or wounded. Instead, they are to be found primarily in the retreat from common ideals, in basic cultural values abandoned or under siege, and in institutions floundering in a sea of shrill and conflicting demands. At issue is whether it is possible or desirable to preserve the strengths of a common heritage in the face of insistence from some quarters that our past has resulted in a culture worth tearing down to build over, rather than one worth keeping and building on. It is a conflict over the viability of American culture and identity itself.

The Decline of American National Identity

America has become the land of paradox as well as opportunity. The twentieth century has been called the American century (Evans 1998), and perhaps it is accurate to so name it. The United States has emerged as the predominant world power, economically, militarily, politically, and culturally. Yet, freed by the end of the cold war from a need to focus on external enemies, America appears have arrived at a crossroads. We live in a time of unprecedented prosperity, but Americans continue to be uneasy about the quality of their leaders, the competence of their institutions, and the larger meaning of their lives.

Domestically, America appears to present a mirror image of its international standing. It is the single most powerful country in the world, and yet it is beset domestically by fractious disagreements about its values, history, culture, and policies. Divisive issues such as affirmative action, abortion rights, English as America's basic language, homosexual marriage, and many more matters of heated contemporary debate raise important questions of political and psychological equity. Yet they also raise profound questions of national psychology, purpose, and identity.

Must cultural, psychological, and political diversity lead to a fragmented and thus dysfunctional national identity? Some worry it might. Is the opposite of fragmentation Anglo-Western domination? Some apparently think so. James Hunter (1997, 52, italics his) argues in his book *Cultural Wars* that *"cultural conflict is ultimately about domination."* The word domination implies subjugation. And if he is correct, it's not surprising that our "culture wars" are fought with no quarter given to a state of exhaustion and stalemate.

Is it true, though, that the goal of all cultural conflict is domination? Not necessarily. I'm well aware that the United States has a mixed, in some cases bad, historical record in its treatment of American Indians, Americans of African and Asian descent, women, and others. Yet the strong and ultimately more historically successful tradition in the United States has been *inclusionary pluralism*, not domination and subjugation. Those who believe otherwise have the difficult task of explaining how a "hegemonic," "dominating" elite no longer dominates.

A better and more useful question is not whether a society must have a dominant culture, but whether in a democratically pluralist country like the United States it is still important to have a *primary* one. Is democratic inclusionary pluralism compatible with the cultural *primacy* of certain core American traditions like individualism, opportunity, merit, and responsibility? The wager that this country has made for two hundred plus years is not only that it's important, but necessary and possible.

The question, What does it mean to be an American? has never been easy to answer. It is much less so now. While numerous elements of American national identity have been identified over the years, a focus remains on ideals, customs, creeds, emotional attachments, values, and psychologies.[1]

In the past four decades new, more troubling questions have emerged. Some ask: Is there an American national identity? Others ask: Should there be one? What purpose does it serve in a "postmodern" era when allegiances ought to be global? Immigration advocates and their political allies ask: Is it legitimate to ask immigrants to subscribe to what Americans ought to be leaving behind? Their answer is no (Takaki 1993).

Somewhat paradoxically, arguments over assimilation assume a stable, coherent culture into which immigrants are assimilated. This is increasingly not the case. The major traditions and values that underlie American national culture have themselves become contested. That is the meaning of the phrase "culture wars," though the reality is that there exist a series of wars: "science wars," "history wars," "testing wars," "school wars," "military culture wars," and so on.

Some observers (Maharidge 1996; Isbister 1996, 1998) applaud these developments. They view the decline of key American cultural traditions, and especially its "dominant elites," as a necessary step in developing a less "hegemonic," more democratic society. Others (Schlesinger 1992; Miller 1998), including myself, worry about an America whose central traditions, many of which are critical to supporting a free democratic society, seem in danger of being lost—perhaps past the point of recovery.

The Decline of Cultural Stability? Immigration, Diversity, and National Identity

Sometimes, it seems, members of the American community do not live in the same country. It is not only that "whites" and "blacks"[2] profoundly disagree about the guilt or innocence of O. J. Simpson, the fairness of the criminal justice system, or whether Bill Clinton is an appropriate public role model, although there are strong "racial" differences in all three areas. What's more troubling is that this "perceptual divide" is mirrored by those whose work entails knowing the meaning of the most basic facts.

Hacker (1995) examines his data and hypothetical anecdotes and finds two nations, one "black" and one "white," divisively unequal. Stephen and Abigail Thernstrom (1997) examine their data and find enormous progress toward making Americans of African descent and others one nation indivisible. Feagan (2000) entitles his book *Racist America*, with no further real analysis apparently necessary. And Orlando Patterson (1995, 24–25) reaches the paradoxical conclusion that while "there is no denying the fact that in absolute terms, African Americans, on the average, are better off now than at any other time in their history . . . it is also no exaggeration to say that . . . these are the worst of times, since the ending of Jim Crow, for the African American population." How it can be both the best and worst of times for the same group is not fully explained.

The same ambiguity permeates the important and highly contentious issue of immigration. Immigrants are idealized by some, even as their increasing numbers are greeted with concern by many others. Meanwhile, political leaders of all sides prefer not to deal with a large array of important concerns raised by historically unprecedented rates of legal and illegal immigration. Democrats view these rates from the vantage point of their own partisan advantage, extol the virtues of our "immigrant nation," and have been implicated in rushing to confer citizenship. Their allies go further and condemn any questions about these issues as inherently racist.

Republicans, on the other hand, fearful of being labeled "anti-immigrant," follow the lead of former Senator Spencer Abraham (R-MI), chair of the Senate Immigration committee "to accentuate the positive" (Lewis 1997). With this view cemented in position, hard questions are not asked, and data that are inconsistent with a rosy outlook can be ignored or misstated.[3]

Meanwhile, political pressure is building for another amnesty for illegal, or as their advocates prefer, "undocumented,"[4] aliens. Some (Sierra et al. 2000, 539, italics mine) argue that "the reality of free trade and regional economic integration presents a challenge that *demands* moving beyond the confines of nationalism and addressing transnational problems with innovative solutions." In that vein, Vicente Fox, president of Mexico, has proposed solving the problem of illegal immigration from his country and region simply by making the U.S.-Mexico border an open one (Sullivan and Jordan 2000; Thompson 2000). President George W. Bush has declined to endorse this option.

There is no doubt that record levels of immigration have increased America's ethnic, racial, and cultural diversity. The latest figures from the 2000 Census show that "ten percent of those living in the United States are foreign born, the majority of them from Latin America" (Rodriguez 2000). The number of immigrants living in the United States has almost tripled since 1970, far outpacing the growth of the native-born population, rising from 9.6 million to 28.4 million today, *the highest number in American history.*[5] The new figures dramatically affirm that "the country is going through a remarkable transformation in just a generation's time, one that will reshape the nation's demographics and social landscape for years to come" (Escobar 1999).

One of these dramatic changes concerns the racial and ethic composition of the country. By 2050, by some estimates, America will contain no majority racial or ethnic group.[6] Some advocates, counting on a coalition of what they see as the oppressed, are hoping to turn James Madison's warning about the tyranny of the majority on its head. Others are wondering how America will manage to integrate so many culturally diverse newcomers while retaining its core identity as a country built primarily, but not exclusively, on western European intellectual, legal, ethical, and cultural traditions.

America's traditional answer to this question has been assimilation. Yet assimilation,[7] with its implications—that there is a national American identity and immigrants choosing to come here should, in good faith, try to embrace it—is "contested," to borrow a somewhat dainty postmodern term that hardly does justice to the fierce assault on it as a normative and descriptive model. Some sociologists see the term as harboring "deep layers of ethnocentric pretensions" and they associate with it physically and emotionally harmful experience (Rumbaut 1977). Many multiculturalists see it as an attempt to strip immigrants of their identity. Not unimportant to some, this would make immigrants less available for purposes of further deconstructing a common American identity to an amalgam of ideologically bonded advocacy groups.

Is it fair to ask those who wish to live here to live within the cultural frameworks provided by these traditions? Yes, if immigrants want to continue to enjoy the benefits for which they came here. Most immigrants come to the United States seeking political and economic freedom. Those benefits are built on, and supported by, the very same primary cultural traditions that traditionally have led to, and reinforced, the very opportunities for freedom and advancement that draw so many immigrants here.

Assimilation to those primary American cultural traditions would seem, on its face, to be instrumental in helping immigrants achieve the goals for which they came. They are important as well to our country because reconfirming the viability of this traditional path, through the incorporation and use of traditional American cultural values, reaffirms these values and their usefulness as a path to the realization of immigrants' and citizens' aspirations.

If there are good reasons for immigrants to assimilate and incorporate themselves into America's primary culture, there are hazards in doing so uncritically. Even immigrants who arrive in this country with values and beliefs that parallel those of traditional American culture might wonder whether assimilation to a debased national culture is beneficial (Portes and Zhou 1994). Studies show, for example, television and adversarial youth culture undermine the values of hard work and family values with which many immigrants arrive (Rumbaut 1977, 17; see also Salins 1977, 56–57). Rumbaut found that length of residence for immigrant children in San Diego was associated with spending less time on homework and more time watching television, which, not surprisingly, led to lower grade point averages (GPAs). Paradoxically, then, immigrant groups who might be helpful in revitalizing traditional American cultural values like hard work, the importance of merit, and feelings of pride and attachment to the nation are faced with becoming integrated into a culture in which these very basic ideals are themselves under attack or in decline.

Nor can Americans count on immigrant groups to answer problems that Americans already here have not addressed themselves. A study, "Births of Hispanic Origin, 1989–95" (National Center for Health Statistics, February 1998), showed soaring birthrates among teens of Mexican origin that were more than twice the rate of the nation's teens as a whole, and more than three times the rate of "white" teenagers (Healy 1998; Holmes 1998). Equally disturbing is that the figures revealed that Hispanics born in this country were more likely than Hispanics who moved here from their homeland (primarily Mexico) to give birth as teenagers and to have babies outside marriage (Vobejda and Constable 1998). Clearly, not every immigrant group can be counted on to equally contribute to the revitalization of traditional American values. Indeed, these disturbing figures suggest that continuing high levels of this immigration stream may contribute to the development of an Hispanic/Mexican "underclass" in a country that has had little success in addressing or resolving similar problems among Americans of African descent.

As this is happening, most public debate has centered on whether and to what extent new immigrants are an economic asset or liability to the country. Economic analysis, while important, completely misses a much more pressing, controversial, and critical issue, however: How will it be possible to integrate enormous numbers of new immigrants into a national culture and identity that are themselves increasingly questioned?

Leaderless Politics in a Divided Society

Divisive policy issues such as affirmative action, abortion rights, immigration and assimilation, English as the primary language, same-sex marriage, and educational standards, to name a few, permeate our politics. Paradoxically, most Americans tend to be in general agreement about many of these matters (see, for example, DiMaggio, Evans, and Bryson 1996; Wolfe 1996, 1998). How can that be so?

Americans live in a country where there is enormous and increasing interconnectedness but far less relatedness. They live in a country where indicators of economic and cultural well-being go in opposite directions. And they live in a country where, in spite of its success, many—in most polls, a majority—of its citizens are profoundly troubled by the direction in which it appears to be going (Wysocki 1999; Pew Research Center 1999).

Not surprisingly, America's politics are no less paradoxical than its public psychology. The United States is a country that hungers for policy moderation and bipartisanship, goals its leaders and institutions ritually promise while engaging in the most extreme forms of partisan trench warfare. It is a country where a departing president's excesses while in office and in leaving it have exhausted the public. And it is a country hungry for authenticity but increasingly subject to large doses of spin and the politics of appearance.

One almost might argue that the more political agreement there is among ordinary Americans, the more savage the battles become. Why? Part of the answer surely must be located in an examination of American political leadership—or, more precisely, the lack of it.

Declining Social Capital and the Culture of Leadership

The controversies swirling around the cultural foundations of American national identity have been paralleled, not surprisingly, by debates about the decline of "social capital" (Putnam 1995, 2000; Norris 1996; Ladd 1999). Decreasing levels of trust in social and political institutions, declining political participation, and declining public interest in and attention to many spheres of public life remind us that healthy democracies are as much a function of their publics' psychology as they are of formal constitutional documents (Lasswell 1959; see also Almond and Verba 1963).

Social capital, therefore, is a useful term because it calls attention again to the critical link between public psychology and the support of democratic social and political institutions. Yet in doing so, it risks ignoring the other half of this seminal democratic equation: *leadership capital.*

Political leadership itself is a form of social capital and, like its public psychology counterpart, is absolutely indispensable to the well-being of democracies. Like social capital, evidence of its decline and the consequences of that decline permeate and complicate our present circumstances.

The term "capital," as in social or leadership capital, suggests a surplus—something you have beyond sufficiency that enables you to do something else of value. Greater wealth for example, provides the means to support materialism, opportunity, or disengagement. Social trust provides the means to find common ground and undertake common purpose. Character and competence provide the building blocks of surplus leadership capital.

Leaders who earn, through their words and actions, a public reputation for honesty, integrity, competence, good judgment, and a steady capacity to put the public's interest first and their own, or party's, interest thereafter will accumulate leadership capital (Renshon 2000). Yet, consider in this respect the modern presidency. Of eight post-Eisenhower presidents, five were unable to gain or serve through a second term because of their own failings, and the sixth barely managed a second term in spite of them. Lyndon Johnson repeatedly lied about Vietnam and squandered his leadership capital. Richard Nixon committed felonies and squandered his. Gerald Ford squandered his by pardoning his predecessor. Jimmy Carter failed to combine honesty with competence and squandered his, and George Bush demonstrated inspired leadership abroad and modest leadership at home. Bill Clinton managed a second term, but left a legacy so marred by avoidable controversy that his presidency can hardly be considered a success. Indeed, only Ronald Reagan managed to serve two terms and leave the office with the stock of presidential leadership capital enhanced and his reputation intact. It remains to be seen which category President George W. Bush will join.

This problem and its development owe as much to the past as the present. The joint depletion of leadership and social capital has been underway for decades. If, as is repeatedly said, political leadership is best understood as the fit between the leader, citizens, and their times, then it has been a hard era for them all.

The Decline of Leadership Capital: A Brief Political History of a Dizzying Decade

The conflicts that permeate our national culture cannot be understood apart from their relationship to contemporary American politics. Our national political culture has reached an unstable plateau, arrived at through the most wrenching, dizzying political reversals.

In 1991, George Bush stood at the pinnacle of his public approval. Not only had he immediately and correctly grasped the implications of Sadaam Hussein's grab for land, oil, and power, but he successfully demonstrated that leadership with the courage of its convictions can mobilize the support of the American public in spite of its understandable anxieties. Unfortunately for President Bush, after this leadership triumph both his courage and his convictions appeared to the public, not without reason, to be less intensely stimulated by the myriad problems facing this country than they were in stopping Sadaam Hussein. Primarily for that reason, in 1992 Mr. Bush became another in a long line of modern presidents (Lyndon Johnson, Richard Nixon, Gerald Ford, Jimmy Carter) who were unable to serve a second term. Americans, beset by economic, political, and cultural uncertainties, turned to Bill Clinton, who promised to avoid the pitfalls of the left and right and govern smartly from the political center as a "New Democrat."

However, immediately upon his election, Mr. Clinton declared himself the heir not only of the votes he received, but also those of one of his rivals as well, and stated that an overwhelming majority of Americans had voted for change. That may have been so, but it is an open question whether the change Americans wanted is the change they received. With a decidedly left-of-center Democratic Congress as his partner, the president temporarily lost track of his promise to govern as a New Democrat and increasingly began to look to many like an old one. The result was a cataclysmic repudiation of the president and his party in the 1994 congressional, state, and local elections. Republicans gained control of both houses of Congress for the first time since the early years of the Eisenhower administration (Berke 1994, A1). In the House they won fifty-two seats (Wilcox 1995, 1) and in the Senate, eight additional seats.

Equally striking were Republican gains at the state and local levels. Republicans picked up twelve governorships in addition to the eighteen they already held (Verhovek 1994, A1). No Republican incumbent who sought reelection to the House, the Senate, or to a governorship lost (Wilcox 1995, 1). At the state legislature level, Republicans picked up at least fifteen chambers that had been in Democrats' hands. In no case did Democrats pick up chambers that had been held by Republicans. Before the election the Democrats controlled sixty-four chambers, the Republicans thirty-one (three were tied). After the election the figures were forty-nine and forty-six, respectively (again, with three tied). For the first time since Reconstruction, the number of Republican state legislators (3,391) approached the number of their Democratic counterparts (3,847). There is some evidence that these changes filtered down to the local level as well.

In North Carolina for example, Republican county officials increased their numbers by fifty-six, to 217 seats from 161. Of that state's one hundred counties, Republicans became the majority in forty-two local governments, up from the twenty-seven they had controlled before the election (Smothers 1995, A16).

It was clearly a Republican electoral landslide. However, its meaning was another matter. Was 1994 a classic realignment election? Was it just one more indication of the country's dealignment? Was it only a repudiation of the Clinton administration, or a repudiation of government itself? Twenty-five years before that, Theodore Lowi (1969) had confidently predicted the end of the welfare state. Was this election a confirmation of that assertion?

Those questions were soon answered. Republicans, flushed with victory and confidence, declared that realignment was at hand, liberalism a historical relic, and a Republican in the White House just a matter of time. However, borrowing a well-worn page from Mr. Clinton's political career, Republicans, in some ways understandably, began to confuse the opportunity given to them to create a mandate with already having been given one. Americans may have wanted less government in some areas, but apparently they were not prepared to do without any government. As a result of Republican miscalculations, and President Clinton's and his party's extremely adroit political use of them, an almost fatally weakened presidency was revived and transformed.

Democrats were immeasurably aided in this process in the 1996 presidential election by the selection of a basically decent, but terminally inarticulate, Republican candidate. Democrats were now not the only political party to scarcely survive a near-death political experience. Having allowed themselves to become associated with that most dreaded of all new political words, "extremism," Republicans barely managed to hold on to their majority in the House. This ensured that the newly re-elected and newly moderated President Clinton could count on, and make use of, ample Republican anxiety at being portrayed as "harsh" every time he and they disagreed about anything. Democrats were understandably delighted at their newfound ability to support both balancing the budget and increasing government spending, ending big government as we know it even while expanding government programs and cutting and raising taxes at the same time.

Republicans, on the other hand, were understandably distraught at their inability to agree among themselves, much less provide an effective alternative to President Clinton. They had not yet figured out, as President Clinton had, how to be for less government but not against it, how to be for affirmative action but opposed to racial preferences, and how to appear favorable toward immigration while expressing legitimate concerns about accommodating and integrating vast numbers of newcomers economically and culturally.

This state of acute political vertigo brought about by the dramatic and abrupt changes of the past years has resulted in the development of a new, somewhat puzzling, perhaps even bizarre, form of political extreme combat: bipartisan trench warfare. Its purpose is to mask as well as inflict lethal political wounds. It requires that each party appear to accept the most publicly popular assumptions of their opponents: Democrats present themselves as prudent and Republicans as compassionate. However, at the level of real politics, every hearing, every issue, every bill, every press conference, and every leak is initiated or scrutinized for what each side hopes will be decisive partisan advantage.

In these circumstances, raw, often ugly, partisanship always trumps civility. Not surprisingly, public confidence in Congress, a reflection of the depletion of leadership capital, dropped. For example, in February 1997, a Harris poll found that only 38 percent of the American public approved of the way Congress was doing its job. By October 1999, only 32 percent approved.[8] By September of 2000, that number had climbed to 45 percent, but the highest it had ever been in the last decade had been a bare majority approving (51 percent), and its low had been a dismal 22 percent.[9]

Republicans appeared to be losing ground in this fight. They seemed to be biding their time, hoping that if they didn't suggest, or stick with, anything that appeared too controversial or that could be mischaracterized by a president who didn't hold their best interests at heart, they might, just might, hold on to their congressional majority and even pick up the presidency in 2000. What they would do with national control was an unanswered question, even for Republicans. It was unclear just what the party and its leadership wished to stand for or, if necessary, stand against. In order to show the public you have the courage of your convictions, you first need to have some.

Democrats, sensing Republican vulnerability, labeled every policy difference "extremist," or another example of favoring "the powerful" instead of "the people," a theme Albert Gore adapted, with mixed results, in the 2000 presidential election. They feared that a tarnished president continued to damage their prospects. They also feared being put back on the wrong side of issues like crime or national defense.

The American public, however, is far less timid in expressing its concerns. Social issues—crime, drugs, the decline in moral values, and problems in education—have topped the list of public concerns. A 1997 *Washington Post*-ABC poll (Morin 1997) found that in spite of a booming national economy and a soaring stock market, 57 percent of those interviewed said the country was headed in the wrong direction, while 75 percent didn't trust the government or its leaders to do what was right. Almost all that thought so mentioned the decline of the nation's moral health and well-being, as well as problems in education, race, and immigration.

This concern persists. A September 2000 poll conducted by *The Wall Street Journal* and NBC found that moral standards and ethics were the top concern of Americans, tied with the economy. Education, health care, and social security followed. Lest there be any doubt that Americans were concerned about these qualities not only in their society but in their leaders, consider the following evidence: 70 percent of the American public rated the quality of "being trustworthy enough to do the right thing" as very important. This far outranked the qualities of being knowledgeable (43 percent), being compassionate enough to understand average people (46 percent), and even having strong leadership qualities (61 percent).[10]

The Public's Psychology and the Decline of Leadership Capital

The decline of leadership capital in the United States owes much to the actual psychology and behavior of the leaders who depleted it. Yet it would be unfair to attribute all our misfortunes to them. We, the public, share a substantial part of the responsibility as well. To understand that responsibility, we must first ask some questions about the public's psychology, or as I will argue is the case, the different psychologies to be found in a more differentiated view of "the public." What are the public's expectations of our political leaders? How, if at all, have they changed? What are the implications of these changes for the accumulation or reduction of leadership capital, and, how do they affect the capacity to, and the methods by which one might, govern in a divided society?

Discussions of the relationship of leaders to their "followers" repeatedly invoke the assumption of a unified public psychology. Winston

Churchill, it is assumed, spoke to the need of *all* the British people for heroic leadership that was necessary to defend the country. Likewise, discussions of Franklin D. Roosevelt assume that *all* Americans (rich and poor) welcomed the heroic leadership that was required to save our economic and political system.

In times of overriding systemic crisis, it makes sense to think in terms of a unified public psychology. But does it make sense to assume that in less catastrophic times? I think not. At least in the United States, it is useful to think in terms of several public psychologies rather than a single public psychology. This country was founded by people who were willing to take great risks to advance their personal freedoms and economic circumstances. They were willing to strike out on their own and adapt to the circumstances they encountered, which were clearly quite different from those they left behind. Yet, we are no longer a country made up primarily of rugged individualists, except in our public symbolism. Surely such people still exist. But they now share the stage with other, larger groups, governed by different psychologies.

In a prescient book, Boorstin (1987 [1961], 3–4) pointed out a disturbing trend in American political life: the use of the country's enormous individual and public resources to "create a thicket which stands between us and the facts of life." What did he mean? He referred to the demand of illusions that flood our experience, which in turn are fueled by our extravagant expectations. Americans, he argued, have become accustomed to expect "anything and everything."

In response, no small number of political leaders (and others) have hastened to assure us that it is possible to keep both our illusions and our reality without becoming disappointed, cynical, or hopeless. Some of our leaders tell us that it is possible for government to tax less, spend more, and save. They tell us it is possible for schools to promote both merit and inclusion painlessly, and for families to be constituted in any way adults choose without harmful effects on children. It is not.

Given these developments, some see Bill Clinton as the perfect embodiment of the age. They look around and see evidence of the erosion of the values and beliefs that were instrumental in developing this country. They see America fast becoming a country in which people want dispensations from inconvenient rules and standards. Pruden (1998), for example, puts it this way:

Can't get into the college of your choice because of low test scores or poor grades? No problem, we'll simply create a new special category for you that exempts you from the standards that others need to surmount. Are you a young woman a point shy of a scoring record who breaks her foot? No problem, we'll arrange a special uncontested shot for you. You live in a commonwealth that would like to become America's 51st state, but your official language is Spanish and you are not anywhere close to meeting the requirements of the other 50 states? No problem, some in Congress hoping for political advantage will create special rules for your admission.

It is not a far stretch from these examples to tolerance of a president whose behavior and subsequent attempt to cover up a relationship with a twenty-one-year-old intern would not be tolerated in any C.E.O., professor, military commander, or person in a position of power and responsibility.

Boorstin's insight provides an important window into the forces shaping public psychology and thus leadership capital. However, it reflects a view of the public as somewhat undifferentiated. In fact, like most social and psychological currents that permeate society, this one, too, plays out differentially because there is not just one American public, but a number of them.

In the two centuries since de Creveceour (1997 [1783], 43–44) famously asked, "What, then, is the American, this new man?" there has been no shortage of answers (Renshon 2000). The first, and most basic, was that he was motivated by the desire to do what had not been possible in his or her country of origin: to make use of his talents in the service of his ambitions to improve the material (and social) circumstances of his life.

A primary goal of achievement was "success," made possible by freedom (psychological, social, and political). Not surprisingly, later theorists of American national character (Mead 1942; see also Gorer 1948) viewed success as a double reflection on mobility. Americans could, were expected to, and expected themselves to make every effort to take advantage of the opportunities enshrined as cultural ideals and for many, though not all, in actual fact. Success was measured by mobility—the distance between start and finish, or in a word, achievement.

Following Freud, "culture and personality" theorists saw the family as the primary institution of American cultural and psychological preparation.

It both prepared children for the culture into which they were born and, in doing so, reflected in those children the internalization of the culture's predominant values. Yet American culture provides no specific formulas for "success" other than general admonitions to work hard, do your best, and so on. So mobility has been, and remains, infused with anxiety (the exact point made by de Tocqueville in 1848).

According to Horney (1937, 14–33) this leads to "compulsive competitiveness" and its emotional siblings, interpersonal aggressiveness and hostility. At the same time, the competitive life is a lonely one; intimacy and competition are difficult to reconcile. Horney notes that competition and conflict are accompanied by fear of failure and of others. These fears weaken self-esteem and, as a result, the "neurotic" craves love. These patterns are fueled, in part, by parents' concern for their children's success. As a result, parents tend to reward their children's performance, not their existence. Given these circumstances, it is difficult for children to develop an inner anchor for their own self-identities. They are oriented, rather, in substantial part toward others—parents, peers, teachers—who provide them with conditional cues of their success. In short, more than a decade before David Riesman and his colleagues (1950) brought the phrase "other-directed" into our cultural and political vocabularies, Horney and Mead were documenting the same feature in the unfolding circumstances of the interplay between American culture and psychology.

American economic success, paradoxically, both mediated and exacerbated these problems. Expanding financial security and the mass production and distribution of an increasingly large number of symbols of success through most strata of American society represent real psychological as well as economic changes. However, with abundance came a problem: How do you tell where you stand in Levittown? The answer: You keep up with the Joneses, but you don't stand out by standing apart.

On the other hand, the achievement ethic of the 1960s was quite different. "Tune in, turn on, drop out" is an invitation to withdraw from traditional cultural codes surrounding achievement. From that vantage point, achievement certainly is not measured by the accumulation of wealth, but of "inner peace" and understanding. The realization of one's own unique internal blueprint is the goal and self-enlightenment is the means. Conformity to "conventional" values or views is seen as absolutely antithetical to achieving self-realization. Cole Porter's signature composition,

"Anything Goes," seems an apt theme song for a cultural movement in which "do your own thing" and "let it all hang out" were taken as core personal values, and that shaped how cultural cues favoring achievement would be understood and enacted.

Yankelovich (1981, 163–218), surveying Americans in the 1980s, a time of economic insecurity, found us increasingly turning away from the fusion of relentless ambition for mobility and the work ethic that had been part of American culture for centuries.[11] Following the lead of de Tocqueville, Turner, Erikson, and Riesman, he found cultural values responsive to structural circumstance. He (1981, xviii–xix) viewed the turn inward as a response to diminished economic opportunities and expectations. Yet he also saw in this turn inward a new effort to resolve the dilemmas raised by a firm commitment to ambitious self-advancement in a context of stagnant mobility. In these circumstances, the "rat race" seemed less attractive than the ambiguous but still ambitious phase "self-fulfillment."

Somewhat paradoxically, yet "emphatically," Yankelovich (1981, xviii) insisted that this form of self-fulfillment was not the middle class's version of countercultural narcissism, although he did note that in its more extreme forms, "the new rules simply turn the old ones on their head, and in place of the old self-denial ethic [delay of gratification], we find people who refuse to deny anything to themselves—not out of bottomless appetite, but on the strange moral principle that 'I have a duty to myself.'"

How are the duties to one's self reconciled, if they are, with the traditional American commitment to community and interpersonal ideals and values? Easily. Self-fulfillment, being an entirely personal matter, requires those who pursue it simply to adapt the cultural code: "Live and let live." Or, as Yankelovich (1981, 88) notes, "Traditional concepts of right and wrong have been replaced by norms of 'harmful,' or 'harmless.' If one's actions are not seen as penalizing others, even if they are 'wrong' from the perspective of traditional morality, they no longer meet much opposition."

Unlike the 1960s, in which counterculture adherents dismissed traditional values as bourgeois and confining, this "live and let live" approach to personal values and convictions has lead to a new ethic that can be summed up by what has become almost an eleventh commandment: "Thou shall not judge." The "non-judgmentalism of middle class Americans" in matters of religion, family, and other personal values emerges as the major finding of Wolfe's (1998) in-depth interviews with Americans across the country. He attributes it to an emphasis on pragmatism rather than values in making tough personal decisions, a reluctance to second guess the tough choices of other people, and ambivalence or confusion as the "default" moral position.

Yet there is an important distinction to be drawn between being slow to judge and being averse to making judgments. Why Americans now seem more averse than slow is a question left unanswered by Wolfe but nonetheless is critical in understanding the public's response to the loss of leadership capital over the past two decades. Needless to say, a strong ethic of self-fulfillment coupled with the view that whatever I do, or anyone else does, that doesn't directly harm anyone else is all right "often collides violently with traditional rules, creating a national battle of cultural norms" (Yankelovich 1981, 5).

It is within these overlapping layers of American cultural and public psychology that a disturbing loss of leadership capital has been and is unfolding. Leaders must be able to mobilize citizens in support of their mutual goals. However, mobilization is not synonymous with simple arousal. The capacity to harness ambition to ideals and values that resonate with, but which sometimes may require the moderation of, citizens' more unreflective "demands" or "needs" is one example of the link between leadership and citizen capital. How this is possible when Americans have become accustomed to expecting "anything and everything" (Boorstin 1987 [1961], 3–4) is no small question.

Other questions regarding political leadership arise as well in these circumstances. What role, if any, have leaders' practice played in the depletion of their own capital? What has been leadership's role in the development of this apparent paradox of substantial conflict and shallow divisions? How is it possible to govern or to lead in these conditions? How are such divisions related to the accumulation or depletion of leadership capital?

Leaderless Politics

Ambition is a core element of any leader's success. As the building block of public accomplishment, it is, as noted, a key resource for the accumulation of leadership capital. Yet it is also necessary to distinguish among ambitions, from the simply motivational to the dangerously grandiose. But how? One answer is to examine the relationship between ambition and character integrity. A consolidated set of ideals and values for which one is willing to stand can anchor and temper ambitions, even large ones. Without them, self-interest has no constraints.

If character integrity is the capacity to maintain fidelity to ideas and values, even at the risk of personal or political harm, then it is clear that to have the courage of one's convictions, you need both. In short, personal and political courage is the key link between the two elements of leadership capital already discussed, ambition (and the skills to realize it) and a well-grounded sense of ideals and values. The three together, ambition and ideals consolidated by the courage and other key personal resources to sustain them, are the key to the accumulation of leadership capital. I term failures of either having convictions or the courage of them, coupled with strong ambition, *leaderless politics*.

The rise of leaders anxious for office and lacking either the skills to realize their ambitions or strong principled convictions coupled with the courage to follow them leads to a mismatch between ambitions and performance. Contemporary leaders often aspire to more than they are able to accomplish or are willing to explain publicly. It is a paradox of our contemporary recruitment of top-level political leaders that we require of them enormous ambition to endure the rigors of gaining high office, but limit our support of their large initiatives once they are there.

One result is that leaders are tempted to finesse their plans with spin rather than direct and honest public explanation. This essentially was Bill Clinton's problem. He was a man who believed in large plans but was forced to campaign on modest ones. Once in office he tried to mask, but still pursue, the large scope of his policy ambitions, with the result that he became a moderate after the 1994 elections by necessity, not choice (Renshon 1998a). President George W. Bush, in his first months in office, appeared to prefer candor, even when it means a political fight (Bell 2001; Balz 2001).

Some believe the gap between leadership ambitions and a combination of high but skeptical public expectations provides room for governing in a politically contentious environment. I think not. Masking ambitions runs the risk of violating public performance standards that underlie the accumulation or depletion of leadership capital. The public appears to prefer leaders who combine competence and integrity, not those for whom the two are inversely related. Leaders unable or unwilling to risk honesty with the public deplete their own capital when caught, while also depleting the reserve of social trust and capital on which they must often draw.

Conclusion

The question this country is left with in the aftermath of the Clinton presidency is whether our present and future leaders can be honestly articulate, reconcile, and carry through their promises and ambitions. Our country faces enormous issues arising from our dramatically increased racial, ethnic, and cultural diversity. The importance of leadership in times of no national consensus is not solely, perhaps not even primarily, an ability to propose and pass legislation. But, then, what is it?

We have divisive national arguments. Yet on many matters, we don't disagree. What has been leadership's role in the development of this apparent paradox of substantial conflict and shallow divisions?

Americans appear to have confounded large ambitions with "heroic leadership." Yet ambition unanchored by the capacity for fidelity to deeply held values and ideals runs the risks of grandiosity or dishonesty. Torn between their ambitions and public skepticism, presidents and candidates have tried to negotiate these treacherous currents for a decade, primarily by trying to finesse rather than engage them. Michael Dukakis famously suggested in 1988 that his presidential campaign was about competence, not ideology, and was soundly trounced by the most publicly ideological president of the decade. George Bush lacked a discernible domestic political or policy center and failed to get a second term. Bill Clinton ran and won the presidency as a "New Democrat," governed as an old one, and won reelection by declaring "the era of big government is over," even while copiously adding new programs to it. President George W. Bush has a limited electoral mandate, but bold policy ambitions. Can policy ambitions be bold without being heroic? We shall see. While "heroic leadership" is one of the central political myths of our time, "leaderless politics" seems a more realistic description of our civic condition.

That is one reason why, as the 2000 presidential election unfolded, the public proved hungry for authenticity. Regarding Republican presidential candidate John McCain, for example, Balz (1999, A1) wrote, "the McCain rise owes to other factors as well: [including] a direct style in year when 'authenticity' has become a buzzword for what voters want." The accumulated loss of leadership capital over decades of squandered opportunity appears to have created its own public momentum for its restoration.

The question that we are left with is whether it is possible to find and field any leader who has courage and convictions both, one who is not afraid to raise and address difficult issues, even with those least likely, his political allies, to want to hear them. In our present and foreseeable circumstances, there is a need, one might say a desperate one, for postpartisan political leadership—leadership that combines principles with proportion and integrity with competence. We need leaders whose pragmatism is a function of their psychology, not their strategy, and whose moderation is a reflection of their character, not their persona. If we don't get these leaders, we will no longer be worrying about whether Democrats or Republicans dominate our future, but whether as a country we have a good one.

Notes

*This essay draws on Renshon (1996 [1998a], 2000).

1. Historical views of American national identity, coupled with a modern reformulation of the concept and its nature in contemporary American society, can be found in Renshon (2000).

2. I put the term in quotes to underscore that there are conceptual categories with mixed, at best, empirical grounding. Geneticists have argued that "race" is not a scientifically viable concept given the mixtures of genes, and that the term and its associates (e.g., black, white, etc.) suffer from the same major drawbacks. In doing so, I depart from the adapted convention of organization like that of the American Psychological Association, which has reified murky scientific categories by mandating capitalization of terms like "black" and "white" whenever they are used. Race and its associated categories are, of course, important categories of political analysis, but that is clearly a matter of convention and politics, not molecular and genetic science. Matters are complicated by the fact that the terms have some predictive validity. "Race" in the form of an observer's ascription or a respondent's self-identification does carry some predictive weight. The reason for this, however, cannot necessarily or appropriately be ascribed to "race." Other possibilities include shared experience, shared outlooks, ethnicity, and strategic, political self-identifications. Moreover, as rates of intermarriage in the United States increase among almost all ethnic groups, the question of how "pure" race categories are not only scientifically misleading but politically injurious is also important to consider. For an analysis of how racial categories came to be used and misused in the federal government's effort to count by race, see Skerry (2000). For a very thoughtful examination of classification systems, including racial ones, see Bowker and Star (1999).

3. George J. Borjas and Richard B. Freeman (1997), two senior members of a panel examining the costs and benefits of immigration, dispute the misuse of their study by Senator Abraham. The study in question was conducted by a panel of the National Research Council (1977).

4. These terms reflect the attempt to control the frame of discussion, much as the "prochoice" and "prolife" terms have sought to do so in the abortion debates. Advocates prefer the term "undocumented," because it diverts attention from the fact that these persons have entered the country in violation of our immigration laws, and have done so purposefully. Those with concerns about this type of immigration prefer the term "illegal" precisely because it places that unlawful act directly in the path of natural sympathies for those who want a "better life."

5. The 2000 Census survey counted 28.4 million foreign-born Americans, the highest number in the nation's history. They accounted for 9.7 percent of the nation's population in 1999. Of that number, 51 percent arrived from Latin America, 27 percent from Asia, 16 percent from Europe, and 6 percent from other areas of the world. America had its highest percentage—14.7 percent—of foreign-born Americans in 1910. But since the population itself was small, the number of foreign-born Americans was 13.5 million (Camarota 2001).

6. The relevant statistics are available from the U.S. Bureau of the Census (1992; 1995, Table 12).

7. On assimilation in general, see Kazal (1995). On the question of the demise of assimilation, see Glazer (1993).

8. The data can be found at pollreport.com <http://www.pollingreport.com/congjob.htm> (October 20, 1999).

9. Data are drawn from the *Wall Street Journal*/NBC poll (Study #6008), September 14, 2000, available at <http://www. WallStreetJournal.com> (September 15, 2000).

10. Ibid.

11. For example, he reports (1981, 38–39) data that in the mid-1960s, 72 percent of college students agreed that "hard work always pays off." By the early 1970s, this figure had dropped to 40 percent. These findings were paralleled in adults for whom, between the late 1960s and the late 1970s, the percentage of adults agreeing with that aphorism fell from 58 to 43 percent.

References

Almond, Gabriel, and Sidney Verba. *The Civic Culture*. Boston: Little Brown, 1963.
Balz, Dan. "President's Words Belie His Tactics, Democrats Charge." *The Washington Post* (March 4, 2001): A1.
———. "McCain's Rise Alters Dynamics of Race." *The Washington Post* (November 6, 1999): A1.
Bell, Jeffrey. "Keep Up the Tough Talk, Mr. Nice Guy." *The Washington Post* (March 4, 2001): B1.

Berke, Richard L. "G.O.P. Wins Control of Senate and Makes Big Gains in House: Pataki Denies Cuomo 4th Term." *The New York Times* (November 9, 1994): A1.

Boorstin, Daniel. *The Image.* New York: Vintage, 1987 [1961].

Borjas, George J., and R. B. Freeman. " Findings We Never Found." *The New York Times* (December 10, 1997): A29.

Bowker, Geoffey C., and Susan Leigh Star. *Sorting Things Out: Classification and Its Consequences.* Cambridge, Mass.: MIT Press, 1999.

Camarota, Steven A. *Immigrants in the United States—2000: A Snapshot of America's Foreign-Born Population.* Washington, D.C.: Center for Immigration Studies, 2001.

Clinton, William. J. "Presidential Debate in San Diego" (October 16, 1996). *Weekly Compilation of Presidential Documents* 21, 32:42, 2091–92.

————. "Remarks and Question and Answer Session with the American Society of Newspaper Editors" (April 11, 1997). *Weekly Compilation of Presidential Documents* 14, 33:15, 509.

————. "Remarks at the University of California at San Diego Commencement Ceremony" (June 14, 1997). *Weekly Compilation of Presidential Documents* 23, June, 33:25, 1997, 877.

de Creveceour, J. H. St. John. *Letters from an American Farmer,* ed. Susan Manning. New York: Oxford University Press, 1997 [1783].

DiMaggio, Paul, John Evans, and Bethany Bryson. "Have Americans' Social Attitudes Become More Polarized?" *American Journal of Sociology* 102 (1996): 444–96.

Escobar, G. "Immigrants' Ranks Tripled in 29 Years." *The Washington Post* (January 9, 1999): A1.

Evans, Howard. *The American Century.* New York: Knopf, 1998.

Feagan, Joe R. *Racist America.* New York: Routledge, 2000.

Glazer, Nathan. "Is Assimilation Dead?" *Annuals* 530 (1993): 122–36.

Gorer, Geoffrey. *The American People: A Study in National Character.* New York: Norton, 1948.

Hacker, Andrew. *Two Nations in Black and White.* New York: Ballantine, 1995.

Healy, M. "Latina Teens Defy Decline in Birthrates." *Los Angeles Times* (February 13, 1998): A1.

Holmes, Stephen A. "Hispanic Births in U.S. Put at Record High." *The New York Times* (February 13, 1998): A15.

Horney, Karen. *The Neurotic Personality of Our Time.* New York: Norton, 1937.

Hunter, James Davidson. *Cultural Wars: The Struggle to Define America.* New York: Basic Books, 1997.

Isbister, J. " Is America Too White?" In *What, Then, Is the American, This New Man?"* compiled by E. Sandman. Washington, D.C., Center of Immigration Studies, 1998, 25–32.

————. *The Immigration Debate: Remaking America.* New York: Kurnarian Press, 1996.

Kazal, R. A. "Revisiting Assimilation: The Rise, Fall, and Reappraisal of a Concept in American History." *American Historical Review* 100, no. 2 (1995): 437–71.

Ladd, Everett C. *The Ladd Report*. New York: The Free Press, 1999.

Lasch, Christhopher. *The Culture of Narcissism: American Life in an Age of Diminishing Expectations*. New York: Basic Books, 1979.

Lasswell, Harold D. "Political Constitution and Character." *Psychoanalysis and the Psychoanalytic Review* 46 (1959): 3–18.

Lewis, Anthony. "Accent the Positive." *The New York Times* (October 10, 1997), A23.

Lowi, Theodore J. *The End of Liberalism: Ideology, Policy, and the Crisis of Public Authority*. New York: Norton, 1969.

Maharidge, Dale. *The Coming White Minority: California's Eruptions and America's Future*. New York: Times Books, 1996.

Mead, Margaret. *And Keep Your Powder Dry*. New York: William Morrow, 1942.

Miller, John J. *The Unmaking of Americans: How Multiculturalism Has Undermined America's Assimilation Ethic*. New York: The Free Press, 1998.

Morin, Richard. " Poll Finds Wide Pessimism About Direction of Country." *The Washington Post* (August 29, 1997): A1.

Myrdal, Gunnar. *An American Dilemma*. New York: Harper, 1944 (1964).

National Center for Health Statistics. *Births of Hispanic Origin, 1989–95*. Washington, D.C., February 1998.

National Research Council. *The New Americans*. Washington, D.C.: National Academy Press, 1977.

Norris, Pippa. "Does Television Erode Social Capital? A Reply to Putnam." *PS: Political Science and Politics* 29 (1996): 474–80.

Patterson, Orlando. *The Ordeal of Integration*. Washington, D.C.: Civitas, 1998.

———. "The Paradox of Integration." *The New Republic* 24 (1995): 24–27.

Pew Research Center for the People and the Press. "Technology Triumphs, Morality Falters" (July 13, 1999).

Portes, A., and M. Zhou. "Should Immigrants Assimilate?" *The Public Interest* 116 (Summer, 1994): 18–36.

Pruden, Wesley. "Pruden on Politics: A Perfect Expression for a Gelded Age." *The Washington Times* (March 13, 1998): 22.

Putnam, Robert. *Bowling Alone*. New York: Simon and Schuster, 2000.

———. "Bowling Alone: America's Declining Social Capital." *Journal of Democracy* 6 (1995): 65–78.

Renshon, Stanley A. "American Character and National Identity: The Dilemmas of Cultural Diversity." In *Political Psychology: Cultural and Cross-Cultural Foundations*, ed. Stanley A. Renshon and John Duckitt. London: Macmillan, 2000, 285–310.

———. *High Hopes: The Clinton Presidency and the Politics of Ambition*. New York: Routledge, 1998a.

———. *The Psychological Assessment of Presidential Candidates*. New York: Routledge, 1998b.

Riesman, David. "Egocentrism: Is the American Character Changing?" *Encounter* 55 (August/September, 1980): 19–28.

Riesman, David, with N. Glazer and R. Denny. *The Lonely Crowd: A Study of the Changing American Character*. New Haven, Conn.: Yale University Press, 1950.

Rodriguez, Cindy. "Latino Influx Boosts Number of U.S. Immigrants to All-time High." *Boston Globe* (September 12, 2000): A1.

Rumbaut, Ruben G. "Assimilation and Its Discontents: Between Rhetoric and Reality." *International Migration Review* 31, no. 4 (1977): 923–60.

Salins, Peter J. *Assimilation American Style*. New York: Basic Books, 1977.

Schlesinger, Arthur A., Jr. *The Disuniting of America: Reflections on a Multicultural Society*. New York: Norton, 1992.

Sierra, Christine Maria, Teresa Carrillo, Louis DeSipio, and Michael Jones-Correa. "Latino Immigration and Citizenship." *PS: Political Science and Politics* 33, no. 3 (2000): 535–40.

Skerry, Peter. *Counting on the Census: Race, Group Identity and the Evasion of Politics*. Washington, D.C.: The Brookings Institution Press, 2000.

Smothers, Ronald. "G.O.P. Gains in South Spread to Local Level." *The New York Times* (April 7, 1995): A16.

Sullivan, Kevin, and Mary Jordan. "Fox Seeks New Cooperative Era For N. America." *Washington Post Foreign Service* (August 14, 2000): A1.

Takaki, Ronald. *A Different Mirror: A History of Multicultural America*. Boston: Little Brown, 1993.

Thernstrom, Stephan, and Abigail Thernstrom. *America in Black and White: One Nation Indivisible*. New York: Simon and Schuster, 1997.

Thompson, G. "Fox Urges Opening of U.S.–Mexican Border to Build New Partnership." *The New York Times* (August 14, 2000): A1.

U.S. Bureau of the Census. "Projections of the Population of the United States, by Age, Sex, and Race: 1992–2050." *Current Population Reports*. P-125-1092. Washington, D.C.: U.S. Government Printing Office, 1992.

U.S. Bureau of the Census. *Statistical Abstract of the United States*. 115th ed. Washington, D.C.: U.S. Government Printing Office, 1995.

Verhovek, Sam Howe. "Republican Tide Brings New Look to Legislatures." *The New York Times* (November 12, 1994): A1.

Vobejda, Barbara, and P. Constable. "Hispanic Teens' Birthrate Ranks 1st of Ethnic Groups." *The Washington Post* (February 13, 1998): A10.

Wilcox, Clyde. *The Latest American Revolution: The 1994 Elections and Their Implications for Governance*. New York: St. Martin's Press, 1995

The Wirthlin Report. "Mood of the Nation." August/September, 1997, p. 4.

Wolfe, Alan. *One Nation, After All*. Chicago: University of Chicago Press, 1998.

————. *Marginalized in the Middle*. Chicago: University of Chicago Press, 1996.

Wysocki, Bernard, Jr. "Americans Decry Moral Decline." *The Wall Street Journal* (June 24, 1999): A9.

Yankelovich, Daniel. *New Rules: Searching for Self-fulfillment in a World Turned Upside Down*. New York: Random House, 1981.

TWO

Which America?

Nationalism among the Nationalists*

Noah M. J. Pickus

What a difference a decade makes. As recently as 1990, debates over American identity were characterized by a divide between universalists and multiculturalists. Universalists stressed abstract American ideals while multiculturalists emphasized plural American cultures. In contrast, the mid-1990s witnessed an explosion of a remarkably wide variety of opinion writers, scholars, and, in John McCain, a serious presidential candidate, who objected to both the universalist and the multiculturalist positions. These nationalists contend that America is more than an idea and that it is more than a federation of cultures. At the same time, they insist, American nationalism is based on neither racial nor religious superiority. As Peter Spiro, writing in *The Stanford Law Review*, observes, "a liberal nationalist school of American citizenship is now emerging around the twin precepts of inclusiveness and national vitality" (Spiro 1999, 599).

This liberal, nationalist school combines ideas often considered antithetical—inclusiveness and nationalism—and covers a significant swath of the political spectrum from left to right. Proponents of newly nationalist politics include, for instance, T. Alexander Aleinikoff, a prominent law professor who held high policy positions at the Immigration and Naturalization Service in the mid-1990s, and David Hollinger, a well-known historian, both of whom traditionally have been identified on the liberal side of the political divide. The school also includes the prolific public intellectual Michael Lind, currently a Senior Fellow at the New America Foundation, a public policy institute that aims to transcend the conventional political spectrum, and the duo of William Kristol, former chief of staff to Vice President Dan Quayle and currently the editor of *The Weekly Standard*, and David Brooks, a senior editor at *The Weekly Standard*.

This new ordering of the intellectual and, potentially, the political universe in the United States is reminiscent of a similar period in American history: the Progressive Era. Then, as today, Americans were pressed to address the nature of their union by a complex concatenation of economic dislocation, cultural upheaval, demographic change, and challenges to established moral and scientific paradigms.

Opinion makers and political leaders in the Progressive Era were deeply concerned about weakening party loyalties and a decline in voting, the rise of an increasingly secularized Protestantism, the mass migration of Europeans, the movement of blacks from the southern to the northern cities, and the ever more vigorous entry of women into politics. These fears were compounded by worries about the concentration of authority in large, corporate entities. Progressive reformers believed that unbridled economic power was corrupting the political system and undermining the capacity of citizens to be self-sufficient and independent in their political judgments. Some leaders further despaired that the disintegrating effects of science, technology, and complex social relations meant that the possibility for independent, virtuous citizens to live by a set of common values had been lost. The fundamental changes reconfiguring American life thus unsettled their sense of a stable social order at the same time they revealed a society made of contending groups (Brandeis 1915; Lippmann 1929; Higham 1955; Lears 1981).

Modern liberal nationalists often note the parallels between the Progressive Era and today. They draw extensively on writers and political leaders from that period in articulating their solutions for our time. Yet, for all their agreement, they draw on distinctly different ideas of national identity developed at the beginning of this century: the "New Nationalism" of Theodore Roosevelt and Randolph Bourne's vision of a "Trans-National America." The Progressive coalition was a fractious one, capable, for a while, of including the conservative nationalism of Roosevelt and the liberal pluralism of Bourne. Many Progressives supported Roosevelt's third-party bid for the presidency in 1912, but by the 1916 election the coalition had fallen apart and had been superceded by the 1920s (Gerstle 1994; Rodgers 1982).

Can liberal nationalism today offer a coherent and compelling vision that avoids that fate? Or is it merely a cover for a wide range of views that are fundamentally incompatible? If the latter, then, like its Progressive predecessor, it may prove unable to offer a convincing ideology or build a broad-based political coalition. My purpose here is not to criticize liberal nationalists because their visions involve risks and tradeoffs—what vision does not?—but rather to map the implications of each view, to analyze its particular promise as well as the perils it invites, and to gauge the prospects for building a more robust version. In doing so, I mean to press the question: If we are to be "One America," which America are we to be?

Roosevelt and the New Nationalism

In response to the challenges presented in the early decades of the twentieth century, Theodore Roosevelt called for a "New Nationalism," one that reflected the unique nature of American life and pressed citizens to achieve great things. He worried that a series of economic and political trends—materialism, localism, and globalism—were causing citizens to place the interests of the nation second and that this would make them incapable of managing America's growing authority in the world. In an era dominated by industrialists and political bosses, Roosevelt urged and acted as if larger projects of national solidarity mattered.

Roosevelt anticipated later Americans' concerns about "prosperity without purpose" when he took aim at the notion that material success and laissez-faire government were the purpose of individual life and a free society. American elites' fawning attention to European luxury and fashion, he charged, was weakening the internal fortitude necessary to maintain the nation's morals and form of government. At the same time, the absence of real equality of opportunity and "social and industrial justice" for average citizens was undermining their ability to believe in America's higher ideals. Roosevelt celebrated economic development and personal advancement, but he insisted that politics, patriotism, and duty were more important than finance. "[O]ur country calls not for the life of ease but for the life of strenuous endeavor," he told the Hamilton Club in 1899. "[I]f we shrink from the hard contests where men must win at hazard of their lives and at the risk of all they hold dear, then the bolder and stronger peoples will pass us by" (Roosevelt 1899, 331).

Roosevelt recognized that patriotism was a dangerous idea, one that could lead citizens to blindly celebrate only what was their own. He acknowledged that the United States should be willing to learn from ideas developed in other nations, as long as such ideas were compatible with

America's fundamental ideals and were adapted to the nation's particular circumstances. Those broader ideals, however, were not subject to adaptation or negotiation. His understanding of American nationalism mixed a psychological emphasis on individualism, an economic focus on equality of opportunity, and a structural concern with the separation of church and state. Roosevelt regarded these ideas as distinctive hallmarks of a specifically American nationalism, one that could serve as a singular force for individual emancipation and social progress.

He thus defended American patriotism against those he derided as "parochialists" or "cosmopolitans." "Parochialism," Roosevelt argued, is the "patriotism of the village," the exaltation of the little community over the broader needs and purposes of the nation. The parochialist's impulse to love the particular was justifiable, he acknowledged, but the object of his affection was too insular. In the present age, to remain committed to a narrow, regional sensibility served only to undermine America's capacity to express its truly national greatness and thus accomplish projects of historic significance. Just as the patriotism of the village was destructive of American strength, so too was a philosophy of cosmopolitanism that promoted the extinction of national feeling. Such a future might one day be possible, Roosevelt conceded, "where our patriotism will include the whole human race and all the world." But since that age "is still several eons distant," proponents of cosmopolitanism "are of no practical service to the present generation." In fact, they threaten the development of a robust American identity as the primary source for achieving good at home and abroad. "Nothing will more quickly or more surely disqualify a man from doing good work in the world than the acquirement of that flaccid habit of mind which its possessors style cosmopolitanism," he charged. "The patriotism of the village or the belfry is bad, but the lack of all patriotism is even worse. . . . Such a man is not a traitor; but he is a silly and undesirable citizen" (Roosevelt 1894a, 15–17).

The primary intellectual force behind Roosevelt's nationalism was Herbert Croly, a pre-eminent journalist and editor who founded *The New Republic* in 1914. In 1910, Croly helped draft Roosevelt's "New Nationalism" speech, which Roosevelt delivered at the dedication of the John Brown Cemetery at Osawotomie, Kansas. That speech drew on Croly's recently published *The Promise of American Life*, a book that set the broad moral agenda for centrist Progressivism. In it, Croly sought to square a Jeffersonian commitment to democracy and individual emancipation with the

scale and complexity of modern life. In his view, only a Hamiltonian vision of expanded national authority could control the economic forces
that threatened to overwhelm democratic institutions and undermine citizens' opportunities for individual emancipation. Such expanded authority required a commensurate sense of national identity to undergird it.
Croly rejected the possibility that an American national identity could im-
itate the European nations' emphasis on shared blood, soil, or race. He
also doubted the liberal universalist idea that Americans could be held together on the basis of their ideas alone.

Instead, Croly sketched a national identity that simultaneously reached
backward into American history and looked forward to a new age of individual emancipation. In America, individual rights depended on a sense
of identity that is "chiefly a matter of actual historical association," he asserted. "A people that lack the power of basing their political association on an accumulated national tradition and purpose is not capable of
either nationality or democracy" (Croly 1909, 257). Citizens exercising
their rights then had to understand that they would only achieve true independence by finding their place, economically and morally, as contributors to a broader national life. Economically, citizens had to find their
particular niche in a modern industrial order. Morally, they had to identify with the needs and aspirations of their fellow citizens. As Alan Ryan
has observed, the emphasis in Croly's book was on the future, on the *promise* of American life. That promise was individual emancipation, but such
emancipation depended entirely on a national state that could adequately
meet social needs. Thus, for Croly, individual freedom and national purpose were intimately linked. "The task of individual and social regener-
ation," he wrote, "must remain incomplete and impoverished until the
conviction and feeling of human brotherhood enters into the process of
the human spirit" (Croly 1909, 453; Ryan 1996).

Roosevelt and Race

Roosevelt merged with Croly's economic and moral nationalism a distinctly racial vision of history and American culture, one that drew heavily on prevailing social ideas about neo-Lamarckism. He drew from his
study of history and natural science an understanding of social competition in which both heredity and environment played crucial roles. In
his 1910 Oxford Lecture, Roosevelt rejected racial determinism in favor of

a Lamarckian view in which nations and races could both advance and regress depending on the mix of racial traits and environmental influences (Dyer 1980, 33–44). Americans, in his view, combined the best racial traits of the English, German, Irish, and Norse, traits that then had been strengthened and improved by the hard frontier environment. From these racial strains, Roosevelt understood that Americans had inherited the capacities to be "bold and hardy, cool and intelligent, quick with their hands and showing at their best in an emergency." Americans also possessed a special capacity for ruling themselves, for combining liberty with self-control, a trait they had inherited from their Teutonic ancestors (Roosevelt 1882, 23, 30; Roosevelt 1888, 324–25).

Nonwhite races, on the other hand, represented inferior racial strains that would dilute Americans' special combination of self-assertion and self-control. Thus the destiny of the white race, its "domineering masterful spirit," justified the seizure of Texas from Mexico. Mexicans were alien from whites in "blood, language, religion, and habits of life," incapable of self-government, and thus naturally subject to dominion (Roosevelt 1887, 114). Similarly, the Chinese had lost their manly virtues and lacked the proper capacity for self-assertion. Roosevelt therefore supported the exclusion of Chinese immigrants in 1882 and reiterated his support for significant restrictions during his presidency. Although he supported emancipation, Roosevelt doubted that blacks would ever be capable of self-government. In contrast, he expressed tremendous admiration for the achievement of Japanese civilization, even suggesting at one point that the Japanese had reached a higher degree of development in some respects than Americans. Nonetheless, he supported the Gentleman's Agreement of 1907 barring further immigration from Japan. He did so, in part, owing to his aversion to racial mixing with the Japanese and his doubts that America could assimilate those whose origins and customs were so fundamentally alien (Roosevelt 1909; Dyer 1980, 134–40).

Despite these views, Roosevelt rejected the more extreme nativist thinking and policies that were common currency in the late nineteenth and early twentieth century. His preoccupation with racial differences did not "translate into a full-blown hysteria about a 'yellow peril,'" as Thomas Dyer points out. "[T]he association of barbarism with yellow skin made little sense" to Roosevelt. He lampooned plans to provide separate railroad cars for Japanese, calling them "silly" and "indefensible" (Dyer 1980, 139). Japanese who already were present in the United States had to be incorporated into the nation. Indeed, part of Roosevelt's decision to exclude Japanese immigrants from entry issued from a compromise he engineered to limit racial exclusion at home. In 1906, the year prior to the Gentleman's Agreement, the state of California had begun segregating Asian students in their public schools. Roosevelt promised California officials to limit Asian immigrants in return for an end to such segregation. In other words, national immigration laws restricting entry to Asians were enacted, in part, in the context of protecting Asians already living in the United States.

Roosevelt often condemned the Know-Nothings and Native-American parties of the nineteenth century as un-American and contravening the spirit of the Constitution. Americans, he held, should neither persecute nor support anyone on the basis of their religion or ethnicity. He objected to voting against a man because of his religious creed, and he objected to voting for him on the same grounds. In either case, Roosevelt asserted, one imposes a religious test that violates the spirit of the Constitution (Roosevelt 1915, 13–15). In 1912, pressed by social workers and motivated in part by political needs, Roosevelt's Progressive Party pledged to protect the welfare of immigrants and to incorporate them as part of its nationalist ideology. This position earned Roosevelt the ire of the nativist Junior Order of United American Mechanics and secured for him a significant proportion of the immigrant vote. Three-quarters of the districts in New York City in which Roosevelt won a plurality were heavily populated by immigrants from eastern Europe (Higham 1955, 190).

Cultural Assimilation and Ethnic Nation-Building

The historical and scientific theories of civilization development that had led Roosevelt to embrace imperialism abroad and restriction at home also caused him to reject or modify the dominant forms of nativist thinking. He believed that America was developing its own distinct nationality. "We are making a new race, a new type, in this country," he wrote in 1906. This new ethnic type owed its development to the unique American environment, both "physical and spiritual," as well as the mixture of blood found among the original settlers. He further contended that this new race "has never been fixed in blood," and could continue to absorb immigrants of appropriate racial stock, as each group "adds its blood" and, in the process of doing so, "changes [the nation] somewhat" (Dyer 1980, 131–32).

Roosevelt thus promoted a distinctly ethnic process of nation-building. He worried that economic and social modernization was hastening the general tendency of races to reach "a stationary state" where their fecundity and virility began to decline. These concerns resulted in his relentless championing of a traditional notion of motherhood in which women had a duty to their race to procreate. His support for restrictions on Asian immigration also reflected his project of nation-building. More than merely a reflection of his doubts about the wisdom of racial mixing, Roosevelt aimed to promote an ethnic and nationalist unity among working class whites by limiting the entry of nonwhites. He wanted to provide a buffer against both lower class resentment and upper class domination. By protecting whites from economic competition from imported labor, he argued, American democracy could avoid the class conflict that had destroyed aristocratic governments. He thus pursued restriction as part of an explicitly economic and ethnic nation-building strategy, a strategy that differed from the more explicitly white supremacist proponents of race-based exclusion (Roosevelt 1894b, 213; 1897, 250; see also Lind 1995, 73).

Roosevelt heartily approved of Israel Zangwill's 1908 play *The Melting Pot*, which Zangwill had dedicated to him. The idea and image of the melting pot seemed to suggest a fusing of nationalities into a new nationality that drew from all its ingredients. Roosevelt's own understanding was closer to the notion that non-Anglo-Saxon nationalities would be purified in the melting pot and shaped in the image of the majority culture. In his view, a single standard of behavior was necessary to reinforce a sense of commonality and a willingness to sacrifice. Immigrants therefore had to shed their foreign speech, habits, dress, and, especially, language. The most important demand American nationalism placed on its adherents was a sense of identification with America itself. Allegiance "is a matter of the spirit and of the soul," Roosevelt told the Knights of Columbus. "The only man who is a good American is an American and nothing else. . . . There is no room in this country for hyphenated Americans" (Roosevelt 1915, 392–93).

To achieve this uniform nationality, immigrants required a formal process of Americanization. Initially, that meant a policy that was simultaneously generous in outlook and practical in outreach, and swift and harsh if standards were not met. Immigrants' rights had to be protected so that they felt neither bitterness nor resentment toward their new identity. In 1915, Roosevelt objected to a literacy test as barring many new-comers who might make excellent citizens. In its stead, he proposed ad-mitting illiterate aliens and giving them an opportunity to learn English and to work (Roosevelt 1915, 398).

They would also be expected to participate in civic life. "The policy of 'Let alone' which we have hitherto pursued is thoroughly vicious from two standpoints," he declared.

> By this policy we have permitted the immigrants, and too often the native-born laborers as well, to suffer injustice. Moreover, by this policy we have failed to impress upon the immigrant and upon the native-born as well that they are expected to do justice as well as to receive justice. . . . We can-not secure . . . loyalty unless we make this a country where men shall feel that they have justice (Roosevelt 1915, 402).

Immigrants had to prove themselves willing to take up the duties of their new civic status. Roosevelt advocated deportation for those who, after a period of time, had not at least begun to acquire the language. As part of a broader transformation of identity and sentiment, he urged immi-grants "to bear the most honorable of titles" by Americanizing their names. He made clear that U.S. citizenship was an all-or-nothing propo-sition, one in which devotion to the American flag not only came first but also was singular—"no other flag should even come second." "Above all," Roosevelt demanded, "the immigrant must learn to talk and think and *be* United States" (Roosevelt 1894a, 22–24). This view shaped much of the initial federal effort to formalize the rules governing naturalization and to consciously mold immigrants into citizens. In contrast to the restric-tionist agenda, the movement to Americanize immigrants reflected Roo-sevelt's confidence in the absorptive capacities of nationalism in the United States (Pickus 2001).

Nationalism Unbounded

As much as Roosevelt tied personal virtue and democratic politics to na-tional solidarity, his vision of nationalism could also be remarkably vague. Allegiance to the American nation was crucial, but crucial to what end? Nationalism was necessary, but what was a nation for? At times, Roosevelt named moral greatness, civilizational and racial superiority, and individual freedom among other purposes the American nation was devoted to achieving. But his nationalism, his celebration of America and American deeds above all else, was ultimately unclear as to what, if any, limits should or could be placed on that nation and on its exploits.

Roosevelt expanded the reach of the presidency by rooting executive power in direct appeals to the people rather than in formal constitutional authority. Those appeals enlarged the president's power while contravening limits on governmental authority (Tulis 1985). A similar dynamic was at work in Roosevelt's New Nationalism. His ideas about racial evolution, and devolution, in combination with his conception of allegiance as singular and unbending, untethered him from the American Founders' emphasis on limited government. Roosevelt's nationalism, his zealousness, and his devotion to a life of conflict could lead in a myriad of directions. His form of nationalism was at odds with that of Washington and Lincoln, even though he claimed them as his heroes. He did not take to heart their concerns for a polity balanced between reason and reverence and dependent on moderate habits of character. Instead, as Charles Kesler observes, he revered them for "their greatness of soul, wholly apart from the ends or the understanding of justice to which they devoted their greatness" (Kesler 1998; see also Croly 1909, 174).

The unboundedness of Roosevelt's nationalism can be seen in the coercive turn taken by the Americanization movement and in the triumph of racially based immigration policy. Roosevelt had sought to defend a uniquely American nationalism, one that rejected the notion of hyphenation for native white Americans as well as for ethnics. As part of his ideology, and as initially articulated by the Americanization movement, native-born Americans were obligated to accept and help new immigrants, to demonstrate tolerance even as they demanded assimilation. In practice, Americanization programs and propaganda were directed entirely at immigrants and ethnics. Under the pressure of politics, especially the concerns for national unity generated by the First World War, a second stage of Americanization reinforced the exclusionary vision of citizenship advocated by proponents of immigration restriction. As the exhortations for Americans to become more tolerant waned, efforts to deracinate newcomers gained strength. The dominant vision of citizenship in the Progressive Era thus came to depend on both limiting the entry of newcomers and coercing those already present (King 2000; Pickus 2001).

At the same time that Roosevelt's assimilation approach turned increasingly coercive, it proved insufficiently powerful as an alternative simply to restricting immigration from southern and eastern Europe. Immigrants whom Roosevelt had considered assimilable were regarded as racially deficient by a wide range of legislators, opinion leaders, and the public (Grant 1918; King 2000). Such views contributed heavily to the establishment in 1924 of a yearly quota of 150,000 immigrants from European countries based on the proportion of foreign-born residents in the United States in 1890, a practice that discriminated against southern and eastern Europeans. This statute also excluded the Japanese altogether. Roosevelt died in 1919, but by then, even his confidence in the absorptive capacities of American nationalism had been shaken. His "booming, belligerent optimism," as Thomas Dyer neatly summarizes Roosevelt's final years, gave way to a sense of "impending racial disaster" (Dyer 1980, 168).

Randolph Bourne and Cultural Pluralism

As a journalist and essayist, Randolph Bourne brought a distinctly cultural dimension to his analysis of ethnicity and American identity during the Progressive Era. Published in July, 1916, his "Trans-National America" essay opened with a frontal assault on the notion that immigrants were un-American because they felt deeply attached to their countries of origin. "We are all foreign-born," he announced, "or the descendants of foreign-born, and if distinctions are to be made between us they should rightly be on some other ground than indigenousness." Bourne pointed out that the early settlers did not come to the New World to adopt the culture of Native Americans. Indeed, he contended, "[i]n their folkways, in their social and political institutions, they were, like every colonial people, slavishly imitative of the mother-country" (Bourne 1916, 109).

Bourne acknowledged a positive side to the Americanization movement. He believed that mastering English, naturalizing, even learning to salute the flag, were important aspects of joining the nation. He lauded American elites for their work in the schools and settlement houses seeking to help immigrants adjust to a new life. Well before Americanization had taken its more coercive turn, however, he rejected what he saw as its tendency to substitute a "petrified" English culture for the development of a genuinely American one. "The Anglo-Saxon element is guilty of just what every dominant race is guilty of in every European country," Bourne wrote. "[T]he imposition of its own culture on the minority peoples." He thought that immigrants had good reason to think of Americanization as based primarily on a "predominance of priority" rather than the establishment of a truly American culture (Bourne 1916, 111–12).

The reverence for all things English had misled both native-born and naturalized citizens into missing what was genuinely unique about the new nation, its "distinctively American spirit." This spirit was fundamentally "pioneer," it was about "bigness [and] action," and it was the "adventurous, forward-looking drive of a colonial empire." Whitman, Emerson, and James constituted its own creators and celebrators, native geniuses who had been made to "exist on sufferance alongside of this other cult, unconsciously belittled by our cultural makers of opinion" (Bourne 1916, 110). At least these creators of a distinctly American sensibility in verse, essay, and philosophy had managed to emerge at all; in drama, fiction, and architecture, Bourne lamented, "we are inarticulate of the very values which we profess to idealize." A conception of nationalism defined as the melting pot misunderstood that the American cultural tradition, paradoxically, lay in the future. This tradition had to be created, not formed in imitation. Bourne was excited by the prospects of creating something genuinely new, by the "incomparable opportunity of attacking the future with a new key" (Bourne 1916, 115–16).

His excitement at creating a new culture was tempered by what he regarded as American elites' insistence on "Anglo-Saxonizing" newcomers. He observed that the South remained the most purely English and compared it unfavorably to the "wisdom, intelligence, industry, and social leadership" that had come out of the Midwestern states that had absorbed more immigrants (Bourne 1916, 112). What Bourne most worried about was that immigrants would be pressed to lose the very traditional cultures that provided them with cultural substance and thus helped orient them in a rapidly changing world. The homogeneity and uniformity so sought after by the most ardent nationalizers threatened to create "cultural half-breeds, neither assimilated Anglo-Saxons nor nationals of another culture" (Bourne 1916, 113).

This, in fact, was what Bourne believed had already started to take place, replacing native culture with no culture. He foreshadowed future debates over commercialization and anomie in describing immigrants as having substituted for their traditional culture "only the most rudimentary American—the American culture of the cheap newspaper, the 'movies,' the popular song, the ubiquitous automobile." By forcing newcomers to throw off their native traditions, Bourne feared that they would become lost, "men and women without a spiritual country, cultural outlaws, without taste, without standards but those of the mob. We sentence them to live on the most rudimentary planes of American life" (Bourne 1916, 113–14).

Bourne distinguished between what he called centripetal and centrifugal forces in cultural life. He praised the distinctive qualities of individual cultures as centripetal, as providing the values that make it possible to locate oneself in the world, to make judgments, and, as such, to be better able to contribute to the American community. Americans should respect rather than denigrate "the Jew who sticks proudly to the faith of his fathers and boasts of that venerable culture" and the "Bohemian who supports the Bohemian schools in Chicago." Centrifugal forces, in contrast, operate at the fringes of particular cultures, such that immigrants who are detached from their cultures become mere "fragments of peoples.... This is the cultural wreckage of our time, and it is from the fringes of the Anglo-Saxon as well as the other stocks that it falls" (Bourne 1916, 112–13). Bourne thus joined his concern that a backward-looking Anglo-Saxonism stood in the way of the truly American pioneer spirit with his worry that immigrants were being pressed to lose the only identity that could keep them anchored in the absence of a new American nationalism. Yet America had not yet developed an "impelling, integrating force." It still lacked a clear enough sense of its national purpose or cultural traditions.

Cosmopolitanism

The dominance of English tradition and the de-culturation of newcomers, in fact, stood in the way of forging a radically new transnational identity. This identity simultaneously would be pluralist and cosmopolitan. The pluralist dimension would issue from the centripetal forces operating from the left side of the hyphen that joins subgroup to national identity. In contrast to European nationalism, America would make a place for groups to mingle but not to become uniform. Thus, what Roosevelt and other Americans recoiled from in horror, the ostensible "failure of the melting pot," Bourne regarded as the beginning of the great American experiment in democracy. "In a world which has dreamed of internationalism, we find that we have all unawares been building up the first international nation. America is already the world-federation in miniature, the continent where for the first time in history has been achieved the miracle of hope, the peaceful living side by side, with character substantially preserved, of the most heterogeneous peoples under the sun" (Bourne 1916, 117).

While Bourne marveled at the possibility that European cultures would "merge" but not "fuse," he clearly thought that in the intersections among cultures citizens would engage in a dynamic "weaving back and forth" of traditions (Bourne 1916, 121). On the American side of the hyphen a cosmopolitan culture would develop as a result of this cultural engagement and interaction. A new generation of Americans would regard national provincialism in the same manner Roosevelt viewed regionalism, as a useful feeling whose time had passed. Bourne coined a distinctive term for this process: citizens would be "acclimatized," rather than assimilated. He hoped a new generation would reject the "stale and familiar attitudes of those whose ingrowing culture has scarcely created anything vital for his America of today." In this process, even the "eager Anglo-Saxon" would be liberated to breathe "a larger air. In his new enthusiasm for continental literatures, for unplumbed Russian depths, for French clarity of thought, for Teuton philosophies of power, he feels himself a citizen of a larger world" (Bourne 1916, 118).

The hyphen functioned for Bourne "as a plus sign," to use Michael Walzer's phrase (Walzer 1990). Individuals' distinctive cultural heritages would be precisely what makes them, in Bourne's view, "more valuable and interesting to each other." These differences would serve as spurs to the development of an "intellectual sympathy" that aims to get to "the heart of the different cultural expressions, and [feel] as they feel." Bourne believed that, under these circumstances, it would be possible to understand other views and traditions while retaining ones' own. Indeed, those differences would be made "creative" because they constituted the foundation of a "new cosmopolitan outlook." This outlook would be America's true gift to the world even as it bound Americans together by their equal possession of it. "For Bourne," David Hollinger notes, "cosmopolitanism implied strength and resilience rather than a lack of deep character. Cosmopolitans engaged a world the complexity of which rendered provincial tastes and skills inadequate and uninspiring" (Hollinger 1995, 94). Bourne was an American nationalist who saw America serving a greater purpose, not one who saw preserving the nation as the primary aim. American nationalism would draw on subnational identities in the service of establishing a transnational identity. It would be the crucible through which acclimatized Jews, Germans, Italians, and Anglo-Saxons created "an intellectual internationalism [that makes] . . . understanding and not indignation its end." "Such a sympathy," Bourne assured, "will unite and not divide" (Bourne 1916, 118–19).

Allegiance

Although Bourne despised the ideology of patriotism and the machinations of the Americanization movement that he associated with the First World War, he did not favor "a policy of drift" (Bourne 1916, 119). Bourne wanted an "integrated and disciplined" American nation, but he conceived of this unity and how to achieve it in radically different terms from Roosevelt. Bourne differed even from fellow Left Progressives like John Dewey, whom he bitterly criticized for supporting the war (Bourne 1917). "War is the health of the state," he famously declared, arguing that what would follow from the conflict in Europe was not a unified nation but an overdeveloped state apparatus (Bourne 1919, 71). Instead, Bourne proposed that America had a unique role to play in the world. It would become the "first international nation" by a set of policy ideas that coordinated rather than eradicated its diverse elements.

In his 1916 essay "Trans-National America," Bourne's main concern was the integration of immigrants in America. He was willing to treat questions of immigration policy as matters of "expediency," as practical determinations based on economic need and the country's physical capacity for absorption. He insisted, however, that "we must have a policy and an ideal for an actual situation [of cultural pluralism]. Our question is, What shall we do with our America?" In place of Americanization, Bourne argued for policies that engaged new immigrants in social and political life coupled with a powerful antidiscriminatory ethic. Effective integration, he contended, required a spirit of joint cooperation. A free society was one in which all its members had an equal chance to determine its "ideals and purposes and industrial and social institutions." New and native-born citizens must feel a sense of enthusiasm and purpose and this depends on no ethnic group sensing "that its cultural base is being prejudged." Immigrants were more likely to embrace a country that included them as equal participants in an ongoing process of national self-definition, rather than one that believed they had to lose their sense of self and ideals by a process of Americanization.

Bourne believed that multiple allegiances and identities strengthened American identity, as long as they were properly engaged in a process of acclimatization. He therefore did not regard becoming an American citizen as the kind of transformative event that could or should sever an individual from his previous allegiances. He saw little purpose in demanding that immigrants escaping the exclusive nationalism of Europe adopt an equally narrow American nationalism. Instead, Bourne favored dual citizenship as a practical basis for strengthening the new cosmopolitan identity he envisioned America developing. He further advocated "free and mobile passage of the immigrant between America and his native land" because it would enable America to spread its new ideology of cosmopolitanism. Rather than seeing immigrants who shuttled between the United States and their country of origin as parasites, Bourne saw them as "a symbol of the cosmopolitan interchange which is coming, in spite of all war and national exclusiveness." "Only the American," he wrote confidently, "and in this category I include the migratory alien who has lived with us and caught the pioneer spirit and a sense of new social vistas— has the chance to become that citizen of the world" (Bourne 1916, 121).

Process and the Pioneer Spirit

Despite his confidence, Bourne was easily shouldered aside in the frenzy of nationalism during the First World War. As a literary and cultural critic, he had little organizational support for his ideas. When he died at age thirty-two in the flu epidemic of 1918, rumor held that opposition to his pacifist views had left him without any means of support or outlets for his writing (Lasch 1965, 74). The ultimate vagueness of his own views also contributed to his inability to make headway against the juggernaut of hypernationalism. Bourne's powerful critique of Americanization and evocation of a new cosmopolitanism gained some ground in the 1930s and 1940s, especially among socialists and modernists (Hollinger 1995, 95). But he never developed a systematic, coherent theory of transnational America, a point he acknowledged (Bourne 1916, 122).

Bourne wrote prior to the ethnic, racial, and identity movements of the mid- to late twentieth century. He was eager to castigate the fear and illiberalism he believed undergirded the dominant culture's reaction to the growing ethnic diversity of the United States. This focus on the perils of Americanization came at a price. He avoided questions about the conflicts that might develop between the left and the right side of the hyphen, about whether the group consciousness he applauded would overwhelm the cosmopolitanism he sought to engender, and about whether the cosmopolitanism would corrode the group consciousness. Bourne's attention to the importance of inherited identities often seemed at odds with his emphasis on the dynamic "weaving back and forth" between new and native-born citizens. This confusion between the persistence of difference and the emergence of a genuinely new culture still characterizes debates over multiculturalism today (Hollinger 1995, 94).

What did Bourne imagine would change and what would remain the same in the first international nation? He wrote of "a future America, on which all can unite, which pulls us irresistibly toward it," and he set out a process for arriving at this destination. But he never gave it substance. His America was a nation devoted to the pioneer spirit. Bourne thus never fully addressed the potential conflict between a polity founded on a set of self-evident truths and a culture devoted to a continual process of becoming. Nor did he confront the question of whether a dynamic national culture would require some greater sense of stability and form. Bourne made it easier for his views to be swept aside because he left unanswered the question of how a national identity based on the "pioneer spirit" could become the integrating force he thought necessary as well.

Bourne shared with Roosevelt a concern for the cultural, psychological, and conceptual dimensions of citizenship, even as he offered radically divergent conceptions of allegiance, nationality, and ethnicity. At critical junctures, each of their views was ambiguous and unclear as to its limits. Roosevelt could not compete with the more exclusionary and coercive forces of nationalism that he had helped to unleash, even as his own visions and associated social movement became more restrictive. Bourne was tossed aside more easily than Roosevelt, in part because he was not allied with any significant political movement, and, in part, because of the inscrutability of his ultimate vision of American life. Neither view prevailed and both died depressed and dispirited within two weeks of each other. What are the implications of Bourne and Roosevelt's fate for modern proponents of their versions of liberal nationalism? Do they offer coherent visions that are capable of withstanding countervailing pressures?

Multicultural Nationalism

Alexander Aleinikoff advances an explicitly Bourneian conception of American nationalism and citizenship. He argues that a multicultural nationalism is consistent with both the new realities of global life and the highest aspirations of the American people. His aim is to "develop policies that foster a nation at peace with its constituent groups and groups that identify with the nation." Aleinikoff's nationalism, like Bourne's, is characterized by its confidence in the capacity of America to emerge enriched from controversies over multiculturalism and globalism. "A progressive American nationalism must be forward-looking," he writes, "welcoming an America becoming rather than bemoaning an America lost. . . . America is an open-ended proposition" (Aleinikoff 1998a, 80).

Like Bourne, Aleinikoff regards a unitary American identity as neither possible nor desirable. Improved communication, better transportation, free trade laws, the proliferation of dual citizenship, and a prevailing discourse celebrating universal personhood and cultural difference now mean that the link between migrant and home country will persist and may even strengthen over time. These changes have led to greater sociocultural, economic, and political exchange between migrant groups and their home communities and government. Furthermore, immigrants now enter an America whose growing polyethnism and multicultural ideology doom any attempts to create a nation by traditional means of assimilation. The acceptance of a more multicultural society undermines the Rooseveltian aim "to mold new immigrants into an American stock, reasserting Western values and excluding people who do not abide by them" (Aleinikoff 1998a, 83). Indeed, Aleinikoff celebrates rather than laments the proliferation of multiple loyalties. In his view, attachment to one identity does not necessarily mean less attachment to another. Nor is it clear that one's national allegiance crowds out all other commitments. "People talk about symbolic problems of dual nationality," Aleinikoff notes. "It's very hard to identify concrete problems with it. . . . People are a bundle of allegiances, to families, nations, even the schools they attended" (Cheng 2000, A3; see also Aleinikoff 1990, 28; 1998b, 25–40).

The proliferation of subnational and transnational loyalties does mean that a revived sense of national identity is more, rather than less, important. As a practical matter, the nation-state remains the primary vehicle for protecting rights and practicing democracy. It is also the best means to encourage "us to look beyond the immediate demands of those alive today to the interest of future generations." Moreover, the fact that Americans disagree about what it means to be an American gives added impetus to ensuring that those disagreements take place within a larger whole. "[T]he central idea," Aleinikoff writes, "is that a person be committed to this country's continued flourishing and see himself or herself as part of that ongoing project. The allegiance, the common identification, need not be exclusive, but it must be paramount" (Aleinikoff 1998a, 83, 85). His articulation of this vision itself reflects the significant changes in public debate over the last decade—as recently as 1990 he memorably referred to the idea of a national community as an "oxymoron" (Aleinikoff 1990, 30).

Aleinikoff distinguishes his notion of allegiance from an emphasis on "timeless civic values." In his view, a commitment to shared political principles produces only an agreement to disagree, rather than a more robust sense of identification. What is needed, instead, is a sense of "mutuality," a Bourneian commitment to go beyond mere nondiscrimination and to actively engage others on their own terms. Aleinikoff, like Bourne, does not ask that citizens suspend judgment, but he does insist that they seek to understand those whose views and cultures differ from their own. "Tolerance is a politics of peaceful coexistence; mutuality is a politics of recognition," he writes (Aleinikoff 1998a, 84).

Aleinikoff's emphasis on mutuality and on identification with the whole over the parts diverges from a multiculturalism that emphasizes the permanency of groups' differences. He favors a principle of permeability in which group identity is understood as voluntary and fluid, a quality neither to be eradicated nor frozen. Aleinikoff thus sets his nationalism against any view that would interfere with the "open-ended interaction [that changes] both immigrant and native cultures." He embraces Bourne's notion of a dynamic relationship between new and old, a process that rejects the idea of America as a fixed entity. Rather, he argues, America is a "contract under constant renegotiation" (Aleinikoff 1998a, 84). In addition to his principles of mutuality and permeability, the conditions that make possible that process of renegotiation include immigration policies that ensure control over the nation's borders and that place greater emphasis on skills-based immigration, and immigrant policies that provide a social safety net for newcomers and that promote English as the de facto national language.

For all Aleinikoff's updating of Bourne's vision, key elements remain unclear. In the first place, what does it mean to say that America remains an "ongoing project" and an "open-ended proposition"? The examples Aleinikoff gives of a two-way relationship between new immigrants and native-born citizens seem rather mild: the enlargement of standard English to include words derived from other languages and the way in which a Protestant work ethic of individualism has been supplemented by the communal efforts of immigrant groups. Aleinikoff also seems to set limits on change when he argues that a commitment to liberal political principles is a necessary, though not sufficient, condition for being American.

Yet Aleinikoff also seems to advance a conception of American identity and ideals that is radically open to change. He stresses that Americans have different ideas about what being an American means and emphasizes a process of dynamic interaction that privileges flux over fixity. This preference for process raises the same two questions as Bourne's emphasis on the "pioneer spirit": How does an emphasis on process and change relate to the idea of the nation as embodying specific purposes and particular ideals? Does an identity based on commitment and process have sufficiently integrative force?

Aleinikoff says little about what limits on change liberal principles actually set, a crucial issue in the context of current conflicts over the meaning of those principles. Writing in 1990, he argued that fashioning citizens on the basis of citizenship in the nation-state would compel conformity to a "dominant liberal discourse [that] is neither neutral nor all-inclusive." Scholars such as Martha Minow, Derrick Bell, and Patricia Williams, he contended, have demonstrated that claims to national community reflect "the norms and culture of dominant groups" (Aleinikoff 1990, 31, n. 84; see Minow 1990; Bell 1987; Williams 1991). Aleinikoff's vagueness on this key issue in 1998 has prompted some observers to question what liberal nationalists mean by calling America "an open-ended proposition." "All societies change over time and there is always some reinterpretation of civic norms," notes John Fonte. "However, the major issue is what is open to reinventing and what is not. If the core principles of the American Founding are fluid, porous, and always being recast, then the moral-cultural foundation of the American regime is a hollow shell" (Fonte 1998, 9).

Aleinikoff clearly rejects any notion of ethnic federalism, yet he describes America as a "contract under constant renegotiation." A contract is an agreement based largely on bargaining in which each side seeks to improve its position. This view contrasts with Aleinikoff's notion that what is needed is identification with the whole beyond the parts. It implies a self-interested, tactical set of maneuvers rather than a process of democratic persuasion. Moreover, he characterizes the parties to the contract as groups rather than individuals. This characterization suggests that Aleinikoff means to do more than simply acknowledge the role group consciousness and group effort have played throughout American history; it suggests a continuing and publicly acknowledged and rewarded role for group rights. This possibility raises the question of whether "a commitment to the continued flourishing of the country" is sufficient to bind when views of the country's meaning and values are sufficiently divergent and the process for managing them is negotiation among groups.

Aleinikoff's principles of mutuality and permeability are meant to inoculate Americans against too strong an emphasis on groups' inwardness and group rights, but they raise questions of intent and practice as well. What, in the end, does it mean not to prejudge a group's "cultural case" as urged by Aleinikoff and Bourne? Does it allow for a cultural defense of spousal abuse? Does it mean that bilingual education is appropriate as a means to preserving an individual's cultural context? Does it encompass justifications for affirmative action on the grounds of expanding racial diversity? Furthermore, what is the process by which real differences among groups or values are explored and resolved? Aleinikoff's principles of mutuality and permeability evoke the ideal of a liberal education. But on campuses as well as in courts and legislatures, the politics of recognition has often been associated with preserving differences rather than engaging them in a manner that sustains a sense of common commitment. Aleinikoff offers a complex picture of what he describes as "tender times, when assertions of sub-national or trans-national affiliations are too frequently read as disloyalty and claims about the value of the nation-state are too frequently dismissed as nativist" (Aleinikoff 1998a, 86). The unresolved question in these tender times remains how to attend to the role of group identity while engendering commitment to the nation and the values of individual liberty and human equality.

Cosmopolitan Nationalism

David Hollinger, like Aleinikoff and Bourne, criticizes a singular, un-contested conception of American identity. He is suspicious of attempts to draw group identity too tightly on the basis of nationality. Against universalists, Hollinger rejects the notion that American identity is defined by an unchanging set of civic values. He contends that Americans are deeply divided over what it means to live up to the principles embodied in the U.S. Constitution. Hollinger also shares with Aleinikoff a Bourne-like cosmopolitanism that emphasizes the dynamic interaction among groups rather than the static vision of inherited identities proffered by some multiculturalists. He supports "the renewal and critical revision of those communities of descent whose progeny choose to devote their energies to these communities even after experiencing opportunities for affiliating with other kinds of people" (Hollinger 1995, 13; see also Hollinger 1998b).

Hollinger presses beyond Bourne, and differs in emphasis from Aleinikoff, in the attention he devotes to the American side of the hyphen. He sees the American nation as the best vehicle for advancing the values of a "rooted cosmopolitanism." Those values include "recognition, acceptance, and eager exploration of diversity" as well as "a push for solidarities less all-inclusive than the species-wide 'we'" (Hollinger 1998b, 92–93). A sense of shared American purpose is necessary, in his view, for redistributing resources within the United States, helping minorities achieve greater equality, and expanding the circle of humans whom Americans care about and feel responsible toward.

Hollinger emphasizes the possibilities for combining individual rights and national identity in the United States. For him, the United States is more than a set of institutions, procedures, and abstract liberal values. It is also "a finite historical entity with a record of specific tragedies, successes, failures, contradictions, and provincial conceits . . . " (Hollinger 1998b, 94). This record makes it possible for Americans to conceive of their common citizenship as based in a dynamic conception of a historically significant people, a people committed to an ongoing debate over their collective identity. American national identity, in Hollinger's work, serves common purposes without obscuring our differences. He believes Americans can accomplish this difficult task by recognizing that they share a past that consists of quarrels over the meaning of American identity as well as a common project of expanding human freedom.

"[C]oercion is obviously a large part of the story of American belonging," Hollinger acknowledges. As a consequence, he recognizes that there are risks in stressing the centrality of national solidarity. But he questions whether a cosmopolitan vision of nationalism necessarily depends on a significant degree of coercion. "The suppression of cultural diversity and political liberties in the Progressive Era and early 1920s is indeed a cautionary tale for our own time. But what lessons this often-told story should offer us today is less certain. . . ." Boundaries, Hollinger contends, "are not always evil; what matters is which boundaries, where and for what purposes they are drawn and by what authority" (Hollinger 1997, 562, 564; see also Wolfe 1989, 246–56; Pickus 1998b, 130–33). He further emphasizes that the presence of so many ethnic and racial identities in America makes the dangers of nationalism less pronounced. In addition, the United States' commitment to liberal political principles in the 1990s means that loyalty to America can coexist with a commitment to the broader human community.

Hollinger's attention to the evolving and contentious nature of American nationhood, like Alienikoff's emphasis on flux, also brings to light a very different set of risks: it raises crucial questions about the relation of self-government, constitutional politics, and national identity. Most fundamentally, is a commitment to shared quarrels, or to interpretation, sufficient to bind a heterogeneous population? What, if any, limits are there on a transformative conception of national solidarity, one in which citizens may believe in new principles and ideals and the nation may be reconfigured? These broad conceptual questions require answers, and not simply as a matter of political theory. A project that invites significant change must demonstrate that it can generate sufficient commitment to sustain itself.

On the other hand, Hollinger risks engendering a different sort of alienation if he makes the nation a vehicle for achieving a set of goals defined too narrowly. If his embrace of nationalism is primarily directed toward building a larger welfare state, or at transcending the nation itself in favor of broader forms of governance and identification, why should current citizens who disagree with those aims subscribe to his vision? Is it possible for citizens to regard their nation with deep affection and attachment while also viewing it simply as instrumental to some other purpose? This question further raises the critical issue of how American national identity might change. Will it, for instance, come as a result of elite politics, of international courts and bureaucracies imposing a set of transnational rights (see Jacobson 1996)? Or will Americans, as a self-governing people, consciously decide to alter what they mean by citizenship and national identity? The answers to these questions will be crucial to determining how well any changes are accepted.

Hollinger's focus on history and narrative hints at one possible response to some of these questions. He finds historical narrative the best vehicle for addressing both our differences and our similarities: the history of Americans as a specific people grounds, and limits, their debates; it allows them to connect to the sense that many have of belonging to the nation as well as to their devotion to broader principles and cosmopolitan commitments. Hollinger believes that one can render an honest picture of American history that is, all told, inspirational. Indeed, teaching new and native-born citizens that American history is an epic tale of the conflict over who they are as a nation may have great potential to inspire commitment to liberal principles and the American nation.

Hollinger's project calls for a delicate balancing act between inspiration and criticism, idealism and alienation. It remains an open question whether such a balance is possible to achieve in theory, let alone in practice. As the essence of an ideal national narrative, he offers the claim that: "The United States now finds itself in a position to develop and act upon a cultural self-image as *a national solidarity committed, but often failing, to incorporate individuals from a great variety of communities of descent, on equal but not homogeneous terms, into a society with democratic aspirations inherited largely from England*" (emphasis in original). This is a carefully wrought sentence that might draw agreement across a range of views. Yet it, too, demands further clarification, such as what it means to incorporate individuals from different groups on "equal but not homogeneous terms" (Hollinger 1998b, 95; see also Hollinger 1998a, 325–26; Ravitch and Schlesinger 1996).

Democratic Nationalism

In 1995, Michael Lind published *The Next American Nation*, a bold, slashing book advocating a radical revival of liberal nationalism. Lind shares Hollinger's emphasis on the historical nature of American nationalism.

But where Hollinger draws on Randolph Bourne and is wary of too tri-umphalist a vision of American identity, Lind derides Bourne and favors Theodore Roosevelt as his exemplar of an American cultural hero. Lind's view contrasts even more with Aleinikoff's, whose use of Bourne to empha-size an America constituted by mutually respecting groups is at odds with Lind's faith in the melting pot and his sharp criticism of affirmative action.

Lind believes that America has been held in the grip of a white "over-class" bent on religious and racial domination. From 1789 to 1861, Protes-tant Anglo-Saxons and Germans dominated; from 1875 to 1957, this group expanded to a more generic European nationality and Christianity. In its third and current incarnation, this overclass has used group-based poli-cies such as affirmative action to include minority elites while avoiding "the dramatic reforms of American government and business that are nec-essary to integrate working-class and poor blacks and Hispanics, along with the absolute majority of the poor who are white, into the larger so-ciety." Lind is not concerned about the danger of balkanization along racial lines. Rather, he worries about "Brazilianization" in which the United States is divided by strict class lines that consign nonwhites and poor whites to the bottom of the social hierarchy. Such a system is char-acterized by the withdrawal of elites, including some minorities, into pri-vate neighborhoods, schools, police, and health care—"a nation-within-a-nation" (Lind 1995, 14).

Proponents of a faux multiculturalism, this white overclass and its mi-nority partners, along with neoconservative universalists who insist that America is an idea, have succeeded in obscuring the true nature of Ameri-can nationalism. The American nation, like all other nations, is formed by language and by habits, what Lind calls "common folkways and a com-mon vernacular culture." This is not a patriotism based on ideology, he argues; "it has more to do with family, neighborhood, customs, and his-torical memories than with constitutions or political philosophies." For Lind, the American cultural nation preceded the state, whereas for Aleinikoff the state constructed a nation of citizens (Lind 1995, 5, 7; Aleinikoff 1998b, 58). As Peter Skerry has observed, Lind's argument shares similarities with more traditional conservatives, such as Peter Brimelow and John O'Sullivan writing in *The National Review*, but he "builds his case on a subtler, more persuasive understanding of America culture that acknowledges its diverse elements and allows for its syncretic growth. So, for example, Lind quite rightly puts the history of black Americans at the center of the American experience . . ." (Skerry 1995, 81; Lind 1995, 274–76).

It is this patriotism of ordinary Americans that Lind wants to draw on in forging an alternative to both laissez-faire capitalism and multiculturalism. He aims to establish a new "Trans-American Melting Pot" by means of "universal miscegenation and upward-leveling, race-blending, and class-blurring." To create this Fourth Republic, Lind mandates a "continual churning of the social classes, abetted by a radical (and race-neutral) restructuring of the political, economic, and educational orders" (Lind 1995, 260). He supports massive state-led programs that cut across traditional lines of liberalism and conservatism, ranging from orphanages and boarding schools for inner-city youth to equalizing spending on education across the nation. On immigration, Lind would limit the flow of unskilled labor and "require a high degree of acculturation as a condition of immigration," though he opposes "coercive and repressive methods" (Lind 1995, 285, 287). These measures reflect his Rooseveltian concern for nation-building and for maintaining a social compact with American labor.

Lind's historical narrative and radical mixing of policies seek to break with the orthodoxies of left and right and establish a new national center to American politics. He offers a conception of American identity as more than abstract ideals but less than a racial or religious nationalism. Yet his vision also risks feeding an American propensity to veer between the extremes of too weak and too strong an emphasis on national identity, both of which can enhance the coercive powers of the state over the individual.

In the first case, Lind's notion of a "vernacular" culture that draws on common folkways and language may prove too weak too support his grand designs. In *One Nation After All*, Alan Wolfe suggests that Americans have come to value tolerance as their primary virtue (Wolfe 1998). If true, then it is difficult to imagine how current American "folkways," especially as those are increasingly shaped by participation in a modern consumer culture, provide a sufficiently robust basis on which to draw in the face of conflict (see Galston 1998). This difficulty is compounded by changes in American institutional life since the Progressive Era. The institutions of civil society, such as churches, unions, and political machines that mediated cultural differences, incorporated immigrants, and maintained vital links between elites and citizens today play a quite different and, generally, more attenuated role (Skerry 1993; Pickus 1997).

As a result, Lind cannot rely on the same civic sinews as Roosevelt did to link Americans across the divides of color and class, and there is little discussion of these institutions in Lind's prescriptions. He often praises the great political organizer, Bayard Rustin, and advocates a broad social policy in line with Rustin's vision, but he but does not identify the organizations that today could support such a figure. Under these conditions, it is hard to see how invoking figures like Roosevelt can knit together a nation of nonjudgmental, middle-class citizens who are increasingly disconnected from one another and estranged from their poorer, racially diverse fellow citizens. The problem to be overcome here is not active exclusion but passive neglect.

These difficulties raise the possibility that Lind's project may open the door to more coercive forms of cultural conformity even as it is forced to become more exclusionary itself in order to compete. Roosevelt's example is especially relevant here. Lind distinguishes too neatly between a nativist "dark side" to nationalism and Roosevelt's "constructive and inclusive current" (Judis and Lind 1995, 21). He does not sufficiently address the dangers presented by the unbounded nature of Roosevelt's devotion to the nation or by their shared definition of the American people in cultural terms. Nor does he confront the kinds of questions Aleinikoff raises as to whether it is possible or desirable to enforce a singular and unbending conception of allegiance in the modern world. Lind's views differ from Roosevelt on some of these matters. Moreover, simply because the Progressive Era ended in coercive, exclusionary policies does not mean such a dynamic will repeat itself today, as critics of liberal nationalism often suggest that it will. These differences and changed conditions do, however, require more forthright acknowledgment and discussion if Lind is to convince others that his tradition of nationalism is simultaneously robust *and* inclusive. He needs to explain how his milder version of nationalism can accomplish the same assimilation and nation-building as Roosevelt's more coercive one (see Gerstle 1997a; Smith 1997; Spiro 1999; King 2000).

The dangers of coercion and exclusion inherent in any process of nation-building, in combination with the current conditions of civic neglect and institutional anemia, may explain the disjunction between Lind's history and his proposals for reform. Those proposals do not depend on Americans' shared sensibility or the creation of social institutions populated by actual citizens. Instead, they tend to be of the silver bullet type that bypasses the process of democratic persuasion and the steady work of political organizing. These proposals range from democratizing schemes, such as campaign finance reform and proportional representation, to top-down reforms that require massive state intervention to achieve, such as an "unsubtle, crude, old-fashioned redistribution of wealth," the banishment of religion from public life, and, in its stead, the creation of an ethic of "civic familialism." Whatever one thinks of Lind's particular proposals, his broader vision threatens to erase some of the fundamental ideas the American nation is meant to serve: individual liberty and equality of opportunity.

Despite his populist stance, Lind clearly has little faith that Americans are capable of their own political reformation. His iconoclastic nationalism stakes out new ground; it also risks proving too weak to support his grand designs while opening the door to more exclusionary and coercive versions of nationalism, and giving rise to the dangers of an overly intrusive state.

National Greatness Conservatism

Like Lind, William Kristol and David Brooks invoke the tradition of Alexander Hamilton, Henry Clay, and Theodore Roosevelt. They do so in the service of what they call "National Greatness Conservatism." Their aim is to redirect the conservative movement in America. Roosevelt in particular captures the proper mixture of domestic activism and foreign engagement that Kristol and Brooks believe will enable conservatives and the Republican Party to "shape the next century as an American century" (Kristol and Brooks 1997). They first widely broached the idea of "National Greatness Conservatism" in 1997, and promoted it especially actively in connection with John McCain's run for the Republican presidential nomination in 2000. Kristol and Brooks helped shape the language and direction of McCain's campaign, such that, in writing about his candidacy, they were often working out their own ideas as much as describing his (Foer 2000; Chait 2000). They shared with McCain a central question: "How can Americans love their nation if they hate its government?"

In their most conscious echo of Teddy Roosevelt, Kristol and Brooks argue that an antigovernment, libertarian philosophy is insufficient. While the ideology of "leave us alone" made sense both substantively and tactically in moving the American people away from the liberal view of a large, active federal government, "wishing to be left alone isn't a governing doctrine," they declare (Kristol and Brooks 1997). That ideology is merely a politics of resentment at a time when conservatives should be inspiring citizens to enlarge their aspirations. Without larger purposes, Brooks fears, "democracy has a tendency to slide into nihilistic mediocrity" (Brooks 1997). In their view, conservatives have rightly emphasized that devolving authority to voluntary associations and smaller forms of government is critical to forging a sense of civic responsibility. But, they add, local communities must be linked to national projects to ensure that their interests are broadened.

Like Roosevelt, Kristol and Brooks celebrate economic development and personal advancement while insisting that politics is not merely about self-interest. Politics is a noble calling because its fundamental aim is to get Americans to "think of ourselves as citizens, not merely consumers; we should serve the public good, not merely private interest. We should be represented in Washington as Americans, not merely as members of interest groups or taxpayers." They saw in McCain's call for campaign finance reform "a more comprehensive ambition to reinvigorate citizenship." It reminded Americans that "citizenship entails more than just voting, and the business of America is more than just business" (Kristol and Brooks 2000a).

Kristol and Brooks also saw in McCain a crucial second component of a modern conservatism based on national greatness: a moral appeal rooted in patriotism rather than directly in religion. A robust religious faith, in their view, is necessary to protecting citizens from liberalism's overemphasis on individual choice. But, in a liberal democracy, appeals to shared values should focus on "public virtues, like courage, honor, integrity, and duty," the virtues necessary to national greatness. They pointed approvingly to the shift in McCain's speeches "from religious faith to the Declaration of Independence, from the cross to America." This shift from religion to patriotism signaled to them a Roosevelt-like stance against selfish private interests—"tobacco companies, pork-barrel spenders, special interests, overreaching federal regulators"—rather than a crusade to regulate morality in private life (Kristol and Brooks 2000b).

Like Lind and Croly, Kristol and Brooks want to distinguish their brand of patriotism from the European "blood-and-soil-nationalism," a form of which they see in a figure like Patrick Buchanan. They conceive of American nationalism as the interrelation of a universalist emphasis on abstract ideals of equality and liberty and a particularist history of supporting those principles. This understanding of America's national greatness, they argue, is the best bulwark against the appeal of European-style nationalism. Unlike Lind's denigration of an American exceptionalism built on ideas, Kristol and Brooks contend that "[o]ur pride in settling the frontier, welcoming immigrants and advancing the cause of freedom around the world, is related to our dedication to our principles" (Kristol and Brooks 1997).

What does Kristol and Brooks's argument for an energetic government that respects limits on its authority mean in the modern era? In foreign policy, Kristol and Brooks would pursue a more expansive approach, featuring, for example, a more critical engagement with China; in domestic policy, their suggestions range from policies that "preserve and enhance our national patrimony—the parks, buildings and monuments that are the physical manifestations of our common heritage"—to workfare, standards in education, efforts to reduce abortion by increasing adoptions, and Roosevelt-like campaigns to "bust the great public trusts of our time—the education, health, and Social Security monopolies" (Kristol and Brooks 1997). Brooks is especially taken by the example of the original Library of Congress and its "grand interiors" as a way to "lift Americans above the petty concerns of bourgeois life and put them in touch with aristocratic virtues and transcendent truth" (Brooks 1997).

How do these policies differ from those of other conservatives today, particularly in the domestic arena? Kristol and Brooks acknowledge that their program is vague, calling it "silly to try to lay out some sort of 10-point program for American greatness." Their purpose is to get Americans "to think differently about politics," not to provide a detailed policy agenda (Kristol and Brooks 1997). "It almost doesn't matter what great tasks government sets for itself," notes Brooks, "as long as it does some tangible thing with energy and effectiveness" (Brooks 1997). This Roosevelt-like view of public life suggests that the same questions raised about the purposes of Roosevelt's nationalism can be addressed to Kristol and Brooks and to the McCain candidacy they championed. What ideological or institutional limits exist to their broader themes of nationalism and patriotism? When McCain stressed that we "live for America" in his Republican Convention speech, does it not sound, as Ramesh Ponnuru observes, "uncomfortably close to idolatry"? (Ponnuru 2000).

At the same time that Kristol and Brooks's nationalism raises questions about limits on the activities of government, the modest nature of their initial proposals indicates that they face an entirely different problem: whether their policies are sufficient to invoke and sustain a robust national sensibility. "Grand American projects," such as the Library of Congress, seem rather pallid compared to building the Panama Canal, ending the Great Depression, or launching a war against poverty. "At least liberals emphasize important issues," grumbles the libertarian Doug Bandow. "[C]onservatives apparently believe they can achieve greatness on the cheap" (Bandow 1997). Will a new nationalist conservatism have to pursue ever-grander projects to sustain itself? This possibility is precisely why Kristol and Brooks' invocation of Roosevelt has been welcomed by some liberals. "Using government on behalf of 'national greatness,'" notes *Washington Post* columnist E. J. Dionne, "could get you right back to the New Deal" (Dionne 1997).

Kristol and Brooks are noticeably silent on an area of public life that Roosevelt considered a fundamental threat to national greatness: the market. Roosevelt sought to build a more robust sense of national identity to undergird the federal government's authority to regulate national commerce. While an ardent believer in capitalism, he subjugated economic development and personal advancement to national greatness. Roosevelt worried that rising social inequality would make it impossible for American workers to actively support national projects. And he believed that the values of the market, if extended too far, would undermine the moral and civic values necessary to sustain a free government. Can Kristol and Brooks spark a broad scale national revival today without addressing the effects of global markets on domestic inequality, the social compact, and American culture? As Jim Sleeper observes: "Conservatives, defending even global investments that accelerate the social decay they decry, sacrifice Madison to Madison Avenue. . . . Many Americans whose lives are less charmed are left with a sinking feeling that the old decencies driving the McCain and World Trade Organization insurgencies are little more than doomed, wistful gesturings of a lost civic love" (Sleeper 2000).

Kristol and Brooks's "national greatness" manifesto also has little to say directly on issues of diversity and American citizenship. Like Roosevelt, they clearly want a vigorous sense of unified, national identity to guide American politics and they counterpose this project to "talk about building a bridge to a multicultural, diverse and politically correct twenty-first century" (Kristol and Brooks 1997). Their magazine, *The Weekly Standard*, has opposed bilingual education, affirmative action, and other group-based policies. Unlike Roosevelt, they have devoted less attention to whether any special policies or processes might be necessary to actively shape a new American identity with regard to minorities, and especially toward new immigrants. Roosevelt argued that a policy of "Let alone" is especially pernicious in the case of immigrants; he believed that the federal government had to prevent resentment from developing among new arrivals by actively incorporating them into American political life. Yet those policies led, in part, to more coercive, exclusionary forms of nationalism and Americanization. The incorporation of immigrants into the American nation thus offers Kristol and Brooks an ideal place to spell out the content, and the limits, of national greatness conservatism.

Bridging Intellectual and Institutional Gaps

If we are to be One America, which America are we to be? When liberal nationalism burst onto the scene in the mid-1990s it offered to transcend traditional political divisions. Within our hypereconomy of ideas, the fissures have rapidly become apparent. Across the wide range of nationalists who are simultaneously committed to vitality and inclusion many of those fissures cannot be bridged. A multicultural nationalism, to take one example, is a goal for some and an oxymoron for others. The segmentation of American intellectual life into the separate realms of academia, the media, and think tanks makes these divisions even more difficult to cross (Lind 1999). Still, these nationalists all speak a broad public language, and they differ from ardent multiculturalists and fervent globalists in their shared view that America is a remarkable nation. To some, it is an exceptional nation, unique in human history; to others it occupies a special, if not entirely unique, position among nation-states. Like both Roosevelt and Bourne before them, they believe America must create its own traditions and play a distinctive role in the world. There is thus considerable room for useful discussion and fruitful disagreement.

At the beginning of the twentieth century, the Progressives sought to forge a felt sense of national identity and shared citizenship. While neither Roosevelt nor Bourne prevailed at the time, an inchoate, broadly defined liberal nationalism that drew on their views did emerge from the crucibles of the Depression, the Second World War, the Civil Rights movement, and the Great Society. During the last thirty years, that nationalism has been challenged internally by group discontent and individual alienation and externally by the globalization of markets and the movement of people. Over the course of the twenty-first century, that identity will be further tested by simultaneous trends toward political devolution and supranational evolution, massive demographic shifts and mounting cultural tensions, and the advent of new technologies and the perils of economic dislocation.

These trends present new challenges, including how to develop a shared vision for public life in which institutions and citizens collaborate effectively to create healthy communities; how to maintain democratic authority over increasingly globalized economic and political power; how to regulate ethnic and religious clashes within and between nations; and how to navigate the changing and complex interrelationships among the public, private, and nonprofit sectors. If liberal nationalism is to fulfill its promise to offer new approaches to old problems and creative solutions to new ones, its already raucous membership will have to forthrightly confront these challenges in all their complexity. Three interlocking questions seem particularly crucial for liberal nationalists to address.

What does loyalty and allegiance mean in the modern world? The proliferation of multiple identities flows in part from the liberal freedom to choose one's associations. These associations, as Bourne understood, also serve as a source of meaning, a personal mooring, in a market-oriented, liberal society. Yet, while loyalty may be hard to define in a free society that depends on multiple identities and conflicting allegiances, those identities and allegiances can easily prove destructive if they are not also integrated in some manner. Liberal democracies must attend to the conditions that make multiple identities possible, conditions that necessarily limit some choices. Liberal nationalists believe that some kind of integration is necessary. The question is whether multiple identities must be integrated within a single national allegiance or whether the nation itself can be treated as one among many commitments. Is it plausible for national identity to be paramount, but not exclusive, as Aleinikoff puts it, or does being paramount require some degree of exclusivity (see Fletcher 1993; Wolfe 1997; Aleinikoff 1998a, 1998b; Pickus 1998a; Renshon 2000)?

These questions about exclusivity raise a related question: *To what degree does a renewed emphasis on nationalism require coercive or exclusionary policies?* Some scholars contend that building national community in the United States has often proceeded in tandem with repressive and exclusionary policies. They worry that illiberal American political traditions lurk closely beneath the surface and want to limit the opportunities for the resurgence of a narrow brand of nationalism. The fate of Progressive reformers certainly suggests caution in embarking on exercises in nation-building. At the same time, America today is clearly a more tolerant nation compared to the Progressive Era. The nation's capacity to launch a coercive Americanization program, for instance, seems greatly reduced. In 1995, as chair of the Commission on Immigration Reform, Barbara Jordan unsuccessfully called for reviving even a moderate form of those programs. Indeed, that lack of interest indicates not that traditions of American illiberalism are too strong but, rather, that *any* effort to forge a cohesive national identity may necessitate massive social engineering. Under current conditions, is such engineering possible or desirable? Lind's "Trans-American Nationalism," for instance, is hardly a vision for the timid; it requires a "continual churning" of racial identity, class status, and the political system. Such ambitious plans help focus attention on defining more carefully the content of a renewed nationalism and the groups toward whom it is directed, as well as the process by which that renewal might be carried out, and the safeguards that can be built in for dissent and disagreement (see Hollinger 1997; Gerstle 1997a, 1997b; Smith 1998; Pickus 1998b; Aleinikoff 1998b).

These matters of substance and of process suggest a third key question: *Can a revived nationalism strengthen the mediating institutions of American public life?* Liberals and conservatives have devoted significant attention in recent years to reviving the voluntary associations of civil society. Among other virtues, such associations are the best place to develop the habits of belonging and participation. But, as Kristol and Brooks stress, local associations must be linked to broader communities to ensure that those habits do not become simply parochial and defensive. In turn, a robust civic life at the state and local levels can moderate swings between too strong and too weak a sense of nationalism. For liberal nationalism to contribute to this process of mutual interaction, it cannot remain the province of academics, opinion-makers, and the occasional political leader. Its proponents must heed Peter Skerry's warning that the preoccupation of "the chattering classes [with] overarching historical themes and contemporary value conflicts" has tended to "give short shrift to the messy and sometimes arcane details of the institutions that make society work." If liberal nationalism is to avoid this error, its proponents will need to forge links to religious institutions, immigrant associations, trade unions, small businesses, and high-tech corporations. They will need to help fill the gaps between national policy and community renewal (see Kristol and Brooks 1997; Skerry 1995; Brinkley 1996; Skocpol 1996; Putnam 2000).

We can see the beginnings of these linkages between intellectuals and institutions in a number of areas. The movement to address the ills of the inner city through faith-based programs, for instance, has brought together conservative policy analysts with organizers in minority communities. Foundations are addressing the social consequences of the information economy by connecting technology entrepreneurs to policy thinkers. On the one issue of greatest concern to both Roosevelt and Bourne, the integration of immigrants, however, an unhealthy divide remains between groups that work directly with immigrants and groups concerned about the declining value of citizenship. Many organizations that aid newcomers focus on protecting immigrants' rights. On the other hand, organizations that decry the dissolution of a common American identity have had very little to do with newcomers.

If a modern American nationalism is to engage citizens in a dynamic sense of shared purposes, its proponents will need to carefully consider what intellectual and institutional gaps they mean to bridge. Without undertaking such a project, the liberal nationalism that emerged at the end of the twentieth century risks going the way of its predecessor at the beginning of that century. Its intellectual usefulness will run its course and its political potency will be pushed aside, either by the same racial and ideological forces that Roosevelt and Bourne contended with or by the multiple subnational and transnational forces that are reshaping the nature of politics in the modern world.

* I would like to thank Stanley Renshon, Jim Sleeper, and Maura High for helpful suggestions on this essay; Alex Aleinikoff, Linda Bosniak, Rom Coles, Kim Curtis, Troy Dostert, John Fonte, Gary Gerstle, Johnny Goldfinger, Jennifer Hochschild, Bob Keohane, Scott Kirkhuff, Elizabeth Kiss, Tom Merrill, Alan Ryan, Suzanne Shanahan, Peter Skerry, Rogers Smith, and Peter Spiro for discussions on nationalism; and the H. B. Earhart Foundation for financial support.

References

Aleinikoff, T. Alexander. Winter 1990. "Citizens, Aliens, Membership and the Constitution." *Constitutional Commentary* 7, no. 1, 9–34.

————. January–February 1998a. "A Multicultural Nationalism?" *The American Prospect*, 80–86.

————. 1998b. *Between Principles and Politics: The Direction of U.S. Citizenship Policy.* Washington, D.C.: Carnegie Endowment for International Peace.

Bandow, Doug. October 13, 1997. "Liberals Are Dressing Up in Conservative Clothes." *Cato: This Just In. www.cato.org/dailys/10-13-97/html.*

Bell, Derrick A. 1987. *And We Are Not Saved: The Elusive Quest for Racial Justice.* New York: Basic Books.

Bourne, Randolph S. July 1916. "Trans-National America." *Atlantic Monthly.* Reprinted in Resek, Carl. 1964. *War and the Intellectuals: Collected Essays, 1915–1919.* New York: Harper & Row, 107–23.

————. October 1917. "Twilight of Idols." *The Seven Arts.* Vol. II. In Resek, *War and the Intellectuals,* 53–64.

————. 1919. "The State." In Resek, *War and the Intellectuals,* 65–104.

Brandeis, Louis D. January 23, 1915. "Testimony before the United States Commission on Industrial Relations." *Senate Documents.* 64th Congress, 1st Session, Vol. 26.

Brinkley, Alan. November–December 1996. "Liberty, Community, and the National Idea." *The American Prospect*, no. 29, 53–59.

Brooks, David. March 3, 1997. "A Return to National Greatness: A Manifesto for a Lost Creed." *The Weekly Standard.*

Chait, Jonathan. January 21, 2000. "This Man Is Not a Republican." *The New Republic Online. www.tnr.com/013100/coverstory013100.html.*

Cheng, Mae M. August 7, 2000. "Citizens of the World: New Americans Are Increasingly Keeping Dual Allegiances." *Newsday,* A3.

Croly, Henry. 1909. *The Promise of American Life.* Boston: Northeastern University Press edition, 1989.

Dionne, E. J., Jr. October 24, 1997. "The G.O.P. Finds the Enemy." *Commonweal* 124, no. 18, 7.

Dyer, Thomas G. 1980. *Theodore Roosevelt and the Idea of Race.* Baton Rouge: Louisiana State University Press.

Fletcher, George P. 1993. *Loyalty: An Essay on the Morality of Relationships.* New York: Oxford University Press.

Foer, Franklin. March 20, 2000. "Arguing the GOP: The Neocons Wake Up." *The New Republic. www.thenewrepublic.com/032000/foer32000.html.*

Fonte, John. 1998. "The Progressive Project." Unpublished manuscript, on file with author.

Galston, William A. Fall 1998. Review of *One Nation, After All.* In *The Public Interest.* No. 133, 116 (5).

Gerstle, Gary. October 1994. "The Protean Character of American Liberalism." *American Historical Review* 99 (4): 1043–73.

————. September 1997a. "Liberty, Coercion, and the Making of Americans." *The Journal of American History* 84:524–58.

————. September 1997b. "The Power of Nations." *The Journal of American History.* 84:576–80.

Grant, Madison. 1918. *The Passing of the Great Race.* New ed. New York: C. Scribner's Sons.

Higham, John. 1955, 1988. *Strangers in the Land: Patterns of American Nativism 1860–1925.* New Brunswick, N.J.: Rutgers University Press.

Hollinger, David. 1995. *Postethnic America: Beyond Multiculturalism.* New York: Basic Books.

————. September 1997. "National Solidarity at the End of the Twentieth Century: Reflections on the United States and Liberal Nationalism." *The Journal of American History* 84:559–69.

————. 1998a. "National Culture and Communities of Descent." *Reviews in American History* 26:312–28.

————. 1998b. "Nationalism, Cosmopolitanism, and the United States." In *Immigration and Citizenship in the 21st Century,* ed. N. Pickus. Lanham, Md.: Rowman & Littlefield.

Jacobson, David. 1996. *Rights across Borders: Immigration and the Decline of Citizenship.* Baltimore, Md.: The Johns Hopkins University Press.

Judis, John B. and Michael Lind. March 27, 1995. "For a New Nationalism." *The New Republic,* 19–27.

Kesler, Charles. Spring 1998. "Teddy Roosevelt to the Rescue?" *The National Interest.* www.claremont.org/amer_const/kesler6.cfm.

King, Desmond. 2000. *Making Americans: Immigration, Race, and the Origins of the Diverse Democracy.* Cambridge, Mass.: Harvard University Press.

Kristol, William, and David Brooks. September 15, 1997. "What Ails Conservatism." *The Wall Street Journal,* A, 22, 4.

————. February 14, 2000a. "The McCain Insurrection." *The Weekly Standard* 5, no. 21.
www.weeklystandard.com/magazine/mag_5_21_00/brooks_art_5_21_00.html.

————. March 13, 2000b. "The Politics of Creative Destruction." *The Weekly Standard* 5, no. 25.
www.weeklystandard.com/magazine/mag_5_25_00/kristol_feat_5_25_00.html.

Lasch, Christopher. 1965. *The New Radicalism in America, 1889–1963: The Intellectual as a Social Type.* New York: Knopf.

Lears, Jackson T. J. 1981. *No Place of Grace: Antimodernism and the Transformation of American Culture, 1880–1920.* New York: Pantheon.

Lind, Michael. 1995. *The Next American Nation: The New Nationalism and the Fourth American Revolution.* New York: The Free Press.

————. Spring 1999. "The Three Countries of the American Mind." *The Hudson Review,* 7–17.

Lippmann, Walter. 1929. *A Preface to Morals*. New York: The Macmillan Company.

Minow, Martha. 1990. *Making All The Difference: Inclusion, Exclusion and American Law*. Ithaca, N.Y.: Cornell University Press.

Pickus, Noah. 1997. "Does Immigration Threaten Democracy? Rights, Restriction, and the Meaning of Membership." In *Democracy: The Challenges Ahead*, eds. Yossi Shain and Aharon Klieman. New York: St. Martin's Press.

———. 1998a. *Becoming America/America Becoming: Final Report of the Duke University Workshop on Immigration and Citizenship*. Durham, N.C.: Terry Sanford Institute of Public Policy.

———. 1998b. "To Make Natural: Creating Citizens for the 21st Century." In *Immigration and Citizenship in the Twenty-First Century*, ed. N. Pickus. Lanham, Md.: Rowman & Littlefield.

———. 2001. "Immigration and the Revaluation of American Identity." Unpublished manuscript.

Ponnuru, Ramesh. August 28, 2000. "Hauntings, Visions." *National Review* 52, no. 16. *www.nationalreview.com/28aug00/ponnuru082800.shtml*.

Putnam, Robert D. 2000. *Bowling Alone: The Collapse and Revival of American Community*. New York: Simon & Schuster.

Ravitch, Diane, and Arthur Schlesinger Jr. April 3, 1996. "The New Improved History Standards." *The Wall Street Journal. www.edexcellence.net*.

Renshon, Stanley A. July 2000. "Dual Citizens in America: An Issue of Vast Proportions and Broad Significance." Center for Immigration Studies Backgrounder.

Rodgers, Daniel T. December 1982. "In Search of Progressivism." *Reviews in American History*, 113–31.

Roosevelt, Theodore. 1882. *The Naval War of 1812*. In *The Works of Theodore Roosevelt*, ed. Hermann Hagedorn. Vol. 6, 1926. New York: Charles Scribner's Sons.

———. 1887. *Thomas Hart Benton*. In *The Works of Theodore Roosevelt*, ed. Hagedorn. Vol. 7, 1926.

———. 1888. *Gouverneur Morris*. In *The Works of Theodore Roosevelt*, ed. Hagedorn. Vol. 7, 1926.

———. 1894a. "True Americanism." *The Forum*. In *The Works of Theodore Roosevelt*, ed. Hagedorn. Vol. 13, 1926.

———. 1894b. Review of Charles H. Pearson, *National Life and Character. The Sewanee Review*. In *The Works of Theodore Roosevelt*, ed. Hagedorn. Vol. 13, 1926.

———. January 1897. Review of Brooks Adams. *The Law of Civilization and Decay, The Forum*. In *The Works of Theodore Roosevelt*, ed. Hagedorn. Vol. 13, 1926.

———. April 10, 1899. "The Strenuous Life." Speech before the Hamilton Club, Chicago. In *The Works of Theodore Roosevelt*, ed. Hagedorn. Vol. 13, 1926.

———. May 8, 1909. "The Japanese Question." *The Outlook*. In *The Works of Theodore Roosevelt*, ed. Hagedorn. Vol. 16, 1926.

———. October 12, 1915. "Americanism." Address delivered before the Knights of Columbus, Carnegie Hall, New York. In *The Works of Theodore Roosevelt*, ed. Hagedorn. Vol. 18, 1926.

Ryan, Alan. Winter 1996. "Pragmatism, Social Identity, Patriotism, and Self-criticism." *Social Research* 63, no. 4:1041 (24).

Skerry, Peter. 1993. *Mexican Americans: The Ambivalent Minority*. New York: The Free Press.

————. Summer 1995. "Rebirth of a Nation." *The Wilson Quarterly*, 80–83.

Skocpol, Theda. March–April, 1996. "Unravelling from Above." *The American Prospect*, no. 25, 20–25.

Sleeper, Jim. July 2, 2000. "Yankee Doodle Dandy: Making It in America while Breaking Ranks and Settling Scores." *The Los Angeles Times Book Review*.

Smith, Rogers M. 1997. *Civic Ideals: Conflicting Visions of Citizenship in U.S. History*. New Haven, Conn.: Yale University Press.

————. 1998. *The Policy Consequences of American Illiberalism*. International Migration Policy Program, Carnegie Endowment for International Peace. Occasional Paper No. 2.

Spiro, Peter. February 1999. "The Citizenship Dilemma." *Stanford Law Review* 51, no. 3, 597–639.

Tulis, Jeffrey K. 1985. *The Rhetorical Presidency*. Princeton, N.J.: Princeton University Press.

Walzer, Michael. Fall 1990. "What Does It Mean to Be an American?" *Social Research* 57, no. 3:591–614.

Williams, Patricia. J. 1991. *The Alchemy of Race and Rights*. Cambridge, Mass.: Harvard University Press.

Wolfe, Alan. 1989. *Whose Keeper? Social Science and Moral Obligation*. Berkeley: University of California Press.

————. Autumn 1997. "On Loyalty," *The Wilson Quarterly*, 46–56.

————. 1998. *One Nation, After All: What Middle-Class Americans Really Think about God, Country, Family, Racism, Welfare, Immigration, Homosexuality, Work, the Right, the Left, and Each Other*. New York: Penguin Books.

PART ONE

Political Leadership and the Dilemmas of Diversity

THREE

The Presidency, Leadership, and Race

Russell L. Riley

As Bill Clinton battled to secure the 1992 Democratic presidential nomination, he appeared at a Philadelphia science and technology center to burnish his credentials as a forward-looking New Democrat. The Arkansas governor delivered on that occasion what I remember to be a workmanlike but uninspiring speech on his campaign's major theme, jobs and growth. The rigors of an unusually taxing campaign obviously had taken their toll on even this remarkable candidate. It was, for the most part, an unremarkable performance.

Near the end of his appearance, however, Clinton suddenly found energy and inspiration—on the subject of race. In response to a question from the audience, the candidate sprang into a spirited, impassioned defense of the continuing role of government in protecting minority rights, and voiced an unequivocal commitment to ridding American society of the poisonous vestiges of racism. Here, clearly, was a subject that engaged Clinton's mind and heart, and to which he felt some deep personal conviction to address as a matter of public service. Indeed, Clinton—unlike so many tone-deaf politicians of the post–Voting Rights Act South— had both the words and the music right. Having spent a lifetime watching clumsy attempts by southern politicians to win black votes by mouthing borrowed catch-phrases with artificial cadences, I left that encounter convinced that I had seen the real thing: a southern candidate whose commitment to racial equality, and whose political priorities flowed naturally from his personal encounters with a world most presidential candidates had never seen—and which he was committed to transforming.[1]

Yet as the Clinton presidency ended, there was an air of profound disappointment about what this president had accomplished on the question of race. His signature program—a national dialogue on the issue—

was widely deemed a failure, an initiative producing more weary headshakes than concrete results. Having staked considerable presidential prestige in this enterprise, Clinton and his advisers undoubtedly hoped for more.

What happened? How are we to explain the failure of this significant presidential initiative, especially by a president with a genius for domestic politics and with such an evident commitment to healing the nation's racial divisions?

Most of the public debate on the president's initiative has been divided between two common criticisms. The first—usually voiced by Clinton's critics from the left—has been one of a botched opportunity. This president came into office with generally solid credentials on race, and with a mandate to concentrate on the domestic agenda. Moreover, his exceptional rhetorical skills, and his southern roots, gave him powerful ammunition in dealing with a lingering problem that requires both special sympathies and special powers of persuasion. The first twice-elected Democrat since Franklin Roosevelt thus had an historically unique chance to rid the nation of the vestiges of a dishonorable past—through the initiative or preferably something stronger—and squandered it over his own dishonorable affections. "The spirit was willing, but . . . ." According to this construction, the costs of the president's personal indiscretions are almost incalculable.

The second critique—usually voiced by critics from the right—has generally focused on the president's misplaced faith in the ways of the past. The President's Initiative on Race was flawed primarily because it turned out not to be the true dialogue that the president and his advisors had pledged. According to these critics, the president was right to ask for an open conversation on race, because it promised to reveal the merit of their preferred policies—and the bankruptcy of conventional "liberal" solutions. With the commission's proceedings skewed from the outset, however, an opportunity was lost for an honest, forthright discussion. The president's failure was in not using his own considerable authority on the subject to ensure that the dialogue he promised was truly open, and that those challenging orthodox solutions were not branded as racist. Without the protection he could tender, no rational debate could take place—no new solutions to old problems could be seriously considered.

I will later devote some attention to these two common critiques. But the primary purpose of this essay is to examine the President's Initiative on Race in a third, different way—to look at it from an *institutional* perspective, how it fits into the history of the presidency in general and into patterns of presidential behavior on questions of race in particular. The Clinton record reveals some fundamental features of the presidency at work, features too easily overlooked by simply attributing his failures to personal carelessness or narrow partisanship. These are lessons that transcend party affiliation and that are eminently more enduring than the momentary appetites of an unfaithful husband and undisciplined politician.

The Historical Context: Presidents and the Myths of Heroic Leadership

The Clinton presidency is situated in two historical contexts relevant to this discussion. The first, the issue context, is the long-standing positioning of the presidency in relation to the question of race; the second is this particular administration's position in an identifiable sequencing of institutional power. Given these institutional realities, it is surprising that Clinton attempted the initiative at all—and unsurprising that the effort fared no better than it did.

The nature of the issue context can be summarized this way: The American presidency is an institution that under ordinary circumstances is not well suited to addressing the grievances of racial minorities. Indeed, careful study of the history of the institution reveals that the presidency has typically been used in ways hostile to minority interests, especially with respect to African Americans.[2]

This is an observation that may be vaguely unsettling to many American readers, because it is at odds with popular conceptions of the presidency as a bulwark of liberty and justice. Even in the specific case of African American rights, the presidency looms large in popular conceptions of racial advance, because of the remarkable feats of Presidents Abraham Lincoln, John Kennedy, and Lyndon Johnson, examples that have become legendary and in the process a part of the received political and popular culture. These presidencies have shaped the nation's collective identity, reinforcing the notion that the presidency is the place the nation ought to look for political, and moral, leadership in its ongoing march to equality.

There is, however, a double myth at work in this conventional construction: (a) that the common standards of the presidential institution are most accurately defined by these heroic examples, and (b) that these valorous presidents (valorous, at least, on matters of race) freely led the nation to embrace in each case what Lincoln termed "a new birth of freedom." By deconstructing these myths, we come more fully to an understanding of the presidency's typical position on race. We come to see, as well, that the myths are hardly benign. They have important implications for what Americans even today expect from the White House.

As a beginning, it is helpful to note that organized efforts to advance black equality have been an historically persistent feature of the nation's political landscape. Too, for the vast majority of American history, these efforts have been significant enough (that is, significantly threatening enough) to merit the attention of Washington policymakers—especially the president's. Accordingly, there is a long, rich tradition of presidential engagement with the issue of racial equality. This specific tradition is not, however, a part of what has often been called "the textbook presidency."[3]

The details of this history show an institution routinely employed in the suppression of organized efforts first to rid the nation of chattel slavery and then to secure for the descendants of freed men and women the full measure of equality the Constitution promises. It is this kind of behavior for which—on the evidence—the institution seems to be especially well suited.

An organized antislavery movement rose to national prominence in the United States in the early 1830s. An accurate portrait of presidential behavior on the question of emancipation, then, ought to begin with an examination of Andrew Jackson, mapping trends through to Lincoln's presidency. This history is almost uniformly one of incumbents vigorously exerting their powers to fight off the advances of abolitionism. The heroic Lincoln of popular memory is not at all representative of the antebellum presidency. Neither were the antebellum presidents merely indifferent bystanders to an unfolding drama on the question of slavery. They were instead featured actors, often taking as one of their central missions the eradication of abolitionist threats to the nation's existing social structures.

The Jackson administration, with the president's active complicity, closed down the United States postal system to abolitionist presses, effectively denying them the one avenue all other free presses could use to influence southern opinion. Jackson also made early—and extraordinary—use of the bully pulpit, charging the abolitionists with all manner of offense against the public order and encouraging federal officials to publish the names of those who subscribed to antislavery periodicals in the South, so that they could be subjected to the vigilante justice of their more sensible neighbors. Martin Van Buren, as his first official act as president, promised to veto any measures Congress might send him interfering with slavery in the District of Columbia, a pledge intended to stanch the flow of antislavery petitions then threatening to bury the House of Representatives under a flood of paper. John Tyler took a number of unusual steps, including the generation of a public relations campaign rare for that day, to bring Texas into closer fellowship with the United States, for purposes ultimately of annexing to the country "an empire for slavery."

Subsequent presidents served as the chief executors of the Fugitive Slave Act of 1850, literally becoming responsible for interposing the federal government between individual slaves and the freedom fugitives sought at enormous personal risk. President-elect James Buchanan took it upon himself to lobby the members of the Supreme Court in the case of *Dred Scott v. Sandford*, moving them to adopt the position they eventually announced, that the Constitution's shelter did not extend to people of African descent. Later, as a lame duck after Lincoln's election as his successor, Buchanan also labored feverishly to have the results of the election effectively overturned by trying to have constitutional amendments adopted that would have taken the future of slavery out of Lincoln's meddling hands. Simply put, the presidency of the abolitionist era was hardly an institution friendly to racial equality. This period's presidents creatively used what powers they could muster to stop progress for the nation's black residents.

Race and the Modern Presidency

This long-passed history is salvaged from irrelevancy by the fact that the patterns of presidential behavior seen here were replicated in relation to the civil rights movement, and thus survived well into the era of the modern presidency. Some modifications in behavior became essential to these presidents because black voters increasingly grew to a more prominent presence in the nation's political life, beginning after the Great Migration of World War I. Nevertheless, presidents from Grover Cleveland to John Kennedy used their powers to undermine those racial activists who wanted to make the promise of equality real for all Americans.

The array of weapons deployed was once again extensive. Executive appointments were reserved for those who supported the White House's direction and pace, and were withheld from those who were too aggressive. Booker T. Washington, for example, became a favorite channel of advice and support for successive presidents, because his modest aims for black progress were preferred by white America to the more political, and more radical, intentions of such figures as W. E. B. Du Bois (and later Marcus Garvey). Washington found himself invited to dinner at the White House; Du Bois found himself the object of federal surveillance; Garvey found himself deported, after a series of intensive, FBI-driven investigations. Black activism remained a favored target for J. Edgar Hoover well into the 1960s, when wiretaps and bugs became a primary source of intelligence about the activities of Dr. Martin Luther King Jr. and others. Much of this was driven by White House interest in knowing how best to prepare for, and defer, initiatives that violated the majority community's sensibilities.

Further, presidents helped raise public and private funds to aid those who kept their activism within selected channels, and sometimes secured favored treatment from the Internal Revenue Service. Taking a page from Buchanan's book, Dwight Eisenhower privately lobbied Chief Justice Earl Warren on behalf of the southern interests in the landmark case of *Brown v. Board of Education*—but in this case the president failed. Attorney General Robert Kennedy, in an attempt to channel street activism into safer (and politically useful) channels, promised to secure draft exemptions for Freedom Riders who shifted their energies into a federally sponsored Voter Education Project. Presidents also used their rhetorical powers to boost the preferred civil rights leadership, showering praise on those who might subscribe to White House caution. And, in one richly metaphoric instance, the White House both helped orchestrate changes toning down John Lewis's fiery speech to be delivered at the 1963 March on Washington Rally, and posted junior aides at a toggle switch to shut down the public address system in the event the rhetoric became too incendiary. At the ready, to be cued up to keep the crowd in control, was a vinyl copy of Mahalia Jackson's "He's Got the Whole World in His Hands."[4]

The prevailing patterns of the nineteenth century—presidents actively working to retard advance toward racial equality—were thus repeated deeply into the twentieth. True, some presidents did promote policies intended in small ways to advantage African Americans. But it is worth noting that in virtually every instance of Washington-based racial advance in the twentieth century, the political system was under exceptional duress from racial activists; concessions were made to stem the tide of larger change, to arrest prospects of uncontrolled protest.

Franklin Roosevelt established a Fair Employment Practices Committee only when he became convinced that A. Philip Randolph was on the brink of massing one hundred thousand black demonstrators in Washington—a terrible show of division as the administration prepared for entry into war. Dwight Eisenhower reluctantly moved to sponsor mild civil rights legislation in the late 1950s as a way of shifting the public debate then raging on school desegregation toward the more politically palatable issue of breaking down barriers to the voting booth. Moreover, his celebrated intervention with federal troops into Little Rock occurred only after it became apparent to him that the city might well burn to the ground without this action. Stephen Ambrose has written that Eisenhower, having been implored by the city's mayor to send the troops or risk a spreading chaos, "could not have done otherwise and still been President."[5] Often overlooked is the fact that Eisenhower refused to intervene under almost precisely the same jurisprudential circumstances a year earlier in Mansfield, Texas, because the local officials there managed to keep the peace while denying African American children their rightful place in white schools.

Only Harry Truman appears to have acted significantly to advance the interests of black Americans absent direct, compelling threats to the public order. Remarkably, however, in this case the constitution of the President's Committee on Civil Rights—and then the decision to desegregate the armed forces—reveals a president stumbling into historically important territory. His committee went far beyond anything he expected from them, making a set of recommendations—including desegregation of the military—that was later termed a "political bombshell."[6] He then followed the advice of Clark Clifford and initially decided to embrace the committee's report as a broader effort to position himself to take votes from his presumed 1948 opposition: Thomas Dewey and Henry Wallace. Clifford's logic in encouraging this course of action, he would later acknowledge, contained a crucial flaw: an assumption that southern Democrats would maintain their traditional loyalties to the party despite the president's civil rights package, making this a cost-free gambit. When the consequences of this error soon became manifest, with unexpected enthusiasm in the South for a Dixiecrat revolt, Truman backed off his initial endorsement of the committee's work. Administration insiders subsequently labored to have the 1948 Democratic party platform repeat the innocuous language of 1944 in order to distance themselves further from the alienating effects of the committee's work. Yet Hubert Humphrey and other party liberals succeeded in saddling the Truman camp with a strong civil rights provision, which the administration had fought to kill. In the end, Truman was left with no other viable option than following up with what the committee had recommended. By the judgment of history he did the right thing—but he did so as the result of a miscalculation, a mistake, a dodge, and a political defeat.

The Sources of Presidential Transformation

The general claim made here about the relationship of the presidency to racial progress is given added force by highlighting the fact that even those few heroic presidents who helped usher in transforming change did not escape the fundamental social conservatism of the institution—the institutional imperatives to protect the public order.[7] Abraham Lincoln did not take the oath of office committed to the emancipation of southern slaves. Indeed, just minutes thereafter, in his inaugural address, he asserted, "I have no purpose, directly or indirectly, to interfere with the institution of slavery in the States where it exists. I believe I have no lawful right to do so, and I have no inclination to do so."[8] He devoted most of his first year in office to proving the point, steadfastly refusing to make emancipation a war aim. Indeed, where others, in both Congress and the army, did exert leadership to liberate the enslaved—through either legislative initiative or martial law—Lincoln exerted his considerable, war-enlarged powers to thwart them. He vetoed (or threatened vetoes) of early emancipation schemes, and relieved from their commands officers who were too aggressive in declaring slaves in their regions of authority free. He also employed the moral power of his office to similar effect. In August 1862, he tried to shame a group of black ministers into forming a back-to-Africa movement, and, even after announcing plans to liberate if the Confederacy did not relent, proposed in his December 1862 annual message a compensation plan that might well have delayed the day of freedom indefinitely for southern slaves, had Congress concurred.[9]

In like manner, John Kennedy did not initially embrace the cause of civil rights, and indeed devoted considerable effort to keeping the movement at

arm's length. For example, having run for office pledging to eliminate segregation in housing with the "stroke of a pen," he refused to make that
stroke for so long that some activists took to sending him pens and ink
so he would have no excuse for not keeping his promise.[10] He sanctioned
police state action against movement organizers, and repeatedly worked
to undermine the civil disobedience campaigns of the Freedom Riders and
nonviolent protesters in Georgia and Alabama.

Lyndon Johnson, having pressed ahead with the civil rights act Kennedy
belatedly embraced just before his untimely death, then instructed Martin Luther King Jr. that nothing more could be done. He counseled a
cooling-off period before approaching Congress with a voting rights initiative. The president subsequently did what he could to keep King and
his associates from putting pressure on him to move more quickly.

In each of these cases, the president ultimately decided to sponsor
major civil rights initiatives as a last resort, when virtually every other avenue of recourse had been exhausted. In each of these cases, civil rights
progress came despite the president's best efforts to turn away those pressing for great change. In each of these cases, presidents reluctantly embraced the cause of a mass-based movement because the security of the
nation they were pledged to preserve, protect, and defend had come, they
believed, to depend on transforming the nation's social structures—the
way society was ordered—on the dimension of race.

Lincoln's primary war aim had been, from the outset, the preservation
of the Union. As he plainly put it to Horace Greeley, slavery was an issue
of importance to him only insofar as it bore on this single, simple matter:

> My paramount object in this struggle *is* to save the Union, and is *not* ei-
> ther to save or to destroy slavery. If I could save the Union without free-
> ing *any* slave I would do it, and if I could save it by freeing *all* the slaves I
> would do it; and if I could save it by freeing some and leaving others alone
> I would also do that. What I do about slavery, and the colored race, I do
> because I believe it helps to save the Union; and what I forbear, I forbear
> because I do *not* believe it would help to save the Union. I shall do *less*
> whenever I shall believe what I am doing hurts the cause, and I shall do
> *more* whenever I shall believe doing more will help the cause.[11]

Lincoln ultimately reached a pass in 1862 when he saw that his union-
saving efforts would fail without emancipation as a war aim. The North
needed the reinvigoration that a moral cause would give the fight, and it

needed to make sure that the exploitably narrow difference between the northern and southern positions on slavery did not give France and England the excuse they were seeking to recognize the Confederacy. Diplomatic recognition might well have made permanent the division of the country that began in 1860. This no president could countenance.

Kennedy and Johnson labored under a similar operational code. The Civil Rights Act of 1964 was born of the violence in Birmingham, Alabama, and the Kennedy administration's determination neither to allow racial violence sparked by nonviolent protest to burn uncontrolled across the American landscape, nor to give the nation's communist enemies easy targets for winning the fight for allies among the world's people of color. Fully one-quarter of Radio Moscow's broadcasts during this period dealt with the violence in Birmingham, which sparked almost eight hundred subsequent demonstrations in nearly two hundred communities nationwide.[12] The Voting Rights Act of 1965 was born of the violence in Selma, Alabama, and of Lyndon Johnson's continuing concerns about the nation's domestic and international security positions.

Lincoln, Kennedy, and Johnson ultimately were indispensable in ushering transformational change through the nation's political machinery and the body politic, but none of them acted without compulsion. They were all operating under stresses that quite literally were unbearable without the changes they sought. This is a different kind of portrait from the one that commonly implies presidential direction of social change.

Of course it might be argued that the face of the political landscape was profoundly and permanently altered by the revolutionary developments of the mid-twentieth century, especially those with significant implications for the ballot box. Didn't these transformations reverberate into the presidency, creating significant changes in institutional behavior there?

The answer, undoubtedly, is yes. Post–civil rights era presidents were elected in and governed in a transformed environment, one no longer as hostile to African American interests as before. Accordingly, the standards of typical presidential conduct on racial issues changed, too. Yet these changes have been empirically ambiguous, hardly sufficient to sustain the myth of institutional leadership on racial matters I want to debunk here. The general patterns of active suppression so characteristic for nearly a century and a half did not survive. But the post-1965 presidency is no more a place of great leadership on matters of race than before. Put another way, it is hard to see why Americans ought to expect from the presidency leadership on matters of race based on the strength of the examples set since the Great Society.[13]

Richard Nixon's manipulation of racial politics for his own political purposes, through his "Southern Strategy" preempting George Wallace, is legendary. Even his promotion of race-based affirmative action, in the form of the so-called Philadelphia Plan, was a Machiavellian ploy to sow discord among the Democrats' two most loyal constituencies: labor and African Americans.[14] Gerald Ford was not the manipulator his patron was—and arguably he possessed greater sensitivities to African American rights—but he was a negligible political presence across the board. Jimmy Carter worked in very conventional channels to improve black political access, including a number of significant appointments of African Americans, but he certainly did not leave a legacy of bold action on the question of race. The most charitable reading of Ronald Reagan and race is that the president subsumed his particular policies with respect to civil rights under a general philosophy of retrenchment, which affected adversely those who stood to benefit most from governmental activism. He tolerated within his administration intolerant others, however, for whom a charitable interpretation would be dishonest. George Bush's legacy on race will forever be tainted by his 1988 campaign's traffic in the seedy underside of racial anxiety with the Willie Horton ads, but those politics were not truly representative of Bush as president. Yet it would be a tall order indeed to establish Bush as a leading figure in the development of American race relations on the strength of something like the Clarence Thomas appointment.

At bottom, the reality of the post-1965 presidency is that the institution figures indefinitely in the state of American race relations. Accordingly, the presidency Bill Clinton moved into in 1993 was not a place, one can say on the strength of the accumulated evidence, where leadership for racial progress naturally occurs.

Swimming against the Tide: The Clinton Presidency, Power, and the Politics of Race

Having described the issue context (on race) within which Bill Clinton operated, I now turn to a discussion of the specific power context of the Clinton presidency. That he inherited the institution at a particular point in a recognizable pattern of ebb-and-flow in presidential power also had important implications for his race initiative.

One of the simplest, and generally soundest, models of presidential power holds that in times of system-threatening crisis, Americans rally to the flag to support the incumbent. The accumulation of political power in the presidency generally has been highest during such periods, when the American people—and their representatives in Washington—have accepted centralized direction from the president in order to deal with a clear and present danger. Under these circumstances, a polity usually committed to decentralized power finds merit in what Clinton Rossiter termed a "constitutional dictatorship," or what also might be called a centralized leadership regime.[15] Thus we have seen extraordinary powers devolve onto Abraham Lincoln, Woodrow Wilson, Franklin Roosevelt, and, for very brief intervals for very specific threats, others.

There is, it should be added here, also an important correlation between these kinds of accumulated powers in the presidency and those rare episodes, discussed above, of extraordinary activism on behalf of racial equality. Lincoln's war-enlarged presidency gave him a unique opportunity to make use of powers that few Americans before the Civil War believed anyone could possess. Slaves were a constitutionally protected class of property—in some respects more guarded than any other. Who, under normal circumstances, had the authority to take even a single slave from a "legitimate" owner, much less to execute a mass emancipation campaign so vast in scope as to constitute "the most stupendous act of sequestration in the history of Anglo-Saxon jurisprudence"?[16] Lincoln's emancipation order was issued under color of his war emergency powers, and widely accepted, as he explained, as a necessity of war.[17]

Though the case is less straightforward a century later, the cold war also caused a consolidation of power in the presidency. Here a kind of low-level, persistent crisis prevailed, bearing with it a perpetually enlarged presidency—subject to temporary spikes of power upward, nearing the heights of the wartime Wilson or FDR (as in relation to Korea, Berlin, and Vietnam).[18] It was a protracted era during which presidents effectively had rights of first refusal to speak and act for the nation, especially when, as in the case of civil rights, a policy could be tied directly to America's competition with the communists. That was a trump card that would be played again and again by presidents who sought to put their personal imprint on American policy, foreign and domestic.[19]

The state of national security, however, seemed especially vulnerable in the early 1960s, as domestic turmoil on the question of race combined with the Cuban Missile Crisis (and its afterimage) to leave the nation feeling exposed to threats originating at home and abroad. Kennedy reportedly took little comfort that his approval ratings had soared after the soured expedition at the Bay of Pigs—Americans, he saw, rallied mindlessly to the flag—but that same popular mentality provided him with invaluable resources when he later took to the airwaves to plead for advanced action on civil rights. Americans accustomed to looking to their presidents to resolve a series of serious international security problems in a new internationalized world found it that much easier to turn to the presidency when system-threatening problems arose as well from within. Kennedy and Johnson, then, ultimately found themselves in a relatively favorable position to shepherd significant reform legislation through Congress, and to argue convincingly to the American people that it was essential. The cold war was at once a useful rationale for Americans to accept change in racial structures that hurt the nation's image abroad and a useful source of presidential power in pursuing this end.

The empowerment of the presidency at a time of system-threatening crisis—that is, the establishment of a centralized leadership regime in a polity usually committed to a constitutional diffusion of power—is probably now widely recognized enough to merit designation as conventional wisdom. What is not commonly a part of that conventional wisdom, however, is what happens once the threat has passed, once the security of the system has been firmly reestablished.[20] These postcrisis periods can be especially perilous times for the presidency, as a typical systemic reaction is to reestablish the *status quo ante*. This often means bringing an enlarged presidency back down to size.

The American pattern of postcrisis downsizing of the constitutional dictator is actually older than the Constitution itself. George Washington subjected himself to a formal ceremony in which his Revolutionary War leadership license was officially relinquished back to the Continental Congress that had issued it, placing the great leader once again in a subservient position to the people's representatives.[21] What most distinguishes that episode in retrospect, however, is its harmony—a feature not characteristic of the postconstitutional razings of American leadership regimes.

For exercising a fraction of the authority Abraham Lincoln had employed during the Civil War—and effectively daring Congress to do something about it—Andrew Johnson was impeached. During the First World War, Woodrow Wilson headed a bureaucracy so vast and intrusive that it literally told Americans how much sugar they could put in their coffee.[22] Yet when he tried to direct the shape of the postwar world through the League of Nations, Wilson was shamed at home by a congressional rejection so humiliating that it sent him to an early grave. Shades of these earlier retractions of power were seen once the worst of the Depression had passed, when the American people rejected FDR's efforts to extend his control over the other two branches of the constitutional trinity by packing the Supreme Court and the Congress with people of like mind. The threat of fascism abroad, however, interrupted the usual regime sequencing in this instance, keeping Roosevelt's star ascendant. Yet soon after the Second World War, Harry Truman found himself beleaguered by a resurgent Congress and an American public no longer willing to follow presidential direction. That downward slide was halted by the subsequent outbreak of a hot war in Korea and a protracted cold one globally.

Now to the relevance of this more recent history. With the fall of the Berlin Wall in 1989, and the collapse of the Soviet Union soon thereafter, the cold war concluded. Bill Clinton's presidency subsequently held extraordinarily true to the sequencing pattern typical of postcrisis administrations.[23] With the end of an extended emergency period came the end of an extended leadership regime—with dire consequences for the institution of the presidency. There is, indeed, a remarkable symmetry in what transpired during the troubled Clinton years. The last president to have been impeached before Bill Clinton was Andrew Johnson, as the Civil War leadership regime was demolished. And Clinton's stinging diplomatic defeat in the autumn of 1999, with Senate rejection of the Comprehensive Test Ban Treaty, was a foreign affairs reversal hauntingly reminiscent, as some commentators noted at the time, of Wilson's post–World War I debacle with the League of Nations.

It is commonplace now to blame Clinton's personal foibles for his downfall, and for the low estate into which the presidency fell on his watch. While I do not wish to contest the gravity of his personal misbehavior, it is important not to allow the sensational or lurid to distract us from the larger patterns at work in this instance. Clinton's was a time historically perilous for any president. The institution he inherited in 1993 was, far more than almost anyone recognized, in a state of rapid transition. The nation found that it no longer needed in the White House a robust cold warrior with all the powerful appurtenances of the preceding half-century, a point Clinton himself undoubtedly recognized as he joked in 1993 about missing the cold war.[24] To attribute the evisceration of the millennial presidency to Clinton's personal weaknesses, then, is to miss a more important point—and an illuminating pattern of American political history.

The 1994 "Republican Revolution," when both houses of Congress returned to GOP control, mirrored the midterm election reversals of 1866, 1918, and 1946. In each of those years American voters sent to Washington Congresses extraordinarily hostile to the incumbent and committed to reining in an institution that had become oversized in dealing with a system-threatening crisis. A loss of Congress was the essential predicate for much of what followed in the Clinton presidency. It is especially illuminating that the most proximate factor in generating the 1994 reversal was the popular sense that the Clintons had overextended the White House—creating, via a closed process, a health reform program too easily lampooned as "big government" at a time inauspicious for that kind of initiative.

Further, direct evidence for the power of post–cold war retrenchment on the Clinton presidency is found in the Supreme Court's decision in *Clinton v. Jones*, without which an impeachment proceeding would have been exceedingly unlikely. The Court allowed Paula Jones's sexual harassment lawsuit against Clinton to proceed, notwithstanding claims that a rejection of his request to postpone would undermine the president's power to conduct his official responsibilities. In a critical (but concurring) opinion, Associate Justice Stephen Breyer asserted that his colleagues on the bench had in fact taken far too casual an attitude about the possible debilitating effects of allowing civil lawsuits to proceed during a sitting president's term. He presciently argued that his colleagues—all eight of whom signed the majority opinion—seriously misreckoned the danger to the institution of the presidency in the logic of their ruling. "I do not agree with what I believe to be an understatement of the 'danger'" to the executive branch, he wrote.[25] It is difficult to imagine the Court taking this decision in an environment in which heightened executive power was clearly necessary to deter an ongoing threat to the nation's security. That the Court decided this way in this case is a probative piece of evidence about the extent to which the passing of the cold war influenced perceptions about the need for the nation to defer to the president and to presidential leadership.

The Presidential Initiative on Race: One America

Having now situated Clinton in the proper contexts, it is appropriate to return specifically to his Initiative on Race and the commentary it has generated. What, given this contextual, institutional background, can we make of the liberal critics' claims that this was a missed opportunity? There is more than a grain of truth to this lament. On the historical evidence sketched above, it is clear that the presidency is seldom a place where the matter of race is at the core of the White House agenda—other than when presidential power is actively needed to preserve the majority's preferred status against minority claims. Accordingly, Clinton's voluntary expenditure of even modest political capital in this enterprise may be historically unique. This was by all appearances an unforced venture into the thicket, evidently by one strongly inclined to use the powers of the presidency to favor those not commonly accustomed to it. Liberals may rightly fear, then, that many years will go by before another president is willing to stake his (or her) prestige and reputation in a similar enterprise.

The problem with this critique, however, is that it equates intentions with power—and leadership is comprised of significant measures of each.[26] There was in the most basic sense no "opportunity" for presidential leadership here, because Bill Clinton simply did not have the power resources necessary to accomplish anything significant on race, absent the kind of consensus that would have rendered his initiative superfluous in the first place. That is why the extended digression on presidential power above was necessary. Presidents have succeeded in directing breakthrough racial progress *only* when they have been operating under conditions of system-threatening empowerment. Under conditions of political *normalcy*, presidents may only engage in the sort of bargaining and public posturing that in a deeply divided polity is unlikely to result in the kinds of fundamental changes in social structure we typically associate with race. Yet Clinton governed during an *abnormal* time, one even *less* favorable for bold presidential action than usual.

Positioned in the presidency during an era of post–cold war retrenchment, Clinton was reduced to making extraordinary public appeals for the lowest conceivable standard of presidential power: that he remained "relevant." From this perspective, there hardly appears to have been an opening for presidential leadership on an issue as vexing as race at all. Some might be inclined to read in this interpretation absolution for Clinton—he failed because failure was inevitable. I rather think this evidence makes the president's indiscretions all the more puzzling, all the more objectionable. Cognizant of the fact that he was under intensive scrutiny on the very matter of his personal conduct—and further that the rules of the game no longer sanctioned behavior that earlier cold war presidents may have engaged in with impunity—he conducted himself in a way that was, by virtue of his place in time, absurdly risky. Oddly, Clinton, more than any other president in recent memory, actively sought to retrieve from history useful instruction for his presidency—and yet in a profound failure of intellect or character he missed (or dismissed) instructive, but discouraging, lessons. In his defense, it appears that the many historians he consulted over the years for advice about governing did not communicate to Clinton the perils of his peculiar place in time, assuming they recognized them. Instead, advice evidently flowed about how best to mount assertive initiatives, a willing president committed to a progressive agenda being a happenstance too rare to foil with warnings about the inaptness of such enterprises in the immediate post–cold war years. Here the president was disserved by his friends, failing to recognize Richard E. Neustadt's dictum that no one sees the problems a president confronts in quite the same way he does—everyone else has an agenda, too.[27]

The conservatives' critique of the president's initiative would seem on its face to be unassailable. The free market of ideas works very poorly when important voices are not heard, or when certain alternatives are favored or disfavored depending solely on who is promoting them. The selectivity of the commission with respect to the issues it chose to address—and the voices it consulted—is, by these terms, impossible to defend.

Yet in one important respect the commission's selectivity was not just intellectually defensible—it was necessary. An essential ingredient of true dialogue, of civil conversation, is a shared sense among the participants of goodwill toward one another, or of common cause. On few questions is this element more important than on that of race, where so many sensitivities are exposed. Absent a presumption of goodwill and the development of the rapport it fosters—that is, a willingness among the participants to give others the benefit of the doubt—an inclusive conversation will either be marked by evasions, with participants circling around the real issues, or by anger and frustration, with unintended offenses drawing unanticipated reactions. Under the best of circumstances, with perfect rapport, this is a very fragile exercise.

What this kind of enterprise cannot endure are participants with recognizable reasons for benefiting from its failure. This calls into question their good faith, which in turn makes it impossible for rapport to develop. Generic suspicion already rates high in discussions of race, so much so that to give good cause for further distrust is to end any chance of developing the rapport essential for open dialogue. I do not mean to suggest here that the conservative critics of the Clinton initiative, some of whom share the pages of this volume, were motivated to undermine the commission's work. I am merely arguing that enough partisan poison had accumulated in the atmosphere during Clinton's first term—and enough rhetorical excess on the specific issue of race in earlier years—that soberminded commissioners might reasonably have concluded that the only way to proceed civilly, productively, was to invite contributions exclusively from those they knew would not be disruptive. This ruled out the conservative critics, who for partisan or ideological reasons stood to benefit where Clinton, or his agenda, failed.

Having defended the commission in this way, however, I am quick to add that its concession to this reality, too, was at the same time a concession to failure in its essential purpose. This was not a national dialogue. At bottom, the very distrust the panel hoped to address ultimately undermined its purpose, because that distrust was effectively beyond the power of a government commission to dispel. The commission's decision to close off certain avenues of enquiry was at once understandable and justifiable, but the conservative criticism is also at once understandable and justifiable. Alas, that is the enduring reality of an American dilemma.

Conservatives ultimately may comfort themselves, however, not just with the foundering of a skewed Clinton initiative, but also with the fact that the initiative was, on the historical evidence, anomalous. Further, given the troubled reception the Clinton program received, it is hard to see why any president would bother to duplicate it in any recognizable way in the foreseeable future. What the Clinton initiative clearly reveals is that even modest attempts by the government to address the question of race in America with the expressed intent of improving the status of minority communities brings impassioned reactions—yes, even in the twenty-first century. Moreover, whatever else may be true about contemporary conservative remedies for present-day racial tensions in America, they all have one thing in common: They are, relatively speaking, majority-friendly. There's the rub. Majority-oriented politics is the rule, not the exception, in the politics of the presidency; that is the logic *and* the history of the office. From an historical perspective, the White House seldom is occupied by someone who is willing to defy the conventions of the office by freely taking majority-unfriendly initiatives. Until the nature of that majority changes—which may, in fact, be a demographic inevitability of the twenty-first century, as the United States becomes a minority-white nation—the future of the presidency will probably look very much like the past. This, given the portrait of the institution sketched here, cannot be a comforting thought to most liberals.

There is also, however, some reason in this portrait for comfort among those who believe that the vestiges of three centuries of often-vicious discrimination have not been eradicated by three decades of usually irresolute remedy. But it is not in the presidency.

The major advances in racial equality of the nineteenth and twentieth centuries occurred, in the main, not because of presidents, but in spite of them. Presidential leadership in breaking down racial inequality took place because those outside the conventional political institutions succeeded in organizing forces for progress that eventually could not be ignored. It is in this kind of activity that liberals may find room for optimism. Political institutions are inherently, on questions of deep social structure (such as those commonly associated with race), conservative. But change can be wrought through these conservative instruments by those able and willing to use the tools of public opinion creatively to advance their cause. Such efforts are not easy and require long-suffering commitment. William Lloyd Garrison began publication of his seminal abolitionist weekly, *The Liberator*, in January of 1831—and did not see the fruits of his labors fully realized until over thirty years later. The same basic story was replicated in the twentieth century. A. Philip Randolph had a long history of organizing black workers when he confronted Franklin Roosevelt in 1941; when he stood on the steps of the Lincoln Memorial with Martin Luther King Jr. at the March on Washington Rally two decades later, he was still not assured of the success that his efforts eventually won.

Those who would seek leadership in service of greater racial equality, then, are best instructed to do so outside the confines of a formal political order inevitably biased toward majoritarianism. We have, in the United States, seen remarkable exercises of presidential leadership on occasions to deal with what is the most vexing of all American problems. In the final analysis, however, that leadership has been derivative. Those, then, who believe that a national dialogue on race is an essential starting place for the next wave of racial advance must indeed begin that exercise in the public square—with the knowledge that only eventually will it resonate as they would like in political circles.

Notes

1. Clinton's controversial campaign criticism of the rap artist Sister Souljah caused some at the time to question the depth of his commitment to African Americans. That proved to be largely a tempest in a teapot. Before his presidency was completed, black Americans would be among the president's most reliable supporters, with Toni Morrison even venturing that he was the nation's first black president. "The Talk of the Town," *New Yorker*, 5 October 1998, 31–32.

2. The institutional history outlined in this essay is condensed from that appearing in Russell L. Riley, *The Presidency and the Politics of Racial Inequality: Nation-keeping from 1831 to 1965* (New York: Columbia University Press, 1999).

3. Thomas E. Cronin, *The State of the Presidency* (Boston: Little, Brown, 1975), chapter 2.

4. Interview with John Reilly, Salzburg, Austria, 21 December 1999.

5. Ambrose, cited in Chester J. Pach Jr. and Elmo Richardson, *The Presidency of Dwight D. Eisenhower* (Lawrence: University Press of Kansas, 1991), 154.

6. William C. Berman, *The Politics of Civil Rights in the Truman Administration* (Columbus: Ohio State University Press, 1970), 70–72.

7. By the institution's fundamental social conservatism, I simply mean that the presidency is not well designed as an instrument for making changes in basic social structures. It is foremost a majoritarian, nation-keeping implement, and as such is seldom deeply involved in disrupting the basic social structures that the majority considers essential to its well-being. Indeed, the presidency is vastly better suited to preserving those structures against attack by those who would change them. A more elaborate treatment of this claim appears in Russell L. Riley, "The Limits of the Transformational Presidency," in Robert Y. Shapiro, Martha Joynt Kumar, and Lawrence R. Jacobs, eds., *Presidential Power: Forging the Presidency for the 21st Century* (New York: Columbia University Press, 2000), 435–55.

8. Don E. Fehrenbacher, ed., *Abraham Lincoln: Speeches and Writings, 1859–1865* (New York: Library of America, 1989), 215.

9. In this meeting, Lincoln asserted that the terrible war then being fought was caused solely by the presence of the black race on American soil, and claimed that the only way it would end was for their removal to Liberia or Central America. Those who elected the route of greatest "comfort"—remaining in the United States—Lincoln charged with holding "an extremely selfish view." See "Address on Colonization to a Committee of Colored Men, Washington, D.C.," in Fehrenbacher, ed., *Speeches and Writings*, 353–57. On the last-ditch compensation proposal, see David Herbert Donald, *Lincoln* (New York: Touchstone, 1996), 397.

10. Carl M. Brauer, *John F. Kennedy and the Second Reconstruction* (New York: Columbia University Press, 1977), 205.

11. Fehrenbacher, ed., *Speeches and Writings*, 358.

12. See Brauer, *John F. Kennedy*, 240; Taylor Branch, *Parting the Waters: America in the King Years, 1954–63* (New York: Simon and Schuster, 1988), 825.

13. A useful summary of this period is provided by Kenneth O'Reilly, *Nixon's Piano: Presidents and Racial Politics from Washington to Clinton* (New York, Free Press, 1995), 277–423.

14. John David Skrentny, *The Ironies of Affirmative Action: Politics, Culture, and Justice in America* (Chicago: University of Chicago Press, 1996), chapter 7.

15. Clinton Rossiter, *Constitutional Dictatorship: Crisis Government in the Modern Democracies* (New York: Harcourt, Brace & World, Inc., 1948).

16. Charles A. and Mary R. Beard, *The Rise of American Civilization* (New York: Macmillan, 1930), part 2, 100.

17. See Arthur M. Schlesinger Jr., "Abraham Lincoln and Franklin D. Roosevelt," in Gabor S. Boritt, ed., *Lincoln, The War President: The Gettysburg Lectures* (New York: Oxford University Press, 1992), 145–78.

18. This is what Richard E. Neustadt refers to as "emergencies in policy with politics as usual." *Presidential Power and the Modern Presidents: The Politics of Leadership from Roosevelt to Reagan* (New York: The Free Press, 1990), 5.

19. See John Kenneth White, *Still Seeing Red: How the Cold War Shapes the New American Politics* (Boulder, Colo.: Westview Press, 1997).

20. My understanding of this sequencing pattern comes from the unpublished work of James Sterling Young at the University of Virginia.

21. See the description in Barry Schwartz, *George Washington: The Making of an American Symbol* (Ithaca, N.Y.: Cornell University Press, 1987), 137–43.

22. Robert Higgs, *Crisis and Leviathan: Critical Episodes in the Growth of American Government* (New York: Oxford University Press, 1987).

23. Arguably George Bush was the initial victim of the postwar retraction of power. His exceptional foreign policy credentials became all but a liability in the 1992 campaign, when the American public seemed increasingly uninterested in commitments abroad. Ironically, the remarkable ease with which Bush directed success in the Gulf War may have contributed to a sense among the American people that international threats were no longer worth keeping an empowered presidency around to handle.

24. White, *Still Seeing Red*, 256.

25. *Clinton v. Jones* (95-1853), 520 U.S. 681 (1997), Concurrence (by Justice Breyer), <http://supct.law.cornell.edu:8080/test/hermes/95-1853.ZC.html>.

26. James MacGregor Burns, *Leadership* (New York: Harper Torchbooks, 1978), 12–17.

27. Neustadt, *Presidential Power*, chapter 1.

FOUR

President Clinton's Race Initiative

Promise and Disappointment

Richard D. Kahlenberg

President Bill Clinton's Initiative on Race, launched in 1997, sought to promote, at long last, the elusive goal of "One America." In soaring language that reached back to Lincoln and even the nation's founding, the president asked the American people to join him "in a great national effort to perfect the promise of America for this new time as we seek to build our more perfect union. . . . That is the unfinished work of our time, to lift the burden of race and redeem the promise of America" (Clinton 1997a, 4, 8). Kicked off with grand hopes, the initiative appeared to have three important things going for it.

First, Bill Clinton, a politician often accused of having no core, appeared deeply committed to racial reconciliation. He had told Bill Moyers in an often-cited interview during the 1992 campaign that race was the one issue he would never compromise for political gain (Stephanopoulos 1999). Clinton's One America advisory board praised him in extraordinary terms, declaring, "No other President in the history of this Nation has had the courage to raise the issue of race and racism in American society in such a dramatic way" (Advisory Board 1998, 9). Aide Harold Ickes said, "If there is a true north to Bill Clinton, it is race" (Burns and Sorenson 1999, 242).

Second, in sharp contrast to the 1968 Kerner Commission appointed by President Lyndon Johnson in the wake of racial rioting, Clinton launched his initiative in an era of economic prosperity and racial peace. The timing appeared right to elicit a generous response from the American public—in contrast, say, to the recession in the early 1990s, when Republicans bludgeoned Democrats on the "quota" issue.

Third, as a political moderate, Clinton had a better chance than most to break the logjam in American race relations. For years, liberals had correctly pointed out that unless we address the wide economic gulf between America's white majority and its less-fortunate African-American and Latino communities, we are unlikely to be one nation. But since 1968, the left had pursued race-specific policies that often had the side effect of sharpening and enforcing differences, thereby undercutting the goal of unity. Conservatives, meanwhile, had rightly pointed out that the left's reliance on race-conscious policies was divisive, but offered no affirmative program to deal with the tough economic realities that leave large numbers of poor people—many of them people of color—out of the American mainstream. The laissez-faire approach, which helped freeze an unequal status quo, did not offer the promise of One America either.

Clinton stood poised to pursue what he called a "third way" on these issues. As this chapter will make clear, throughout his public career, his campaigns, and his presidency, Clinton had intermittently returned to the theme that the best way to promote greater racial harmony was through need-based programs that were nonracial in character but disproportionately beneficial to people of color. Such an approach would at once address the history of slavery and segregation indirectly while at the same time eschewing the balkanizing side effects of race-specific policies. It represented the path not taken by progressive politicians following the 1968 assassinations of Martin Luther King Jr. and Robert Kennedy.

But as may be true of the Clinton presidency as a whole, Clinton on race is a portrait of unfulfilled promise and missed opportunity. The race initiative was almost universally viewed as a failure, and the president's handling of the crisis over the future of affirmative-action programs brought only temporary peace and left major questions unaddressed. Rather than espousing a breakthrough policy based on economic need, Clinton responded to short-term political concerns and muddled through only by obscuring larger issues.

This essay proceeds in two parts. Part I briefly reviews the history of the Clinton presidency's record on key racial issues, culminating in the president's Initiative on Race. Part II then evaluates the strengths and weaknesses of the president's effort to promote racial harmony. (In chapter 11 of this volume, I continue this thread of thought and make recommendations for an alternative economic-based approach to pursuing One America.)

The Narrative: What Happened

The Clinton Campaign in 1992

During the 1992 campaign for president, Arkansas Governor Bill Clinton made racial healing an important priority, but he appeared to believe that the traditional Democratic approach was not the most promising way of achieving racial harmony. Rather than emphasizing race-specific policies, he emphasized programs to address common economic concerns. In 1990, when Clinton chaired the Democratic Leadership Council, the group endorsed a policy of equal opportunity over equal results, drawing the ire of Jesse Jackson (Brown 1991, 146–47). Clinton was clearly uneasy with the inherent divisiveness of racial and gender preferences, and his campaign book, *Putting People First*, never used the phrase "affirmative action" and declared his opposition to racial quotas (Clinton and Gore 1992, 64). In the 1992 New York Democratic primary debate, when Clinton famously revealed his ambivalence over marijuana, he revealed a similar (though underreported) ambivalence about affirmative-action preferences. He said he supported affirmative-action goals, but then also said that contracts should not go to minority firms that bid above the lowest offer, backtracking, Thomas Edsall notes, "from the actual practice in many set-aside programs" (1993).

Clinton knew that a central reason for the string of Republican presidential victories beginning in 1968 was the way in which Richard Nixon, Ronald Reagan, and George Bush had successfully convinced white working class voters that Democrats did not respect their values. On issues like crime, busing, welfare—and affirmative action—many so-called "Reagan Democrats" believed that the Democratic Party had abandoned them. Many observers believed that Robert Kennedy was the last Democratic politician to simultaneously have credibility with working class whites and blacks, who, together, had once stood at the center of the New Deal coalition. In the early 1990s, Clinton knew the political imperative of defusing the racial issue.

Clinton's campaign aide George Stephanopoulos believed Clinton was uniquely positioned to draw "black and white workers together in common cause. Just like Bobby Kennedy had tried to do before an assassin's bullet struck him down. Then came court-ordered busing, urban decay, the Democrats' drift toward identity politics, and a generation of Republican candidates from Nixon to Bush whose winning formula was crime, quotas, and welfare queens. By 1991, RFK's 'black and blue' coalition was a distant memory. Maybe Clinton could put it back together. That was his dream and mine" (1999, 38–39).

In the Democratic primaries, Clinton's nonracial message centering on common economic needs appeared to be resonating. In a March 1992 editorial, *The New York Times* said Clinton's Super Tuesday primary showings "give healthy evidence, probably for the first time since Robert Kennedy's Indiana primary campaign in 1968, that it is politically possible to bring poor blacks and blue-collar whites together" (Editorial 1992). William Julius Wilson wrote that a media preoccupied with Clinton's private life had "failed to appreciate the significance of Mr. Clinton's remarkable biracial coalition" of lower and middle income whites and blacks (1992).

The First Term

After Clinton's election, his ambivalence about race-specific remedies continued. At a Camp David retreat shortly following the election, when it was noted that Clinton had not done as well as hoped with southern, white, blue-collar males, Hillary Clinton said, "Screw them. Let's move on." But President Clinton responded, "Those bubbas, I grew up with them. I understand them. I know what they're going through. We can't win this thing unless the bubbas are respected too" (Burns and Sorenson 1999, 257).

Clinton sought to be inclusive, famously calling for a government that "looks like America." But he also railed against "bean counters" who pushed for more women in the top posts. And he abandoned his nominee for the position of assistant attorney general for civil rights, Lani Guinier, after conservatives accused her of being a "Quota Queen."

In September 1993, Vice President Al Gore's Reinventing Government initiative went so far as to suggest eliminating affirmative-action preferences in government procurement. Stephanopoulos raised objections with Gore, saying "I can't make an argument on the merits," but politically, ending affirmative action in procurement is "like throwing a cluster bomb into the middle of our base" (1999, 208). Gore, who would later become an ardent champion of race-based affirmative action, responded that Clinton had already signed off on the proposal, but in fact the president had not, and the plan was eventually shelved (Stephanopoulos 1999, 209).

In the 1994 congressional elections, the white male vote went 62–38 for the Republicans, an overwhelming margin that helped land the GOP a majority in the House for the first time in forty years ("Portrait," 1994). Conservative plans to place an anti–affirmative action initiative on the California ballot in 1996 (later dubbed Proposition 209) had the White House deeply concerned. Some within the administration believed Clinton should endorse the anti–affirmative action initiative and Assistant Attorney General Deval Patrick was asked to prepare an analysis of the effects of such an endorsement (Lemann 1999, 296). In February 1995, Clinton announced a "review" of affirmative-action programs—a defensive step, journalist Nicholas Lemann notes, that no president since Lyndon Johnson had taken, "even those Republicans who had campaigned against affirmative action" (1999, 297).

In an early March 1995 press conference, Clinton suggested that affirmative action should be based on economic need rather than race, a move urged by presidential pollster Dick Morris (Stephanopoulos 1999, 369). Clinton said, "I want to emphasize need-based programs where we can because they work better and have a bigger impact and generate broader support." *The Washington Post* headline declared, "In Shift, President Supports Affirmative Action Based on Needs" (Devroy 1995).

But Clinton's suggestion that "we should move to an 'alternative' based on economic need rather than race" Stephanopoulos notes, "sent a shock wave through affirmative action supporters" (Stephanopoulos 1999, 365). A political firestorm erupted among organized Democratic interests, particularly feminist and civil rights groups. Meanwhile, interest groups like labor, and populist political figures like Rep. Richard Gephardt, who might be expected to support a shift from race to class, did not. Perhaps most important, Jesse Jackson threatened to challenge the president for the Democratic nomination if he didn't "stand firm" on affirmative action (Stephanopoulos 1999, 364). A serious primary challenge, Stephanopoulos noted, was "the surest predictor of a single-term presidency" (1999, 336).

Still, within the White House, Morris continued to push for a new approach to affirmative action based on need. In the weekly campaign strategy meeting with the president and vice president on March 16, 1995, Morris pointed out that a need-based approach was consistent with policies espoused by Martin Luther King Jr. toward the end of his life, and indeed, with Jesse Jackson's Rainbow Coalition. Morris noted that if

Jackson insisted on opposing the class-based, race-neutral approach, he should be pressed, "was he kidding about [the] rainbow?" (Morris 1998, 378). Acknowledging the significance of the Jackson threat, however, Morris urged in a May 4, 1995, memo to the president to make some defense of affirmative action for now, and then: "After filing dates for primaries pass, move emphasis to the right and stress color blindness" (1998, 435).

In April 1995, Clinton addressed the California Democratic convention, which was split between pro– and anti–affirmative action camps. Clinton declared, "We don't have to retreat from these affirmative-action programs that have done great things for the American people and haven't hurt other people. We don't. But we do have to ask ourselves, are they all working? Are they all fair? Has there been any kind of reverse discrimination?" Democratic supporters of affirmative action were heartened, as were Democratic opponents. Clinton advisor Stephanopoulos thought, "Good, he stayed on script" (Lemann 1999, 299).

In July 1995, as the administration's review of affirmative-action programs came to a close, Clinton delivered a speech at the National Archives building, in which he said affirmative action should be "mended" rather than "ended" (Clinton 1995). He announced four core principles by which affirmative-action programs should be judged, and directed all federal agencies to abide by those principles. "The policy principles are that any program must be eliminated or reformed if it: a) creates a quota; b) creates preferences for unqualified individuals; c) creates reverse discrimination; or d) continues even after its equal opportunity purposes have been achieved" (*Affirmative Action Review* 1995). Clinton also adopted Morris's call for "a system of race-neutral incentives for businesses to locate in poor neighborhoods," but only as a supplement to rather than a replacement for race-based affirmative action (Stephanopoulos 1999, 371).

Critics pointed out that in practice, the Clinton guidelines involved little, if any, affirmative-action mending. His first principle, "no quotas," simply codified existing law that finds quotas illegal. The second principle, "no preferences for the unqualified," was also meaningless since no one argued for advancing genuinely unqualified candidates. The universe does not divide neatly into qualified and unqualified: the tough issue is whether racial preferences should benefit the *less* qualified over the *more* qualified, which Clinton's careful language clearly allowed. The third limiting principle, no "reverse discrimination," was also insignificant because Clinton defined the term not to mean, as commonly understood, preferences against whites, but much more narrowly, as "illegal discrimination," which meant many affirmative-action preferences were fine. The final principle, that preferences should be "retired when the job is done," meant for Clinton that preferences would literally continue until all discrimination was eradicated—a far cry from Lyndon Johnson's notion of limited compensation for past discrimination. Clinton pointed to not a single example of a program that had gone too far, and even the most ardent advocates of affirmative action could not argue that they were for rigid quotas, for preferences for the unqualified, for illegal reverse discrimination, or for continuing affirmative action once the job was done (Kahlenberg 1996b, 1048–56).

Nevertheless, the speech was an enormous political success. Morris found in a survey following the speech that "over three-quarters of blacks *and* three-quarters of whites felt that Clinton did not favor one race over the other" (Morris 1998, 215). Though Clinton prescribed very little mending of affirmative action in practice, the public liked his rhetoric about the need to curb abuses. For the public, apparently, the presidential word was equated with the deed.

For supporters of affirmative action, Clinton's National Archives speech was all they could ask for: it neutralized the issue politically without giving an inch on substance. But as the election neared, they were highly disappointed that Clinton did so little to fight Proposition 209 in California and that the administration pulled the plug on a more circumscribed counterinitiative that might have saved affirmative action. Lemann notes, "If [the counterinitiative] moved forward, the President would have to endorse it, which would make affirmative action a central issue in his reelection campaign, which was not in his political interest" (Lemann 1999, 313). Instead, Lemann says, the Clinton people appear to have struck a covert deal with the Prop 209 advocates: they wouldn't link Clinton to affirmative action if he didn't raise big money for the initiative's opponents (Lemann 1999, 330; Connerly 2000, 181). In a late October 1996 speech to a largely black audience in Oakland, Clinton reiterated his opposition to Prop 209 but also told his listeners that there comes a time to move beyond racial grievance. The president said: "We've got to get to the point in this country where we can let some of this stuff go and say, you know, if you believe in the Constitution and the Declaration of Independence and the Bill of Rights, if you show up for work every day or you show up for school every day and you do what you're supposed to do, and you're doing the best you can, we don't need to know anything else about you" (Kahlenberg, 1997, xx).

In the end, Morris notes, Clinton "defused the issue politically" so that "[r]ace played no role in the 1996 presidential election even though anti-immigrant and anti–affirmative action ballot propositions threatened to make it the most racial of recent contests" (Morris 1998, 215).

The Second Term: The Race Initiative

While Clinton easily won reelection, the same California electorate that gave him a handy victory passed the anti–affirmative action initiative by 56 percent to 44 percent. It was in this context that during the second term Clinton began searching for a "legacy" and concluded that he could make a significant contribution by launching a national dialogue on race, an idea originally suggested by Lani Guinier (Burns and Sorenson 1999, 256). He appointed a seven-member advisory board on race, consisting of Duke history professor John Hope Franklin (chair), Linda Chavez-Thompson of the AFL-CIO, Reverend Dr. Suzan D. Johnson Cook of the Bronx Christian Fellowship, former New Jersey Governor Thomas H. Kean, attorney Angela E. Oh, former Nissan Motors president Bob Thomas, and former Mississippi Governor William F. Winter.

In a speech at the University of California at San Diego in June 1997, Clinton outlined what he hoped to accomplish with his One America initiative. He continued to wrestle openly with the affirmative-action question. On the one hand, he caricatured opponents of affirmative action, claiming, "There are those who argue that scores on standardized tests should be the sole measure of qualification for admissions to colleges and universities" (Clinton 1997a). On the other hand, he went on to say, "I know that the people of California voted to repeal affirmative action without any ill motive." And he opened the door to new and better ways of achieving diversity: "To those who oppose affirmative action," he challenged, "I ask you to come up with an alternative. I would embrace it if I could find a better way" (Clinton 1997a).

From the beginning, the initiative foundered. At the very first meeting, in July 1997, Chairman Franklin engaged in a sharp public exchange with Angela Oh over the proper focus of the board's work. Oh wanted to move the discussion beyond black and white, to reflect America's new diversity. Franklin responded, "This country cuts its eye teeth on racism in the black/white sphere" (Advisory Board 1998, 33). The sight of squabbling between people of color was, of course, fundamentally at odds with the board's mandate of helping to promote racial reconciliation, and it raised serious questions about whether an explicit racial focus was the best way to achieve unity in an increasingly diverse America.

Critics also noted that while the majority of Americans opposed racial preferences, the Advisory Board included only members who favored such policies. A November 1997 hearing on affirmative action in higher education at the University of Maryland featured a unanimous chorus of supportive witnesses. Chairman Franklin dismissed the idea of including the leader of the affirmative-action rollback in California, black businessman Ward Connerly, saying "I'm not certain what Mr. Connerly . . . could contribute to this discussion" (Holmes 1997). The initiative came under further attack when Clinton cabinet member Rodney Slater appeared at an initiative-sponsored community meeting in Dallas that barred nonblacks from participating (Hutchenson 1997).

In response to the criticism that the administration was conducting a "monologue" rather than a "dialogue," Clinton invited conservatives to the White House (Baker 1997). He also asked affirmative-action critic Abigail Thernstrom to participate with him in a town hall meeting in Akron, Ohio, in December 1997. The press played up Clinton's confrontation with Thernstrom, in which the president bullied her about whether she favored affirmative action in the military. But overall, the president displayed a fair amount of ambivalence. During the discussion, he said the "real issue" was whether a "class-based affirmative opportunity agenda" should supplement or replace race-based affirmative action: "that's the nub of the affirmative action debate" (Clinton 1997b, 14). Astonishingly, he answered his own question differently than he had in formal policy speeches, noting "politically and substantively you'll help more people and build more unity by having an economic basis for social policy now" (Clinton 1997b, 14). Clinton declared, "the biggest problems that minorities have in this country today are problems that are shared with disadvantaged white people, too—access to education, access to jobs, and that we've got to find a way somehow to talk to each other and to work on this so that we're coming together" (Clinton 1997b, 13).

Over the next nine months additional meetings were held, and in September 1998 the Advisory Board issued its final report, which included a broad range of recommendations, from strengthening laws against hate crimes, to improving K-12 education, reducing housing discrimination, institutionalizing the racial dialogue, and holding a presidential event to discuss stereotypes (Advisory Board 1998, 4–6). In the area of K-12 education, the report did not include any concrete recommendations on creative ways to promote more school integration and instead focused on ways to make racially separate schools work better through enhanced early learning, better teacher preparation, and more school construction (Advisory Board 1998, 4). The board did endorse affirmative action as "an important tool for overcoming racial discrimination and promoting the benefits of diversity in education, employment and other contexts" (Advisory Board 1998, 12, 94–95).

The report was widely seen as a disappointment and a squandered opportunity. *The New York Times*, for example, reported, "After 15 months of work, President Clinton's advisory board on race relations has produced a modest report whose chief recommendation is the creation of a permanent Presidential council on race. The voluminous report breaks little new ground" (Holmes 1998). Board member Tom Kean acknowledged, "There is a timidity on this question. . . . We were not encouraged to be bold" (Holmes 1998).

On the issue of affirmative action, where the board did take a strong stand, the country wasn't listening. Two months later, in November 1998, the state of Washington passed an anti–affirmative action initiative despite strong opposition from the business and political establishment in the state. A liberal electorate, which overwhelmingly supported an initiative to raise the minimum wage, rejected race and gender preferences by a margin even larger than the margin in California two years earlier (Kahlenberg 1998).

The Advisory Board's recommendations were just that, and were meant to be followed up with the president's own report "by the end of the year" (Holmes 1998). Some believed the president's report, which came to be referred to as a book, would revive the flagging effort. In January 1999, White House Deputy Chief of Staff Maria Eschaveste told *The National Journal* that, "the ambition is great for it. The hope is that 10 years from now, someone could take this book off the shelf and say, 'This advanced the cause of race relations in America'" ("Advancing the Cause" 1999). In March of 1999, when asked about the overdue book, Clinton said he hoped it would be ready "in the next couple of months" (Clinton 1999, A9). But by June 1999, *The Washington Post* was pessimistic, noting in a headline, "Like Commission, Clinton's Book on Race Languishes" (Babington 1999). As of this writing (May 2001) there is still no book. In the end, Bill Clinton's commission and national dialogue on race, which was meant to define his mark as president, is viewed by all corners as a major disappointment.

The Clinton Legacy

What is the Clinton legacy on race? As the 2000 presidential campaign loomed, Clinton appeared to have failed in his earlier efforts to move the Democratic Party beyond race. Quite the opposite: nonracial initiatives were being pitched as race based. In January 1999, for example, Vice President Gore unveiled an administration program called the Hispanic Education Action Plan. A report in *The Washington Post* noted dryly that in fact the increased spending outlined in the plan were for programs that "generally do not designate benefits according to ethnic or racial categories: they target students or schools according to economic standards, or to meet specific challenges such as concentrations of students who speak little English or schools with high dropout rates" (Suro 1999). In a triumph of identity politics, Gore's campaign manager, Donna Brazile, identified the "four pillars" of the Democratic Party as women, blacks, organized labor, and ethnic minorities (Bennet 2000).

Worse, Clinton's candidate for president appeared to have little appreciation for the moral complexity of affirmative action. Gore dropped his reservations about affirmative action dating from the Reinventing Government days and took to ridiculing opponents of affirmative action. "They're in favor of affirmative action if you can dunk the basketball or sink a three-point shot" (Gore 1999), he declared in a speech to the Detroit NAACP, an absurd charge since affirmative-action preferences have never been employed in professional basketball, where blacks are enormously over-represented, constituting 80 percent of professional players (McKinley 1999).

At the same time, Clinton had not done much to salvage the long-run prospects of race-specific policies. In early 2000, Florida joined Texas and California in eliminating racial preferences—so that three of the four largest states in the country had dispensed with such public policies. Nor did the administration do anything to support politically and legally viable alternatives. In September 1999, when the Educational Testing Service floated a program to identify "Strivers," low income students who did better on the SAT than expected given their economic background, the administration stood by silently as college officials moved to kill this promising program (Kahlenberg 1999). Clinton did almost nothing to shape the future of nonracial affirmative action, leaving it to conservative and moderate governors in Texas, Florida, and California, who pushed a geographic class-rank approach to university admissions, which satisfied some constituencies, but lacked the moral force of need-based affirmative action (Kaus 1999).

Surely even more disturbing from the perspective of forging One America, the nation's public schools—which are our primary institutions of social cohesion—continued to grow more segregated under Clinton's watch. Clinton symbolically held open the door to adults who had desegregated the Little Rock schools as students forty years earlier, but his primary education strategy was to improve economically and racially separate schools, an enormous challenge since school quality almost always depends on having a core of middle-class families (Kahlenberg 2001). While forced busing in many ways exacerbated racial tensions, particularly when confined to poor and working-class whites and blacks, Clinton offered astonishingly little leadership on creative new ways to bring together children from all backgrounds into economically and racially integrated common schools.

The Problem with the Clinton Approach

President Clinton's laudable goal of promoting greater racial unity foundered for a number of reasons: some, like the impeachment proceedings, wholly unrelated to race. [As Philip Klinkner quipped, the president hoped to launch a dialogue on race and instead began a "national conversation on oral sex" (Klinkner 1998).] But many of Clinton's other second term programs did prevail. Fundamentally, the race initiative appeared to disappoint because the trio of favorable factors that were thought in 1997 to offer the opportunity for a breakthrough did not pan out. The president placed short-term politics above the larger goal of One America; the nation's economic prosperity did not guarantee consensus on issues of racial policy; and the president ended up not pursuing his often-stated strategy of bringing different races together around common economic needs.

Politics

Where, in 1992, some blacks feared that Clinton was quite capable of selling them out for politics, in fact the record of the Clinton administration on race may mark a new peak in African American political strength. In Clinton's original cabinet, there were five African Americans, two Hispanics, and twelve whites, which means blacks were overrepresented by 100 percent. Clinton's cabinet didn't look like America; it looked like the Democratic electorate (Kahlenberg 1996c, 49).

Likewise, Clinton's frequent flirtation with class-based affirmative action, fostered by the ever-political Dick Morris, was rejected, ironically, at least in part for political reasons—the threatened challenge from Jesse Jackson. As Stephanopoulos put it, "Remembering the rule that primary challenges almost always cripple incumbent presidents, I was convinced we'd lose if Jackson ran" (1999, 370).

In a further irony, while Jackson was the one person most responsible for keeping Clinton from pursuing a class-based approach, he had in fact based his 1988 campaign around class-based populism. Jackson spoke of the need to "leave the racial battle ground and come to the economic common ground." He told his black and white audiences, "When a baby cries at midnight because it has no supper, that baby doesn't cry in black or white or brown or male or female. That baby cries in pain." His campaign literature announced, "Twenty years ago racial violence in the Old South was not only constant, but legal. Today racial violence still occurs but it's illegal, so we can struggle effectively to end it. But economic violence is legal and is devastating the lives of Americans of all races" (Kahlenberg 1996a, 196–97). George Packer, writing in the *New York Times Magazine*, said of Jackson's campaign: "There had been nothing like his interracial movement of the disenfranchised since Robert Kennedy's 1968 campaign, maybe since the original Populists in the early 1890's" (1999, 76).

Economic Prosperity

Clinton's initiative surely benefited from the country's relative economic prosperity, but if the initiative's backers thought economic well-being would smooth over white opposition to race-based programs, they were wrong. Good economic times did not prevent voters in California and

Washington from passing voter initiatives to ban race and gender preferences, in part, perhaps, because the opposition went beyond interests (will I lose my job to affirmative action?) to values (is it right for people to receive benefits and burdens based on immutable factors like race and gender?).

There is some evidence to suggest Clinton may have underestimated the relative importance of values to the success of the race initiative. According to one report, he told his staff that the initiative was really about economic success in a global economy. "Empowering American minorities would ensure that America would continue to be the leading economic power in the world. American blacks who were in business in America could relate better to the African blacks wanting to do business with America. Asian Americans empowered in this country could be more competitive and do better deals with Asians in Asian countries. 'That is the value of a diverse workforce,' Clinton said, 'making sure enterprises are globally connected. It's not just "let's all live together in harmony." It's about enhancing our economic power in the twenty-first century'" (Klinkner and Smith 1999, 314–15). But the success of voter initiatives to ban racial preferences suggests the issue reached deeper than economics.

Beyond Race to Need

For a variety of reasons, Clinton never served the transformative role on issues of race that many believed to be within his grasp. While he frequently flirted with programs to move the country beyond race-specific programs to more radical economic programs, he ultimately settled instead on a strategy of obfuscating the real nature of race-specific programs rather than mending and broadening them. Clinton's reluctance to introduce need-based principles directly into race-based programs was problematic for three reasons.

First, Clinton left major progressive programs highly vulnerable to judicial attack and did little in the way of contingency planning. Many legal observers now believe that when the Supreme Court is given the opportunity to revisit the *Bakke* decision, which upheld the use of race-based affirmative action in college admissions to promote diversity, a majority of the Court will reverse the decision ("Race Sensitive Admissions" 2000). Worse, racial desegregation orders are being lifted in city after city, and voluntary programs to promote racial integration are being successfully challenged by white parents. Not to have a backup plan to promote inte-

gration through nonracial means is foolish if one is serious about fostering One America.

Second, because the president's initiative focused primarily on racial
remedies, it had little to offer in the way of bold new policy proposals.
Unlike the mid-century reports on race relations, Gunnar Myrdal's *An
American Dilemma* or the Kerner Commission's *Report of the National Advisory
Commission on Civil Disorders*, both of which made sweeping public policy
recommendations about race-specific problems, Clinton's initiative came
at a time when strong laws addressing discrimination in employment, education, and housing were already on the books. Critics on the right
ridiculed the board's primary recommendation—make the board permanent—while critics on the left ridiculed the board's "all talk, no action"
approach. Leonard Steinhorn and Barbara Diggs-Brown, for example, labeled Clinton "the Oprah Winfrey of our racial conversation" (1999, 212).
In reality, the board had little bold to say because the issue of equal opportunity had long ago shifted from race to class. In that sense, the initiative was fundamentally backward rather than forward looking.

With the legal infrastructure to combat discrimination in law enforcement, housing, employment, and education largely in place, the new
challenge is bringing people of color into the economic mainstream. As
Orlando Patterson has written, "ethnic segregation now increasingly
masks the real story: class segregation. The middle class is increasingly divided from the lower classes" (1999). In the twenty-first century, he argues,
issues of race will subside; "this will be a century of class and class consciousness, forcing the nation to finally take seriously its creed that all
are created equal" (2000).

Class will increasingly come before race not simply because laws are on
the books to address issues of racial discrimination, but because those
laws are helping to shape attitudes and behaviors in significant ways. The
rise of a black middle class has loosened the once tight bond between race
and disadvantage. More and more Americans were born after passage of
the 1964 Civil Rights Act; their "liberal guilt" is more likely to be based
on unfair economic advantages enjoyed than the shame of personally benefiting from racial prejudice. Increasing rates of intermarriage also make
the whole concept of race more arbitrary and harder to define, as the Advisory Board itself acknowledged (Advisory Board 1998, 51).

Third, at its root, the initiative's focus on race before class was in tension with the stated goal of creating One America. For some who

espoused the race-specific policies backed by the president and the Advisory Board, the whole notion of One America was absurd. The multicultural left long ago abandoned the term "integration" for "diversity," because the latter emphasizes difference rather than assimilation. The Advisory Board itself noted, "There has been some criticism of the use of the term 'One America'" (1998, 105 n.1). Surely, the organizers of the Dallas meeting who excluded all who were not black did not subscribe to the One America theme.

Outside these circles, most backers of race-specific policies may very well subscribe to the ultimate goal of One America, but the fact remains that the race-specific means can conflict with the ends of racial unification. Particularly today, as the rationale for affirmative action has shifted from a program of temporary compensation for past discrimination to the more open-ended goal of maintaining diversity, the vision of unending color-consciousness is highly unappealing and divisive.

On one level, if universities admit students based on difference—they will add a different perspective—it is not surprising that these students then seek to affirm difference through separate group houses that promote racial solidarity. On another level, research suggests that the resentment race-specific policies breed among whites is impeding the goal of One America. Political science professors Paul M. Sniderman and Edward G. Carmines conducted an experiment in which they asked one-half of a group of respondents what they think about blacks and subsequently asked questions about affirmative action. For the other half of respondents, the order of the questions was reversed, and individuals were asked first about affirmative action and then what they think of blacks. The two groups were matched by education, levels of prejudice, social background, and political outlook. Sniderman and Carmines found that when the affirmative action question appears first in the survey, the mere mention makes the percentage of whites agreeing with negative stereotypes about African Americans increase: that "most blacks are lazy" rises from 20 percent to 31 percent and "most blacks are irresponsible" increases from 26 percent to 43 percent. The experiment involves varying the order of only one question in a survey of more than one hundred questions, yet triggers a statistically significant jump in white hostility (Sniderman and Carmines 1997).

The use of race-specific policies also raises the awkward specter of intraminority squabbling, a taste of which the Advisory Board saw in the clash between members Franklin and Oh. Michael Lind predicts that the rubric "people of color" will increasingly become less relevant in the new century and we are likely to become divided socially and economically as African Americans vs. everyone else—that is to say, Latinos and Asians are likely to "become white" just the way the Irish "became white," where white is a synonym for the dominant middle-class group (Lind 1998, 38). If this happens, policies that benefit all people of color are likely to increasingly benefit the most advantaged subgroups: Latinos and Asians, along with middle-class African Americans. This is not a hopeful scenario for promoting One America.

Conclusion

The primary focus of this essay has involved an evaluation of President Clinton's efforts, but it should be noted that conservatives have done little to promote One America apart from attacking race-specific policies. At one point, some conservatives appeared to back the class-based alternative to affirmative action. Newt Gingrich said race-based programs should be replaced with special help for people "who come out of poor neighborhoods, who come out of poor backgrounds, who go to school in poor counties." And 1996 presidential candidate Bob Dole declared toward the end of the campaign: "The real focus should be on helping citizens who are economically disadvantaged, to provide assistance based on need and not on skin color—in other words, needs-based preferences, not race-based preferences" (Kahlenberg 1997, xx).

But over time, conservatives have instead embraced the class-rank approach, led by the Bush brothers in Texas and Florida, in which students in the top 10 percent or 20 percent of every high school class are guaranteed admissions to the state university. There are positive aspects to these plans, in that they will promote greater integration without using race per se. In this sense, Jeb Bush's decision to label his proposal the "One Florida" plan is appropriate. But these programs are also limited, and far less promising, than economic-based affirmative action.

First, the class-rank approach is less meritocratic than class-based affirmative action—overinclusive of undeserving middle-class kids who happen to attend low-performing high schools and underinclusive of deserving disadvantaged kids who attend more rigorous high schools.

Second, dropping standardized tests entirely is risky. It may mean more underprepared kids will be admitted and fail out of college, which does no one any good. Third, the plans don't apply to elite private colleges—or public graduate schools—where much of the affirmative-action battle is joined. In adopting what is in effect a geographic rather than need-based preference, conservatives appear to have cut a deal that would produce a clear racial dividend, rather than providing a leg up to the most deserving.

At this junction, leaders in neither political party appear willing to take the bold steps necessary to take us closer to the goal of One America. Trapped in polarized positions for and against race-conscious policies, no one seems willing to address the growing class divisions that underlie so much of our nation's disunity.

References

"Advancing the Cause—But What Cause." 1999. *National Journal* (16 January): 79.

Advisory Board of the President's Initiative on Race. 1998. *One America in the 21st Century: Forging a New Future.* Washington, D.C: U.S. Government Printing Office (18 September).

Affirmative Action Review: Report to the President. 1995. Washington, D.C.: U.S. Government Printing Office.

Babington, Charles. 1999. "Like Commission, Clinton's Book on Race Languishes." *The Washington Post* (20 June): A2.

Baker, Peter. 1997. "Reaching Out to Revitalize Race Panel." *The Washington Post* (20 November): A14.

Bennet, James. 2000. "Al Gore Moves Beyond Meta." *New York Times Magazine* (23 January): 25ff.

Brown, Peter. 1991. *Minority Party.* Washington, D.C.: Regnery Gateway.

Burns, James MacGregor, and Georgia J. Sorenson. 1999. *Dead Center: Clinton-Gore Leadership and the Perils of Moderation.* New York: Scribner.

Clinton, Bill. 1995. "Remarks by the President at the National Archives and Records Administration." The White House Office of the Press Secretary (19 July).

———. 1997a. "Remarks by the President at University of California at San Diego Commencement." The White House Office of the Press Secretary (14 June).

———. 1997b. "Discussion Remarks in Town Hall Meeting on One America, University of Akron." The White House Office of the Press Secretary (3 December).

———. 1999. "If We Don't Act the War Will Spread" (excerpts from press conference). *The Washington Post* (20 March): A8–A9.

Clinton, Bill, and Al Gore. 1992. *Putting People First: How We Can All Change America.* New York: Times Books.

Connerly, Ward. 2000. *Creating Equal: My Fight against Race Preferences*. San Francisco: Encounter Books.

Devroy, Ann. 1995. "In Shift, President Supports Affirmative Action Based on Needs." *The Washington Post* (4 March): A1.

Editorial. 1992. "Bill Clinton, in Black and White." *The New York Times* (11 March): A22.

Edsall, Thomas B. 1993. "The Special Interest Gambit." *The Washington Post* (3 January): C2.

Gore, Al. 1999. "Remarks to NAACP Detroit Metro Chapter." Gore 2000 Speeches (25 April).

Holmes, Steven A. 1997. "Race Panel Excludes Critics of Affirmative Action Plans." *The New York Times* (20 November): A24.

———. 1998. "Clinton Panel on Race Urges Variety of Modest Measures." *The New York Times* (18 September): A1.

Hutchenson, Ron. 1997. "Blacks-Only Gathering for Race Initiative Faulted." *Fort Worth Star-Telegram* (9 December): 1.

Kahlenberg, Richard D. 1996a. *The Remedy: Class, Race, and Affirmative Action*. New York: Basic Books.

———. 1996b. "Class-Based Affirmative Action." *California Law Review* 84 (July): 1037–99.

———. 1996c. "Defend It, Don't Mend It." *Washington Monthly* (December): 48–50.

———. 1997. *The Remedy: Class, Race, and Affirmative Action* (including a new preface to the paperback edition). New York: Basic Books.

———. 1998. "Lessons from the Other Washington." *Intellectual Capital.com* (5 November), www.intellectualcapital.com/issues/98/1105/lcopinions3.asp[11/18/98]

———. 1999. "The Colleges, the Poor, and the SATs." *The Washington Post* (21 September): A19.

———. 2001. *All Together Now: Creating Middle-class Schools through Public School Choice* (Washington, D.C.: The Brookings Institution).

Kaus, Mickey. 1999. "Yes, There Are Easy Answers." *Slate* (1 December).

Klinkner, Philip. 1998. "The 'Racial Realism' Hoax." *The Nation* (14 December): 34.

Klinkner, Philip, and Rogers Smith. 1999. *The Unsteady March: The Rise and Decline of Racial Equality in America*. Chicago: University of Chicago Press.

Lemann, Nicholas. 1999. *The Big Test: The Secret History of the American Meritocracy*. New York: Farrar, Straus & Giroux.

Lind, Michael. 1998. "The Beige and the Black." *New York Times Magazine* (16 August): 38.

McKinley, Jesse. 1999. "Out of the Ball Park: For Black Americans, Baseball Loses Its Luster." *The New York Times* (10 October): 43.

Morris, Dick. 1998. *Behind the Oval Office: Getting Reelected against All Odds*. Los Angeles: Renaissance Books.

Packer, George. 1999. "Trickle Down Civil Rights." *New York Times Magazine* (12 December): 75–79.

Patterson, Orlando. 1999. "What to Do When Busing Becomes Irrelevant." *The New York Times* (18 July): 17.

———. 2000. "Race Over." *The New Republic* (10 January): 6.

"Portrait of the Electorate: Who Voted for Whom in the House." 1994. *The New York Times* (13 November): sec 1, 24.

"Race Sensitive Admissions in Higher Education: Commentary on How the Supreme Court Is Likely to Rule." 2000. *Journal of Blacks in Higher Education* (Winter 1999/2000): 97–100.

Sniderman, Paul M., and Edward G. Carmines. 1997. *Reaching Beyond Race.* Cambridge, Mass.: Harvard University Press.

Steinhorn, Leonard, and Barbara Diggs-Brown. 1999. *By the Color of Our Skin: The Illusion of Integration and the Reality of Race.* New York: Dutton.

Stephanopoulos, George. 1999. *All Too Human: A Political Education.* New York: Little, Brown and Co.

Suro, Roberto. 1999. "Gore Proposes School Funds for Hispanics." *The Washington Post* (25 January): A10.

Wilson, William Julius. 1992. "The Right Message." *The New York Times* (17 March): A25.

FIVE

Affirmative Action and the Failure of Presidential Leadership*

John David Skrentny

One of the threats to the formation of a harmonious "One America" is the continuing problem of ethnic and racial discrimination in America. Ironically, another threat to harmony comes from the "affirmative action" policies meant to aid ethnic and racial minorities. These policies categorize and bestow special opportunities to Americans on the basis of race or ethnic background.[1] Affirmative action regulations and programs have been highly controversial and divisive since the early 1970s. What affirmative action needed—desperately—was strong presidential leadership in the form of clear, consistent advocacy and education for the American people, especially the affirmative action–ineligible Euro-American men. Instead, the story of affirmative action is the story of the failure of presidential leadership.

One of the most fascinating aspects of the affirmative action debate is that affirmative action regulations are older than the affirmative action debate; that is, the affirmative action debate occurred after affirmative action for African Americans, women, and other minorities had already become national policy in employment, higher education, and government small business assistance. All of these affirmative action policies began in the 1965–1969 period. The public debate began in the early 1970s. The presidents in power during affirmative action's formative period, Democrat Lyndon Johnson and Republican Richard Nixon, never explained to Euro-Americans why it was necessary to single out African Americans, Latinos, Asian Americans, and American Indians for special consideration and opportunities. Later presidents also failed to mount an education campaign, leaving affirmative action advocacy to civil rights leaders, newspaper columnists, and a few academics.

This means that Euro-Americans were told why they should accept affirmative action *after* the government had already adopted it. In other words, the policy developed "behind the backs," so to speak, of Euro-Americans. This alone could have led to the resentment of the policy that is shown in many (though not all) polls on the topic (Hochschild 1999). Furthermore, advocates never settled on consistent reasons why Euro-Americans should accept affirmative action. Justifications and emphases varied from compensation for past discrimination, to the need to stop present discrimination, to the rights of all groups fully to take part in American society, to a value on ethno-racial "diversity." The justification that received the most currency—that African Americans and other minorities deserved preferences as compensation for past discrimination extending back hundreds of years—mystified working class or struggling Euro-Americans who felt they were not in a position to oppress anyone. Mystification and resentment at the past-discrimination justification was doubled for descendants of eastern and southern European immigrants, mostly Catholics and Jews, whose parents or grandparents were fleeing poverty or persecution and believed they had no ethnic or geographic relation to past American racial oppression. Many could recall instances of severe discrimination or prejudice against their own groups.

Rather than remaining mostly silent as affirmative action developed, Johnson and Nixon could have made clear and consistent arguments that did not only rely on morality. They further could have shown leadership by explaining why it might be in Euro-American interests to support a policy that categorically excludes them on such a sensitive basis as race or ethnicity.

In this chapter, I will argue that affirmative action was doomed to a shaky, uncertain existence and great controversy in part because of a failure of presidential leadership. Modern affirmative action was born during the Johnson and Nixon administrations, but both presidents allowed the policy to be born almost in secret. To be sure, there were other important issues in the middle and late 1960s crowding affirmative action off the agenda, most notably the Vietnam War and bussing to achieve primary and secondary school integration. Still, it was obvious that minority preferences would be greeted with hostility by Euro-Americans, and neither president used the "bully pulpit" of the presidency to explain and advocate the policy to the American people. Presidents *have* done so with other potentially controversial policies in the past, however.

After first explaining the affirmative action story, I examine the cases of presidential support for color-blind civil rights and nondiscrimination in immigration policy. The comparison to the lack of support for affirmative action shows how leadership on the issue could have occurred. Affirmative action may never have been popular, but this most divisive of social regulations never really had a chance.

American Presidents and Affirmative Action

Lyndon Johnson and Affirmative Action

As I have argued elsewhere,[2] what we now know as affirmative action began during the Johnson administration with a focus on African Americans in employment. Its original justifications were very different from the justifications that we know today, and were usually not intended for the public. Thus, the original advocacy of affirmative action occurred through different government officials justifying the policy primarily to each other, not to Euro-American citizens. This was a behind-the-scenes, often secret process occurring in the privacy of the White House or in the workings of civil rights bureaucracies.

First, government elites in the Johnson administration were drawn to affirmative action as a way to stop and prevent African-American rioting in the nation's cities. Also, administrators in the civil rights enforcement agencies (specifically the Equal Employment Opportunity Commission [EEOC] and the Office of Federal Contract Compliance [OFCC]) were drawn to affirmative action as a pragmatic—that is, efficient and effective—tool for protecting rights to nondiscrimination. The alternative "color-blind" method was an enormously time-consuming and frequently fruitless practice of investigating individual complaints of discrimination. It was much easier to analyze statistics of minority representation and to pressure companies to increase minority proportional hiring than to send bureaucrats to company offices to root about for "smoking gun" evidence of discrimination.

Perhaps the earliest example of this process actually comes from the Kennedy administration. In a secret 1963 meeting involving the president,

Vice President Lyndon Johnson, Attorney General Robert Kennedy, and Secretary of State Dean Rusk, the top leaders of the executive branch met with the Business Council, an organization of leaders of America's largest corporations, to urge them to hire more African Americans. The perspicacious Kennedy team foresaw great racial violence in American cities in the coming years, and asked the business leaders of America to head it off by color-consciously bringing in more African-American workers.

Later, when the cities really were going up in flames, Johnson continued the secret policy. The Johnson administration quietly urged the National Guard and some local police forces to hire more African Americans. Johnson also privately met with business leaders and urged them to relax traditional standards of merit in order to hire some of the large numbers of African-American unemployed in the nation's largest cities. Many did so without presidential persuasion.[3] To the American people, Johnson was saying only that the government must not reward rioters, but it also must not let the poverty conditions in the cities continue. Publicly, he used color-blind language, referring only to residents of ghettoes. Thus, when President Johnson *did* advocate color-conscious policies, he did so in secret. He never clearly told Americans that antiriot policy included what we now understand as affirmative action.

Johnson's EEOC and OFCC also moved toward affirmative action. It is obvious that policy developments in bureaucracies are less likely to get public attention than a presidential project such as Johnson's War on Poverty, but for something as controversial as affirmative action, Johnson could have exercised leadership by telling Americans what was happening in the bureaucracies. He could have told Americans why it was in their interests to accept what appeared to many observers as a violation of one of Johnson's great achievements, the Civil Rights Act of 1964. He did not.

Title VII of the Civil Rights Act prohibited discrimination on the basis of race, national origin, religion, and sex. It created the EEOC to enforce the law. Complaints of discrimination quickly overwhelmed the young EEOC, and administrators looked for a better way to enforce the law than investigating each individual complaint that came in through the door. In late 1965 and 1966, they decided to collect data on the numbers of EEOC-designated minorities hired at companies with at least one hundred workers, and hold hearings with firms in particular industries or geographical areas that did not hire enough of those minorities to pressure them to hire more. The EEOC's strategy made a lot of sense given its meager resources and massive caseload, but this strategy was not outlined in the law, and in its overt color-consciousness, seemed to go against the law. Furthermore, the law said nothing at all about which groups were America's minorities, but the EEOC designated some groups (African Americans, Latinos, American Indians, and Asian Americans, to go along with women of all groups) for their minority-hiring data collection.

Meanwhile, the Office of Federal Contract Compliance in the Labor Department, charged with enforcing Johnson's 1965 Executive Order 11246 (forbidding race, national origin, and religious discrimination by government contractors and requiring an undefined "affirmative action"), was following a similar course. Contractors simply could say that they did not discriminate and they would try to make special "affirmative" efforts to avoid discriminating, but still not hire any African Americans. The OFCC could thus proceed on its merry way approving contractor promises and not ever clearly accomplish anything. To show that the law mattered, it began to require contractors (first in the construction industry, an area with particularly few African-American workers) to show minority hiring goals and timetables when they submitted a bid for a government contract. The "goals" were percentages of minorities the contractors would try to hire, and the "timetables" were the dates they would try to do this hiring. Contractors still only had to show a "good faith" effort that they tried to meet those goals, but if the OFCC decided it was not good enough—not enough minorities were hired—they could cancel the contract. From the point of view of the administrators, the policy made sense. But in its color-consciousness, color-proportionalism, and designation of official minorities (the same as the EEOC's), the policy was not even hinted at in Johnson's original executive order. It developed and became government practice nevertheless without Johnson's input.

At the same time, the Small Business Administration (SBA) also began affirmative action by offering grants, technical assistance, favorable loan terms, and preferential procurement for businesses owned by the EEOC's official minorities, though the SBA temporarily dropped Asian Americans from the program (Graham 2001; La Noue and Sullivan 1994, 2001). The SBA's program was initially justified as riot control. Again, from the point of view of administrators and Johnson officials, the policy made sense. They believed that since some African Americans in America's cities were burning neighborhood stores and businesses owned by Euro-American outsiders, a policy that encouraged African-American ownership in those neighborhoods might create a class of persons in the neighborhoods who would discourage violence. Still, Johnson never announced either of these policies to the American people, never told them why they were necessary, never told them why nonrioting Latinos, American Indians, and Asian Americans were being included (or excluded), and never told them why they should support it or why it was in their interests to support it.

In fact, it is difficult to show clearly that Johnson even knew that affirmative action policies were developing in his own administration under his watch. The term "affirmative action," in his 1965 executive order, simply had no clear content or meaning at the time and did not until later implementing regulations (Skrentny 2001). In my research, I have never found a single instance in which Johnson uttered "affirmative action," or "goals and timetables," the key phrase that gave meaning to the term (Glazer 1987). I have never found him to utter "preferences" or "quotas," either. Perhaps a future researcher will find such instances, but their very obscurity proves the point: Johnson did not exercise leadership on the delicate issue of selling affirmative action policy to the Euro-American people. His behind-the-scenes efforts to manage the racial crisis in the cities were informal and always disconnected from civil rights policy.

There is no evidence that he directed the EEOC or the OFCC to put pressure on firms to hire with an eye toward racial proportions. The only evidence that he knew that such developments were taking place were letters that EEOC chairmen Franklin Roosevelt Jr. and Stephen Shulman sent to Johnson describing the new developments.[4] Given the hundreds of pages that cross a president's desk everyday, we cannot assume he paid close attention. In fact, Johnson mostly ignored the civil rights agencies, even letting the EEOC go several months without having a chairperson when chairs left, and letting it languish without its full leadership of five appointed commissioners (Blumrosen 1971; Graham 1990). Johnson did not propose or encourage the EEOC hearings or the OFCC's goals and timetables.

There is a sliver of evidence that he directed the SBA to give preferences in loans and other help to African American–owned businesses. SBA director Howard Samuels sent letters to Johnson regarding SBA activities along these lines, and in one June 22, 1968, memo Samuels mentioned a Johnson directive to "to take the lead in the development of minority entrepreneur programs through the available resources of the Federal Government and the cooperation of American business" (Johnson Library,

Gaither Papers, Box 21). But again, I could not find Johnson's original statement; if he did make it, he made it only once, it may have been private, and at any rate it received no significant publicity.

Many advocates of affirmative action can of course point to Johnson's 1965 commencement address at Howard University as evidence of presidential support for affirmative action. It is unlikely that most advocates of affirmative action who have cited the speech have ever read it in its entirety. Given the later importance and controversy that has swirled around affirmative action, the Howard speech is a very weak example of presidential support and public relations for the policy. The problem is not just that the Howard speech was only *one speech*. The bigger problem is that the speech does not contain the words "affirmative action" and never described anything like the policies and programs that have been practiced in the name of affirmative action. Furthermore, I have not been able to uncover any evidence that Johnson even had employment regulations or preferences in higher education or special help for minority-owned businesses in mind when he made the speech.

To be sure, what Johnson said could indeed be interpreted—as countless affirmative action advocates and commentators have done—as support for affirmative action. In the oft-cited passage, Johnson said:

> [F]reedom is not enough. You do not wipe away the scars of centuries by saying: Now you are free to go where you want, do as you desire, choose the leaders you please. You do not take a person who for years has been hobbled by chains and liberate him, bring him up to the starting line of a race and then say, "you are free to compete with all the others," and still justly believe you have been completely fair (Rainwater and Yancey 1967, 126).

Johnson added that the next frontier was "equality as a fact and as a result" (Rainwater and Yancey 1967, 126), but there is no evidence that he had in mind the racial hiring goals, timetables, or quotas of affirmative action.[5] The speech, written by Richard Goodwin and Daniel Patrick Moynihan, went off in another direction, reciting statistics of African-American poverty, unemployment, and infant mortality, and described the "legacy of slavery" that produced the "special nature of African-American poverty." Johnson also described the problem of family breakdown among African Americans. Regarding policy, Johnson only mentioned that African Americans lacked job training and skills, adequate housing, and health care, and said, "We are trying to attack these evils through our poverty program, through our education program, through our medical care and our other health programs and a dozen more of the Great Society programs that are aimed at the root causes of this poverty" (Rainwater and Yancey 1967, 128). He ended his speech with a vague recitation of potential answers to African-American problems, saying that, "Jobs are part of the answer," "Decent homes in decent surroundings, and a chance to learn—an equal chance to learn—are part of the answer," and "Welfare and social programs better designed to hold families together are part of the answer" (Rainwater and Yancey 1967, 130–31). It does not stretch credibility, then, to assert that the most often-cited justification for affirmative action was *not about affirmative action*. At best, it was an oblique, implicit justification uttered only once. Needless to say, to be accepted by Euro-Americans, affirmative action needed much more than this.

Richard Nixon and Affirmative Action

Richard Nixon would not offer much more leadership, though he did push for a new program of affirmative action for minority-owned businesses and for a limited affirmative action in employment. Nixon's efforts were in part rather desperate attempts to win office in 1968. When that was just barely successful (Nixon was elected in 1968 in a three-way race, winning with only 43 percent of the vote), he continued to use creative, risky efforts to disrupt the Democrats' efforts to build a winning coalition for 1972.[6]

During his campaign, when that slim victory was still in doubt, Nixon made a speech on the radio advocating a new program to aid African-American businessmen, stating he wished to create

> the bridge of black success—a bridge that can only be achieved by those [African Americans] who themselves have overcome, and who by their help or their example can show the way to the American dream. The bridge of black capitalism—by providing the technical assistance and loan guarantees, by operating new capital sources, we can help blacks to start new businesses . . . and to expand existing ones. . . . What we need is imaginative enlistment of private funds, private energies, and private talents, in order to develop the opportunities. . . . It costs little or no money, government money, to set in motion many of the programs that would in fact do the

most . . . to start building a firm structure of [African-American] economic opportunity (Stans 1991, 239–40).

Nixon made few other promotional statements about the program. He followed through with his campaign pledge, creating the Office of Minority Business Enterprise (OMBE) in 1969. The program expanded to include other minorities with no public justification or explanation. Its early years were filled with frustration and turf battles with the parallel program in the SBA (Graham 1990, 314–15). Nixon continued to support this program that promised to develop Republicans among various officially designated minorities, but rarely in high-profile circumstances and never with any clear justification for the policies. In October 1971, he made a statement to Congress stressing his support and asking for more funds for the program that was originally not supposed to cost anything. He requested only $43.6 million for OMBE, mainly for technical assistance, but wanted another $700 million for grants, loans, and guarantees. His strongly worded message to Congress recited statistics of the underrepresentation of African Americans, Latinos, and American Indians in business. Asian Americans were either left out accidentally or their statistics of representation were not compelling. He described the increases from 1969 to 1971 in grants and loans to minorities ($200 million–$566 million) and a growth in purchases from minority companies from $13 million to $142 million. With an argument uttered far too rarely, Nixon explained that the preferences for minority capitalists were self-help for the poor: "The best way to fight poverty and to break the vicious cycle of dependence and despair which afflicts too many Americans is by fostering conditions which encourage those who have been so afflicted to play a more self-reliant and independent economic role" (Nixon 1972, 1041–46).

While helpful, this statement offered no real justification of minority preferences or why "dependent" and "desperate" Euro-Americans should be excluded, and did not even connect to any arguments of discrimination. A struggling, aspiring Euro-American entrepreneur hearing such an announcement (though it is very unlikely that any did in fact hear Nixon's statement, as it was directed to Congress and was not a televised speech)[7] was, we must assume, supposed to take solace in the fact that his or her racial group already was well represented in the business class in America.

Affirmative action for minority-owned businesses expanded considerably throughout the 1970s, including congressional action to have "set-asides" of massive procurement bills. These programs, in such areas as transportation and defense, would contain provisions that required states to make efforts to set aside 10 percent of funds for minority-owned contractors. Many states and municipalities copied these laws in their own procurement bills. Though minority set-asides have run into trouble with the Supreme Court,[8] they have otherwise received little publicity. Since they only affect the relatively small section of the population seeking government contracts for their businesses, they have not factored greatly in the resentment over the policy. They do represent, however, another advance of affirmative action that came without a campaign of education and advocacy.

Nixon also supported affirmative action aimed—apparently exclusively—at construction unions. The construction industry was a good target because construction workers were overwhelmingly Democrats, and in this context affirmative action could split the labor–African American–Democratic alliance. It further offered the advantages of giving Nixon a pro–civil rights policy at a time when he was slowing down school integration, and expanding the labor pool and driving down wages, thus lessening inflationary pressures (Kotlowski 1998).

Nixon supported the OFCC's "Philadelphia Plan," the first strong "goals and timetables" regulation. It was aimed at integrating the Philadelphia construction unions. The policy ran into some trouble with the obscure congressional officer known as the comptroller general, an overseer of government contracting, during the last months of the Johnson administration. Some members of Congress, mostly southerners such as North Carolina Democrat Sam Ervin, also attacked the policy. They argued that the goals and timetables requirement ran afoul of the Civil Rights Act (a law the southerners had strongly fought against only five years earlier).

Nixon's main defense of this affirmative action came in a statement during a press conference in September 1969, when he stated:

> [I]t is essential that African-American Americans, all Americans, have an equal opportunity to get into the construction unions. . . . We intend to continue through the Department of Labor to attempt to make progress in this field, because in the long run, we cannot have construction unions which deny the right of all Americans to have those positions. America

needs more construction workers, and, of course, all Americans are entitled to an equal right to be a member of a union (Skrentny 1996).

Nixon did not, however, clearly explain to the American people why a new, color-conscious approach was needed. On the contrary, he downplayed that such a radical shift in policy was even occurring.

Nixon won a little-known Christmas Eve battle with Congress over the Philadelphia Plan—and then hardly mentioned the policy again for the next three years. Perhaps it is not fair to expect great advocacy and education in Nixon's support of affirmative action aimed at construction unions, because available evidence suggests Nixon's support came largely as a result of his desire to divide the Democratic-voting African Americans from the Democratic-voting construction unions. However, in the second year of Nixon's presidency, there was also a *major* policy development and expansion of the goals and timetables requirement beyond construction unions. The OFCC expanded the goals and timetables affirmative action policy designed for the construction industry to all major government contractors with at least a $50,000 contract and more than fifty employees. The February 1970 directive, "Order No. 4," stated they were to make efforts to "correct any identifiable deficiencies" in the utilization of minorities (Graham 1990, 342–43). How did Nixon justify the expansion? He did not. Nixon never made any announcement explaining "Order No. 4." Neither did he explain December 1971's "Revised Order No. 4," which expanded the goals and timetables concept to women. In fact, it is not at all clear that Nixon even knew that affirmative action goals and timetables had expanded to all government contracts. In 1972, he referred to the Philadelphia Plan when talking about affirmative action during that year's campaign.

By 1972 and 1973, affirmative action was beginning to attract some attention, much of it negative, from the media (see, for example, Seabury 1972; Seligman 1973). One area where it attracted much attention was not a government policy at all. The Democrats had embraced minority goals for their delegate selection process for the 1972 party convention. Nixon criticized this reform as un-American "quotas." To defend himself from charges of hypocrisy, he claimed his Philadelphia Plan required only "goals and timetables" and not quotas. Nixon's comments may have been the first time most Americans even heard about color-based preferences. And what they heard was criticism—coming from Nixon's bully pulpit.

Alternative Programs for Presidential Leadership

What could Johnson and Nixon have done differently? Is it fair to have expected more from them?

Most Euro-Americans never have been generous with social policy to benefit African Americans. A policy like affirmative action that specifically recognizes African Americans and some others for some special, positive treatment regardless of economic class, and that may compromise traditional (if not necessarily valid) standards of merit, should have been propounded with a careful strategy. To have Euro-Americans accept affirmative action, our leaders could have explained that it was good for everyone. There could have been a solid, consistent public relations effort spanning at least a year, preferably more. Presidents could have shown the leadership that they did with two other controversial measures, one very successful, and the other almost as successful.

Presidential Support for Color-Blind Civil Rights

There was a time in the 1940s when the idea of simply outlawing overt, malicious racial discrimination was very controversial and garnered the support of less than 50 percent of Euro-Americans. For example, in 1942, only 32 percent of Euro-Americans thought African Americans and Euro-Americans should go to the same schools, and 46 percent supported segregated transportation. In 1944, only 45 percent thought African Americans should have as good a chance as Euro-Americans to get any kind of job. In 1945, only 43 percent supported a state law to have employers hire without regard to race. While data is sparse, it is clear that this support on the equal chance for jobs question began steadily moving upward, so that it had reached 83 percent in 1963, 87 percent in 1966, and 95 percent in 1972 (Schuman, Steeh, and Bobo 1985, 74; Burstein 1998 [1985], 44, 46). As sociologist Paul Burstein has shown, the rise in public opinion support was the crucial factor in getting the Congress to pass Title VII of the 1964 Civil Rights Act (Burstein 1998 [1985], 180). It likely had similar effects for other titles of the law. Why did public opinion change? Even a social scientist as astute as Burstein can only speculate (Burstein 1998 [1985], 92, 120). The courageous civil disobedience of the civil rights movement was

a likely major factor, especially as its peacefulness was contrasted in television and newspaper pictures with the weapons and ruthlessness of some
southern police and pockets of resistance (Garrow 1978). But I think it
would be wrong to discount the leadership shown by American presidents
on this issue. Their support was not eager; it was slow in coming and proceeded with much hand-wringing.[9] Compared to leadership on affirmative action, however, it was magnificent.

One can point to many statements and activities of the postwar presidents on civil rights, but I will focus on an aspect of their leadership
sorely lacking in the affirmative action issue: they advocated "color-blind"
civil rights for African Americans to Euro-Americans by explaining why
it was in their interests to support civil rights. Of course, the historical
context was different, and allowed for arguments that could not be made
today. But a strong effort was made, as can be seen most clearly by examining the efforts of President Harry Truman.

Historians rightfully do not see the Truman administration as being a
time of great flourishing of civil rights protections. African Americans
made few gains in the 1945–1952 period. But this soft-spoken man from
Independence, Missouri, offered a model in how to advocate controversial civil rights policy. One excellent strategy can be seen in the report of
his President's Committee on Civil Rights (PCCR). Appointing a temporary organization to examine civil rights is hardly a master stroke, and
it would have been preferable if the committee had been more ideologically inclusive in its membership. Still, Truman had the right idea: change
public opinion to get Congress to act. In his memoirs, he wrote the purpose of the committee was to "get the facts and to publicize as widely as
possible the need for legislation" (Truman 1956, 180). The committee's
major publication, *To Secure These Rights* (PCCR 1947), was smart public relations, precisely what affirmative action has lacked.

This remarkable little report explained in simple, no-nonsense terms
why Euro-Americans should support basic civil rights for African Americans. It explained the concept of civil rights in criminal justice, employment, and politics. It provided facts of African-American and other
groups' inequality, including easy-to-read graphs and charts that showed
the facts of lynching, the devastating impact of the poll tax on voter
turnout, African Americans' lack of participation in the military hierarchy, the bases of employment discrimination complaints to the wartime

Fair Employment Practices Commission, nonwhite unemployment rates, segregation in the military and in Washington, D.C., and possible areas where civil rights legislation might help.

An especially distinctive feature of the report was that it clearly offered and elaborated three basic reasons for Americans to support civil rights. The first was the "moral reason," which was necessary to communicate that offering equal opportunity was simply the right thing to do from an ethical standpoint. The report rather strongly states, for example, "The pervasive gap between our aims and what we actually do is creating a kind of moral dry rot which eats away at the emotional and rational bases of democratic beliefs" (PCCR 1947, 139). At the least, stating the moral reason first reassured African-American readers that their full citizenship was a good in its own right. Such moralistic arguments are, unfortunately, where most advocates of affirmative action begin and end. Truman's report did more.

The second reason to support civil rights laws was the "economic reason." It appealed to the Euro-American pocketbook. Readers learned that bringing more Americans into the economy, and using their skills to the fullest, would have benefits for everyone, as African Americans gained more purchasing power, leading to greater demand and a higher standard of living for all. In other words, whites gained from African-American rights. The report did not stop at making this simple assertion. It supported the economic reason with a quotation from the president of the United States Chamber of Commerce, statistics of the high rates of African-American overrepresentation in Depression-era relief programs, and graphic charts illustrating the economics of civil rights. It was oversimplified, but its strength was that the economic reason used a conservative discourse for a liberal end. Unlike the moral reason, this argument sailed over the heads of the many believers in African-American inferiority; it was against the economic interests even of white supremacists to oppose civil rights. Any counterargument would be economic in nature, and less laden with emotion.

The third reason also used a conservative discourse and appealed to Euro-American self-interest. It was "the international reason." Readers learned, supported with a quotation from Secretary of State Dean Acheson, that racial discrimination seriously damaged American foreign policy. America and the Soviet Union were in a contest to win the hearts and minds of the peoples of Asia, Africa, and Latin America, Acheson and the report explained. Nations in these areas were throwing off the yoke of colonialism and striking out as nation-states on their own. With independence came choices—the way of the West, or Communism? Many of these new nations were nonwhite; many of them were, in fact, African. Their citizens were keenly interested in how America treated its nonwhites. With so much blatant discrimination occurring in the United States, the Soviet Union could easily describe it and photograph it for propaganda to be broadcast and disseminated all over the globe. With such propaganda, the Soviets could convince third-world peoples that Marxism-Leninism was the way of equal rights and that the Americans could not be trusted. The international reason for civil rights was that allowing racial discrimination would lead to a domino effect, as more and more nations would turn away from the United States and fall to communist control, further isolating the United States and leading eventually to communist world domination. The report stated, "The United States is not so strong, the final triumph of the democratic ideal is not so inevitable that we can ignore what the world thinks of us or our record" (PCCR 1947, 148).

It was indisputable that the Soviet Union (and later China) used such propaganda, and Asian and African peoples were greatly concerned with American racial discrimination. The "international reason" was real—and also a stroke of public relations genius. It further took the civil rights debate away from moralism and appealed to a goal of conservatives—taking the communist threat with utmost seriousness. Those who opposed civil rights were, therefore, "soft" on communism and taking needless risks. At a time when fear of Soviet expansion had a powerful effect on American social policy, leading to federal involvement in formerly local or state activities (as shown by the later National Defense Education Act in 1958), anti–civil rights forces would have to somehow make an exception that civil rights were not important to fight communism. Given the abundance of evidence (Dudziak 2000; Skrentny 1998; Klinkner with Smith 1999), it was a very powerful argument. Like the economic reason, the international reason had the twin advantages of educating Americans and uniting them. Furthermore, neither relied on simple goodwill and morality, both of which could evaporate when the economy turned downward.

Truman himself repeated many of these arguments in his strong statement to Congress in support of the committee's recommendations (Truman 1960a), and his campaign adviser in 1948 even instructed him to emphasize the "international reason" when on the stump advocating civil

rights (Clifford 1991). It became more prominent than the "economic reason," though both were excellent arguments. Truman's successor, Dwight
D. Eisenhower, was not as committed to civil rights as was Truman, but
he continued to advocate color-blind civil rights protections to Americans by explaining it was in their self-interest. This was most prominent
during the school integration crisis in Little Rock, Arkansas, when citizens strongly resisted allowing African Americans into formerly white
schools and Governor Orval Faubus did nothing to enforce the law. Eisenhower's televised speech to the nation on the matter framed civil rights
in terms of Truman's international reason (Eisenhower 1958).

In the 1960 election, Republican Richard Nixon and Democrat John F.
Kennedy both discussed civil rights in terms of geopolitics. Thereafter,
with the drama of the civil rights movement becoming ever more salient
and compelling, the international reason fell out of presidential discourse,
and the moral reason achieved dominance. But by then, public opinion
was already becoming strongly supportive of color-blind civil rights. This
was not only the result of presidential effort; obviously, as mentioned
above, the civil rights movement had an impact. Also, social scientists
formed a near-unanimous block in support of civil rights (Klinkner with
Smith 1999, 137–38; Scott 1997, 125), and other public commentators supported civil rights. But compared to affirmative action, presidential leadership on color-blind civil rights was impressive. It *preceded* the development of policy, it was clear, it was convincing, and it was consistent.
Presidents united the country and took the edge off of resentments by
appealing to national self-interest.

Immigration Reform

Presidents showed similar public relations savvy on another controversial
issue—immigration. Beginning in the 1880s, the United States cut off immigration from Asia, and in the early 1920s, it severely curtailed immigration from eastern and southern Europe as well. Except for some of the
nationalities involved, Americans either supported this discrimination or
did not care. The 1965 Immigration Act, however, eliminated these discriminatory restrictions.

On this issue Truman also showed leadership. He urged Congress to
eliminate the national origins discrimination in the law. When Congress
did reform the nation's immigration law in 1952, it tinkered with some

provisions, but left the national origins restrictions intact. In response, Truman vetoed the law, complaining that the restriction system "is a constant handicap in the conduct of our foreign relations" and creates "a pattern that is insulting to large numbers of our finest citizens, irritating to our allies abroad, and foreign to our purposes and ideals" (Truman 1960b, 77). Congress overrode the veto, passing what became the McCarren-Walter Act. Truman did not let the matter rest, creating another commission that released another report similar to *To Secure These Rights*. The President's Commission on Immigration and Naturalization (PCIN) issued *Whom We Shall Welcome*, on January 1, 1953 (PCIN 1971 [1953]). The report, while more technical than the civil rights report, made similar arguments in arguing for an open, nondiscriminatory, and friendly immigration policy.

The report offered great detail on how the national origins system worked and explained how immigration affected the economy and foreign relations, in effect reprising the economic and international reasons from the civil rights battle. It summarized hearings held around the country by the commission. It also explained in detail why reform was in all Americans' self interest. Chapter 2 of the report argued that America needed more immigrant manpower, especially in certain areas of shortage "both for the needs of defense and of an expanding peacetime economy," and because it would "continue to supply us with the talents and skills from abroad that have so strengthened and enriched our civilization." The report emphasized that "an increase of immigration from 154,000 to 250,000 per year could scarcely present serious problems of absorption" for the American economy (PCIN 1971 [1953], 44). While not directly addressing the discrimination, this economic reasoning did suggest that it was not in America's interest to exclude some talented potential immigrants solely because of their national origin.

In chapter 3, on "Immigration and Our Foreign Policy," the commission specifically addressed the discrimination issue. It argued that Japanese exclusion in the 1924 Immigration Act "contributed to the growth of the nationalistic, militaristic, and anti-American movement in Japan which culminated in war against the United States." The Japanese ambassador had warned that the exclusion could have serious consequences, and America's own Secretary of State Charles Evans Hughes had similarly warned Congress that it should not "affront a friendly nation" with such a stigma (PCIN 1971 [1953], 45). The commission then extended this line of argument to the present situation, where the United States, in a position of world leadership, should show "a decent respect to the opinions of mankind" if it wanted to win the struggle against communism (PCIN 1971 [1953], 46–47). The commission buttressed this view with strong support from a variety of participants at hearings, from labor organizations to women's organizations to religious organizations to officers of the foreign service. This last group made arguments virtually identical to those used to support civil rights for African Americans. For example, W. Averell Harriman, director of the Mutual Security Agency, argued, "The kind of immigration policy we adopt is a factor in the world struggle between democracy and totalitarianism." United States Special Representative in Europe William H. Draper said, "In endeavoring to strengthen the economic and military defense of the free world, and particularly of the North Atlantic Community, we should recognize immigration policy as one of the elements in achieving economic and political stability as well as social equilibrium" (PCIN 1971 [1953], 47). A better immigration policy should abolish the national origins system, set an overall maximum annual quota for immigration that "should reflect the needs and capacity for absorption of the United States" (this figure was said to be 250,000 in 1952), and priorities should be based on emergency situations abroad, "such as continued distress and suffering among refugees, expellees, escapees, displaced persons and other victims of communism and other forms of totalitarianism," as well as the "special and general needs of the United States" (PCIN 1971 [1953], 13).

Though not running for president, Truman prominently campaigned for the Democratic candidate, Adlai Stevenson, and criticized Republican support of the McCarran-Walter Act. He criticized Republicans for supporting "a philosophy of racial superiority developed by the Nazis, which we thought we had destroyed when we defeated Nazi Germany and liberated Europe." But the opponent, retired General Dwight D. Eisenhower, also promoted reform. Eisenhower linked the need for reform to national security and cold war issues (Tichenor 1996, 377–78).

In office, Eisenhower did not strongly pursue the immigration reform issue, though he continued a practice, begun under Truman, of allowing special admissions where it served American foreign policy purposes. Kennedy picked up the issue, even writing a book on the subject, *A Nation of Immigrants* (Kennedy 1964), though this was a romantic portrait and less of a hard-edged argument of why reform was in the interest of Americans. But Kennedy was not alone, as leadership also came from the Senate.

Senator Philip A. Hart (D-MI) had ensured that Kennedy would be an ally with his own immigration reform legislation. In December 1962, before he submitted his bill, Hart asked Kennedy aide Theodore Sorensen for help in the form of a section on immigration reform for the upcoming State of the Union address. Hart informed Sorensen that numbers of immigrants admitted was less important than having "a system which will select the best immigrants without prejudice because of race or nationality." Worried about arguments that stressed negative economic impacts of immigrants, on December 14, 1962, Hart asked Kennedy aide Theodore Sorensen to have the Labor Department develop material on the relationship between immigration and employment (Kennedy Library, White House Central Subject File, Box 483). By April, the Hart staff was informing the Kennedy administration of the coordinated effort to sell the bill, with various senators making speeches in Detroit, Toledo, New York, Bridgeport, Connecticut, and along the West Coast, and thanking them for the Labor Department's efforts. "It is important," Hart staffer William B. Welsh explained to Kennedy aide Myer Feldman on April 29, 1963, "that we get a good message from the President to the Congress in the very near future and certainly before the Senate hearings begin" (Kennedy Library, White House Central Subject File, Box 482).

Kennedy was happy to oblige; he would send both a message and his own bill. Kennedy sent a letter to the Congress explaining, "The most urgent and fundamental reform I am recommending relates to the national origins system of selecting immigrants." Reform would not solve all problems but it would, however, "provide a sound basis upon which we can build in developing an immigration law that serves the national interest and reflects in every detail the principles of equality and human dignity to which our nation subscribes." On July 23, 1963, Kennedy wrote a letter to Congress, explaining:

> The use of a national origins system is without basis in either logic or reason. It neither satisfies a national need nor accomplishes an international purpose. In an age of interdependence among nations, such a system is an anachronism, for it discriminates among applicants for admission into the United States on the basis of accident of birth (Kennedy Library, White House Central Subject File, Box 482).

Kennedy was assassinated, but the issue remained on the agenda. A 1964 bill stalled, but both parties supported reform, and over the next year, interest group support for reform would also be strengthened by the formation of the National Committee for Immigration Reform, which included two former presidents (Truman and Eisenhower) and some leading figures of corporate America. Robert Murphy, chair of Corning Glass International, and a former undersecretary of state and U.S. ambassador, formed the group. George Meany, president of the AFL-CIO, also was a member of the organization, as well as of several ethnic organizations.

The National Committee for Immigration Reform worked closely with the Johnson administration (Johnson even thanked Murphy for forming the group [Johnson Library, Statements of Lyndon Baines Johnson, Box 150]), helping with the public relations campaign. In its June 15, 1965, "Statement of Purpose," it listed as its first reason for reform that "by discriminating among nations on the basis of birthplace, the national origins provision is detrimental to our international interests, breeds hatred and hostility towards the United States, blocks comity among nations, and is a hindrance to our nation's policy of peace among nations, without serving any national need or serving any international purpose of the United States" (Johnson Library, Statements of Lyndon Baines Johnson, Box 150). Committee Director of Information Gladys Uhl told a Johnson aide on the same day, "We plan an intensive campaign—through the use of all communications media, through personal contacts with Members of the Congress—to help win widespread support and dispel the general public apathy and misunderstanding concerning the bill" (Johnson Library, Statements of Lyndon Baines Johnson, Box 150).

In fact, Americans now favored doing away with the national origins system. The persuasion apparently had some impact. A May 31, 1965, Harris poll showed that when asked whether immigration laws should be based on skills or national origin, a plurality chose "Base more on skills of individual" (36 percent), while 20 percent chose "Base more on country quotas," 15 percent said it "makes no difference," and 20 percent were "not sure" (U.S. Congress 1965, 3014–15). Two months later, using somewhat different wording, Harris conducted another poll. When asked, "What is the most important criteria for admitting new immigrants to the U.S.?," those favoring occupational skills numbered 71 percent, relatives in the U.S. 55 percent, and country in which born was only 33 percent. The poll posed another question: "The U.S. currently has a quota system based on the country of origin. Should this policy be changed to one of occupational skills rather than the country in which the immigrant was born?" For this question, the numbers for reform were somewhat less overwhelming, but still suggested improvement over the May poll, as 50 percent chose "should change," while 33 percent said "should not change" and 17 percent had no opinion (Johnson Library, Bill Moyers Files, Box 1).

Reform came in 1965, though that year's Immigration Act was not what the Kennedy or Johnson administrations really wanted. Advocates of reform sought elimination of the national-origin restrictions and first-immigration preferences for persons with skills in short supply in the United States. But antireform members of Congress, especially Michael Feighan (D-OH), who controlled the House immigration subcommittee, as well as southerners, demanded compromises from the Johnson administration. To hinder immigrants from eastern and southern Europe and the developing world, the final bill gave first preference to immigrants who already had relatives in the United States (Reimers 1985, 72). Of course, this would favor persons from northern and western Europe, who would have more relatives in the United States than others. But there was little demand for immigration from these regions of Europe, and neither was there great demand from eastern and southern Europe, where communist governments made immigration difficult. On the other hand, there was great demand from other parts of the world, especially east and south Asia and Latin America, and the family preferences became the method for immigrants to bring in unskilled relatives, competing or at least appearing to compete with America's lower classes.

Given its unintended consequences, immigration reform is not an ideal example of president-led policy making. On the one hand, it shows a failure to adequately anticipate what the compromise reform would accomplish. The number of immigrants arriving now, about 900,000 a year, is much larger than anyone foresaw or advocated in 1965, and the percentage from the third world is tremendously higher than anyone said would be the case in 1965.

On the other hand, this is not entirely the fault of the pre-1965 presidential advocates of the law, as the final law was not what they intended. And the reform *is* an example of successful leadership in terms of education and advocacy in eliminating national-origin discrimination. In 1965, the public supported specifically eliminating national-origin discrimination in immigration. Presidents likely played a major role in getting this support. The reasoning was consistent, and the arguments told Americans why it was in their interests to support the new policy. Presidents worked with a variety of political actors, and in the case of Truman and Eisenhower, continued a bipartisan drive for reform even after their terms of office had expired.

Applying the Models: How Could Presidents Have Led on the Affirmative Action Issue?

I do not mean to accuse Johnson and Nixon of incompetence, negligence, or malfeasance for their failure to properly advocate affirmative action and educate the Euro-American people about the issue. Truth be told, they were operating in difficult circumstances. Nearly every major American city was a scene of violence in its African-American neighborhoods. Johnson had little time to find the cause of the problem, and many African-American leaders likely would have perceived a protracted, grassroots public relations campaign for affirmative action as stalling, possibly further exacerbating the violence. Further, both Johnson and Nixon operated during other crises, such as the Vietnam War and the climate of protest and insurrection related to the war. Courts were beginning to order bussing to force school integration in the South, leading to great political turmoil there. Nixon was also in a precarious electoral situation, contributing to a kind of political paranoia and the ultimate downfall of his presidency in the Watergate scandal. Last, both presidents would have had to go against, or modify, the hard-won public acceptance of color-blind civil rights.

We also should not let Johnson and Nixon off the hook completely. Though times were tough, it is also true they made almost no effort at all to explain the need for affirmative action. In the Johnson administration, the policy was essentially a secret, receiving no official and public recognition by Johnson that I have been able to find in years of research. Nixon did better, but flip-flopped, offering no consistent support. It is quite possible that these presidents knew affirmative action was controversial, and rather than confront and reduce the controversy, they simply refused to risk their popularity on it.

What could they have done better? Most obviously, Johnson, Nixon, and all later presidents could have clearly maintained a moral reason to support affirmative action, but also told Americans why it was in their interests to support the policy. Johnson did not have to offer his true rationale of riot prevention to support the policy. If he did, he could have combined it with Truman's "international reason," stressing the need for an America that appeared egalitarian to be a model for other nations to look up to and to counter continuing communist propaganda. Indeed, it was concerns of geopolitics that led Johnson to affirmative action as riot control in the first place, since Soviet propaganda showing America using repressive measures on its African-American population would have been a foreign relations nightmare (Skrentny 1998).

For Johnson, the international reason was available, but as the cold war thawed, it would have been less compelling for Nixon. Certainly as Nixon made overtures to China and otherwise pursued "détente," the international reason would have seemed inconsistent. Both Johnson and Nixon could have used Truman's "economic reason." Johnson and Nixon could have explained that it served no economic purpose to have some ethno-racial groups frozen out of the economic mainstream, and that it could serve positive benefits to bring them in, have more earn good wages, increase consumer demand, and create a bigger "economic pie" for everyone. Or they could have explained, as Nixon did on too few occasions, that affirmative action was an alternative to expensive job training and welfare programs, as it rewarded the American value of hard work. They might have been able to mitigate the social costs of affirmative action (Euro-American resentment) by emphasizing that affirmative action was relatively costless, from a budget standpoint, since it was only a regulation and not a transfer of government revenues. And they could have developed other programs to assuage the fears of the economically insecure Euro-American working class, who felt no responsibility for past oppression of African Americans but were told that they were racists and should bear the initial brunt of affirmative action. Nixon's policy of integrating construction unions never came with any serious inquiry into the matter of why the Euro-American construction workers fought so hard for these jobs, resisted integration, and did not try to move into white collar or professional positions higher in socioeconomic status. The threat of affirmative action in blue collar fields could have been softened if it came with a special scholarship or technical training program for workers already in blue collar or construction work, or aimed at their sons, who often followed them into the construction trades.

Other reasons of self-interest were possible. Americans may be alone in the developed world in their tolerance for city regions that are so crime-ridden that persons of any race fear car trouble when driving through them. These areas are usually segregated African-American neighborhoods where unemployment is extremely high and citizen morale is extremely low.[10] Even without the rioting that was occurring in these neighborhoods in the late 1960s, Johnson and Nixon could have advocated affirmative action as an inexpensive way to mitigate these centers of urban crisis by offering help for African-American businesses, African-American workers, and African-American students that could ultimately relieve much of the crime in these neighborhoods. It was and is in all Americans' interest to eliminate the fear of a car breakdown, or a mistaken subway trip, into a high-crime neighborhood.

Johnson or Nixon could have appointed a Truman-style commission to publish a high-profile report advocating affirmative action.[11] Ideally, the commission would be bipartisan, like the citizens' group advocating the end of national-origins restrictions in immigration policy that included Truman and Eisenhower. Political leaders could have stuck to a consistent rationale for affirmative action, and if they did not have time to justify the policy and educate Americans before they implemented it, they could have at least done so *while* they were implementing it.

The leadership of Ford, Carter, Reagan, Bush, or Clinton on affirmative action is no more impressive than that of Johnson and Nixon. Of course, the GOP had turned away from affirmative action and the Democrats were in that difficult position of justifying the policy after the fact. But none offered clear reasons why affirmative action was in Euro-American interests.

The latest rationale for affirmative action, that it creates valuable "diversity," is a step in the right direction, as it usually comes with arguments of self-interest. Affirmative action advocates have been arguing since the late 1980s that a firm's diverse workforce brings in fresh ideas and can better connect with an increasingly diverse customer base (the unintended result of the 1965 immigration reform!), benefiting all who work for the firm. In education, it is argued that different skin colors or Latino heritage serve as proxies for diverse viewpoints and offer a richer education for all students.

Despite the continued repetition of the value on diversity, there was remarkably little evidence to support it. Much of the existing solid evidence is only now trickling in—years *after* the argument had been made (e.g., Bowen and Bok 1998). In contrast, Truman's economic and international reasons to support civil rights always were backed up by clear logic and evidence. In fact, the diversity goal was first sold to American businesses by human resources professionals as a way to justify their jobs during the years when the Reagan administration was removing much of the pressure on firms to use affirmative action (Kelly and Dobbin 1998; Lynch 1997). In education, university deans and administrators fashioned the diversity rationale during the riot years of the late 1960s and without any comprehensive study. Furthermore, poor or working class Euro-Americans are supposed to support a racial diversity policy that does not benefit them. The diversity that is valued, despite the inclusive language and arguments, is limited to skin color and Spanish surnames. There is, for example, no talk of the benefits of religious diversity, political diversity, or achieving a diversity of Euro-American groups. And few in politics or university admissions talk about class diversity.[12] Bill Clinton and many others have claimed that America gains strength through some types of ethno-racial diversity, but they do not clearly explain why and how. That diversity is a national strength is simply asserted; we are to accept it primarily on faith. It is hard to see how "diversity" policies that benefit minorities and allow well-off Euro-Americans to continue to assume elite positions in American society will produce support among middle- and working-class Euro-Americans.

Conclusion

In the economic good times of the late 1990s, affirmative action declined in salience in American politics. But there is no denying that it always has been a public relations failure. Presidents never provided a public relations campaign as they did with other controversial measures. Presidents implemented this most contentious of techniques to create opportunity for African Americans, women, and other designated minority groups without explanation or justification. Many Euro-Americans complained in the 1970s and still do today of feeling that affirmative action was forced on them. This survey of presidential leadership on the issue suggests they were right.

* I wish to thank Stanley Renshon for helpful comments on an earlier draft of this paper and Sara Samuels for expert research assistance.

Notes

1. Many affirmative action programs also benefit women of all ethnicities, but these will not be discussed here since the theme of the book is focused on ethnicity. Also, affirmative action for women has not been nearly as controversial, or even acknowledged, as that for ethnic minorities.

2. Unless otherwise specified, the following details on the development of affirmative action are taken from Skrentny (1996). On the development of affirmative action, also see (Graham 1990) and Blumrosen (1971; 1993).

3. Universities also sought to change admissions standards to allow more African-American students to enroll in law and medical schools, partly in response to the urban crisis, though this was done independent of federal government policy. There is no evidence that President Johnson or Nixon urged the creation of these programs.

4. Shulman, for example, sent a letter to Johnson on March 4, 1967, describing a new program that "utilizes the Commission's 'arm of persuasion' as you termed it, in a wholesale approach to new job opportunities for Negroes, Mexican Americans and other Spanish-speaking, and American Indians." The program was "an effort by the Commission to seed the country with demonstration programs for recruiting, hiring and promoting minority group members in substantial numbers" (EEOC Papers, Shulman Files, Box 9). There is no record of Johnson ever discussing the EEOC's "arm of persuasion" that I have been able to find (and certainly not in the way Shulman interpreted it), no record of him responding to Shulman's letter, and it is in fact uncertain that he ever read Shulman's note.

5. See Davies (1996) for a discussion of the origins of the speech.

6. On the type of "preemption politics" needed by presidents in Nixon's situation, see Skowronek (1993).

7. While *Time* and *Newsweek* magazines ignored the message, *The New York Times* gave it front-page coverage. The story, however, devoted only one sentence to Nixon's justification of the program, quoting him as saying, "The opportunity for full participation in our free enterprise system by socially and economically disadvantaged persons is essential if we are to obtain social and economic justice for such persons and improve the functioning of our national economy" (Delaney 1971, 1).

8. See *City of Richmond v. J.A. Croson Co.* 488 U.S. 469 (1989); *Adarand Constructors v. Peña,* 115 S. Ct 2097 (1995).

9. See Riley (1999) for a critique of presidential leadership on civil rights. I do not disagree with Riley's argument; my claim is that *relative to* presidential action on affirmative action, presidential leadership on color-blind civil rights appears as a worthy model.

10. These are the places where the "truly disadvantaged" live. See Wilson (1987).

11. The United States Commission on Civil Rights did not have the high profile needed to successfully sell affirmative action, and it in fact paid no attention to the policy development until 1970, when it published a massive and rather technical report on civil rights enforcement (U.S. Commission on Civil Rights 1970). A similar follow-up report was published the next year. The higher profile *Report of the National Advisory Commission on Civil Disorders* (National Advisory Commission on Civil Disorders 1968), also known as "The Kerner Report," contained much useful information on the deplorable conditions that African Americans faced, but unfortunately got off on the wrong foot, from a political standpoint, by alienating struggling, insecure lower middle class and working class Euro-Americans with the blunt claim that "white institutions" and "white society" were responsible for the conditions of the ghetto. It instead limited its claims to help for "ghetto residents" and the "hardcore unemployed."

12. The best statement on the role of class in affirmative action is Kahlenberg (1996). The most influential defense of "diversity" in university admissions is Bowen and Bok (1998). Bowen and Bok discuss the benefits for diversity of admitting poor students of all backgrounds in a few sentences (Bowen and Bok 1998, 50). Clearly, more promotion of class diversity is needed to make lower middle class whites feel that the value of diversity will benefit them in any way.

References

Blumrosen, Alfred. *Black Employment and the Law.* New Brunswick, N.J.: Rutgers University Press, 1971.
———. *Modern Law: The Law Transmission System and Equal Employment Opportunity.* Madison: University of Wisconsin Press, 1993.
Bowen, William G., and Derek Bok. *The Shape of the River: Long-Term Consequences of Considering Race in College and University Admissions.* Princeton, N.J.: Princeton University Press, 1998.
Burstein, Paul. *Discrimination, Jobs and Politics.* Chicago: University of Chicago Press, 1998 [1985].
Clifford, Clark M. for the President. 17 August 1948. In *Civil Rights, the White House and the Justice Department,* ed. Michal Belknap. Vol. 1. New York: Garland Publishing, 1991, 64–71.
Davies, Gareth. *From Opportunity to Entitlement: The Transformation and Decline of Great Society Liberalism.* Lawrence: University Press of Kansas, 1996.
Delaney, Paul. "Nixon Acts to Strengthen Aid to Minority Business." *The New York Times* (14 October 1971): section 1, 1.
Dudziak, Mary L. *Cold War Civil Rights.* Princeton, N.J.: Princeton University Press, 2000.
Eisenhower, Dwight D. "Radio and Television Address to the American People on the Situation in Little Rock, September 24, 1957." *Public Papers of*

the Presidents of the United States: Dwight D. Eisenhower. Vol. 5. Washington, D.C.: U.S. Government Printing Office, 1958, 689–94.

Equal Employment Opportunity Commission Papers. Files of Stephen Shulman. National Archives, College Park, Md.

Garrow, David. *Protest at Selma.* New Haven, Conn.: Yale University Press, 1978.

Glazer, Nathan. *Affirmative Discrimination.* Cambridge, Mass.: Harvard University Press, 1987.

Graham, Hugh Davis. *The Civil Rights Era.* New York: Oxford University Press, 1990.

————. "Affirmative Action for Immigrants? The Unintended Consequences of 1960s Reforms." In *Color Lines: Affirmative Action, Immigration, and Civil Rights Options for America,* ed. John D. Skrentny. Chicago: University of Chicago Press, 2001, 53–70.

Hochschild, Jennifer L. *Facing Up to the American Dream.* Princeton, N.J.: Princeton University Press, 1997.

————. "Affirmative Action as Culture War." In *The Cultural Territories of Race: African-American and White Boundaries,* ed. Michèle Lamont. Chicago: University of Chicago Press, 1999, 343–70.

Johnson, Lyndon. Files of James Gaither. Lyndon Johnson Library, Austin, Tex.

————. Statements of Lyndon Baines Johnson. Lyndon Johnson Library, Austin, Tex.

————. Files of Bill Moyers. Lyndon Johnson Library, Austin, Tex.

Kahlenberg, Richard D. *The Remedy: Class, Race, and Affirmative Action.* New York: Basic Books, 1996.

Kelly, Erin, and Frank Dobbin. "How Affirmative Action Became Diversity Management: Employer Response to Antidiscrimination Law, 1961 to 1996." *American Behavioral Scientist* 41 (April 1998): 960–84.

Kennedy, John F. *A Nation of Immigrants.* Revised and enlarged edition. New York: Harper & Row, 1964.

————. White House Central Subject File. John F. Kennedy Library, Boston, Mass.

Klinkner, Philip, with Rogers Smith. *The Unsteady March.* Chicago: University of Chicago Press, 1999.

Kotlowski, Dean. "Richard Nixon and the Origins of Affirmative Action." *The Historian* 60 (1998): 523–41.

La Noue, George, and John C. Sullivan. "Presumptions for Preferences: The Small Business Administration's Decisions on Groups Entitled to Affirmative Action." *Journal of Policy History* (1994): 439–67.

————. "Deconstructing Affirmative Action Categories." In *Color Lines: Affirmative Action, Immigration, and Civil Rights Options for America,* ed. John D. Skrentny. Chicago: University of Chicago Press, 2001, 71–86.

Lynch, Frederick. *The Diversity Machine.* New York: The Free Press, 1997.

National Advisory Commission on Civil Disorders. *Report of the National Advisory Commission on Civil Disorders.* New York: Bantam Books, 1968.

Nixon, Richard M. "Special Message to the Congress Urging Expansion of the Minority Business Enterprise Program, October 13, 1971." In *Public Papers of the Presidents of the United States: Richard M. Nixon*. Vol. 3. Washington, D.C.: U.S. Government Printing Office, 1972, 1041–46.

President's Commission on Immigration and Naturalization. *Whom We Shall Welcome: Report of the President's Commission on Immigration and Naturalization.* Washington, D.C.: U.S. Government Printing Office, 1953, reprinted by New York: Da Capo, 1971.

President's Committee on Civil Rights. *To Secure These Rights.* Washington, D.C.: U.S. Government Printing Office, 1947.

Rainwater, Lee, and William L. Yancey. *The Moynihan Report and the Politics of Controversy.* Cambridge, Mass.: MIT Press, 1967.

Reimers, David M. *Still the Golden Door: The Third World Comes to America.* New York: Columbia University Press, 1985.

Riley, Russell L. *The Presidency and the Politics of Racial Inequality: Nation-Keeping from 1831 to 1965.* New York: Columbia University Press, 1999.

Schuman, Howard, Charlotte Steeh, and Lawrence Bobo. *Racial Attitudes in America.* Cambridge, Mass.: Harvard University Press, 1985.

Scott, Daryl Michael. *Contempt and Pity: Social Policy and the Image of the Damaged Black Psyche, 1880–1996.* Chapel Hill: University of North Carolina Press, 1997.

Seabury, Paul. "HEW and the Universities." *Commentary* (February 1972): 38–44.

Seligman, Daniel. "How 'Equal Opportunity' Turned Into Employment Quotas." *Fortune* (March 1973): 160–68.

Skowronek, Stephen. *The Politics Presidents Make.* Cambridge, Mass.: Harvard University Press, 1993.

Skrentny, John David. "Introduction." In *Color Lines: Affirmative Action, Immigration, and Civil Rights Options for America,* ed. John D. Skrentny. Chicago: University of Chicago Press, 2001, 1–28.

———. "The Effect of the Cold War on African-American Civil Rights: America and the World Audience, 1945–1968." *Theory and Society* 27 (1998): 237–85.

———. *The Ironies of Affirmative Action: Politics, Culture and Justice in America.* Chicago: University of Chicago Press, 1996.

Stans, Maurice H. "Nixon's Economic Policy Towards Minorities." In *Richard M. Nixon: Politician, President, Administrator,* ed. Leon Friedman and William F. Levantrosser. New York: Greenwood Press, 1991, 239–40.

Tichenor, Daniel. "Regulating Community: Race, Immigration Policy and American Political Development." Unpublished Ph.D. dissertation. Brandeis University, 1996.

Truman, Harry S. *Memoirs.* Vol. II. Garden City, N.Y.: Doubleday, 1956.

———. "Civil Rights Message." In *Freedom and Equality: Addresses by Harry S. Truman,* ed. David Horton. Columbia: University of Missouri Press, 1960a, 9–18.

————. "Veto of the Immigration and Nationality Act of 1952." In *Freedom and Equality: Addresses by Harry S. Truman*, ed. David Horton. Columbia: University of Missouri Press, 1960b, 75–85.

United States Commission on Civil Rights. *The Civil Rights Enforcement Effort.* Washington, D.C.: U.S. Government Printing Office, 1970.

U.S. Congress. *Congressional Record.* Washington, D.C.: U.S. Government Printing Office, 1965.

Wilson, William Julius. *The Truly Disadvantaged.* Chicago: University of Chicago Press, 1987.

PART TWO

American Culture and the Dilemmas of Diversity

Moving beyond Racial Categories*

Richard J. Payne

An attempt to have an honest national conversation on race, the central objective of President Clinton's Initiative on Race was bound to fail, largely because most Americans cannot honestly talk about race. This is due to the ideological and deeply emotional nature of race. Race is so intertwined with personal identity that most Americans tend to perceive discussions of race as intrinsically accusatory. Under these circumstances, an emphasis on racial differences instead of what we have in common as human beings and as Americans is generally counterproductive. It was obvious from the beginning that those involved in leading the national dialogue on race viewed race relations primarily in terms of black and white, with the growing number of Asians, Latinos, and others relegated to the sidelines. Perhaps the most serious flaw in this regard was the initial exclusion of Native Americans, the people whose encounters with Europeans helped to shape contemporary American race relations.

As this essay shows, the national dialogue on race failed because its basic premises and focus were out of touch with the rapidly changing and complex realities of race in America today. The voices of the young generation of Americans were not equally represented or listened to by those in charge of the Initiative on Race. But the foundation of the failure of the national dialogue on race was the uncritical acceptance of the very concept of race. The participants subscribed to the primitive notion of different races of human beings, thereby reinforcing the problem they wanted to solve, or at least diminish. The social construction of race is challenged by generational and demographic changes, increased educational opportunities and achievements, the growth of a strong black middle class, increased interaction of people from diverse backgrounds, and the erosion of racial categories due to the growth of interracial relationships and transracial adoptions.[1] These developments and strong presidential leadership can help create One America. This positive assess-ment does not overlook developments that impede efforts to move beyond race. Race will continue to matter more in some regions of the country than in others. Many individuals and groups will continue to resist social change.

Nevertheless, most Americans are likely to place less emphasis on racial categories and will increasingly interact with people from different racial backgrounds. Just as ethnicity has declined in significance due to increased interaction among ethnic groups, race also will become less important as individuals get to know each other on a personal basis.

The Social Construction of Race

Race is an arbitrary label that is wrapped in pseudoscientific doctrine to legitimize socioeconomic and political power. In the process of exagger-ating small, superficial, and highly selective differences among people, such as skin color, pseudoscientists ignore the fact that human beings have a common origin in Africa. In the most comprehensive scientific study of human genes, L. Luca Cavalli-Sforza, Paolo Menozzi, and Alberto Piazza collected genetic material from tens of thousands of individuals from ap-proximately five hundred ethnic groups. They concluded that the super-ficial characteristics that form the foundation of the concept of race can be explained by different environmental conditions. Based on these phys-ical differences, they further concluded that the number of distinguish-able races can range from three to sixty-three, depending on the criteria used.[2] The concept of race is rejected by most scientists, a development that is weakening the social construction of race.

There is ample genetic variation in all populations, even in relatively small ones. Furthermore, the differences among these small groups are in-significant when compared to differences within the major groups called races. This is partly due to the fact that, contrary to the fiction of a pure race, human beings have been mixing for many centuries. Narrow stud-ies of so-called racial groups often obscure common characteristics of dif-ferent races. There are numerous examples demonstrating that people who are classified as racially different have many genetic similarities. Equatorial Africans, Italians, and Greeks could be regarded as one race because they all carry the sickle cell gene. Asians and the San or Bushmen of South Africa have similarly shaped eyes. Asians, Native Americans, and Swedes have similarly shaped teeth. Norwegians, Saudi Arabians, and the Fulani of northern Nigeria could fall into the same racial category because they are lactose tolerant. Depending on the traits selected, Swedes, the Fulani, the Xhosa of South Africa, the Ainu of Japan, and many Italians could be regarded as a single race.[3] In other worlds, racial classification is an extremely arbitrary cultural construct that is not scientifically valid.

Americans and others have used race to distinguish among those who are regarded as belonging to the dominant cultural circle and others who are excluded, different, and culturally distant. Distinctions based on superficial facts acquire deeper significance when deliberate efforts are made to make social, economic, and political reality conform to ideas embodied in the theory of racial divisions among human beings. Consequently, although race is a scientific fantasy, it is an unfortunate, socially and politically constructed, fact. But this social fact is highly dependent on the widespread acceptance of the erroneous assumption that, biologically, race is fixed, measurable, concrete, and objective. The idea of race is reinforced by those who benefit socially, economically, and politically from it.

The social construction of race is facilitated by obvious superficial differences and concerted efforts to treat those regarded as "others" in such a way that their behavior and way of life conform to what amount to self-fulfilling prophecies. For example, the belief that some races are not as intelligent as others is followed by the allocation of resources in ways that help make this assumption true. An essential aspect of the social construction of race is the creation of institutions that perpetuate the socioeconomic and political order. In other words, even though race is believed to be a natural phenomenon, maintaining the status quo cannot be left to chance. Race becomes an institutional fact that cannot survive without a conscious effort to sustain it. The national dialogue on race, by accepting artificial and arbitrary racial divisions as scientific facts, actually contributed to maintaining race as an institutional fact.

The social and political construction of race clearly depends to a large extent on its acceptance by both those who benefit and those who suffer from it. To accomplish this objective, both groups must be enculturated to regard this artificial social arrangement as natural, as objective reality. For a variety of reasons, everyone learns the rules of racial classification and internalizes race as social identity. As time passes, race becomes common sense, a way of comprehending, explaining, and acting in the world.[4] Those who benefit from the racial system as well as those who are constrained by it cooperate to maintain much of the status quo, even as some of them complain about problems caused by the unnatural arrangement. But new conceptions of social, political, economic, and scientific realities invariably challenge old ways of thinking and the social, political, and economic relationships based on them.

Race as a hierarchical divider of human beings did not emerge until the spread of European colonization of Asia, Africa, and Latin America and the development of the institution of slavery in the Americas. In the United States, the issues of slavery and territorial expansion played a pivotal role in the social construction of race. The English, who settled what would later become the United States of America, were relatively isolated in Europe from people with different skin color. Their reaction to Native Americans was much more negative than that of the Spanish, Portuguese, and French. English culture had conditioned the English to see ugliness and evil in black, a perception that inspired both fear of and hostility toward Africans and Native Americans. Although the Spanish, French, and Portuguese also viewed Native Americans and Africans as inferior, the English emphasized the importance of racial differences to a much greater degree than the other Europeans. This is evidenced by the racial problems in contemporary American society and the relative racial harmony in Latin American countries. This background helped to pave the way for the adoption of a racial prism that would become central to the organization and functioning of American society. By 1850, America's economic success and its expansion westward were seen as evidence of the innate superiority of the American Anglo-Saxon branch of the Caucasian race in relation to other races.

Whiteness was socially constructed to unify previously divided Europeans who now lived together in America, a country in which enslaved Africans made up a significant proportion of the population, especially in the South. Whiteness became an asset. To be white meant that one belonged to a socially, economically, and politically advantaged group. Poor Europeans, who had little understanding of the concept of whiteness previously, were elevated to the white race and given unprecedented civil, social, and economic privileges vis-à-vis Native Americans and Americans with African ancestry. These privileges required those who were designated as white to oppress and exclude those designated as black.[5] Systematic efforts were made to strengthen racially constructed boundaries by downplaying differences among whites and highlighting differences between whites and excluded groups, especially those designated as black. During the late nineteenth and early twentieth centuries, the United States accomplished the cultural homogenization of whites through social reform movements, education, and a combination of incentives and disincentives.[6]

Ironically, it is in America, the embodiment of freedom, that slavery and skin color became permanently intertwined. In ancient civilizations as well as in premodern western Europe, there was no link between slavery and skin color. Captured Africans in Greece and Rome were not assigned a fixed inferior status in those societies. There does not appear to have been much prejudice against Africans because of their skin color in either Greece or Rome.[7] Slavery flourished throughout southern Italy and Sicily. German, Celtic, Jewish, Gaelic, and North African slaves were treated more or less the same way by their Roman masters. In some cases, slaves were both darker and lighter in terms of skin color than those who enslaved them. Similarly, slavery in ancient Egypt encompassed a wide range of skin colors, and slaves and slaveholders often traded places as their fortunes changed due to wars and other factors.[8]

Confronted by the glaring incongruity between America as a beacon of freedom and America as a slave society, those with an economic interest in perpetuating the institution of slavery made a concerted effort to demonstrate that the concepts of freedom and natural equality of mankind were not applicable to enslaved Africans. Therefore, if all men were created equal and endowed by their Creator with certain unalienable rights, then enslaved Africans could not be men. Americans with African ancestry were not only perceived to be outside the boundaries within which whites lived and enjoyed freedom, but they also had to be seen as not fully human.

This combination of America's position as a bastion of liberty in a world characterized by oppression on the one hand and Americans' strenuous efforts to protect an economic system based on the enslavement of Africans on the other helped generate an extreme form of racism. Thomas Sowell observes, "in despotic countries no special ideology needs to be invoked in defense of slavery. Although racial arrogance and racial oppression occurred throughout Latin America, it never approached the pervasive fanaticism reached in the United States."[9] Yet, as those in charge of President Clinton's Initiative on Race demonstrated, preoccupation with the past, racial divisions, and the politics of racial identity can be counterproductive. A more constructive approach is to focus on and to support developments that are undermining the social construction of race.

Generational and Demographic Changes

Generational change is one of the most potent challenges to racial inequality based on the social construction of race. President Clinton embodied many of the racial attitudes of a new generation of Americans, which partly explained his efforts to focus the nation's attention on racial problems. The fact that a majority of Americans in many parts of the country grew up with segregation is bound to influence the overall racial climate. Older Americans exercise considerable power in many of America's institutions, decide who will be hired and promoted, and play a crucial role in shaping public policies. On one hand, their enculturation could be viewed as being conducive to perpetuating the status quo in race relations. On the other hand, many older Americans have seen the negative aspects of racism and have become, if they were not already, active agents of change.

What is often overlooked, which was a major problem with the national dialogue on race, is that younger people do not have the same preoccupations with race as many older Americans do. Their view of the world is less determined by a racial prism than that of earlier generations of Americans. Many young Americans acknowledge the existence of racial problems and the reality that America is not yet a society that is color blind, but they believe that the future will be characterized by racial equality and integration. Most Americans in their twenties have never experienced officially approved segregation and many are horrified to learn of past segregation and discrimination. They are increasingly uncomfortable with racial categories, a cornerstone of the social construction of race. They often refuse to classify themselves racially when required to do so by schools, colleges, and universities. Their friends and often their parents are from diverse backgrounds. Their teachers are generally sensitive to racial concerns, and in many cases, their parents were firmly committed to the civil rights movement.

Young people between the ages of fifteen and twenty-four have attitudes that are conducive to undermining the social construction of race and building a more unified American society. For example, 85 percent of black youths, 84 percent of Latinos, and 79 percent of whites say they are comfortable with the idea of being roommates with someone of a different race. Approximately 72 percent of young Americans believe that there is nothing wrong with people of different races dating each other.

Fifty-seven percent of teenagers who date have dated interracially. Only 28 percent said their parents would disapprove of such relationships but not admit it. About 62 percent of the parents of teenagers say they would be "totally fine" if their children dated interracially.[10] Old Americans who grew up in a racially segregated society and experienced the racial strife that accompanied the civil rights struggle have much different perceptions on race. Although many younger people segregate themselves, their relationships are much more complex than the simplistic racial prism used by many older Americans in the academic world, government, and elsewhere. Younger Americans tend to judge each other on an individual basis. They make distinctions among people based on many factors, of which race is not always the most significant. Educational, class, political, and regional differences often form the basis of interracial coalitions among young Americans. However, it is important to point out that older Americans still possess institutional power. They exercise significant control over the country's economic, social, and political life.

Data from the U.S. Census Bureau show dramatic changes in America's racial and ethnic composition, a development that has serious implications for traditional approaches to the race issue and national unity. By 2050, the non-Hispanic white population is projected to decline to about 52.7 percent; 16 percent of the population will be black, 20.1 percent will be of Hispanic origin, 10 percent will be Asian and Pacific Islander, and 1.2 percent will be Native American.[11] In many parts of the United States, including California, Texas, Arizona, and Florida, the demographic shift is readily visible. The growth of minorities is already influencing candidates for national political office to emphasize racial inclusiveness. Most candidates represent a new generation of Americans for whom racial division is less acceptable. Race, however, continues to play an important role in American politics. During the presidential primaries in 2000, for example, George W. Bush advocated bringing people from different racial backgrounds together, but visited Bob Jones University, which banned interracial dating, to shore up his conservative Republican credentials. He also did not oppose South Carolina's decision to fly the Confederate flag on government buildings. Controversy surrounding his election as president further damaged his relationship with most Americans with African ancestry. These examples do not change the larger reality that generational replacement and demographic change combine to dramatically alter not only race relations, but also the very concept of race itself. Presidential leadership can play a pivotal role in building a more united America by suggesting ways to take advantage of these positive developments.

Immigration

As an immigrant nation, America has always been shaped by the arrival of large numbers of people from throughout the world. For most of its history, however, the United States strongly encouraged immigrants from northern and western European countries to settle the vast country, while barring large-scale nonwhite immigration. Europeans brought with them, or quickly learned in America, values and beliefs that influenced the very definition of America and the identity of Americans. Immigrants from Latin America, Asia, the Caribbean, Africa, and the Middle East are not only changing the racial composition of the United States but also are altering some aspects of American culture. Many of these new arrivals challenge the concept of race, which is seen primarily as black and white. In so doing, they strengthen the forces of change that are already present in the country. Newer immigrants come from diverse cultural backgrounds. Because of their different worldviews, they might look at society in terms of ethnic and class differences instead of race. Racial categorization, a foundation of the social construction of race, is further weakened by the growing rate of interracial marriages, many of them occurring between immigrants from Africa, Asia, and Latin America and white Americans. Overall, there were 1.3 million interracial married couples in the United States in 1994, compared to 964,000 in 1990, 651,000 in 1980, and 310,000 in 1970. Between 1970 and 1994, the number of black-white married couples grew by roughly 450 percent. In 1970 there were 65,000 black-white couples, compared to 296,000 in 1994.

Immigration also contributes to undermining the concept of race by strengthening the power of American minority groups. In many important metropolitan areas, racial minorities are fast becoming majorities. The rapid growth of non-European immigrants creates the potential for intraminority conflicts; it also underlines the need for Americans of all racial backgrounds to establish interracial coalitions to secure shared interests. Another important way in which immigrants are helping to move the country beyond race is by challenging racial stereotypes through their economic success and their ability to build bridges across black-white boundaries. As more immigrants from Asia, Africa, and Latin America achieve positions of power, they are likely to make society more sensitive to racial problems and to weaken the racial prism.

Immigration is a major contributor to the demographic shift discussed earlier. A dramatic alteration in the racial composition of the United States is bound to have a significant impact on race relations. Waves of immigration from Latin America, together with high birth rates among Latinos, will downgrade the status of blacks as the nation's largest racial minority. Latinos already outnumber blacks in Los Angeles, Houston, Phoenix, and San Antonio, and they are likely to overtake blacks in New York. While these developments have already engendered conflicts between blacks and Latinos, the need for interracial cooperation remains strong. Blacks, in order to avoid being further marginalized, will increasingly be forced to place less emphasis on race to form coalitions across racial divisions that are based on concrete interests. But these racial groups are not monolithic, and conflicts within groups are as likely to occur as conflicts among them, making it increasingly obvious that race is not always the most important factor determining human relations. For example, Latinos were divided over the Elian Gonzalez issue, with Cuban Americans holding views that were not supported by most Latinos. Similarly, the position of most Cuban Americans in Miami was opposed by Miami's white and black populations. In other words, other issues were more important than race in this particular case.

Challenging the social construction of race is the fact that the new immigrants are much more connected to their places of origin. The immigrants are arriving at the height of a technological revolution that facilitates travel and communication among people who are separated by great distances. To a much greater extent than earlier, waves of immigrants from Europe, Asians, Africans, Latin Americans, Middle Easterners, and people from the Caribbean maintain strong connections with relatives and friends they left behind. The new immigrants are essentially transmigrants in the sense that they maintain multiple and constant connections across international boundaries.[12] In the process, they forge links between their societies of origin and the places where they settle. Furthermore, they bring with them multiple identities, of which race might be relatively insignificant. Immigrants are likely to focus on national, regional, religious and economic, and educational identities.

Latinos and Caribbean peoples, because of their home countries' geographic proximity to the United States, have the most thorough and wide-ranging contacts with their countries of origin. But fax machines, e-mail connections, televisions, telephones, and rapid and relatively inexpensive transportation enable immigrants from more distant places also to remain in contact with their families and cultures. Many immigrants from Mexico sometimes cross the border daily. Instead of simply being assimilated into American culture, the new arrivals are changing American culture to a greater extent than earlier immigrants. Dominican and Puerto Rican newspapers are on sale in Manhattan the day of publication, and Mexican newspapers arrive in Los Angeles just as quickly. Immigrants have direct access to papers and other publications from their home countries because of the Internet. Computers have made distance meaningless. Radio and television stations broadcast foreign-language programs throughout the United States, and Spanish in Miami, Los Angeles, and an increasing number of American cities is more prevalent than English. This ability to function in two or more cultures simultaneously reduces the incentive to fully assimilate into America's culture. The sense of separateness also allows many new immigrants to evaluate America's racial assumptions more carefully and objectively. Constant contact with their old cultures reminds them that race is not always the dominant consideration. In fact, they often clearly see the fallacy of race as divider of human beings. However, these very same factors also have significant implications for building One America. While race is likely to become less important, the national loyalties of new immigrants could undermine their commitment to the United States and their American identity.

Many immigrants from the Middle East and parts of Asia bring with them the view that religion is the dominant factor in human relations and that race is not as significant as most Americans believe. Islam, which is fast becoming a major force in American society, boasts of an ability to bring people of all races together. The reality of relations between Muslims and others, however, is much more complex than the religious beliefs. The number of Muslims in the United States is rapidly increasing, due primarily to immigration and conversions among Americans with African ancestry. As Islam becomes more prominent in American society, its central tenet of racial harmony has the potential to contribute to the erosion of racial boundaries and the concept of race itself.

The perpetuation of the concept of race and racism depends on widespread public acceptance of the binary or dichotomous black-white view of race. Immigration, by further complicating an already racially diverse society, erodes the dichotomous approach that characterizes race. The vast majority of new immigrants are neither black nor white. Many of them are mixtures of different racial groups and do not perceive themselves as belonging to any of America's narrowly defined racial categories. Their refusal to accept the American concept of race, combined with other important cultural changes, helps undermine the consensus on which the social construction of race depends. Who is white or who is black becomes more difficult to determine because of the increasing range of skin colors and intimate bonds among Americans of all colors. Under these circumstances, the meanings of and benefits that flow from conventional perceptions of race diminish.

Immigrants also challenge conventional ideas on race by devising alternative ways of categorizing individuals and by focusing on nonracial sources of identity. Immigrants augment the resurgence of ethnicity and culture as alternatives to race as primary determinants of identity. Although these might be as divisive as race, they are likely to be less durable, as the integration of different European ethnic and cultural groups in America clearly shows. Distinctions among immigrants from the Caribbean and Latin America, for example, are largely based on nationality, language, and class. Puerto Ricans, Haitians, Dominicans, Jamaicans, Cubans, and Mexicans are likely to emphasize ethnicity, partly because racial mixing in these regions has rendered attempts to neatly categorize people based on skin color virtually futile. These realities are increasingly becoming part of America's reality. Younger Americans, less concerned about race and less dependent on skin color as the main source of their identity, are speeding up the process. Sharp black-white distinctions are weakened and the system of racial classification is made more difficult to maintain by the injection of immigrant values and attitudes into society.

Racially categorizing people from throughout the world is becoming almost impossible. For example, immigrants from the vast region between Morocco and Afghanistan encompassing the Middle East, North Africa, and Turkey are regarded by the United States as "white, non-European." In other words, Egyptians, Sudanese, Saudi Arabians, and Libyans are "white" despite extensive racial mixing in those countries and the fact that many of them have darker complexions that most Americans with African ancestry. The illogic of this system is obvious and confusing to many younger Americans. While many older Americans and some organizations that represent various groups will continue to support racial classification, the growing refusal of younger Americans to be racially classified is likely to eventually undermine this system.

Public schools struggle with trying to fit multicultural children into official racial categories. Some administrators arbitrarily classify children. Others allow parents to provide their own label. But this whole system, and the social construction of race, is disintegrating. The Census Bureau now allows Americans to check as many racial categories as they like to reflect their racial mixture. This development threatens not only the social construction of race but also those who benefit from it. However, this is only a beginning. Anyone who checks any box that is a minority is counted as a minority, regardless of their complex racial background. For example, a racially mixed person who checks the black box is counted as black even if he or she also checked the white and Asian boxes. Many Americans seem confused about the differences between race and ethnicity. For some of them, multiracial means having parents or grandparents from different national backgrounds. The challenges posed by immigration to America's racial definitions is made clearer by examining various immigrant groups' views of race.

The fastest growing minority group in the United States, people of Hispanic background, does not generally subscribe to the American concept of race. As Dominick La Capra puts it: "The notion of race is particularly elusive with reference to Hispanics. No color definition actually applies."[13] Immigrants from Latin America and the Caribbean try to make sense of U.S. racial categories through the prism of their own experiences with and definitions of race. Puerto Ricans, for example, are predominantly a mixture of Europeans, Africans, and Caribbean Indians. Although they, like other Latinos, have developed their own racial categories, their definition of race is flexible and intertwined with economic considerations. Many Puerto Ricans who are regarded as white in the Caribbean are often categorized as black in the United States. Focusing principally on culture and national identity, most Hispanics attempt to downplay the significance of race in their communities.

Similar to Latin America, the Caribbean has a flexible definition of race and generally does not focus exclusively on racial characteristics when making social distinctions. Historically, the small white populations, which were made up primarily of men, not only produced racially mixed children but also often recognized and educated them. Racially mixed people became an intermediary group between blacks and whites, thereby helping to bridge racial divisions. Instead of a rigid distinction between black and white, Caribbean societies emphasize many gradations of skin color. This approach encourages people to claim all of their relatives. Recognizing one's own complex racial background works against the acceptance of America's binary view of race. It makes one more willing to accept others.

In sharp contrast to the United States, where slavery was equated with race, Middle Eastern countries enslaved non-Muslims of all races, including whites. Military slaves came primarily from central Asia and the Caucasus. Millions of Africans were enslaved in Saudi Arabia, Iraq, the Gulf States, and other countries in the Middle East, but slavery was a comparatively flexible institution. Slaves fought for various countries and supported and founded dynasties. Slaveholders recognized their children with enslaved women, and many slaves converted to Islam and were freed. Once freed, a former slave could marry anyone, including his former master's daughter.[14] Similar to Latin America, slaves were fully assimilated into Middle Eastern societies. Although Middle Eastern immigrants are not without racial prejudices, they are more inclined to elevate religion above race in their social categorization of individuals.

Many Asian immigrants come from cultures that generally stress social hierarchy and their own perceived superiority over other racial groups, including Europeans. The Chinese are usually confident of their cultural superiority, largely due to their country's historical achievements. Many Japanese hold similar perceptions. Moreover, Asians are more inclined to concentrate on national identity and social class than on race to distinguish themselves from each other. Consequently, many regard the concept of an "Asian American" as a myth. They know that there are significant ethnic, cultural, religious, and regional differences among Asians. The Japanese and Chinese hardly think of each other as belonging to the same racial category.

Educational Achievements and the Growing Black Middle Class

Another cornerstone of the social construction of race was the deliberate effort by both the state and individuals to keep blacks poor, uneducated, and noncompetitive with whites. The gap in educational achievements and income between whites and blacks only helped to justify separating people into racial categories and to maintain economic, social, and political advantages for the white group. One of the most potent challenges to the idea of race is the educational and economic success of members of the marginalized racial group. Educational achievement has long been regarded as instrumental in overcoming barriers of race and class. A strong education is positively associated with income; generally, the more education one has, the higher one's earning power. Equally important, education strengthens one's self-confidence, one's sense of entitlement, and one's ability to redefine himself or herself. Blacks have made extraordinary gains in education, despite the popular tendency to view blacks through the experiences of the black underclass. Whereas only 51 percent of blacks twenty-five years old and over had graduated from high school in 1980, by 1994, 73 percent had a high school diploma. In 1995, the high school completion rate for blacks between the ages of twenty-five and twenty-nine increased to an unprecedented 87 percent, five percentage points above the national average and equal to the rate of whites.[15]

College enrollment for blacks has been steadily improving. The proportion of blacks twenty-five years old and over who had completed at least a bachelor's degree grew from 8 percent in 1980 to 13 percent in 1994. This is in contrast to an increase from 18 percent to 23 percent for whites. Similarly, the number of Americans with African ancestry receiving doctorates has risen. In 1995, blacks earned 1,287 doctorates, the most since the National Research Council began collecting data on the race and ethnicity of doctoral recipients in 1975. The implications of education for black success, and the social construction of race, are obvious. A 1996 survey by the Illinois Department of Higher Education found that 81 percent of black students who graduated from state universities in Illinois in 1994 found full-time jobs within a year of graduation, a figure that was three percentage points higher that that for white graduates.[16]

Success in education has been matched by economic progress and a growing black middle class whose members are likely to pass on tangible and intangible aspects of success to their children. The strong performance of the American economy for much of the 1990s and the beginning of 2000 has greatly enhanced economic conditions for many Americans with African ancestry. Unemployment for this group is now, at the beginning of 2000, the lowest it has ever been. It is increasingly common to see growing numbers of blacks in the financial world managing millions of dollars. The number of black households making more than $100,000 has doubled in the past two years, reaching approximately 400,000 families in 2000. Census Bureau data show that blacks, especially women, with a college education earn about 86 percent or more of the earnings of white men. In some professions, black women earn about 10 percent more than white women. In cities such as Vineland, New Jersey; Brentwood, New York; Cleveland Heights, Ohio; Southfield, Michigan; Carson, California; and the borough of Queens in New York City, black median household income was greater than white household income more than ten years ago. Growing black economic success is directly linked to educational achievements, as it is for other Americans.

Black success in education is matched in virtually all other areas of American life. Between 1987 and 1992, black-owned businesses, including manufacturing, finance, retail, construction, and services, grew by 46 percent. The increase for all businesses in the United States was 26 percent. Total revenue for black businesses rose 63 percent during the same period to $32.2 billion. The strong economy of the 1990s clearly benefited all ethnic and racial groups, including black Americans. Black home ownership increased significantly between 1993 and 2000, due largely to market forces and reduced discrimination in lending. U.S. Attorney General Janet Reno and the Clinton administration in general vigorously attacked lending practices that were designed to diminish black access to home ownership. Mortgages approved for blacks increased by 38 percent between 1993 and 1996, compared to 30.9 percent for Latinos, 27.1 percent for Native Americans, 17.0 percent for Asians, and 12.0 percent for whites.[17] Ample evidence of black success in both education and income suggests that separating people into racial categories is becoming increasingly meaningless.

Increased Interpersonal Contacts

Racial separation is an essential component of the social construction of race because it reinforces erroneous perceptions of insurmountable differences among racial groups. Those who view the world through a racial prism tend to ignore the extensive and growing contacts between members of various racial categories throughout the United States. If preventing interpersonal contacts strengthens racism, increased interaction among blacks, whites, Latinos, Asians, and others contributes to eliminating racial boundaries as well as to eroding the premises upon which race is socially constructed.

Gordon Allport, in *The Nature of Prejudice*, articulated the view that prejudice may be reduced by equal-status contact between majority and minority groups in pursuit of common goals. He believed that social norms, laws, institutional supports, and environments that engender trust, respect, and friendship were essential to this endeavor.[18] Eventually, close contacts often give rise to the realization that individuals from socially constructed racial categories share a common humanity and the same basic human needs. Extended intimate contact encourages the development of empathy: the ability to feel another person's suffering and to put oneself in another's position. Contact characterized by ongoing cooperative activities often promotes improved interpersonal communication and attraction, trust, greater feelings of similarity, and a growing tendency to help one another. Extensive positive interaction among individuals from various racial categories often leads to perceptions of individuals as unique human beings as opposed to racial stereotypes. The more contacts that blacks, whites, Latinos, Asians, and Native Americans have with each other in a wide range of different circumstances, the greater the chances are that they will make distinctions among individuals who belong to a racial group. In other words, they will not automatically see individuals as members of a racial group but as persons with unique attributes. This personalized interaction influences individuals to focus on specific information about each other instead of using category identity to determine the character of their interactions.[19]

Americans have become more tolerant of each other as contacts have increased. There is more socializing among members of different races than at any other time in American history. Approximately 68 percent of Americans live in at least partially integrated neighborhoods, and 66 percent of whites have black friends, compared to 80 percent of blacks who have white friends. These personal contacts have done more to erode racial boundaries than is generally acknowledged. Bill Clinton, both as a young man and as president, demonstrated how influential early contacts with blacks had been on his life and his formulation of national policy, especially his call for a national dialogue on race. When Clinton's father died, his mother moved to New Orleans to pursue a degree in nursing, leaving her one-year-old son with his grandparents, Eldridge and Edith Cassidy. His grandparents taught him to respect people of all races. His daily contacts with blacks enabled him to develop strong personal relationships with them. Ordinary Americans also stress the importance of personal contacts in their attempts to improve relations with people of different races—driving a school bus, working with teachers and students of different races, playing golf in mixed-race groups, volunteering on projects such as Habitat for Humanity, and attending workshops.

In a country as diverse as the United States, sports play an integrative role and serve as a vehicle of upward mobility. The cooperative nature of sports guarantees that members of the team, in order to ensure the team's success, have to trust and protect each other to a large extent. Players on integrated sports teams follow the same rules, thereby developing common values and a shared understanding not only of the game but also of the larger society. Sports demonstrate that racial cooperation is not only possible but also essential for success. Sports help improve race relations by bringing players from diverse backgrounds into close contact with each other. Although many southern universities had integrated their classrooms by the late 1960s, integrating athletic teams took longer, partly because segregationists understood that close contact between the races would foster the development of deep friendships and feelings of equality, thus shattering the myth of the superiority of one race over another. Both the 1996 Republican vice presidential candidate Jack Kemp and the former Senator Bill Bradley, who challenged Al Gore for the Democratic nomination for the 2000 presidential campaign, credited sports with bringing them into closer contact with blacks and exposing them to the prejudice many of their teammates experienced.

White and black players often room together partly because coaches group players according to their positions on the team. These experiences, when positive, help destroy prejudice on both sides. Coaches often counsel players on personal matters, acting in many instances as substitute parents. Many interpersonal relationships that develop because of sports usually draw in relatives and friends, thereby expanding the number of individuals who are confronted with racial stereotypes—their own as well as those of others. Sports also promote equality by leveling the playing field and stressing achievement and talent instead of skin color. Sports divert attention away from skin color to ability, a measure of the individual and not race. Finally, sports command a wider societal influence. Outstanding athletes such as Michael Jordan and Tiger Woods are regarded by Americans of all ages and races as role models. Sports, by challenging myths about abilities of different races, weaken the social construction of race.

With the exception of the military, college campuses provide the most numerous opportunities for students to develop interpersonal contacts and to transform those contacts into lifelong relationships. Colleges, universities, and other institutions of higher education bring together students from diverse backgrounds, many of whom had never interacted with individuals of other racial categories prior to arriving on campus. Colleges bring students into situations where cooperation is required. They room together, visit each other's homes, eat in the same cafeterias, participate in study groups, study on the same floor of the library, play sports together, and engage in many of the same extracurricular activities. The potential to challenge the social construction of race is great on college campuses. Many college administrators, however, do not take full advantage of this opportunity. Many of them cave in to the most vocal students who demand separate organizations, activities, and even separate dormitories.

Interracial Relationships: Crossing Racial Boundaries

The social construction of race is dependent on acceptance of the fallacy of racial purity and rigid racial boundaries. As discussed earlier, all human beings are descendants of a common ancestor in Africa and the so-called races have been mixing for a long time. It is ironic that the concept of racial purity, though not usually articulated as such, has an incredibly strong grip on most Americans who live in one of the most racially mixed societies in the world. Because of such a widespread assumption of racial purity, or an unwillingness to admit obvious racial mixture, interracial relationships represent a significant challenge to the concept or race. Proponents of racial segregation have always understood that interracial relationships and the children they produce eventually undermine racism by challenging the assumption of monolithic, fixed, and inherently incompatible races. The clear demarcation of the races, which is an essential cornerstone of the social construction of race, is weakened by the existence and social recognition of widespread racial mixing.

Acceptance of interracial relationships and the development of language that recognizes the offspring of such relationships as part of two or more racial categories are clear indicators that American society has achieved a significant degree of social, racial, and economic equality. The social construction of race assumes economic inequality among races. People who marry each other generally come from similar economic backgrounds. Thus, acceptance of interracial relationships implies an acknowledgment of both racial and economic equality. Public opinion polls show an increasing acceptance of interracial relationships, with the younger generation of Americans more supportive of them than older Americans. The wide disagreement between the old and the young on the issue of racial mixing is evidence of the radical alteration of racial attitudes over the past few decades. It also underscores the fact that race is less important to younger people than to their parents or grandparents. By overlooking this crucial difference, President Clinton's advisory panel on his national dialogue on race demonstrated how disconnected they were from the real nature of race relations in America today. This does not mean that young people are exempt from racial thinking. However, race for them is not what it used to be, or is, for their parents and grandparents.

Whereas only 27 percent of American over fifty years of age approve of marriage between blacks and whites, 56 percent of those between thirty and thirty-nine years of age approve. But the most important finding, which supports the thesis that the social construction of race is being seriously undermined, is that 64 percent of Americans between the ages of eighteen and twenty-nine approve of interracial marriages.[20] Generational replacement is clearly conducive to significant changes in racial attitudes and behavior.

Public approval of interracial marriages has steadily increased among both whites and blacks since 1968. Whereas only 17 percent of whites of all ages favored interracial relationships in 1968, by 1991 the number had grown to 44 percent. In the case of blacks, 48 percent approved of mixed marriages in 1968, compared to 70 percent in 1991. Education, interpersonal contacts, income, and region also influenced attitudes on this issue. For example, whereas 70 percent of college graduates approve of interracial marriage, only 26 percent of Americans who did not graduate from high school approve.

Similarly, whereas 65 percent of Americans who live in large cities are supportive of interracial marriages, only 32 percent of rural residents approve. Sixty-one percent of Americans with annual incomes over $50,000 favor racially mixed marriages, compared to 37 percent of those with incomes under $20,000. Whereas 60 percent of Americans living in the West approve of interracial marriages, only 32 percent of those living in the South support them.[21] Based on these and other findings, it is reasonable to conclude that higher levels of education, increased interpersonal contacts, growing urbanization, and generational change combine to weaken the consensus on which the social construction of race depends.

Interracial relationships contradict racial assumptions, draw attention to similarities between individuals from different racial backgrounds, and create intimate ties that cut across racial boundaries. They increase sensitivity to and awareness of racial problems; provide greater access to social, economic, and political opportunities; and challenge the concepts of racial superiority and inferiority. The children of such relationships complicate the categorization of individuals based on the assumption of innate biological and cultural distinctions. Stated another way, interracial marriages, because of their intimate and long-term nature, test racial boundaries and the willingness of individuals from different racial groups to accept each other in essentially long-lasting egalitarian relationships.[22]

Because the maintenance of racial boundaries depends on an acceptance of exclusive racial group membership, an "us-versus-them" viewpoint, and the ability to easily distinguish between insiders and outsiders, interracial relationships effectively erode racial boundaries by making it more difficult to determine who belongs to a particular racial circle and who does not. Interracial relationships are about inclusion of individuals in what are generally seen as exclusive racial groups. Marriage brings the families, friends, and acquaintances of the marital partners into close interpersonal contact. Ultimately, race problems break down when individuals of different races share common family members.

So thoroughly have interethnic and interfaith marriages weakened ethnic and religious boundaries that it is no longer a remarkable event when an American of Polish ancestry marries and American of English ancestry, or when a Jew marries a Catholic. But older Americans recall how ethnic and religious hostilities were almost as bitter as racial hostilities and still are in some parts of the country today in relation to intermarriage. Just as blacks are not monolithic, whites are not homogeneous. Creating a degree of harmony among white ethnic groups, many of whom had been in open conflict with each other in Europe, was a gradual process, at the heart of which was an increase in interethnic marriages. As such marriages were gradually accepted, they created greater momentum toward increased rates of intermarriage.

As more Americans became multiethnic, ethnicity diminished as a social force. Group membership became more flexible and the children of interethnic relationships helped bridge the divide between two or more ethnic groups. Because intermarriage often reduces the strength of affiliation people of mixed ancestry have for any one group, interethnic marriages directly threaten the traditional bases for ethnic groups.[23] Although the process is taking longer, the same logic applies to racial groups.

Interracial relationships challenge the widely accepted view that physical characteristics determine group membership and identity. Equally important, mixed relationships strengthen individualism and freedom of choice, which help erode a central component of the social construction of race—namely, externally imposed definitions of who belongs to which particular group. A more highly educated population is embracing individualism to a much greater extent than before. Authority from above has clearly diminished and the idea of keeping people in line is strongly resisted. Economic prosperity and the mobility of individuals, often to areas where they have no family members or social networks to enforce social rules of any kind, strengthen this growing individualism. Technology has also contributed to the erosion of centralized authority and the weakening of rigid group identity. Interracial marriages weaken racial cohesion even further, complicate racial group membership to the point that it ceases to be significant, and facilitate movement across racial boundaries. Strong crosscutting ties that emanate from interracial marriages undermine the assumption of the existence of sympathizers based on racial identification, which is crucial to maintaining racism. Physical characteristics alone are not enough to determine who belongs to or supports socially constructed racial categories when a significant number of people from various racial groups develop intimate relationships.

Children of interracial relationships have always been a major concern for supporters of racial segregation because their very existence demonstrates the erosion of racial boundaries and the concept of race. As their numbers grow and their self-confidence strengthens, these children question the logic that forms the foundation for a binary approach to race in relation to blacks and whites. In her book *Notes of a White Black Woman*, Judy Scales-Trent discusses the unique views that multiracial people have of America's racial categories. She writes: "My position does not allow me the luxury of thinking that the notion of race makes any sense."[24] As more children of racially mixed couples reject the system of racial classification and declare their membership in two or more groups, they shake the foundation of the concept of race by challenging whiteness and blackness as pure categories. Changes in the census for 2000, which allowed people to check as many racial categories as they liked, were influenced by the growing number of racially mixed Americans who refuse to follow the traditional views of race. Eventually, racial mixture will make the fallacy of the racial classification system so painfully obvious that it will be abandoned altogether.

Family members and friends of racially mixed children and people involved in interracial relationships play a vital role in augmenting the movement toward greater racial harmony. Despite their initial opposition to interracial marriages, many Americans eventually confront their prejudices and often end up embracing the interracial couple and their children. The arrival of grandchildren significantly modifies the attitudes of most grandparents, who recognize that racially mixed grandchildren are blood relatives. This acknowledgment is facilitated by wider public approval of interracial marriage, a sharp decline in society's tolerance of racism, and greater societal respect for the individual's freedom of choice.

Perhaps one of the greatest implications of interracial relationships is their tendency to heighten awareness of racism and unequal opportunity and treatment, especially among white Americans. Being involved with a person from a racial minority group was cited as one of the most important experiences in helping whites understand the problems that racial minorities sometimes face. The intimate nature of their interaction, especially when children are involved, often exposes white partners to the kind of unfair treatment that many blacks receive simply because of their skin color.

Interracial relationships and the recognition that the resulting children belong to more than one racial group have serious implications for the one-drop rule, which is at the heart of the concept and practice of racism. The one-drop rule essentially designates as black anyone who has any trace of African ancestry, regardless of physical appearance. The United States is the only country in the world that has institutionalized such a rigid definition of who is black and who is white. Incidentally, the rule applies only to blacks; one drop of Japanese blood, for example, is not enough to transform a white person into an Asian.

Although the one-drop rule remains a reality in American society, it is being challenged by the growth of interracial relationships and by greater public awareness that this cornerstone of America's social construction of race is seriously flawed. The simple act of claiming one's relatives from different racial backgrounds is an important departure from the one-drop rule. To a large extent, the survival of the one-drop rule depends on the willingness of Americans, especially those of racially mixed ancestry, to accept society's definition of them as belonging to racially pure categories.

Constructing a New Paradigm: From Race to Universal Virtues

The social construction of race is a deliberate effort to influence people to see others in a certain way and to justify societal arrangements. To create One America, the social construction of race must be replaced with a new frame, a new point of view, a new way of looking at things. Framing refers to how a problem is conceived, the kinds of evidence that are considered, the cognitive strategy that is employed.[25] The frame determines to a large extent how we interpret what happens in our environments, what judgments we make, and how we perceive what we regard as reality. Since most of us are sensitive to contextual cues when making decisions, formulating judgments, forming opinions, and taking action, framing is a significant determinant of behavior.[26] Stated another way, framing determines what we deem to be important.

A racial frame influences many of us to view ordinary human problems in racial terms. Race is only one of several ways of perceiving, interpreting, and dealing with human differences. The habitual use of terms like "race" and "racism" almost guarantees that a racial worldview or perspective will be perpetuated.[27] The stereotypes that are integral components of a racial perspective are often subconsciously accepted not only by those who gain but also by those who are disadvantaged by their existence. This is particularly true of groups in conflict.

Reframing an issue challenges prevailing thinking and the power and advantage that emanate from it. By perceiving the world in nonracial terms, one can be empowered to achieve one's aspirations and to participate more fully in American life. To accept a racial frame is to accept the status quo. The degree to which disadvantaged individuals accept the status quo is a measure of the dominant group's success in controlling the relationship. To become full participants in their society, disadvantaged groups must change their frame from one that is particular and confining to one that is universal.

Reframing suggests the adoption of a different language when discussing race. Language is a powerful agent of change. It influences perception, thoughts, and actions in subtle but potent ways. To a large extent, language plays a pivotal role in one's perception of reality. The language used reflects a society's thinking, its values, and its method of structuring human relations. Language defines us; it signals who we are.[28] To say

"I am white" is another way of saying "I am not black and therefore I am entitled to different treatment." To say "I am American" is another way of saying "I am similar to people whose skins are a different color." Reframing must be the responsibility of the individual.

The racial frame must be replaced by a new frame that emphasizes universal virtues. Racism is about vices, about the lack of certain universal virtues. In all human societies there is, to greater or lesser degrees, an acknowledgment of fundamental virtues such as treating others in a way that you would want to be treated. Other such virtues include self-responsibility, self-discipline, perseverance, honesty, forgiveness, tolerance, loyalty, lawfulness, justice, and courage. Skin color or physical traits obviously do not determine virtue.

The genius of the civil rights movement was that it embraced universal virtues and emphasized a framework that was inclusive. It inspired people of all colors by recognizing the common humanity of all Americans. Instead of focusing on differences, it drew attention to common universal virtues, thereby allowing blacks, whites, Latinos, Asians, and others to unite for a common purpose. As Roger Fisher and Scott Brown point out, "The greater the extent to which you and I share values and perspectives, the fewer differences we will have and the more easily we will find a basis for dealing with them."[29] Framing racial issues in universal terms facilitates the perception of shared values. It also moves us closer to the goal of creating One America.

*This chapter is based on *Getting Beyond Race: The Changing American Culture* (Boulder, Colo.: Westview Press, 1998). The author wishes to thank Julie Edmunds for assisting with research.

Notes

1. Richard J. Payne, *Getting Beyond Race: The Changing American Culture* (Boulder, Colo.: Westview Press, 1998); William Julius Wilson, *The Declining Significance of Race* (Chicago: The University of Chicago Press, 1980); and Orlando Patterson, "Race Over," *The New Republic*, January 10, 2000, 6.

2. L. Luca Cavalli-Sforza, Paolo Menozzi, and Albert Piazza, *The History and Geography of Human Genes* (Princeton, N.J.: Princeton University Press, 1994), 19.

3. Sharon Begley, "Surprising New Lessons from the Controversial Science of Race," *Newsweek*, February 13, 1995, 67–68.

4. Michael Omi and Howard Winant, *Racial Formation in the United States* (New York: Routledge, 1989), 67.

5. Theodore W. Allen, *The Invention of the White Race, vol. 1* (London: Verso, 1994), 14.

6. Ruth Frankenberg, *White Women, Race Matters: The Social Construction of Whiteness* (Minneapolis: University of Minnesota Press, 1993), 203.

7. Thomas E. Gossett, *Race: The History of An Idea in America* (Dallas, Tex.: Southern Methodist University Press, 1963), 7.

8. Roger Sanjek, "Enduring Inequalities of Race," in *Race*, ed. Steven Gregory and Roger Sanjek (New Brunswick, N.J.: Rutgers University Press, 1994), 4.

9. Thomas Sowell, *Race and Economics* (New York: David McKay Co., 1975), 20.

10. Karen S. Peterson, "For Today's Teens, Race Not an Issue Anymore," *USA Today*, November 3, 1997, 1.

11. Bureau of the Census, *Population Projections of the United States, by Age, Sex, Race, and Hispanic Origin: 1992 to 2050* (Washington, D.C.: U.S. Department of Commerce, 1992), xvii.

12. Nina Click Shiller, Linda Basch, and Christina Blanc, "From Immigrant to Transmigrant," *Anthropological Quarterly* (January 1995), 48.

13. Dominick La Capra, "Introduction," in *The Bounds of Race*, ed. Dominick La Capra (Ithaca, N.Y.: Cornell University Press, 1991), 13.

14. Albert Hourani, *A History of the Arab People* (Cambridge, Mass.: Harvard University Press, 1991), 116.

15. Claudette E. Brown, *The Black Population in the United States: March 1994 and 1993*, Bureau of the Census, *Current Population Reports* 9 (Washington, D.C.: U.S. Government Printing Office, 1995), 20–480.

16. "A Benchmark in Black Education," *Chicago Tribune*, September 16, 1996, sec. 1, 12.

17. John R. Wilke, "Mortgage Lending to Minorities Shows a Sharp 1994 Increase," *The Wall Street Journal*, February 13, 1996, A1.

18. Gordon Allport, *The Nature of Prejudice* (Glencoe, Ill.: The Free Press 1950), 150.

19. Miles Hewstone and Rupert Brown, "Contact Is Not Enough," in *Contact and Conflict in Intergroup Encounters*, ed. Miles Hewstone and Rupert Brown (Oxford: Basil Blackwell, 1986) 19.

20. George Gallup Jr. and Frank Newport, "For the First Time, More Americans Approve of Interracial Marriage Than Disapprove," *The Gallup Poll Monthly*, August 1991, 60.

21. Ibid., 62.

22. Richard D. Alba and Reid M. Golden, "Patterns of Ethnic Marriage in the United States," *Social Forces* 65, no.1 (September 1986), 202–03; and Paul C. Rosenblatt, Terry A. Karis, and Richard D. Powell, *Multiracial Couples: Black and White Voices* (Thousand Oaks, Calif.: Sage, 1995), 4.

23. Richard D. Alba, *Ethnic Identity: The Transformation of White America* (New Haven, Conn.: Yale University Press, 1990), 15. See also Paul R. Spickard, *Mixed*

Blood: Intermarriage and Ethnic Identity in Twentieth Century America (Madison: The University of Wisconsin Press, 1989), 15.

24. Judy Scales-Trent, *Notes of a White Black Woman* (University Park: The Pennsylvania State University Press, 1995), 7. See also Maria P. P. Root, " A Bill of Rights for Racially Mixed People," in *The Multiracial Experience,* ed. Maria P. P. Root (Thousand Oaks, Calif.: Sage, 1996), 7; and Stanley Lieberson and Mary C. Waters, *From Many Strands: Ethnic and Racial Groups in Contemporary America* (New York: Russell Sage Foundation, 1988), 163.

25. Samuel L. Popkin, *The Reasoning Voter: Communication and Persuasion in Presidential Campaigns* (Chicago: The University of Chicago Press, 1991), 81.

26. Shanto Iyengar, *Is Anyone Responsible? How Television Frames Political Issues* (Chicago: The University of Chicago Press, 1994), 11.

27. Audrey Smedly, *Race in North America: Origin and Evolution of a Worldview* (Boulder, Colo.: Westview Press, 1993), 7.

28. Elinor Lenz and Barbara Myerhoff, *The Feminization of America* (Los Angeles: Jeremy P. Tarcher, 1985), 20.

29. Roger Fisher and Scott Brown, *Getting Together: Building a Relationship That Gets to Yes* (Boston: Houghton Mifflin, 1988), 5.

SEVEN

Racial Preferences in Higher Education
An Assessment of the Evidence

Stephan Thernstrom

Abigail Thernstrom

One America? Certainly not yet. Too many black Americans, particularly, remain racially isolated by a host of measures. And while members of other groups will become integrated over time, it seems safe to say that the black experience is a story with no happy end in sight.

Not everyone agrees. Harvard sociologist Orlando Patterson, for instance, has predicted that by the middle of the twenty-first century, America will have "no racial problem whatsoever." He sees "the racial divide that has plagued America since its founding . . . [as] fading fast."[1] But his is an unusual voice. Even scholars who celebrate progress (as we do) acknowledge a racial divide that, in important respects, seems remarkably enduring. The workplace has become "diverse," but at the end of the day most blacks and whites head for a drink in different bars.

Some would say that's okay. Equality is essential, but blacks can live and play apart. Our view is quite different. Equal but separate can't work. Those who assume that it can, see blacks and whites as inevitably different. They believe that individuals are defined by the color of their skin—that while Italians can become Americans (no hyphen), blacks will always be African Americans. And yet as long as blacks are seen as a separate people, we believe, they will be judged by the color of their skin. And such judgments are irreconcilable with drive for equality—with the dream of "One America."

We retain the old dream—the one that animated the civil rights movement from before the Civil War through the early 1960s. Individuals should be judged by "the content of their character"; "race has no place in

American life or law." Such were the sentiments of Martin Luther King Jr. and President John F. Kennedy.[2] The question, it seems to us, is not what the ultimate goal should be, but how to get there. And while we have been walking down the road to both greater equality and a more integrated society, the terrain has proven tricky. Indeed, one can ask: have the public policies we have put in place to achieve "One America" in fact backfired? With the best of intentions, have we made a bad problem worse?

We tackle that question in this essay by looking at one aspect of race-related policy: affirmative action in higher education. Specifically, we examine an exhaustive defense of racial preferences in the admission of students to colleges and universities, namely William G. Bowen and Derek Bok's widely celebrated book, *The Shape of the River: Long-Term Consequences of Considering Race in College and University Admissions*.[3] To date, their work is the only full-scale empirical study of racial preferences in contemporary American higher education. How well do their arguments on behalf of race-conscious policies hold up? Are such policies uniting Americans across racial and ethnic lines or further dividing them?

Background

Since the late 1960s, leading American colleges and universities have used racial and ethnic criteria to select a significant fraction of their entering classes. From the beginning, critics attacked such policies as morally wrong and constitutionally suspect. What happened, they have asked, to the core principle so famously articulated by Supreme Court Justice John Marshall Harlan, dissenting in *Plessy v. Ferguson* in 1896? "Our Constitution is color-blind, and neither knows nor tolerates classes among citizens" he said.[4] That was the vision that had animated the 1964 Civil Rights Act as well. In theory, American society was fluid and open; people were free to rise in accord with their demonstrated merit.[5] In fact, African Americans had not been treated as individuals to whom the doors of opportunity were open. The act was an attempt to right that historic wrong, to end the country's sorry history of substituting racial identity for merit. It was thus pure antidiscrimination legislation: no preferences of any kind for members of any racial or ethnic group.[6] Race-conscious policies were permitted under only one circumstance: to remedy proven instances of intentional discrimination.

The notion that every American citizen was to be treated as an individual—that racial group identity was irrelevant "in American life or law"—did not last long. Civil rights organizations and liberal leaders soon adopted the view that Supreme Court Justice Harry Blackmun later articulated in a dissent still frequently quoted today. "In order to get beyond racism," he said, "we must first take account of race. There is no other way. And in order to treat some persons equally, we must treat them differently."[7]

By the time Blackmun wrote his famous 1978 opinion in *Regents of the University of California v. Bakke*, all selective colleges and universities had already traveled far down the road of race-conscious admissions. That was no secret. But the details of the policies, as they were actually implemented, were not known until quite recently. Exactly how much weight was given to racial and ethnic considerations in admissions decisions? The official line was "not much." Race was just one "factor" among many, the formula endorsed by the deeply divided Supreme Court in the *Bakke* decision. But allowing it to be used as a "factor" was a hopelessly elastic standard. No data were ever provided to establish either how substantial that factor was, or what happened to preferentially admitted minority students during and after college. Although higher education officials aggressively defended their policies, they were never willing to release the pertinent facts and stand by them. Secrecy suggesting a lack of moral confidence enveloped rhetoric couched in high moral tones.

In 1991, a corner of the veil was lifted when Timothy Maguire stumbled on the truth at the Georgetown University Law Center, where he was a student. Working part-time in the registrar's office, he found that the college grades and LSAT scores of blacks admitted to Georgetown were dramatically lower than those of their white peers. Race was not just one of many possible "plus" factors being considered by the admissions committee; it was the only consideration that could have explained the acceptance of most black students.[8]

When Maguire went public with his findings, Georgetown's defenders mounted a fierce counterattack. In a *Washington Post* op-ed, a group of Georgetown law graduates charged Maguire with providing only "incomplete and distorted information," perpetuating the "intellectually dishonest myth" that black students are "less qualified than their white counterparts to compete in school."[9] Maguire was in no position to study the matter more systematically, and the school's administrators were unwilling to release any pertinent data; thus, the matter rested there.

The ability to keep the files under lock and key began to come to an end, however, with the *Hopwood* litigation that resulted in the 1996 finding by the U.S. Fifth Circuit Court of Appeals that the University of Texas (UT) law school had engaged in racial discrimination against whites; with the fight in California that ended in the passage of Proposition 209, forbidding racial preferences in the public sector, including higher education; with a similar initiative in the state of Washington; and with a number of freedom of information requests.[10] Tantalizing fragments of evidence have trickled out, all suggesting that the weight given to racial and ethnic considerations was in fact extremely substantial, amounting in most cases to a flagrant double standard.[11]

Thus, the *Hopwood* case, for example, revealed that white students accepted to the University of Texas Law School had been "overwhelmingly drawn from the very top of the national pool," but that to obtain more than a handful of African Americans, the school had been forced to reach down "well into the bottom half of the national pool."[12] Preference advocates had always claimed that minority candidates with weak academic qualifications nevertheless performed well at the Texas law school. But the effect of using such "radically different admissions standards," according to the associate dean, was that "few of our Black students have been able to finish above the bottom quarter or third of the class in terms of law school grades." Worse yet, while some 90 percent of UT's "non-minority students" passed the bar examination on their first try, the figure for blacks was "consistently under 50 percent." Furthermore, half of the minority graduates who failed the bar exam failed "again upon retaking it." Many preferentially admitted students who had devoted three years to studying the law, often going deeply in debt in order to do so, never developed the skills necessary to qualify for their chosen profession.

In the debate over preferences in higher education, opponents remained greatly disadvantaged as long as they were denied access to the facts. But once critics began to accumulate evidence that preferences did not work as advertised, supporters needed empirical information of their own. The gathering of such data was precisely the aim of *The Shape of the River*. With preferences on trial, Bowen and Bok wrote a brief on their behalf—designed to revive the flagging spirits of preference advocates who could not grasp why policies they believed to be moral, efficacious, and legal were coming under strenuous attack in the post-*Hopwood*, post-Proposition 209 era.

That the mood of preference advocates had indeed become dispirited was evident in the sigh of relief that greeted the book's publication. Although it was written in gray bureaucratic prose and was crammed with 147 tables and graphs, it was treated as a major news event. Editorial writers and columnists in leading newspapers and magazines, as well as CBS, CNN, and NPR, hailed it with uncritical enthusiasm. The *New York Review of Books* printed a lengthy two-part review by Ronald Dworkin that read like a publisher's press release. *The New York Times* was not content with simply running a full-page news story and reprinting excerpts from the work itself. It also ringingly endorsed its conclusions in an editorial, which claimed that the study "provides striking confirmation of the success of affirmative action in opening opportunities and creating a whole generation of black professionals."[13]

Bowen and Bok's "massive defense of racial preferences in university admissions," one writer predicted, "will become a primary source in every debate and lawsuit involving affirmative action for the next decade, and maybe longer."[14] That is undoubtedly the case. The book provided extensive new statistical information about the admissions preferences given in elite schools to blacks, their educational performance, and their subsequent career patterns. The authors' findings thus significantly advanced the debate. Alas, however, the book is not an even-handed scholarly study. An assessment of the evidence upon which the authors based their main conclusions reveals many serious flaws. Since Bowen and Bok attempted to provide empirical support for all of the main arguments currently being made in favor of racial preferences in admissions to higher education, a close review of their work amounts to a review of the debate as a whole.

Bowen and Bok: The Argument

In the preface to *The Shape of the River*, Bowen and Bok expressed their desire to "discover the facts. . . . It was important . . . to try to understand and come to terms with any disappointing results as well as to learn from positive outcomes." And in the end, they discovered "an educational process that . . . turned out to be even more subtle and complicated than [they] had imagined it to be when [they] began [their] research."[15]

Happily, it was a "subtle and complicated" educational process that turned out to yield none of the "disappointing results" with which they would have had to "come to terms." None of the arguments advanced by the many critics of racial preferences proved to have any merit at all. What the authors called "racially sensitive" admissions policies were an unqualified success.

The minority students accepted at elite institutions were well qualified, they argued. Race was only one of a great many factors that admissions officers quite properly took into account. On the other hand, if these schools had used race-blind admissions procedures, black enrollments would have declined precipitously and diversity would have disappeared. The preferences were more modest than many had claimed, but many black students needed them to survive the final cut.

Most preferentially admitted students collected diplomas and thus were academically successful, the authors conclude. They found no evidence that black undergraduates felt stigmatized by the racial double standards used to admit them. They were happy with the schools they had chosen. An impressive proportion went on to do graduate work and to enter well-paying occupations. Furthermore, they became unusually active in civic affairs and played key leadership roles both within the black community and in the larger society. Indeed, the economic success and social commitment they owed to their elite educations made them "the backbone of the emergent black and Hispanic middle class."[16]

Preferential policies were not only indispensable to the advancement of African Americans, Bowen and Bok contended. They have had a highly positive effect on all students, as shown by the number of friendships across racial lines and the high level of white support for diversity policies.

If true, these are important contentions. Before accepting them, however, we need to look closely at the evidence and reasoning the authors offered in defense of each of these propositions.

The Politics of Access

If policies are best evaluated by those who design and implement them, then Bowen and Bok were superbly qualified for the task they set themselves. They were present at the beginning of preferential policies a generation ago and presided over their implementation in two schools that rank at the very top of the prestige ladder. William Bowen was provost at Princeton University from 1967 to 1972 and then president until 1988, when he became head of The Andrew W. Mellon Foundation. Derek Bok served as dean of the Harvard Law School from 1968 to 1971 and then as president of Harvard University for twenty years.

In *The Shape of the River*, they evaluated the effectiveness of the preferential policies for which they were primarily responsible at the two institutions they governed. The authors conceded they both had "worked hard, over more than three decades, to enroll and educate more diverse student bodies." Nevertheless, they said, they "were far from certain what the data would reveal" when they began their study.[17]

Perhaps. But it must have occurred to them that it would have been acutely embarrassing if their evidence had revealed that racially preferential admissions policies had not achieved their objectives or had produced unanticipated negative consequences. Critics would have legitimately asked why they had never studied the matter before. At any time in the many years they spent in charge of two fabulously wealthy universities, either one could have commissioned a careful analysis to assess precisely how race-conscious admissions had worked at their own institutions. They did not do so, however, and were thus left with the strongest incentive for giving high marks to a vital part of their own legacy as leaders in American higher education.

The authors had unique advantages that other scholars are unlikely to have in the future. The deep pockets of the Mellon Foundation provided virtually unlimited financial resources. Even more important was their access to student records that schools have never made available to investigators before. Why did these institutions cooperate with Bowen and Bok in the project? It is reasonable to surmise that university administrators agreed to contribute to the foundation's "restricted access database" because they knew preferential policies had come under serious attack, and were confident that the authors could be trusted to view the evidence in the most favorable possible light.

Although the Mellon Foundation claims that it will make the data analyzed by Bowen and Bok available to other qualified researchers, the remarkable guidelines that set forth its policies governing access to this material strongly suggest that no scholar with any reservations about racially preferential policies need apply.[18] One might think that foundations that sponsor scholarly research would at least profess to be committed to the ideal of disinterested, objective inquiry—the pursuit of the truth wherever it is to be found. The Mellon Foundation, however, is quite candid in stating that it seeks to fund research to "support the humanities and affirmative action." Although it is currently funding the work on race, college admissions, and academic achievement by "more than 20 researchers," it seems clear that those researchers are expected to find out things consistent with the foundation's ideology.[19]

It is deplorable but not at all surprising that when the sociologist Robert Lerner, a critic of *The Shape of the River*, presented a well-crafted proposal for further analysis of the data Bowen and Bok used to the Mellon Foundation, his request was denied. He was told that the records he proposed to analyze were "obtained by us on the strict condition that they would never be made available to persons outside the Foundation."[20] One wonders if the investigators currently being supported by Mellon to work on this issue qualify as being "inside" the foundation. If so, why not give Lerner a courtesy title to put him into that category, or even give him some funds to carry out his project?

That the data upon which *The Shape of the River* rests are apparently available only to trusted insiders obviously compromises the search for truth.[21] If the only medical records available to determine whether cigarette smoking causes lung cancer had been controlled by the tobacco companies, and if the companies had restricted access to them to researchers whose minds were closed to the possibility that there was such a link, scientific progress in resolving the issue would surely have been impeded. The Mellon Foundation has erected a similar iron curtain to protect its favored authors from critics who might analyze the data very differently.

It is common social science practice today for scholars involved in large-scale research projects to make the data available for reanalysis by other scholars. For example, it has been proposed that the *American Political Science Review* require that all authors of empirically based articles submit their data as a condition of publication. A classic example of sharing the data is James S. Coleman's 1966 report on educational achievement, which spawned many other publications that utilized his raw material to draw quite different conclusions.[22] *The Shape of the River*, with its "restricted access database," cannot be subjected to searching critical scrutiny of this kind. As a result, critics of the work are limited to the information the authors have chosen to put forward, and must work with the categories that they employ.

Perhaps the schools that provided information to the Mellon Foundation would not have done so without ironclad guarantees that the data would never fall into the hands of any scholar who might reach negative conclusions about racial preferences. If so, that is an appalling commentary on those who administer our elite schools today.

Euphemism 101: "Racially Sensitive" Policies

Bowen and Bok drew their title from a well-known passage in Mark Twain's *Life on the Mississippi*, which notes that the river's steamboat pilots needed to understand "all the million trifling variations of shape in the banks of this interminable river as well as [they knew] the shape of the front hall at home." Evidently, higher education is a tricky river that students navigate with the guidance of "pilots" who seem to be "the parents of prospective students, the high school counselors, college admissions officers, faculty members, and administrators, trustees, and regents responsible for setting policies."[23]

The analogy is impenetrable (is each student a boat on which all these pilots stand?), but the basic point seems clear. Like a river, "the college admissions process and the educational experience that follows it are . . . complex." Those who adhere to "the myth of pure merit" and who believe that the best schools should only accept "book smart, test smart" students are trying to turn tricky waters into a smooth and straight stream. Those who have never stood at the helm of a great paddle-wheeler naively think that the nation's future leaders can be selected by "a series of formulaic calculations" based on test scores and high school grades. In fact, each bend in the educational river is a little different from all the others; admitting students, they said, is "an eclectic and interpretive art" that requires "judgment, experience, and perhaps even accumulated wisdom."[24]

College admissions may be an "art," but Bowen and Bok did not ask for an individualized admissions process that would give less weight to the measurable academic achievement of applicants—if those applicants are white or Asian. Unlike many current defenders of racial preferences, they did not advocate junking the SATs altogether.[25] They argued instead for different standards for different students, depending on the color of their skin.

They did not say so candidly, however. It is revealing and regrettable that Bowen and Bok could not bring themselves to describe the policies they favored as racial preferences. It is very important, they wrote, to avoid "such highly charged words" as "preference," "merit," and "achievement."[26] Instead, they delicately described the process they advocated as "racially sensitive." "Preference" suggests unfair double standards, but who can deny the need for "sensitivity"?

It is a blatantly evasive strategy. When varsity athletes or the children of alumni are given preferences by admissions officers, no one talks about "alumni sensitive" or "sports sensitive" policies. Most selective private colleges in the United States once had Jewish quotas, but at least no one argued that to admit WASPs and Jews by different academic standards was "religiously sensitive."[27] Racial preferences, too, call for straight talk. They may be defensible, but a convincing defense requires candor about precisely what is being defended.

The Missing Context

The core of the Bowen and Bok study is information gleaned from a database that they called "College and Beyond," or C&B. Assembled by the Mellon Foundation in the years 1995 to 1997, it contained data about approximately 30,000 students who began their studies at one of twenty-eight leading colleges and universities in 1976, and more than 32,000 who did likewise in 1989. Data were also gathered about freshmen entering these schools in 1951, to which little reference was made. Twenty-four of the twenty-eight institutions were private, just four of them public. The authors divided the schools into three classes on the basis of their selectivity (SEL) as measured by the mean combined SAT scores of their matriculants.[28]

The most selective schools—SEL-1, they called them—included Princeton, Stanford, Williams, and Yale. (Harvard was not included in the study, for unspecified reasons.) The SEL-2 group consisted of schools like Columbia, Northwestern, the University of Pennsylvania, and Tufts. Only at the SEL-3 level do we find any public institutions—the University of North Carolina at Chapel Hill, the Ann Arbor campus of the University of Michigan, Pennsylvania State, and Miami University of Ohio.[29]

The twenty-eight schools were presumed to be typical of selective colleges and universities, but the sample was heavily weighted toward the most highly selective, SEL-1 and SEL-2 institutions. More than half of the freshmen in the study's 1976 sample attended a school in the top two categories, even though such schools by the authors' own calculations represented only 18 percent of total enrollment in selective colleges in the nation as a whole.[30] (Moreover, since there are over 3,700 institutions of higher education in the United States, most of which require nothing of applicants but a high school diploma and the ability to pay the tuition, the selective colleges are themselves but a tiny fraction of a very large universe.)[31] The generalizations offered about the effects of preferential policies in selective schools were thus heavily skewed toward the most elite institutions, almost all of them wealthy and private. In fact, large and impersonal SEL-3 state institutions like the University of Michigan and Penn State educate more than four times as many students as SEL-1 and SEL-2 schools like Yale, Swarthmore, and Wesleyan.

Furthermore, although twenty-eight schools provided data for this study, the statistical base was even narrower at key points. For reasons not adequately explained, much of the detailed analysis of admissions decisions was based upon records from just five of these schools. The authors said they could not identify the specific schools because they had promised confidentiality, but maintained that the five were "roughly representative" of the twenty-eight schools that made up the C&B database.[32] Very roughly at best, we would say, because not one of them was a public institution. It is not even clear if any were in the SEL-3 category.

The authors did not claim that the universe they examined was the whole of higher education or anything like it. But running through their work was the assumption, perhaps not surprising from two former presidents of Ivy League colleges, that it was only the elite schools, chiefly the elite private schools, that really mattered. One would not know from reading this book that in 1989, the year of their latest sample, just 14 percent of all American college students, and a mere 9 percent of all those who were black, were enrolled in *any* private four-year college or university. Furthermore, even the small fraction of African Americans attending private schools was mostly at institutions with minimal admissions requirements and hence required no preferential policies at all. Substantial numbers were enrolled in the approximately one hundred historically black colleges (HBCs) and universities in the nation, most of which accepted practically all applicants.[33] As we will note later, Bowen and Bok ignored—indeed, deliberately neglected—these important historically black schools.

The extremely narrow focus of their study is also apparent from a National Center for Education Statistics study of 1982 high school graduates. It found that only 10.1 percent of all college-bound seniors enrolled in a selective school; for blacks the figure was just 5.3 percent, for Hispanics 7.7 percent.[34] Elite institutions are certainly worth careful study, but we should not mistake this small tributary for the entire river.[35] Bowen and Bok exaggerated the importance of these schools in American society as a whole, and in the lives of black Americans specifically.

The primary focus on elite private institutions resulted in another serious limitation. The authors barely mentioned Hispanics, a minority group that has grown so rapidly that it now outnumbers the African-American population among those of school age.[36] Bowen and Bok doubtlessly believed that preferential policies were initiated to remedy problems rooted in the historic oppression of African Americans, and that the real test of their efficacy is their impact on black students. But the policies they recommended were not restricted to blacks, and they did not advocate that they should be. That Latinos were missing from their account perhaps reflects the East Coast insularity of the authors. They looked at only two schools (Rice and Stanford) in the region in which two-thirds of all Hispanics live.

Whatever the failings of the American educational system, opportunities for higher education are more widely available than in any other place in the world. Today, six out of seven African Americans graduate from high school, a rate nearly identical to that for whites, and more than six out of ten (61.9 percent) of all black high school graduates go on to college directly after high school. The comparable proportion for whites is less than seven points higher (68.5 percent), a strikingly modest difference in attendance rates given the huge racial gap in academic achievement among high school seniors.[37] Decisions made in admissions offices at places like Princeton, Wellesley, Oberlin, and other selective institutions of the kind Bowen and Bok studied do little to shape the overall structure of opportunity in higher education. It is regrettable that Bowen and Bok made so little attempt to situate the institutions they studied in the national context.

The Weight Given to Race in Admissions to Selective Colleges

How much of an edge is given to black applicants to selective schools because of their race? Diversity advocates have long claimed that schools use race as only one of many factors—that they give black applicants only a small boost in the competition for admission. Critics of preferential policies, on the other hand, maintain that race is of decisive importance, and point out that the combined verbal and math SAT scores of black students who are admitted to selective schools are often 150 or more points below those of their white and Asian peers.[38]

How significant is that gap? Bowen and Bok argued that average black and white SAT scores "are poor indicators of the degree of preference given to minority students." Since black scores are concentrated in the lower ranges, even a school with race-neutral admissions will have a substantial racial gap. A high proportion of the admitted black students will have met only the minimal academic requirements, and few will be in the upper reaches of the distribution. As a consequence, the impact of preferences has not been nearly as great as the racial difference in average SAT scores might make us think.[39] Whatever the formula for admission, there would be a racial gap in those scores—given the fact that the median score for the two groups differs dramatically.

This is a significant point. Given the difference in average SAT scores, the racial gap at the elite schools would not entirely disappear with race-neutral admissions. Nevertheless, that very large gap at their C&B schools cannot be dismissed as a statistical artifact. Race-based admissions clearly widen the disparity significantly.[40] Consider the five private schools Bowen and Bok studied intensively. Among applicants for admission in 1989 with SAT scores from 1200 to 1249, 19 percent of whites and 60 percent of blacks were admitted; in the next bracket up (1250–1299), 24 percent of whites and 75 percent of blacks were accepted.[41] Among applicants with near-perfect scores (1500 or better), over a third of whites were turned down, but every single black got in. Indeed, black students with scores of 1200–1249 were nearly as likely to be accepted at Bowen and Bok's five institutions as whites with scores of 1500 or better! Under race-neutral admissions, clearly the picture would be quite different.

Indeed, any company that hired or promoted *whites* over blacks in proportions like these would be inviting a discrimination suit plaintiffs would find easy to win.[42] But what impressed the authors, oddly enough, was not the magnitude of the racial disparity. Instead, they noted that neither all whites nor all blacks (except those few in the 1500 and up bracket) got in, and concluded that many factors in addition to race entered into the admissions decisions.[43] But if race was not a very big part of the story, then what is the explanation for a black acceptance rate triple that for whites in the 1200–1249 and 1250–1299 SAT brackets? The majority in *Bakke* had sanctioned the use of race as one of many considerations—little more than a tie-breaker.[44] These schools clearly do not conform to the *Bakke* standard; for many black students, race is *the* controlling factor that decides their admission.

Although their own evidence revealed that black students gained entry to elite educational institutions with much weaker academic records than many whites and Asians who were turned down, the authors insisted that these preferred students nevertheless possessed "strong academic credentials" and "were not deficient by any national standard." The problem, they said, was not a paucity of well-qualified African-American students, but rather the abundance of superqualified whites and Asians—students so "spectacularly well qualified," so "extraordinary" that even very strong black applicants would lose out if judged by the same strict standard.[45]

It is hard to take this argument seriously. Words like "strong" and "deficient" are obviously relative terms; whether you are a "strong" or a "deficient" student depends entirely upon the frame of reference. A "strong" student in one context will nonetheless be "deficient" in academic skills in another.

Bowen and Bok did agree that context is important, but suggested that critics of preferences used the wrong frame of reference. African-American students admitted to elite institutions in 1989, they noted, had SAT scores that were slightly higher than the average for all students who enrolled in these schools back in 1951, when they were almost entirely white. Therefore, they said, old grads of that vintage "should have no reason to question the qualifications of the black students of today!"[46]

But unless you make the manifestly erroneous assumption that the competition for entry into these schools has not increased since 1951, their conclusion did not follow. Applicants in 1989 were not competing with those who sought admission in 1951, when the elite colleges drew their students from a limited social stratum, did little national recruiting, and had dramatically lower admissions standards. Today, the academic skills required to be a serious contender for admission to such schools must be much stronger. We doubt that Bowen and Bok believed that a high school runner would be a superbly qualified candidate for the college track team today if his best time would have assured him a place on the varsity in 1951.

A second point the authors made about context is equally strained. To show that preferentially admitted students were not "deficient by any national standard," they noted that three-quarters of the African Americans applying to the highly selective schools in 1989 had higher SAT scores than the *national average* for all white test-takers that year.[47] But again, the comparison is irrelevant. These were not schools for students with academic skills that were only a bit above average. Rather, they were among the most highly selective and competitive campuses in the country. Their white applicants in 1989 had average SAT scores in the top 8 percent of all test-takers on the verbals and the top 9 percent in math. In fact, the whites and Asians they actually accepted ranked in the top 3 to 4 percent.[48] When black students with SATs at the seventy-fifth percentile get into schools at which the average white or Asian is at the ninety-sixth percentile or above, we can say that they are fairly strong students by a "national standard," but are indisputably weak by the standards of the school they will be attending.

Bowen and Bok's figures revealed very heavy preferences in favor of black applicants. Those preferences would have looked even stronger had they employed a different analytical technique that controlled more precisely for the academic qualifications of applicants. Robert Lerner and Althea Nagai recently studied admissions at a number of state university systems for the Center for Equal Opportunity using logistic regression. The method enabled them to calculate the odds of admission for black and white students with the identical high school GPAs, class rank, and scores on the SAT or the ACT. At the College of William and Mary in 1996, the odds of admission were twenty-eight times as great for black applicants. At the University of Virginia at Charlottesville the same year, the black advantage was forty-five to one. In 1999, Virginia favored African Americans by an even more remarkable margin of 111 to 1. But the prize goes to the University of Michigan at Ann Arbor (one of the C&B schools), at which black applicants were favored over whites with the same academic qualifications by a stunning 174 to 1.[49]

Race-Neutral Standards and the Racial Mix

Bowen and Bok minimized the magnitude of racial preferences at highly selective schools. At the same time, however, they stressed the calamitous reductions in minority enrollments that would result from a race-blind process. The two arguments are simply incompatible.

Removing race as a consideration in admissions would have an impact on black enrollment at elite colleges, especially at the very top schools, although it would have no effect on the vast majority of African-American students who do not attend such selective institutions. But even with respect to the C&B schools, Bowen and Bok exaggerated the potential impact of race-neutral policies. They estimate that if students had been admitted in 1989 to SEL-1 schools simply on the basis of SAT scores, 73 percent fewer blacks would have been enrolled. At SEL-2 institutions, the drop would have been 52 percent, and at SEL-3 schools, 32 percent.[50]

These dire enrollment estimates are of little relevance to the current debate, however, because they depend on a peculiar and indefensible definition of a "race-neutral" policy as one that admits students purely on the basis of their standardized test scores. No proponent of race-neutral or color-blind admissions advocates this. Neither the *Hopwood* decision nor Propositions 209 and I-200 bar admissions officials from taking social class and other extra-academic variables into account, even when those variables are correlated with race and disproportionately benefit African-American applicants.

In fact, it is odd that the authors suddenly made such an assumption. In a separate discussion, when they sought to minimize the extent of racial preferences involved in current admissions policies, they acknowledged the importance of other criteria in the admissions process—athletic and musical ability, for instance, as well as socioeconomic disadvantage and leadership skills.[51] By shifting from one definition of race-neutral admissions to another depending upon which one yields results that best fit their argument, Bowen and Bok seriously mislead their readers.

Nevertheless, using race-neutral academic criteria would undoubtedly mean a substantial decline in black admissions at the elite undergraduate schools. How substantial? At the five schools they looked at closely, the authors predicted a drop in black enrollments of 49 percent if admissions officers were allowed to admit students on the basis of athletic ability (and other race-correlated qualities), but could not make racial identity the determining factor.[52] This estimate is not to be taken too seriously. The authors were unable to demonstrate that these five institutions were representative of the large group of twenty-eight schools, much less of the still larger universe of selective colleges. To the extent that the 49 percent is indeed accurate, however, Bowen and Bok confirmed precisely what critics have always maintained: preferences really are preferential.

The Minority Mismatch Theory

Except in the publicly funded institutions of higher education in California, Texas, and Washington, racial preferences are ubiquitous. Bowen and Bok argued that they were fair (only well-qualified black students benefited), necessary (the alternative was a calamitous drop in black admissions), and efficacious: that is, they have worked. Once admitted, black students with weaker academic records do well. The authors saw nothing "disappointing" in the academic performance of students whose race made the difference between acceptance and rejection. Not many flunk out. Almost eight out of ten of the black students in the C&B schools graduated, double the national average for African Americans. At the elite within this elite, the SEL-1 colleges, nearly nine out of ten collected diplomas.[53]

Opponents of racial preferences, however, have long argued that racial double standards "mismatch" minority students to institutions, placing them in competitive academic settings for which they are ill prepared.[54] Bowen and Bok's findings would seem to challenge that argument. If the preferentially admitted students were indeed "mismatched," the dropout rate for blacks should be higher at Yale than at a less selective school. And yet the authors showed the top schools do the best job at retaining their students.

Hold SAT scores constant and the point is clear. Among the 1989 black freshmen with a combined SAT scores under 1,000, for example, 88 percent of those in SEL-1 schools earned diplomas, as compared with 75 percent of those at SEL-2 schools and 65 percent of those at SEL-3 schools. Black students with academic skills that were barely above the national average for all SAT-takers were more likely to make it through Williams College than Tulane or Penn State.[55]

The discovery that the black graduation rate was highest at the most competitive schools only marginally modifies the "minority mismatch" theory (which the authors called the "fit" hypothesis). It is hard to flunk out of Princeton. Most students at all the elite schools finish, and the very best schools do best in this respect. They are wealthy, with ample resources for tutoring and counseling designed to keep every student in school. In addition, grade inflation has turned a D into a B-, and the grading gets easier the higher one goes in the academic hierarchy. At Stanford a few years ago, the median grade was an A-![56]

It is important to note, as well, that only the SEL-3 category included any of the large, bureaucratic, public universities (Michigan, Chapel Hill, Penn State, Miami University)—schools that have limited resources with which to help students in academic trouble. Throughout their volume Bowen and Bok glossed over the glaring differences between public institutions and rich private schools like those they once governed.

Students from relatively affluent black families tend, in general, to have higher graduation rates, and black students at the richest private schools may arrive most advantaged. Socioeconomic status surely accounts in part for the generally high rates of completion at all C&B schools. Although the authors pass over the information hastily, it is startling to discover that fully 64 percent of the African Americans in their 1989 sample had at least one parent who had graduated from college, nearly *six times* the proportion among all black college-age youths. Perhaps even more striking, a mere *14 percent* of the blacks attending elite colleges were from families of low socioeconomic status, defined as those earning less than $22,000 annually and in which neither parent had a college degree. Half of all African Americans of college age in the nation fall into that category.[57]

And yet preferences in higher education are often justified by references to the high proportion of black children living in poverty. Most of the black students attending Haverford, Duke, Northwestern, and Emory are privileged, and wherever they went to school, they would likely graduate at much higher rates than their less affluent peers. And the fact that the most selective schools of all also have the highest graduation rates for African Americans could also simply reflect the higher social status of the black students who attend them. Bowen and Bok unfortunately failed to provide the detailed evidence necessary to confirm or disprove this hunch, though they could easily have done so.[58]

Eight out of ten black students at C&B schools collected their diplomas—by national standards, a high figure, suggesting less of a "mismatch" between student and institution than is sometimes argued.[59] But there is another and more sobering way of looking at the same data. The converse of the graduate rate is the dropout rate. It is the other side of the coin—and the picture is not so pretty. In Bowen and Bok's 1989 sample, only 6.3 percent of the whites failed to get a bachelor's degree (from any school), as compared with 20.8 percent of the African Americans.[60] Hence, the black dropout rate was 3.3 times the white rate, a much larger differential than the overall national gap.[61] Furthermore, the racial difference widened as the selectivity of the school increased, just as the mismatch theory would suggest. The ratio of black to white dropout rates was 2.8 at SEL-3 colleges, 3.6 at those ranked SEL-2, and 4.2 at the SEL-1 level.[62]

To focus on the graduation numbers and ignore the dropout picture is like looking at black employment—rather than *un*employment—rates. In December 1997, 90.1 of the African Americans who were in the labor force were employed, as compared with 96.1 percent of whites.[63] The racial gap in the employment rate was just six percentage points, which seems a quite modest differential. The other side of the same coin, though, is that the black unemployment rate was 9.9 percent, versus only 3.9 percent for whites. African Americans were thus 2.5 as times as likely as whites to be jobless— and joblessness is the important social issue. Likewise, the dropout numbers alert us to an educational problem we cannot ignore.

What would the college completion rates have looked like without race-conscious admissions? Bowen and Bok could have answered this crucial question by classifying the black students in their samples into preferential and "regular" admits. The authors did provide such breakdowns when they estimated how much black enrollment would have declined at the twenty-eight institutions if SATs had been the only criterion. In discussing other matters, in a nifty bit of legerdemain, they let the unwary reader think that all the blacks whose achievements they celebrated were attending the elite schools as a consequence of racial double standards. That is far from the case.

A far less optimistic conclusion about the prospects that students admitted under racial double standards will manage to graduate may be drawn from a 1991 study of freshmen who entered one of eighty-nine accredited engineering schools or programs that enrolled a third of all black engineering students in the country.[64] The overall graduation rate for black freshmen was just 36 percent, little more than half that for white students (77 percent). Some African Americans, though, did much better than the group average. When we compare those with reasonably good SAT scores (500 or better verbals and 600 or better math scores) with those with weaker scores, we find that the former was more than twice as likely to earn a degree (62 percent vs. 29 percent).[65] Ignoring SAT scores and dividing students into a top group with 3.5 high school GPAs and class rank in the top 10 percent had a similar but much weaker effect. Engineering schools that made their admissions decisions on the basis of the "formulaic calculations" that Bowen and Bok regarded with such disdain would have had many fewer black students dropping out than those that accepted black applicants with weak academic credentials in the hope that the handicaps they entered with would somehow vanish during college.

Black "Underperformance" in the Classroom

Graduation rates are an extremely crude and minimal measure of how well a group is faring in college. As John McWhorter has pointed out, to take mere graduation as the test of college performance is like "asking someone how a symphony performance of Beethoven's Fifth was last night and receiving the enthusiastic answer that the orchestra managed to get to the end of the piece."[66] Anyone who gave such a response must have had mighty low expectations for the orchestra. Defenders of preferential policies who are relieved to find that many preferentially admitted students make it through to commencement have similarly low expectations.

Bowen and Bok played up graduation rates, ignoring their own finding that black students in general dropped out of these schools at triple the white rate, a figure that doubtless would be higher if one looked only at the beneficiaries of racial preferences. They devoted much less attention to actual classroom performance. But they did feel compelled to admit a startling and depressing fact: the cumulative grade point average of the African-American students at their twenty-eight schools put them at the twenty-third percentile of the class—the bottom quarter, that is. This is no surprise. Although the matter has been little studied, because schools committed to preferential policies have done their best to keep this depressing information under wraps, black students consistently lag well behind their white classmates academically in institutions across the land.[67]

Even the twenty-third percentile figure is deceptively rosy, because it included many students who met the regular academic requirements for admission and received no racial preference—about half of the black undergraduates at C&B schools, the authors estimated.[68] If Bowen and Bok had examined the classroom performance of only the preferentially admitted, the picture doubtless would have looked even worse.

We were not given such a breakdown, despite its crucial relevance to the central issue in the book. This was an astonishing flaw in the research design, and one that should have been evident to the authors at the outset of their work. It is absurd to credit every academic achievement of

African Americans who attended elite colleges to the preferential policies that affected only about *half of them*, but *The Shape of the River* does precisely that. This glaring analytical blunder means that the accomplishments of all those black students who were not the beneficiaries of racial double standards in admissions were a hidden subsidy that inflated the record of those who owed their admission to their race.[69]

Furthermore, we are never told how many African-American students ranked in the top quarter or the top tenth of their class, graduated with honors, or made Phi Beta Kappa. If the mean was at the twenty-third percentile, however, few could have been near the top. This is another instance of the failure of the authors to supply relevant detail when it might have pointed to conclusions hard to square with their general argument.

Bowen and Bok never asked whether poorly prepared black students showed any signs of catching up with their peers over the course of four years, as preference proponents have often claimed. Does the stimulating environment of a first-class school make up for years of inadequate preparation? The authors ignored an important recent study of four Ivy League schools that found no "late-bloomer" effect at all for black students, no tendency toward convergence in black and white GPAs over the four college years.[70]

Preferentially admitted students clearly had comparatively poor academic records. But, as the authors acknowledged, the fact that many black matriculants entered the C&B colleges unequally prepared for the competition does not entirely explain the black-white gap in class ranking.

> The average rank in class for black students is appreciably lower than the average rank in class for white students *within each SAT interval.* . . . It is one strong indication of a troubling phenomenon often called "underperformance." Black students with the same SAT scores as whites tend to earn lower grades.[71]

Since it is still often claimed that standardized tests are biased against black and other minority students, this passage deserves to be underscored. The authors of the most elaborate defense ever made of racial double standards in admissions in higher education found no support for the view that tests like the SATs underestimate the prospects that black students will succeed: quite the opposite, in fact. African-American students perform *less well* in higher education than would be expected on the basis of their test scores.[72]

The authors devoted a good many inconclusive pages to possible explanations for black underperformance without considering a peer culture problem to which a number of scholars have pointed. African-American students who arrive with marginal academic qualifications may form an alternative subculture that discourages academic achievement as a "white" and "Asian" thing. And perhaps the best-prepared black students, who require no preferences, could be inhibited by peer group pressures from doing as well as they otherwise might have. If so, the "critical mass" of black students that preference advocates want may carry a high cost.

Ronald Ferguson's review of the literature on racial differences in performance at the secondary school level finds evidence pointing to precisely this phenomenon—black students forming "peer groups that disengage from academic competition."[73] Group members "may secretly want to be 'smart,'" Ferguson writes, but "resent any effort by black peers to defect from group norms by *acting* smart." Something similar may be dragging down the performance of even the best-prepared African-American students at elite colleges today, who may be studying less hard than they otherwise might.

This hypothesis could have been explored with the Bowen and Bok database. They had data for the entering class of 1951 at some schools, and could have determined whether the very small numbers of African Americans admitted in the pre-preference era also underperformed. If there were a marked change in the era of racial preferences, it would have been suggestive.

The self-segregation of African Americans that is a prominent feature of campus life today at many places may be related to black underperformance and the formation of "peer groups that disengage from academic competition."[74] Bowen and Bok dismissed the significance of self-segregation by noting that 88 percent of the black students in elite colleges said that they "knew" two or more of their white classmates "well."[75] This survey question had little bearing on the existence of self-segregation, and was too superficial to tap into feelings that are undoubtedly painful and complex.

A glance at the scene at Wesleyan University, one of Bowen and Bok's twenty-eight schools, might have shaken the authors' complacency. Priding itself on being "Diversity University," Wesleyan allows its students the choice of living in houses called Malcolm X, Women of Color, Asian/Asian-American, La Casa, and even one designated "Open," which is the "queer and queer-positive special interest house."[76] When an un-expectedly large freshman class arrived in 1996, the university decided to fill nine empty spaces at Malcolm X house with whites, but backed down when black students objected to living with anyone of another race. The problem was solved by consigning several white students to the basement of the Philosophy building.

Are the black students who reside at Wesleyan's Malcolm X or Women of Color houses more likely to underperform than those at other schools that do not allow such racial and ethnic clustering? It would not have been hard to find out with the data the authors had at their disposal. Yale assigns students to residential units without giving them a choice. Harvard recently departed from tradition and started to make random housing assignments in order to break up the pronounced concentration of African Americans that had occurred when the choice was left to students.[77] Do different college policies on this matter have any discernible educational effects? Bowen and Bok should have explored the issue.[78]

Double Standards and Racial Stigma

The combination of significantly higher dropout rates and under-achievement surely perpetuates stigmatizing myths about black academic talent. When few Jews could get into the Ivy League schools, and Jewish students had to be superqualified to gain admission, a Jewish stereotype was created: Jews are smart. Admitting black students by *lower* standards has precisely the opposite effect: it reinforces the pernicious notion that blacks are not academically talented.

At one point Bowen and Bok did seem to concede that black students may be unfairly stigmatized as a consequence of preferences. "Selective institutions have been reluctant to talk about the degree of preference given black students," they admitted, because they fear that "the standing of black students in the eyes of white classmates would be lowered if differences in test scores and high school grades were publicized."[79]

It is indeed awkward to let out the truth about double standards, though it is remarkable that administrators think that the students will not make invidious comparisons if the statistics are kept under wraps. Knowing or suspecting that some students were treated "differently" in the admissions process because of their race may lead those who are not from groups favored in the admissions process to regard them as less deserving of a place in the class. When black students tend to be at the bottom academically, as Bowen and Bok conceded was the case at the elite schools they studied, those negative attitudes are reinforced.

The authors called this one of the "costs" of preferential policies, but nonetheless denied that the seeming "stigmatization" and "demoralization" of black students was worrisome. The people in the best position to know whether this was true, they said, were the black students themselves, who professed to feel fine. Most were "satisfied" or "very satisfied" with the schools they attended.[80]

This blurs two issues. That black students liked the schools they attended tells us nothing at all about what other students believed about them. Furthermore, the survey question the authors referred to is hardly decisive evidence even when it comes to the feelings of black students. As noted earlier, none of the items in the C&B survey were designed to tap personal feelings of stigmatization. Nine out of ten of all the students who attended one of these schools professed considerable satisfaction with their choice.[81] These campuses are unquestionably very nice places at which to spend four years, with many amenities lacking at less selective and less wealthy institutions and plenty of bright classmates. But students can say, yes, we are pleased we had the opportunity to attend Kenyon College, while at the same time harboring doubts about their own academic abilities.[82]

The psychologist Claude Steele has conducted a number of experiments that show that black college students perform below their capability when tests are administered in a context designed to bring their race to mind and activate negative stereotypes about the intellectual capacity of African Americans.[83] If this is the explanation for the very common phenomenon of black underperformance in higher education, it suggests that preferences in admissions may be a significant part of the problem. What better way to heighten racial consciousness than to announce to the student body that the school is so committed to "diversity" that it happily lowers its admissions standards for blacks and certain other racial minorities? Black students who think, even if mistakenly, that they would never have been accepted at Yale or Stanford if they were white or Asian would have a high degree of what Steele calls "stereotype vulnerability." It is precisely a stereotype—that blacks are different and we need to have a "critical mass" of them—that drives the admissions policies of elite schools today.

Preferences and Success in Graduate School

Bowen and Bok reported with pride that elite colleges send a high proportion of their African-American graduates to "top-rated professional schools," a point central to their argument that preferences "work."[84] Some 40 percent of those in the 1976 entering class obtained professional or doctoral degrees, actually a little higher than the figure for whites from the same schools (37 percent), and dramatically higher than the 8 percent for all black college graduates. Furthermore, blacks from elite colleges are far more likely than their white classmates to attend the most selective and prestigious "top-tier" law, medical, and business schools.[85]

The comparison with black college graduates as a whole proves nothing, of course. Black students at Columbia College are not in the least representative of the nation's African-American students in general. They differ both in the academic skills they brought with them to college and in their social class background.

Nor is the contrast with white graduates of, say, Northwestern telling. Northwestern's black students go on to professional schools that also have highly race-conscious admissions policies. Surely the success of racial preferences in college cannot be measured by how many of the beneficiaries go on to win admission to graduate schools that use precisely the same racial double standards.

Bowen and Bok admitted that "race-sensitive admissions policies" at the graduate level contributed to the success they found so gratifying, but they maintained that credit must also go to the splendid training that such students received as undergraduates.[86] What is the evidence, however, that the elite colleges have done so much to develop the talent of their black undergraduates?

We know, first of all, that the typical African-American students in Bowen and Bok's elite schools ended up in the bottom quarter of their class, and it is reasonable to surmise from other evidence cited above that those with subpar academic qualifications, whose admission was due to the color of their skin, did even worse. That would not seem to make them superb candidates for the best graduate programs.

Perhaps, though, they learned enough to perform outstandingly well on the standard tests used in admissions to the nation's graduate and professional schools. Bowen and Bok did not gather any information about how the students they studied did on such tests. But we do know that, after a full generation of racial preferences at the college level, the pool of black college graduates with the academic skills needed to go on to the best medical schools, law schools, business schools, or Ph.D. programs is pathetically small.[87]

At the very top of the distribution, racial disparities are shockingly large. Of the approximately 70,000 students who applied to law school for the class entering in the fall of 1997, just *sixteen* blacks in the whole country scored 164 or better on the Law School Admissions Test (the 92.3 percentile) and had a college GPA of 3.5 or better. Some 2,646 whites aspiring to become lawyers, 165 times as many, had academic credentials that were that strong.[88]

Data on applicants to business school who took the Graduate Management Admissions Test in 1996 tell the same depressing story. Although more than 10,000 African Americans took the GMAT, only *thirty-three* scored 700 or better, the average at the nation's top business schools. Some 3,238 whites, by contrast, were in the top group, 98 times as many. Although African Americans constituted 8.5 percent of all test-takers, they were a mere 0.8 percent of those scored 700 or higher.[89]

That a good many black graduates of C&B schools go on to graduate schools, many to the top schools, thus is not proof that racial double standards in admissions to elite colleges "work." If they really "worked," these schools should have produced much larger numbers of highly capable students who could compete successfully for top grades in graduate admissions tests without any consideration at all of their race in the admissions process.

Preferences, often glaring preferences, are nonetheless a fact of life in graduate schools, too. In a massive study of more than 27,000 students who entered one of 163 ABA-approved law schools in the fall of 1991, Linda F. Wightman calculated that a total of only *twenty-four* African Americans would have been admitted to any of the top eighteen schools if the decisions had been made purely on the basis of college grades and LSAT scores.[90] But, thanks to preferences, 420 black students got in, a stunning 17.5 times as many.

Compare this with Bowen and Bok's calculation that SEL-1 colleges enrolled 3.7 times as many black students as they would have with admissions based solely on academic qualifications.[91] The law school equivalents to SEL-1 colleges had to put an even heavier thumb—a much heavier

thumb—on the scale to obtain significant African-American enrollments.[92] Are Tufts, Rice, Oberlin, Vanderbilt, and the rest really doing
such a great job training African-American undergraduates? If so, it is
hard to see why their black B.A.s who apply to graduate programs cannot meet the same standards as whites and Asians.

There are still some tests of academic excellence whose results are not
adjusted to take race into account by lowering the standard. Bar examinations, for example, are graded on a color-blind basis, and disproportionate numbers of African-American graduates fail them. For example,
57 percent of the blacks taking the California bar exam for the first time
in 1997 failed, 2.5 times the proportion among whites (23 percent). The
disparity was even wider in New York in 1992—63 percent of African
Americans flunked, more than triple the white figure (18 percent).[93]

In the opening pages of this essay, we cited blunt remarks about this
uncomfortable fact in a confidential memo written by the associate dean
of the University of Texas Law School, a memo that came to light as a result of the *Hopwood* litigation. Remarkably, not a word about bar exams
appeared in *The Shape of the River*, even though one of its authors is a former law school dean who must have been aware of the issue. Furthermore,
the authors repeatedly cited a paper by Linda F. Wightman, while omit-
ting any mention of her detailed discussion of racial differences in bar examination pass rates.[94]

The explanation may be that Wightman's findings on this matter are
inconsistent with the rosy picture painted by the authors. She distinguished black law students who owed their admission to racial preferences
from those who did not, and found that more than a fifth of the former
failed to graduate.[95] Even worse, 27 percent of those who got through
school were unable to pass a bar exam within three years of graduation,
a failure rate nearly triple that for African Americans who were admitted
under regular standards and almost seven times the white failure rate.[96]
Fully 43 percent of the black students admitted to law school on the basis
of race fell by the wayside, either dropping out without a degree or failing to pass a bar examination.[97] These students must be counted among
the casualties of preferential policies. In admitting marginal minority students to make their student bodies more diverse, our law schools are making an implicit promise that they will remedy their academic deficiencies
and supply them with a ticket admitting them to the legal profession.
Their record in delivering on that promise appears dismal.

Bowen and Bok also overlooked very troubling information about how preferences are working in medical school. They regarded it is as a triumph that "about 70" preferentially admitted black students from their 1976 sample went on to graduate from medical school and become doctors.[98] They failed, though, to consider the disturbing results of other relevant studies. A paper in the *Journal of the American Medical Association* reported that in 1988 an appalling 51.1 percent of black medical students failed the required Part I exam given by the National Board of Medical Examiners.[99] The white failure rate was a mere 12.3 percent.

This glaring disparity, the investigators discovered, was almost entirely attributable to preferential admissions policies. Black students who had strong academic credentials as undergraduates were as likely to pass as whites; unfortunately, a high proportion of African Americans entered medical school without strong credentials, thanks to racial double standards in admissions.

Well after graduation from medical school, dismayingly large racial disparities also show up in Board of Medical Examiners tests measuring the competence of practicing physicians in their field of specialization. That was revealed in a RAND Corporation study of a national sample of the medical school graduating class of 1975, including 715 graduates who were classified as minorities, 80.2 percent of them African Americans.[100] Bowen and Bok were familiar with this research, because they cited it as evidence that minority physicians were more likely than others to "work in locations designated as health manpower shortage areas by the federal government."[101] They failed to mention the disturbing and more significant fact that the study also found that only 49 percent of minority physicians were able to qualify as board-certified in their specialty within seven years of graduation, as compared with 80 percent of whites and Asians.[102]

As was the case with the pattern of failure on Part I of the medical boards, the likelihood that minority physicians would have passed the specialty boards depended largely upon their academic records before they reached medical school. A solid 83 percent of those in the top category on an "undergraduate performance index" based on college grades and Medical College Admissions Test scores became board-certified; in the second category, 75 percent did; in the third, 56 percent; in the fourth, 47 percent; and in the lowest group, which received the heaviest preferences, a mere 32 percent qualified.[103] Minority students with weak undergraduate records who had been given a big boost in the admissions process were still conspicuously less skilled than their peers more than a decade after leaving college.

The findings of these careful but little-known inquiries contradict the claims made in a much-ballyhooed 1997 study of graduates of the University of California at Davis School of Medicine, published in the *Journal of the American Medical Association*. This study, however, did not provide any data on performance broken down by race and had other crippling flaws.[104] Thus, in both law and medicine, an alarmingly high proportion of students who benefited from racial preferences in admissions to college and professional school stumbled when that crutch was taken away and they had to pass tough tests that did not take their race into account.

The Historically Black Colleges: Missing in Action

Bowen and Bok certainly did demonstrate in great detail that most of the African Americans who attended the schools included in their study graduated and fared quite well subsequently. Yet again, the conclusion that race-conscious admissions are to be credited does not inexorably follow. The graduates of Yale undoubtedly tend to be much more successful than the graduates of the University of Bridgeport, but did attending Yale make all the difference? There is some brand-name advantage, especially (and perhaps only) when students are looking for their first job. Many other factors influence even short-run outcomes, however. The majority of Yale students arrive in New Haven with assets that very few students at the University of Bridgeport possess—good high school educations, high test scores, and prosperous and well-connected parents.

Bowen and Bok both have spent their entire academic careers at Ivy League institutions and have given countless fundraising speeches about the important role Princeton and Harvard play in training the nation's future leaders. Undoubtedly, they were terrific salesmen. Yet if they really wanted to know precisely how handsomely attending the "best" schools paid off, they needed to use less selective (or unselective) schools as a control group. Although they were aware of the problem, and indeed commissioned a "control group study" to deal with it, the effort added little and is barely mentioned in their analysis.[105] A subsequent study using the C&B data base has demonstrated that, contrary to the argument of *The Shape of the River*, students who attended the most selective C&B schools did not earn significantly more fifteen years out of college than those who attended the least selective ones. If SEL-1 institutions do not yield larger economic benefits than SEL-3 institutions, it is reasonable to wonder if the same holds for SEL-4 or SEL-5 schools.[106]

Bowen and Bok unaccountably missed a tantalizing analytical opportunity by failing to examine a control group readily available to them. The original database collected by the Mellon Foundation included records from thirty-four, not twenty-eight, institutions. Two were excluded from the study because of missing data. The other four were Howard University, Morehouse College, Spelman College, and Xavier University of Louisiana—all historically black colleges (HBCs). These four institutions alone enroll approximately 50 percent more African-American students than do all twenty-eight in the C&B sample, but the authors chose not to examine the records of those who attended them—even though the evidence was already on hand at the Mellon Foundation.[107] It is particularly strange to have dismissed these schools from consideration when evidence indicates that many African Americans hold them in very high regard and believe they offer their children a better education than the colleges and universities Bowen and Bok assumed to be the best for everyone. A recent survey of African Americans in higher education commissioned by the magazine *Black Enterprise* confirms that point strikingly. Nine of the top ten best-for-blacks schools were HBCs.[108]

The four for which Bowen and Bok already had data are among the best of the nation's several dozen HBCs and universities, but they are not very selective by national standards. They accept a majority of their applicants and have median SAT scores that put them at or only slightly above the national average.[109] What happened to the black students who chose to attend Howard, although they had qualifications much like those who went to Duke or Michigan? Bowen and Bok missed the opportunity to explore this vital question.

It happens that the Reverend Martin Luther King Jr. was a graduate of one of the schools Bowen and Bok did not deign to look at—Morehouse College. Bowen and Bok mentioned him (but not his college), but only to support their argument that quantitative measures of academic skills do not help much in predicting "which applicants will contribute most in later life to their professions and their communities."[110] Dr. King, they said, became "one of the great orators of this century," despite having scored in the bottom half of all test-takers on the verbal portion of the

Graduate Record Examination. Yes, indeed—and without having gone to Princeton either. If a regime of preferences had been established a few decades earlier, perhaps he would have attended an elite college and then the Yale Divinity School. Would an Ivy League education have led him to play a more prominent historical role?

The Backbone of the Black Middle Class?

Although their book contains not a shred of evidence about Hispanics, Bowen and Bok came close to suggesting that the black and Hispanic middle classes both owed their very existence to the race-conscious policies implemented by benevolent white educators over the past three decades.[111] "The C&B minority graduates with advanced degrees are the backbone of the emergent black and Hispanic middle class," they wrote.[112]

The numbers don't add up. Only 13,784 African Americans were among the over 300,000 students who entered any SEL-1, SEL-2, or SEL-3 four-year college in the United States in 1976. It can be estimated that just 8,800 of these black students actually graduated, a majority of whom probably would have been admitted to these schools without any racial preferences. Even if we were to make the absurd assumption that the 4,000 or so graduates who had been preferentially admitted would never have gone on to college at all but for the existence of racial double standards in admissions at elite schools, we are talking about a group too minuscule to form the "backbone" of a black middle class that by any reasonable definition includes more than ten million people.[113]

Nor is it correct to claim, as the authors did, that the elite schools are providing African-American students with the skills to rise from lowly origins into the middle class. Their own evidence shows clearly that they are educating young men and women who generally are already economically quite well off. The products of these schools may typically attain higher socioeconomic rank than their parents, but it was their parents who made it into the middle class in the first place, and very few of them did it by going to a highly selective school.

The arguments on this point in *The Shape of the River* were flawed on other grounds as well. In an early chapter Bowen and Bok chronicled the social and economic advances of African Americans since World War II without noticing that much of the progress was made before the institution of preferential policies.[114] Furthermore, to assume that preferences account for subsequent gains is a classic instance of the *post hoc* fallacy. The authors told us that the number of African Americans in Congress rose from four to forty-one between 1965 and 1995.[115] Great news, but what did the Oberlin admissions office have to do with it? A glance at the biographiess of African-American members of Congress in the *Almanac of American Politics* reveals that many were educated at little-known schools, and very few attended elite institutions.[116]

This is not an isolated example. A list of the top fifty African-American federal officials recently compiled by the *Journal of Blacks in Higher Education* shows that only a handful went to a college that Bowen and Bok would define as elite.[117] A similar list of the thirty-three blacks appointed by President Clinton to the federal judiciary looks much the same; four out of ten were graduates of HBCs.[118] A 1996 survey of black officers in the U.S. Army did not distinguish elite institutions from others, but did show that the HBCs had produced 39 percent of the officers, although they account for only a sixth of total college enrollment for blacks.[119]

The contribution of elite schools to the undergraduate training of blacks in the academic profession is even less impressive. A 1996 report by the National Research Council lists the undergraduate institutions that trained the largest numbers of African Americans who earned Ph.D.s between 1992 and 1996.[120] Remarkably, nine of the ten schools that topped the list were HBCs; the tenth was Wayne State, also a heavily black school. Three out of the next eight that completed the list were also predominantly black, and only one—the SEL-3 University of Michigan—ranked anywhere in the Bowen and Bok elite.

This pattern fits the mismatch theory nicely. Getting a doctorate requires enormous commitment and confidence in one's academic ability; those who are inspired to do so are likely to come from colleges where they were academic stars. Students attending schools that gave them a big boost in admissions because of their race are not likely to shine in their studies, as Bowen and Bok's own data show clearly. An African-American student who scored 650 on the math SATs might well stand out as one of the best physics students at Morehouse, Spelman, or Wayne State, while at the University of Chicago he or she is likely to be merely average at best.[121]

A similar picture emerges when we contemplate the educational backgrounds of African-American winners of MacArthur Foundation "genius" awards between 1981 and 1998.[122] Excluding those who never went to college, the forty-four black winners attended no fewer than forty different schools; three-quarters attended institutions that were basically non-selective. And 27 percent were trained at the HBCs that Bowen and Bok chose to ignore.[123]

We have been unable to locate any studies of the educational background of black business leaders, but Stanley Rothman's recent survey found that only a third of the nation's top entrepreneurs in the 1990s had attended elite colleges, and it is hard to believe that the proportion would be notably higher if we could isolate the black members of this group.[124]

Bowen and Bok assumed that elite colleges and universities play the same role in American life that Oxford and Cambridge do in Britain, a fantasy commonly held by those accustomed to breathing those schools' rarefied air. But there are many more avenues to success than they imagined in this huge, complex, and enormously fluid society.

Patterns of Civic Participation

Preferential admissions were responsible for a cadre of African Americans who are making an indispensable contribution to "civic and community endeavors," Bowen and Bok contended. Almost 90 percent of the elite college students in their 1976 sample participated in one or more civic activities in 1995.[125] But this rate, as they conceded, is almost identical to that found in their survey of a nationally representative control group of matriculants at four-year colleges. The United States is a nation of joiners, and it does not appear that attending an elite school makes young people especially civic minded.

Compared to their white classmates, however, black students at elite schools do tend to be somewhat more active, both as participants and as leaders, Bowen and Bok found. Their survey asked whether respondents volunteered to work in or played a leadership role in one or more of thirteen types of activities, including youth organizations, professional associations, political clubs, religious activities, social service or social welfare work, and alumni organizations. Most blacks who attended C&B schools answered yes.

But how can we be sure they would have been any less active at a less selective college? The high level of participation Bowen and Bok discovered might simply reflect the fact that the admissions officers at the C&B schools placed a heavy premium on prior organizational activity, particularly for minority applicants whose academic credentials were weaker.[126] Schools that buy the best possible football players cannot claim credit when many of their former students end up in the National Football League; likewise, colleges that make a big effort to recruit students with leadership skills cannot claim credit for having made them into leaders. Moreover, while it may be desirable to keep the Little League, the Rotary clubs, and the Oberlin Alumni Association strong, participation in such groups seems a questionable way of judging the accomplishments of students from America's most high-powered colleges and universities.

A Model for Race Relations?

Bowen and Bok viewed the elite schools they studied as a model for race relations they hoped the larger society would emulate and maintained that racial double standards are essential to that mission. "Until now," they wrote, "there has been little hard evidence to confirm the belief of educators in the value of diversity,"[127] but their work has filled the void. Their survey data, they said, "throw new light on the extent of interaction occurring on campuses today" and reveal "how positively the great majority of students regard opportunities to learn from those with different points of view, backgrounds, and experiences."[128]

They offered as a key piece of evidence the supposedly high level of interracial friendships they found on elite campuses. For example, they reported that 56 percent of the whites in their 1989 cohort said they knew two or more black classmates "well," and that 88 percent of blacks knew at least two whites well.[129] They marveled that 56 percent of whites in elite schools have two or more black friends. But the import of these numbers is not self-evident. How do they compare with similar evidence about American society in general? Had they looked, they would have discovered that fully 86 percent of all white adults in a 1997 national survey said they had black friends, and 54 percent of whites reported having five or more.[130] Some 73 percent of whites in a 1994 national survey said that they had "good friends" who were African American.[131] And the proportion of blacks with white friends is higher still on every one of these national surveys. The Bowen and Bok survey suggests that the elite campuses may be in the rear guard, not the vanguard.

Former students at C&B schools also said they appreciated studying in a racially diverse environment and wished that the colleges they attended had emphasized racial diversity even more than they had. It is hardly surprising that many of their respondents regarded "diversity" as a "Good Thing"; it has been strenuously celebrated on elite campuses over the past two decades. Nathan Glazer may have overstated the case in titling his recent book *We Are All Multiculturalists Now*, but it is indubitably true of the administrations and much of the faculty at the C&B schools.[132]

In fact, given the prevailing campus climate, it is remarkable that enthusiasm for diversity was as limited as it turned out to be. Bowen and Bok's survey posed an innocuous platitude in the form of a question: How important was the ability to "work effectively and get along well with people of different races/cultures"?[133] Only 42 percent of the white students in the 1976 cohort and 55 percent of the 1989 group said "very important," while the figure for blacks was 74 percent in 1976 and 76 percent in 1989.[134] Surely these figures do not suggest that elite campuses are a national race-relations model.

Moreover, the authors never asked how students who attended less selective schools would respond to such a question. The University of Illinois at Chicago may be a better model than Wesleyan. A May 2000 Zogby poll of a representative national sample of college students found that 84 percent believed that ethnic diversity on campus was important.[135]

Not only is there no evidence that attending an elite school is essential to develop a proper appreciation of diversity, Bowen and Bok also are wrong in assuming that generalized support for diversity means that students strongly endorse the strategies currently used to produce that diversity. Do most believe in lowering admissions standards to ensure a certain percentage of black and Hispanic students on campus? No issue in higher education has generated more controversy in recent years. Bowen and Bok were writing a book about racial preferences in elite institutions of higher education. And yet their elaborate and expensive survey did not include any questions about admissions policies. Why not ask whether or not respondents favored lowering admission standards to increase racial diversity at their schools? Respondents might also have been asked whether they thought such policies made many of their classmates skeptical about the ability of black students. Perhaps most students would say no, but it is also possible that probing such delicate matters might have yielded some of the "disappointing results" the authors never found.[136]

We don't know what students at the C&B schools think about the hotly contested issue of preferences. But we do know what American college students in general think about it. A May 2000 Zogby poll asked students enrolled in institutions of higher education if lowering entrance requirements for some applicants, regardless of the reason, was unfair; 79 percent said yes. Seventy-seven percent said specifically that it was wrong to give preferential treatment to minority students, if it meant denying admission to other students.[137]

How Much Diversity Is Enough?

"Diversity" was Bowen and Bok's mantra. But they failed to provide a searching examination of this slippery and problematic concept. To begin with, there is the question of how much "diversity" is enough. The authors had decades of teaching and administrative experience that might have provided them with some wisdom on the matter, but they stuck very close to their numbers, avoiding any conceptual and philosophical exploration of this difficult question.[138] The operational definition implicit in their work is clear and excruciatingly simple: diversity is the racial mix that exists at their elite schools today. Apparently, it is not a matter of degree. Schools do or don't have it. The C&B colleges get a clean bill of health, but without race-driven admissions policies they will be found wanting.

True "diversity" within a school is, in fact, inevitable—that is, individuals by definition are a diverse lot. But Bowen and Bok—like almost everyone else—fixated on race and ethnicity, thus trafficking in racial stereotypes. (All blacks think alike, as do all whites, all Asians, and all Hispanics; individuals are fungible members of the racial group to which they belong.) They did not ask whether there is a political or religious mix at Haverford—one that includes Evangelicals and Libertarians as well as Catholics and Republicans. Of course, many Americans would feel uncomfortable about giving a preference to applicants on the basis of their religion or political affiliation, but then most are also opposed to picking students on the basis of their skin color.

And what about social class diversity? Although the authors at one point alluded to "persistent gross inequities in wealth, privilege, and position" in American society, and noted that "what people have achieved often depends upon the family they have grown up in, the neighborhoods in which they have lived, and the schools they have attended," they were unable to conceive of the issue of class except in terms of the "racial divide."[139] It never occurred to them that the admission of a white working-class kid from Staten Island might increase "diversity" on an Ivy League campus more than adding another an Exeter-educated African American who grew up in Scarsdale. No observer of elite colleges today can fail to be struck by the homogenously upper-middle-class backgrounds of their student bodies, a fact that arguably impoverishes the educational experience they offer as much as did their racial homogeneity in an earlier era.[140] The obliviousness of the authors to class inequality may explain their endorsement of admissions preferences to the children of alumni.[141] If it is important to make Princeton more "diverse," how can we defend giving an edge in the admissions competition to the son or daughter of a stockbroker who happens to have been a graduate? The two former presidents of Ivy League schools had no problem with such alumni preferences, but surely such policies clashed with their professed desire to overcome the class-based "inequities" in American society.

Even if we accept Bowen and Bok's constricted definition of diversity, it is not clear why we should believe these schools have arrived at the correct racial balance. African Americans, after all, were just 6.7 percent of the students entering Bowen and Bok's elite colleges in 1989, barely half their share in that year's high school graduating class.[142] In the Ivy League schools overall, the figure was a mere 6.1 percent.[143] By national standards, blacks thus remain woefully underrepresented. Bowen and Bok claimed to have demonstrated that students with SATs under 1,000 can do perfectly well at the most selective colleges in America; why, then, do the schools in their study reject four out of five black applicants with such low scores, and why didn't the authors criticize them for doing so? A lower rejection rate would result in a higher diversity score. The answer may be the authors' unspoken acknowledgment that black students with 950 SATs who manage to graduate from Princeton are very special cases. Derek Bok doubtless recalled that in the late 1960s, Harvard conducted an ill-fated experiment when it admitted large numbers of academically unprepared African-American applicants from ghetto schools. Not surprisingly, many floundered.

Their analysis was marred by another striking omission. The mean combined SAT scores of black students at the five schools for which they had detailed data rose by 90 points between 1976 and 1989, cutting the black-white gap from 233 to 165 points.[144] It follows that in 1989 these schools must have rejected a good many black applicants who would have been accepted thirteen years before—a point Bowen and Bok neglected. Elite colleges could have achieved substantially more diversity in 1989 had they been willing to maintain a racial gap of 233 points or so. Were the black students rejected in 1989 "unqualified"? Many must have had scores that made them "highly qualified" in 1976; indeed, Bowen and Bok's entire analysis of the long-term success of black graduates from their twenty-eight schools rested upon the experience of the 1976 entering class—in the workplace for more than two decades. Moreover, they argued elsewhere that African-American students who met the 1951 admissions standards were "qualified" in 1989; what, then, was wrong with the criteria used in 1976?

Diversity at Which Schools?

Most discussions of racially preferential admissions assume that race-neutral policies at elite institutions will mean that fewer black students will be getting a college education. And yet clearly the use of racial double standards at the C&B schools did not increase the total number of black students enrolled in college. Every black student displaced as a result of race-neutral admissions will still have abundant opportunities for a college education at a less selective or entirely unselective institution. Every high school graduate in America can find a school to attend.

Recent developments at the University of California (UC) illustrate the point nicely. The university system was compelled by its regents and the voters of the state to shift to race-neutral admissions for undergraduates entering in the 1998–1999 academic year. The number of African Americans admitted to Berkeley and UCLA dropped sharply as a result, producing a wave of criticism that "diversity" had been diminished. The UC system, it was even said, was becoming "lily white," a truly ludicrous characterization when more than 40 percent of entering students at both Berkeley and UCLA were Asian Americans, and more than 10 percent were black and Hispanic.[145] Bowen and Bok echoed the "resegregation" complaint and claimed that those numbers clearly confirmed their prediction that the abolition of preferences would drastically reduce campus "diversity."[146]

The University of California includes not just Berkeley and UCLA, but six other campuses Bowen and Bok (and most of the media) seem to have forgotten. Although the number of black students who ended up in the freshman class under race-neutral admissions dropped 62.3 percent at Berkeley and 40.1 percent at UCLA, the pattern at other campuses was quite different. At UC Davis, for example, the decline was a mere 2.8 percent. Moreover, black enrollments at Santa Cruz increased by 17.3 percent, by 28.4 percent at Riverside, and by 29.0 percent at UC Irvine.[147]

The net result was not a calamitous decline in diversity at the University of California, but rather a *redistribution* of diversity, with fewer underrepresented minorities at Berkeley and UCLA and correspondingly more blacks and Hispanics at Irvine, Riverside, and Santa Cruz. There is no reason to believe that students who lack the academic qualifications for admission to Berkeley or UCLA under color-blind standards will get an inferior education at these less prestigious but still high-quality schools. They should get a better one, because their academic skills will be on the same plane as those of their classmates. In the year before the end of preferences, only *one* black freshman at the UC San Diego had a GPA of 3.5 or better, as compared with 20 percent of white students. In 1999, 20 percent of the black freshmen at UC San Diego had GPAs of at least 3.5. Indeed, an internal study by the administration found "no substantial GPA differences based on race/ethnicity any longer."[148]

The difference is that, in the days of preferences, minority students with the skills to perform at the same average level as their classmates at a campus like San Diego were admitted to Berkeley because of their race, and most of them were marginal by Berkeley's higher standards. Now that they are at schools to which they are not mismatched, they can be expected to have their share of honors students and no more than their share of those in academic difficulty.[149]

What is more, intensified recruitment efforts by the university system since the end of preferences are paying off in increased numbers of applications by well-prepared minority students since the first numbers came in 1998. A comparison of the students admitted to the University of California in the spring of 2000 to those accepted in the last year of preferences reveals that by now the total number of "underrepresented minorities" (blacks, Hispanics, and American Indians) is actually a bit *higher*, by 2 percent.[150] At Berkeley and UCLA the numbers remained substantially lower than under preferences, but they were rising, and the other six campuses showed dramatic gains.

Hispanics have made greater gains than blacks, whose total numbers admitted to the University of California in 2000 were still 7 percent lower than in the last year of preferential admissions. But not all public institutions of higher education in California are part of the UC system. There is a state college system, which includes such schools as San Francisco State and California State at Los Angeles. It is safe to say that every one of the black students who no longer qualifies for a place at the University of California and who remains eager for further schooling can easily find a place in a state college.

In fact, it is not even clear that the reduction in black enrollments at the University of California will mean a reduction in the number of African Americans who actually graduate. In the past, black students in the system have dropped out at a much higher rate than whites. Of the black students who started as freshmen at Berkeley in 1987, 1988, 1989, or 1990, 42 percent failed to graduate within six years, as compared with 16 percent of whites.[151] Now that the university has begun to accept only those black applicants who meet the same academic standards as other candidates, it is reasonable to expect that the glaring racial gap in dropout rates created by double standards will be narrowed. We have calculated that if the gap in dropout rates were eliminated altogether as a result of color-blind admissions, the number of black graduates of the UC system would actually *increase* by 17 percent, despite their reduced numbers in the freshman class.[152] Even if the gap is only cut in half, which seems a conservative estimate, the number of African Americans earning UC diplomas will still rise by 5 percent.[153] Racial double standards can promote diversity in the freshman class, but surely the goal should be diversity in the graduating class—a very different aim, and one that cannot be achieved by tinkering in the admissions office.

The Morality of Racial Double Standards

Race-neutral admissions are "unworthy of our country's ideals," Bowen and Bok stated in the last chapter of the book.[154] How curious. They seemed to believe that the sorting of American citizens along lines of race and ethnicity is what the framers of the Fourteenth Amendment had in mind. Judging citizens by the color of their skin is indeed as American as apple pie, but the civil rights warriors of the 1950s and 1960s did not put their lives on the line to perpetuate such terrible habits of mind.

Dr. King and the entire civil rights movement believed that the Constitution was color-blind.[155] It was thus the highest duty of the Supreme Court to read the nation's fundamentally egalitarian values—embodied in the Declaration of Independence—into law. But times have changed, and alas, all the empirical data in the world will not resolve the ultimate question of whether racially preferential admissions policies are morally defensible. Is it morally legitimate to distribute benefits to some individuals on the basis of their ascribed racial characteristics?

Bowen and Bok fervently endorsed Justice Blackmun's dictum that "in order to get beyond racism, we must first take race into account. . . . And in order to treat some persons equally, we must treat them differently."[156] Therefore, they saw no problem if a school "needed" more black students and could only fulfill that need by accepting merely "qualified" African Americans while turning down better qualified whites and Asians. This is nothing new for elite colleges, of course, most of which once routinely rejected many superbly qualified Jewish students in favor of merely "qualified" Christian whites in order to preserve a desirable "ethnic balance" in the student body.[157]

Bowen and Bok argued that racial preferences do a great deal for their beneficiaries, but have only the slightest negative effect on any individual white. The gains are concentrated on a group that is small enough to feel the boost; the costs are paid by a group so large as to make the pain for any one of its members trivial. White resentment, they claimed, is like the annoyance many drivers feel at "handicapped parking spaces."[158] Doing away with "the reserved space would have only a minuscule effect on parking options for nondisabled drivers," but many irrationally blame the policy when they have trouble finding a spot.[159] So, too, with spaces in the freshman class at Yale: only a few more whites would get in if the university abolished racial preferences.

The analogy between black students and citizens in wheelchairs is troubling. Furthermore, it is not only whites who are excluded when blacks and Hispanics are admitted to schools by racial double standards. Throughout the book, Bowen and Bok avoided almost any mention of

Asians, who are today a vital presence on elite campuses. Yet surely they knew that in 1996–1997 Asian Americans made up 25 percent of the undergraduate student body at Columbia, 24 percent at Stanford, 18 percent at Harvard, 17 percent at Yale, and 16 percent at Cornell—mighty impressive for a group that is less than 4 percent of the U.S. population.[160]

The cost of racial double standards in admission is currently being paid by many Asian students. When preferences are eliminated, they derive the greatest benefit. Thus Asian American enrollment at the UCLA Law School jumped by 73 percent when race-neutral admissions went into effect.[161] By Bowen and Bok's logic, they are a group small enough to feel the gain from the end of preferences, while the costs have been dispersed widely among blacks, who outnumber Asians more than three-to-one.[162]

In fact, the authors' argument can be used to defend any policy that benefits a minority at the expense of a majority. Six out of seven elementary school teachers today are women.[163] If we were to cut the salaries of each female teacher by 10 percent and give the money this generates as bonuses to male teachers in order to get more male role models in the classroom, the pain any individual woman would feel would be less than the pleasure each man would get from his bigger salary. This logic would also justify any policy that benefits the rich at the expense of the poor—a comparatively very large group.

There is a deeper problem with this entire way of thinking. Bowen and Bok arbitrarily assigned people to racial categories, and then assumed that it is legitimate to offer them different opportunities depending upon the category to which they have been assigned. It doesn't matter that a spectacular white applicant is rejected because the school has "too many" whites already; the young man or woman who is turned down should feel the consolation that the white race is very well represented at that school already. In actuality, it is individuals who suffer from discriminatory treatment, and it does not matter whether the class being discriminated against is a narrow or a broad one.

The X-Percent Solution

After the Fifth Circuit Court of Appeals handed down the *Hopwood* decision in 1996, institutions of higher learning in the state of Texas were forbidden to use race as a basis for selecting students. The state legislature responded to the decision by attempting to "preserve diversity" by another means. It passed the "10 percent plan," which guaranteed any student who placed in the top 10 percent of his or her high school graduating class a place at any public college or university in the state. The University of California has recently adopted but has yet to implement a more modest version of the concept, granting automatic admission to a campus of the state university system for graduates in the top 4 percent of their class. The California plan was more modest in two crucial respects. Four percent is considerably smaller than 10 percent. More important, the students who qualified under this provision were not assured of a spot at the campus of their choice. They might prefer Berkeley or UCLA, but unless their records were strong enough to meet the regular admissions criteria of those schools, they would have to settle for a less competitive place like UC Riverside or UC Davis.

The idea has generated considerable interest elsewhere. In Florida, Governor Jeb Bush is currently implementing a "20 percent plan." Racial preferences will be eliminated at Florida's public colleges and universities; instead, students who rank in the top 20 percent of their graduating class will be assured of a place in college. As in California, students who qualify by virtue of their class rank are not guaranteed a slot at their first-choice school—only at some school within the system. Largely because of the threat of referenda like Proposition 209 and I-200 and the success of constitutional challenges to preferential admissions policies, Pennsylvania and other states are now contemplating similar measures.

It is a clear step forward, in our view, to eliminate race from overt, formal consideration in the admissions process. But it is only a small step if the new policy is designed to identify criteria that are strongly correlated with race, with the process still driven by the determination to achieve a particular racial balance in the student body. Since the impetus behind the various X percent plans came from threats to the old system of racial preferences, and since the backers of the new schemes described the "preservation of diversity" as their principal aim, this appears to be the case with these schemes. It has been claimed, indeed, that Florida made the magic number twenty rather than 10 or 15 percent because its computer models showed that not enough black or Hispanic high school students would have qualified if more stringent cutoffs had been used.[164]

Can this pass muster? Suppose that when the University of Alabama was first compelled by court order to abandon its "whites-only" admissions policy, it had added a new admissions criterion that continued to exclude all, or virtually, all black applicants. This tactic could never have survived the scrutiny of a federal judge, who would have dismissed it as a subterfuge that did not meet the state's obligation to admit qualified applicants without regard for their race. Thus X-percent plans would seem highly vulnerable to constitutional challenge.

The redefinition of merit that is implicit in X-percent schemes is also disturbing. They make the superficially egalitarian assumption that being in the top 10 percent of a mediocre high school is an achievement that is comparable to being in the top tenth at Boston's Latin, New York's Bronx Science, San Francisco's Lowell High, or other superb public secondary schools. Scores on the SAT, the ACT, Advanced Placement exams, or any other test designed to assess college readiness are deliberately factored out of admissions decisions for this entire group of students. Some outstanding minority as well as majority students attending the best schools in the state will not make it into the top X percent, even though their scores on the SATs and the AP exams demonstrate that they are far more accomplished academically than those in the top fifth or tenth of their class at a mediocre school.

The larger the X in X-percent plans, the greater the likelihood that such schemes will mismatch students to institutions for which they are unqualified in the same manner that racial preferences do. How many of these students will be able to overcome the academic deficiencies they have at the age of leaving high school is open to question, and a high dropout rate seems likely.[165] The problem is compounded in the Texas version of the plan, which guarantees a place at the most competitive flagship Austin campus for all top-10-percent graduates who choose it. The colleges will make attempts to provide remedial instruction to those who are floundering, but the evidence about the performance of racially preferred students reviewed above suggests that this is not likely to have much effect. Accepting large numbers of freshmen whose academic preparation is far below the average in the entering class can only have a depressing effect on the level of instruction in general. Given the political pressures that led to the adoption of such schemes in the first place, it will be necessary to adjust demands downward so that most can meet them. This is not a formula that makes for academic excellence.

Conclusion

Bowen and Bok closed their volume with an impassioned plea for "institutional autonomy" on these matters. The leaders of our institutions of higher education, those wise steamboat pilots, have a superior understanding of society's needs, and their schools should have complete freedom to select the students who will allow them to fulfill their "mission." The plea, as Roger Clegg of the Center for Equal Opportunity has said, is "disingenuous." Surely the authors did not favor the repeal of the Civil Rights Act of 1964, which withholds federal money from private institutions engaged in discrimination and thus curtails their autonomy. "More likely," Clegg has noted, Bowen and Bok favored "a regime where discriminating against some groups (whites, Asians) is permissible, but discrimination against other groups (blacks, Hispanics) remains flatly prohibited."[166]

Perhaps the authors' most astounding argument was in their concluding warning. If colleges are forbidden to take race into account—as is now the case for public institutions in California, Texas, and Washington—they will refuse to accept the decline in black and Hispanic enrollment that will inevitably follow, Bowen and Bok claim.[167] If barred from using racial double standards, they will be compelled to lower standards across the board in order to obtain enough non-Asian minorities. Setting the admissions bar very low and then accepting students more or less randomly from a very large pool defined as qualified will yield the desired racial mix. It will also lower the intellectual level of the student body as a whole, of course, but that is the choice that elite schools will make. "It is very difficult to stop people from finding a path toward a goal in which they firmly believe," and the goal they really believe in is diversity.[168] If forced to choose, today's educational leaders will see creating a certain racial mix on campus as more important than maintaining intellectual standards.

Here we have a breathtakingly candid statement of the priorities of two of the most distinguished figures in higher education today—priorities that reflect those of the higher education establishment as a whole. Intellectual excellence should be sacrificed on the altar of diversity.

A February 2001 speech by the president of the University of California, Richard C. Atkinson, revealed that the nation's best state university system was moving that direction. Atkinson called for dropping the SAT verbal and mathematical reasoning test as a requirement for admission, and argued that "narrowly defined quantitative" measures of academic achievement should be given less weight than qualifications that could only be discerned through more "holistic" admissions procedures. It was a thinly veiled effort to get black and Hispanic enrollments up at the university.[169]

This repugnant tradeoff between intellectual excellence and racial diversity would not be necessary, of course, if we concentrated our efforts on closing the yawning racial gap in educational performance among elementary and secondary pupils. As long as the average black high school senior reads at the eighth-grade level, efforts to engineer parity in the legal and medical professions are doomed to failure. For a generation now, preferences in higher education have been a pernicious palliative that has deflected our attention from the real problem.

Notes

1. Orlando Patterson, "Race Over," *New Republic,* January 10, 2000, 6.

2. The phrase was President Kennedy's: "Radio and Television Report to the American People on Civil Rights," June 11, 1963, *Public Papers of Presidents of the United States: John F. Kennedy, January 1 to November 22, 1963* (Washington, D.C.: U.S. Government Printing Office, 1964), 468. It was echoed in Reverend King's 1963 "I Have a Dream" speech, in which he looked forward to the day when his children would be judged by "the content of their character," not by "the color of their skin."

3. William G. Bowen and Derek Bok, *The Shape of the River: Long-Term Consequences of Considering Race in College and University Admissions* (Princeton, N.J.: Princeton University Press, 1998).

4. *Plessy v. Ferguson,*163 U.S. 537 (1896), 551–52.

5. Stephan Thernstrom, *Poverty and Progress: Social Mobility in a 19th-Century City* (Cambridge, Mass.: Harvard University Press, 1964). Chapter 3 describes the mobility ideology that has long been an article of faith with most Americans.

6. The best account of the act is Hugh Graham Davis, *The Civil Rights Era: Origins and Development of National Policy* (New York: Oxford University Press, 1990).

7. *Regents of the Univ. of Calif. v. Bakke,* 438 U.S. 407 (1978).

8. Timothy Maguire, "My Bout with Affirmative Action," *Commentary,* April 1992, 50–52.

9. Anthony T. Pierce, Leslie M. Turner, Steven M. Hilton, "Degrees of Success; With Law School, Graduating Is the Test," *The Washington Post,* May 8, 1991, A31.

10. *Hopwood v. Texas,* 78 F.3d 932 (5th Cir. 1996).

11. The relevant evidence available through the end of 1996 is summarized and evaluated in Stephan Thernstrom and Abigail Thernstrom, *America in Black and White: One Nation, Indivisible* (New York: Simon and Schuster, 1997), ch. 14.

12. Draft of a letter from Dean Mark Yudoff to Clara Meek, 18 May 1988, written by Associate Dean Guy Wellborn, in possession of the author. The associate dean was much more candid than his boss. Dean Yudoff made a great many changes in the draft, all of them designed to obscure the painful truths set forth in the draft version.

13. Editorial, "The Facts about Affirmative Action," *The New York Times*, Sept. 14, 1998, A32. For further documentation on this point, see our essay, "Reflections on *The Shape of the River*," *UCLA Law Review* 46 (June 1999), 1583–1631; see notes 12–14. Much of the material that follows is drawn from this paper. However, we have incorporated new evidence at many points, and also take up certain issues not addressed there.

14. Peter Schrag, "Muddy Waters," *American Prospect*, Mar.–Apr. 1999, 82.

15. Bowen and Bok, *Shape of the River*, xxv.

16. *Ibid.*, 116.

17. *Ibid.*, xxiv–xxv.

18. Andrew W. Mellon Foundation, "Policies Concerning the College and Beyond Database, Aug. 27, 1998" (on file with authors). The document stresses that "the data were obtained from the participating institutions and the surveyed individuals under conditions of strictest confidentiality," and spells out detailed security procedures that would seem more appropriate for the Manhattan Project than for studies of contemporary college life. If those who stand at the helm of our elite institutions of higher education today are as proud as they claim to be of the preferential policies they pursue, why are they so obsessed with preserving confidentiality? For all of their rhetoric about their invaluable contribution to public life, are remarkably secretive about how they select their students.

The guidelines specify that investigators "must be persons of the highest integrity," whose research will be "of the highest quality." One wonders if there is a political test one must pass to measure up to these subjective standards. The foundation will provide access only when the research in question "promises to bring substantial 'added value' to other research that has been done or is in progress," so that "all research done with the College and Beyond (C&B) database will form a research agenda that is at least broadly coordinated." Translation: If you want to lay your hands on this evidence, you better get with the program. Would research by investigators critical of preferential policies be deemed likely to bring enough "added value" and to fit properly in the foundation's research agenda? The president of the Mellon Foundation would not have to be an unusually vain author to feel that research whose conclusions clashed with those he advanced in his book offered little "added value."

Perhaps most striking, the guidelines say that:

> Requests for access to the data for the purpose of replicating results developed by other researchers [that is to say, Bowen and Bok] must go beyond a general desire to recheck results; they should instead offer sound reasons for believing that there is a likelihood of error or

misinterpretation in the work of others, or that the . . . result of one researcher contradicts the result of another, or that certain results are so counterintuitive as to be in need of further verification and/or clarification.

Would an application that sought to evaluate some of the criticisms of *The Shape of the River* set forth in the present article be judged inappropriate as motivated by nothing more than a "general desire to recheck results?" Is not the concept of rechecking and replicating results fundamental to scientific inquiry?

19. John L. Pulley, "Mellon Fund, From the Top Down, Conducts the 'R&D of Education': The Foundation Backs Projects to Support the Humanities and Affirmative Action," *Chronicle of Higher Education*, October 1, 1999.

20. "A Research Proposal Using the College and Beyond (C&B) Database," by Robert Lerner, Ph.D., in association with the Center for Equal Opportunity, November 17, 1999; Letter from Richard E. Quandt of the Mellon Foundation to Robert Lerner, December 14, 1999 (both in possession of the authors).

21. This criticism is well developed in Robert Lerner's "The Empire Strikes Back," in *Three Views of the River* (Washington, D.C.: Center for Equal Opportunity, 1998), 3, 22–23.

22. U.S. Department of Health, Education, and Welfare, *Equality of Educational Opportunity* (Washington, D.C.: U.S. Government Printing Office, 1966). For some of the reanalysis, see Frederick Mosteller and Daniel P. Moynihan, eds., *On Equality of Educational Opportunity* (New York: Vintage, 1972).

23. Bowen and Bok, *Shape of the River*, v, xxii.

24. *Ibid.*, xxi, xxii, 51–52.

25. For the view that the SATs are altogether pernicious, see Nicolas Lemann, *The Big Test: The Secret History of the American Meritocracy* (New York: Farrar, Straus and Giroux, 1999). For a thorough critical appraisal, see Stephan Thernstrom, "Status Anxiety," *National Review*, December 6, 1999.

26. Bowen and Bok, *Shape of the River*, xxiii, n. 6.

27. Marcia Graham Synnott, *The Half-Opened Door: Discrimination and Admissions at Harvard, Yale, and Princeton, 1900–1970* (Westport, Conn.: Greenwood Press, 1979), 225–31.

28. It is interesting that, despite the authors' dismissive comments about selecting students by means of "formulaic calculations" (52), their sole basis for determining which schools qualified as SEL-1, -2, or -3 was the average SAT scores of their students.

29. The full list of schools in each category is supplied in *Shape of the River* at 339, Table B.1.

30. *Ibid.*, 295, Table A.2.

31. In 1995, there were 2,244 four-year institutions of higher education and another 1,462 two-year schools in the United States, for a total of 3,706); U.S. Bureau of the Census, *Statistical Abstract of the United States:1998* (Washington, D.C.: U.S. Government Printing Office, 1999), Table 306.

32. Bowen and Bok, *Shape of the River*, 17 and n. 4.

33. Michael T. Nettles ed., *The African American Education Data Book, Volume I: Higher and Adult Education*, (Fairfax, Va.: Frederick D. Patterson Research Institute of the College Fund/UNCF 1997), 184. Clifford Adelman, "The Rest of the River," *University Business* 2 (Jan.–Feb. 1999): 42–45.

34. Adelman, "The Rest of the River," 44.

35. Consider this analogy. Private elementary and secondary schools educate 11.2 percent of all pupils in the nation (*Statistical Abstract of the US: 1998*, 161.) They are significant in American educational life, but a study of elementary and secondary education that focused exclusively on them would not reveal much about the system as a whole.

36. *Statistical Abstract of the United States: 2000*, 22.

37. In 1999, 88.7 percent of blacks aged 25–29 had high school diplomas, as compared with 93.0 percent of non-Hispanic whites; National Center for Educational Statistics, *The Condition of Education 2000* (Washington, D.C.: U.S. Government Printing Office, 2000), 154, Table 38.1

38. See the scores for 1992 freshmen at thirteen selective institutions given in Table 9, Chapter 13 of Thernstrom and Thernstrom, *America in Black and White*, 408. Such evidence is closely guarded and is very difficult to obtain. However, the Center for Equal Opportunity (CEO) has been using state freedom of information laws to obtain the data from public institutions in several states. Eight reports are now available, examining Virginia, Washington, North Carolina, Michigan, Colorado, the U.S. service academies at West Point and Annapolis, the University of California at Berkeley, and the University of California at San Diego. Racial double standards of this order of magnitude have turned up everywhere that the CEO has looked. At the University of Colorado at Boulder, for example, the average black freshman had an SAT score 205 points below that of his or her white classmates. CEO reports are available at <http://www.ceousa.org>.

39. Bowen and Bok, *Shape of the River*, 17–23.

40. Lerner offers an excellent discussion of this point in "The Empire Strikes Back." The size of the black-white difference in mean scores, he argues, is itself a useful indicator of the extent of racial preferences, even if it is imperfect. Common sense tells us that the larger the difference, the more likely that racial preferences played a part in admissions because such preferences lower the average black score and grade point average (GPA) from what they would have been under a race-neutral system. "When racial preferences are removed, the differences in test scores and grades may not vanish totally but they will decline substantially." All statistical studies of discrimination have a common problem: the somewhat arbitrary nature of the decision that X difference in mean scores provides strong evidence of preferential treatment (i.e., discrimination).

41. Bowen and Bok, *Shape of the River*, 27, Figure 2.5.

42. Farrell Bloch, *Antidiscrimination Law and Minority Employment* (Chicago: University of Chicago Press, 1994), *passim*.

43. Bowen and Bok, *Shape of the River*, 26–27.

44. *Regents of the Univ. of Cal. v. Bakke*, 438 U.S. at 317–18.

45. Bowen and Bok, *Shape of the River*, 19, 256.

46. *Ibid.*, 30. The review that appeared in *The Nation* unaccountably found this comparison "very clever." See David Karen, "Go to the Head of the Class," *The Nation*, November 16, 1998, 46–48.

47. Bowen and Bok, *Shape of the River*, 18–19.

48. *Ibid.*, 375, Table D.2.1; 350, Table B.4.

49. See the Center for Equal Opportunity reports on Virginia and Michigan. Given the overwhelmingly strong preferences at Michigan, it is hardly surprising that the university is presently in court attempting to explain how its discriminatory admissions policies can be squared with the Fourteenth Amendment; Stephan Thernstrom, "Alamo in Ann Arbor," *National Review*, September 13, 1999.

50. Bowen and Bok, *Shape of the River*, 41, Figure 2.11. Although the discussion in the text does not make it clear, these estimates are based on *verbal* SAT scores alone. If *math* SAT scores were used instead, the drop in black enrollments would be appreciably higher—58.5 percent rather than 49.3 percent for the entire sample, and 80.0 percent rather than 73.2 percent at SEL-1 schools (Table B.4). Because it is sometimes asserted that verbal tests are culturally biased against minorities, it is interesting to note that African Americans are even less well represented at the top of the distribution of the math SATs than they are among top scorers on the verbal portion of the exam. Presumably mathematics questions are more culture free than ones designed to test verbal skills.

51. *Ibid.*, 42–44. Although the typical black students attending C&B schools came from middle-class homes, the authors demonstrate, they were still more likely than whites to benefit from any breaks given on the basis of socioeconomic disadvantage; 341, Table B.2. Perhaps more important is the strong correlation between athletic ability and race in the applicant pool of selective institutions. They employ markedly lower admissions standards in judging varsity athletes and provide them with full financial support. It happens that blacks get a highly disproportionate share of these slots; see the evidence in our *UCLA Law Review* essay, note 66.

The substantial presence of black athletes on campus may be an important part of the reason that Bowen and Bok estimated that eliminating race as a factor in admissions but continuing to use extra-academic criteria would do little to narrow the racial gap in SAT scores. The average score of those who would have been rejected would be only 36 points lower than the score of those accepted, they calculate; Bowen and Bok, *Shape of the River*, 42. Putting athletes with very weak academic records into the category of those who would have been admitted under race-neutral standards pulls down the average score of the group, and minimizes the difference between the accepted and rejected groups.

Bowen and Bok admit that if they had followed their earlier method and estimated the SAT gap by assuming admissions based on test scores alone, the gain in the average score of admitted blacks would have been "much greater" (43).

Their failure to specify precisely *how much greater*, though, makes it more likely that readers will miss the changed meaning they give to "race-neutral" at this point.

Thus the authors equate race-neutral standards with SAT-determined standards in projecting a worrisome decline of black enrollment. But when they seek to counter the argument that applying higher academic standards to black applicants will improve their average quality and narrow the racial gap on campus, they redefine race-neutral standards so as to allow the continued enrollment of large numbers of black students with marginal academic qualifications but other strengths (compare 41 with 42–43). They try to have it both ways by playing fast and loose with definitions. For solid evidence that the use of race-neutral standards at the University of California at Berkeley has closed the racial gap in SAT scores far more than Bowen and Bok's estimate, see note 153 below.

52. *Ibid.*, 42.

53. *Ibid.*, 256, 376, Table D.3.1, and 378, Table D.3.2.

54. For a classic statement of the theory, focused on law school admissions, see Clyde W. Summers, "Preferential Admissions: An Unreal Solution to a Real Problem," *University of Toledo Law Review*, 1970, 377. For an equally incisive and prescient statement from the same perspective, see Thomas Sowell, *Black Education: Myths and Tragedies* (New York: David McKay, 1972), particularly Part II, "Black Students in White Colleges." More recent accounts stressing the costs of preferential policies, based partly upon the personal experiences of the authors, include Stephen L. Carter, *Reflections of an Affirmative Action Baby* (New York: Basic Books, 1991); Shelby Steele, *The Content of Our Character: A New Vision of Race in America* (New York: St. Martin's Press,1990); and Shelby Steele, *A Dream Deferred: The Second Betrayal of Black Freedom in America* (New York: HarperCollins, 1998); John McWhorter, *Losing the Race: Self-Sabotage in Black America* (New York: Basic Books, 2000).

55. Bowen and Bok, *Shape of the River*, 61, Figure 3.3. The mean combined SAT score for all college-bound seniors in 1989 was 903; U.S. Bureau of the Census, *Statistical Abstract of the United States: 1991* (Washington, D.C.: U.S. Government Printing Office, 1992), 154. Bowen and Bok draw large conclusions here on the basis of very few cases. Their tables regrettably do not provide the numbers from which the percentages were calculated, but buried in an appendix is the information that just sixty-seven black students entering the eight SEL-1 schools in 1989, a mere 10 percent of the total, had math scores below 500. And only 105, or 16 percent of the total, scored that poorly on the verbals (350, Table B.4). The number whose combined SAT fell below 1000 was thus likely no more than 70–80.

Not only are the numbers from which they generalize very small. We also cannot assume that these few students were indistinguishable from those who had comparably low SAT scores, but attended less selective institutions. How many of them were star athletes, who made it through with a little help from an armada of tutors employed by an athletic department desperately eager to keep up the eligibility of anyone who might help win "The Game"? Others doubtless had something else special going for them, which is precisely why they were admitted to such highly competitive schools despite having test scores that would seem to disqualify them.

56. The median GPA of the college students who had graduated from high school in 1982 was 3.14 in highly selective schools, 2.97 in less selective institutions, and 2.86 in schools that were not selective at all; Adelman, "The Rest of the River," 46. A professor who has spent many years teaching at the University of Michigan Law School has candidly suggested that one cause of grade inflation at elite schools is the reluctance of faculty members to give discouragingly low grades to black students; Terrance Sandalow, "Minority Preferences Reconsidered," *Michigan Law Review*, 97 (May 1999); Editorial, "Making the Grade for Real," *Chicago Tribune*, June 14, 1994, § 1, 22.

57. Bowen and Bok, *Shape of the River*, 49, Figure 2.12 and 341, Table B.2.

58. In a book that is so packed with detail on many points, it is odd and regrettable that this interesting information on the socioeconomic background of black students at C&B schools is not broken down by levels of school selectivity. Impressionistic evidence suggests that black students at SEL-1 schools are overwhelmingly from upper-middle-class families.

59. *Ibid.*, 376, Table D.3.1.

60. Bowen and Bok calculate two graduation rates—a "first-school" rate for those who took a degree at the college they first entered, and an overall rate, which includes those who dropped out of their first school but did graduate from some institution. We use the latter figure in this discussion.

61. National data on graduation rates broken down by race are scanty. The best source is the National Collegiate Athletic Association (NCAA), which publishes an annual report on this subject. The latest such report indicates that 37 percent of the black freshmen who enrolled in an NCAA Division I school in 1992–93 had earned a bachelor's degree by 1999. The figure for whites was 59 percent. Hence the white dropout rate was 41 percent, while the black rate was 63 percent, 54 percent higher; National Collegiate Athletic Association, *1999 NCAA Division I Graduation-Rates Report*, 636.

62. Bowen and Bok, *Shape of the River*, 376, Table D.3.1.

63. *Economic Report of the President:1998*, 331 Table B-43.

64. Thomas R. Phillips, *ABET/EXXON Minority Engineering Student Achievement Profile*, unpublished study for the Accreditation Board for Engineering and Technology, Inc., May 1991. (We are grateful to Scott Miller for providing us with a copy.) The results of this study are reported in considerable detail in L. Scott Miller, *An American Imperative: Accelerating Minority Educational Advancement* (New Haven, Conn.: Yale University Press, 1995), 74–79. Although this very important book appears in the bibliography for *The Shape of the River*, the authors make no reference at all to the minority engineering student evidence, which runs strongly counter to their argument.

65. Phillips, *Minority Student Achievement Profile*, 75.

66. McWhorter, *Losing the Race*, 177.

67. Miller, *An American Imperative*, 79–81 summarizes the literature on this point. Walter Allen's study of 31,000 students enrolled at the University of Michigan between 1975 and 1981 found that the average GPA for white students was 3.24, and 3.22 for Asian Americans. The average for blacks was a dismal 2.24; Allen, "Black Students in U.S. Higher Education: Toward Improved Access," *Urban Review* 20 (Fall 1988).

68. Bowen and Bok estimate (350, Table B.4) that 1,101 of the 2,171 black students entering C&B institutions in 1989 would have been accepted if verbal SAT scores had been the only criterion used, resulting in a decline of 49 percent). Strangely, they also estimate that black enrollment would decline by precisely 49 percent at the five schools they studied in detail if race-neutral policies, but not SAT-driven policies, were implemented (42). That suggests that the five are not representative of the twenty-eight C&B schools, because depending upon SAT scores alone would have produced a much bigger drop than race-neutral polices that allowed other nonacademic factors to operate.

69. At a later point, the authors do divide their 1976 cohort (but not the later one) into those who would have been rejected and those who would have been accepted under a "race-neutral" standard; *Ibid.*, 281. Here they are again using the term loosely to mean admissions based purely on SAT scores. But they offer no consideration of differences in the academic performance of the two groups of black students.

70. Rogers Elliott et al., "The Role of Ethnicity in Choosing and Leaving Science in Highly Selective Institutions," *Research in Higher Education* 37 (1996): 681, 695–96. This is a study of four Ivy League schools that are not named. Judging from the acknowledgments, it would appear that three of the four were Dartmouth, Cornell, and Brown.

71. Bowen and Bok, *Shape of the River*, 77.

72. Miller, *An American Imperative*, 80–81 cites a number of studies that reveal this "overprediction" of black academic performance, and declares that "we should take these findings very seriously." A number of earlier studies that make the same point are reviewed in Robert Klitgaard, *Choosing Elites* (New York: Basic Books, 1985), 160–65.

73. Ronald F. Ferguson, "Teachers' Perceptions and Expectations and the Black-White Test Score Gap," in *The Black-White Test Score Gap*, 300.

74. *Ibid.*

75. Bowen and Bok, *Shape of the River*, 267.

76. Michael Shumsky, "Wesleyan's Example Proves Harvard's Wisdom," *Harvard Salient*, Oct. 26, 1998, 7 (quoting the Wesleyan University Office of Residential Life).

77. "Taking Steps to Curtail Black Student Self-Segregation at Harvard College," *Journal of Blacks in Higher Education*, Spring 1997, 14.

78. Although they agreed not to identify individual schools from their sample, they could have referred to College X and College Y, for example. But

throughout the book the only distinctions they make among C&B schools are between SEL-1, SEL-2, and SEL-3 institutions.

79. Bowen and Bok, *Shape of the River*, 265. Moreover,

> [m]ore than a few black students unquestionably suffer some degree of discomfort from being beneficiaries of the admissions process . . . . It is for this reason that many high-achieving black graduates continue to seek reassurance that they have "made it on their own" and why they complain when job interviewers presume that even the most outstanding black student may well have been helped in this way.

One wonders why Bowen and Bok do not take this damning admission more seriously. It is never mentioned in their conclusion.

80. *Ibid.*

81. *Ibid.*, 196, Figure 7.1.

82. In *Reflections of an Affirmative Action Baby*, Stephen Carter reports that he applied to the Harvard Law School in the late 1970s and received a form letter rejecting him. A few days later, though, he was called by two different officials of the school and by a professor as well, all of whom assured him that the negative decision had been an "error" and apologized profusely for the mistake. They had refused him admission initially, he was told, because "we assumed from your record that you were white" (15). He felt "insulted by this miracle. Stephen Carter, the white male, was not good enough for the Harvard Law School; Stephen Carter, the black male, not only was good enough but rated agonized telephone calls urging him to attend" (16). We see nothing in the C&B survey questions (315–35) that would have given respondents the opportunity to register the feelings that Carter describes here. It is not clear how Harvard Law School officials missed the fact that Carter was an African American in the first place, because the university has been as zealous as others in gathering racial and ethnic data about applicants. Until it abandoned the practice a few years ago out of fear of litigation, the Harvard Graduate School of Arts and Sciences inserted a special green form in each application from candidates identified as being black, Mexican American, Puerto Rican, or American Indian. The form advised departments that the student in question would receive full financial support if judged admissible at all, and that the aid would not be charged to the department's fellowship budget. See Elena Neuman, "Harvard's Sins of Admission," *Weekly Standard*, October 9, 1995, 22.

83. Claude M. Steele and Joshua Aronson, "Stereotype Threat and the Test Performance of Academically Successful African Americans," in Jencks and Phillips, *Black-White Test Score Gap*, 401–27.

84. Bowen & Bok, *Shape of the River*, 99–100.

85. *Ibid.*, 102, Figure 4.4.

86. *Ibid.*, 103.

87. The most recent results on the standard tests required in medical schools, law schools, business schools, and Ph.D. programs are reported in Wayne J. Camara and Amy Elizabeth Schmidt, *Group Differences in Standardized Testing and Social Stratification*, College Board Report No. 99-5 (New York: College Entrance Examination Board, 1999), Table 1. Whether one looks at the Medical College Admissions Test, the Law School Admissions Test, the Graduate Management Admissions Test, or the Graduate Record Examination, the results are the same. On all of these tests, the mean score for blacks is about a full standard deviation below the mean score for whites. That means that the average black test-taker performed no better than whites who scored in the *sixteenth* percentile. Five out of six whites thus outperformed the average black. And only one out of six blacks scored above the average white.

88. John E. Morris, "Boalt Hall's Affirmative Action Dilemma," *American Lawyer*, November 1997, 7. This level of achievement is high, but by no means spectacular. At the law schools ranked as the top six by *U.S. News and World Report*, a student with an LSAT score of 164 would have been in the bottom quartile of those accepted; "Schools of Law," *U.S. News and World Report, Best Graduate Schools: 1998*, 47. The highest-ranked school at which the average student scored below 164 was number fifteen on the list, the University of Southern California.

89. "Calculating the Effect of a Rollback in Affirmative Action on the Nation's Major MBA Programs," *Journal of Blacks in Higher Education* (Winter 1997–98): 6–8.

90. Linda F. Wightman, "The Threat to Diversity in Legal Education: An Empirical Analysis of the Consequences of Abandoning Race as a Factor in Law School Admission Decisions," *New York University Law Review* 72 (1997): 1, 30, Table 6. For an extended critique of this paper that contends that the author has badly misinterpreted the valuable statistical data she provides, see Stephan Thernstrom, "Diversity and Meritocracy in Legal Education: A Critical Evaluation of Linda F. Wightman's 'The Threat to Diversity in Legal Education,'" *Constitutional Commentary* 11 (1998): 13–39. Wightman's top-tier schools, which she designates as "Cluster 1," are the eighteen of the 163 American Bar Association (ABA) approved law schools included in her study that were most selective and had the highest mean LSAT scores and undergraduate GPAs in their entering classes.

Another illuminating study of law school admissions has been conducted by Michael David Shumsky, who examined data on 771 Harvard College undergraduates who applied to one of the top five law schools (Harvard, Yale, Stanford, NYU, and Columbia) in 1997, 1998, or 1999. Looking only at Harvard students controlled for the quality of undergraduate training. He found that, holding GPAs and LSAT scores constant, a black applicant to these top schools was 80.1 percent more likely to be admitted than a white with the same qualifications; Michael David Shumsky, "How Much Does Race Impact the Probability of Admission to an Elite Law School? New Evidence on Affirmative Action from the Law Services Action Reports," unpublished paper, Harvard College, January 1999 (in possession of the authors).

91. Bowen and Bok, *Shape of the River*, 41, Figure 2.11. Of course there are many more freshmen at elite colleges than first-year students at top law schools, but the point still stands. Many black students from the very best colleges do apply to law school.

92. In an article on law schools written since their book was published, Bowen and Bok allude to Wightman's study (without naming it) in support of their claim that race is merely "one factor in making admissions decisions." See Derek Bok and William G. Bowen, "Access to Success," *American Bar Association Journal*, February 1999, 62–63. If preferential admissions serve to multiply the number of black applicants accepted at top law schools more than seventeen-fold, calling race "one factor" seems a considerable understatement

93. Thernstrom, "Diversity and Meritocracy in Legal Education," 32.

94. Wightman's paper is cited no fewer than seven times in *Shape of the River*. In a more recent article written specifically for a legal audience, Bowen and Bok allude to Wightman's estimate that black law school enrollments would drop sharply in the absence of preferential admissions but again ignore entirely the disappointing performance of preferentially admitted black students on the bar examinations; Bowen and Bok, "Access to Success," 63.

95. Wightman, "The Threat to Diversity," 36, Table 7.

96. *Ibid.*, 38, Table 8.

97. Thernstrom, "Diversity and Meritocracy in Legal Education," 40, Table 5. This evidence is tabulated from data supplied in Wightman, "Threat to Diversity," Tables 7 and 8 (36, 38).

98. Bowen and Bok, *Shape of the River*, 281.

99. Beth Dawson et al., "Performance on the National Board of Medical Examiners Part I Examination by Men and Women of Different Race and Ethnicity," *Journal of the American Medical Association* 272 (1994): 674, 675, Table 1. Many of those who fail the Part I exam apparently retake it until they eventually pass; we have been unable to find any figures on the exact proportion. In any event, it is reasonable to wonder if physicians who had to work long and hard just to scrape by after several attempts will be capable of keeping up with the rapid accumulation of knowledge in their specialty in the future. For a sobering personal account from a medical school professor about the controversy over lowering academic standards at a leading medical school in the 1970s in order to keep preferentially admitted students from flunking out, see Bernard D. Davis, "Affirmative Action and *Veritas* at Harvard Medical School," in *Storm over Biology: Essays on Science, Sentiment, and Public Policy* (Buffalo, N.Y.: Prometheus Books, 1986).

100. Steven N. Keith et al., *Assessing the Outcome of Affirmative Action in Medical Schools: A Study of the Class of 1975*, Series No. R-3481-CWF (Santa Monica, Calif.: The RAND Corporation, 1987). The "minority" category in the study consisted of African Americans, Hispanics, and American Indians.

101. Bowen and Bok, *Shape of the River*, 13, n. 56.

102. Keith, *Assessing the Outcome of Affirmative Action*, 36, Table 27.

103. *Ibid.*

104. Robert C. Davidson and Ernest L. Lewis, "Affirmative Action and Other Special Consideration Admissions at the University of California, Davis, School of Medicine," *Journal of the American Medical Association*, 278 (1997): 1153. Among the many glaring flaws in this much-publicized study, the most important is that it does not in fact examine students admitted to medical school as a result of racial preferences—which is, of course, the issue of public concern. It reports on the performance of *all* students admitted to the school for extra-academic reasons. Only 43 percent of the students so classified belonged to an "under-represented" racial group, and the authors fail to provide any numerical break-downs by race. We cannot assume that the same preferences were given to the two groups—those admitted on racial grounds and those admitted for other "special" reasons—nor can we assume that they performed similarly. Wightman's study shows that whites in the category "not admissible" on academic grounds were not at all comparable to African Americans or other racial minorities in that category; "Threat to Diversity," Tables 7 and 8 (36, 38). Wightman's findings about law school completion and bar exam passage rates strongly suggest that "not admissible" blacks were much weaker academically than "not admissible" whites. The failure of the authors of the Davis study to distinguish racial groups within the "special considerations admissions" category renders their study completely irrelevant to current policy debates.

Furthermore, even if we accepted the highly dubious assumption that students admitted to medical school as a result of racial preferences did not differ from those admitted for other reasons under the "special considerations" category, the performance of special admits at Davis was much less impressive than the authors would have us believe. These students had much lower grades in medical school than those regularly admitted, were only a third as likely to be selected for the medical honors society, and were six times as likely to fail Part I of the medical boards (1156). Even the claim of the authors that "special considerations" students performed as well as regular admits in their residencies is questionable; we are not told enough about the rating process to be confident that this is true. For these and other criticisms, see Gail Heriot, Op-ed, "Doctored Affirmative Action Data," *The Wall Street Journal*, October 15, 1997, A22.

105. The investigators commissioned the National Opinion Research Center (NORC) to conduct a national survey of persons who had been eighteen years of age in either 1951 or 1976, to parallel the C&B survey of matriculants; *Shape of the River*, 310–12. For reasons unspecified, no attempt was made to create a similar control group to employ in analyzing the survey of 1989 matriculants. Remarkably little use is made of the NORC information, and the points made from it are unpersuasive; see our *UCLA Law Review* essay, note 121.

106. Stacy Berg Dale and Alan B. Krueger, "Estimating the Payoff to Attending a More Selective College: An Application of Selection on Observables and Unobservables," Working Paper #409, Industrial Relations Section, Prince-

ton University, July 1999. The authors had access to the C&B data because Berg is on the staff of the Mellon Foundation. In this instance, the foundation permitted research by trusted insiders that yielded an unexpected heretical result. This has not made it any more willing to provide access to the data to researchers who do not share the foundation's enthusiasm for racially preferential policies.

107. Bowen and Bok, *Shape of the River*, 291, n.2. The only explanation offered for dropping the HBCs from the study is that examining them "was beyond the scope of this study, which is concerned only with colleges and universities that enroll substantial numbers of white students as well as minority students." This assumes that it would not be of analytical interest to find out how much of a difference it makes to attend an elite white school as opposed to one of the best predominantly black colleges, holding all other factors (family status, SAT scores, and the like) constant.

108. *Black Enterprise* commissioned the survey to develop a list of the "Top Fifty Colleges for African Americans"; Thomas LaVeist and Marjorie Whigham-Désir, "Top 50 Colleges for African Americans," *Black Enterprise*, January 1999, 71.

109. We could not locate a similar guide for 1989, but *U.S. News and World Report*'s "America's Best Colleges: 1998" indicates that Spelman, ranked number one in the *Black Enterprise* survey, accepted 54 percent of its applicants in 1997–98, and that the combined SAT score for a freshman at the seventy-fifth percentile of the class was only 1170. Yale, by contrast, accepted only 18 percent of applicants, and a student at the twenty-fifth percentile had a 1360 SAT, almost 200 points above those at the *seventy-fifth* percentile at Spelman.

110. Bowen and Bok, *Shape of the River*, 277, n.1.

111. *Ibid.*, 6–11.

112. *Ibid.*, 116.

113. For different ways of estimating the size of the black middle class, see Thernstrom and Thernstrom, *America in Black and White*, 183–202. One possible criterion is having attended college; in 1995 some 37.5 percent of blacks aged 25 or older had gone to college, and of those aged 25 to 29, 44.9 percent had gone to college (192, 391). These results square pretty well with the finding that 44 percent of African Americans identified themselves as "middle class" in a 1994 national survey, and 41 percent of those in a 1996 survey did the same (200).

114. Bowen and Bok, *Shape of the River*, 1–3.

115. *Ibid.*, 10.

116. Michael Barone and Grant Ujifusa, *The Almanac of American Politics: 1998* (Washington, D.C.: The National Journal, 1998).

117. "The Higher Education of African Americans in Senior Posts in the U.S. Executive Branch," *Journal of Blacks in Higher Education* (Spring 1998): 58–59.

118. "The Higher Education of President Clinton's Black Judges," *Journal of Blacks in Higher Education* (Autumn 1996): 29.

119. *African American Education Data Book*, 193.

120. National Research Council, *Summary Report 1996: Doctorate Recipients from United States Universities* (Washington, D.C.: National Academy Press, 1998), 42, Table 9.

121. Rogers Elliott notes that "of the top 21 undergraduate producers of black Ph.D.s [in science] during the period 1986–1993, 17 were [HBCs] and none were among the 30 or so most selective institutions that so successfully recruit the most talented black secondary school graduates"; Elliott, "The Role of Ethnicity," 700. He then proceeds to demonstrate, with data from eleven private colleges, that for students with comparatively low SAT math scores, the *less* selective the school the *more* likely it is that they will complete an undergraduate degree in science (701–02). As the evidence in the preceding note suggests, this pattern seems to hold for doctorates in the humanities and social sciences as well.

It should also be noted that Elliott's analysis of patterns of black concentration in science in four Ivy League schools raises questions about Bowen and Bok's finding that black students were about as likely as whites to major in physical science; Bowen and Bok, *Shape of the River*, 71, 382, Table D.3.5. Elliott found that a fairly high proportion of African Americans entered school planning on a science major, but that attrition took a very heavy toll. For one thing, 15 percent of the blacks intending on a science concentration dropped out of school altogether, more than triple the white dropout rate (692, Table 2). Bowen and Bok missed all such cases because they only tabulated these figures for those who graduated, not for all who entered. Second, only 34 percent of the African Americans intending on majoring in science in the Elliott study actually did so; two-thirds of them shifted to a softer field of concentration. By contrast, 61 percent of the whites who began as science majors graduated with degrees in science. We do not know if similar attrition happened at Bowen and Bok's schools as well because the authors only look at what field students ended up majoring in. All of the four schools in the Elliott study were SEL-1s; perhaps black students at SEL-2 and -3 schools were more successful in completing science majors. Bowen and Bok provide no breakdowns of this data by levels of institutional selectivity.

122. "A Review of Blacks Who Have Received the Coveted MacArthur Genius Award," *Journal of Blacks in Higher Education* (Summer 1998): 30–31.

123. *Ibid.*, 31.

124. Stanley Rothman and Amy E. Blac, "Who Rules Now? American Elites in the 1990s," *Society* 35 (September/October 1998): 17–20.

125. Bowen and Bok, *Shape of the River*, 156–57.

126. One of us served on the Harvard College Faculty Admissions Committee for several years and was struck by the heavy weight admissions officers gave to the extracurricular activities of applicants.

127. *Ibid.*, 280.

128. *Ibid.*

129. *Ibid.*, 233, Table 8.3.

130. "Views on Race in America," *Boston Globe*, September 14, 1997, A31 (reporting on a June 1997 poll by KRC Communications).

131. The figure has risen dramatically over the past generation; see the evidence summarized in Thernstrom and Thernstrom, *America in Black and White*, 520–22. Of course, having "friends," or "good friends," of another race is not identical to "knowing well" two or more classmates of another race. But they are not different enough to justify the authors' assumption that elite colleges lead the nation as a whole on this count. In addition, as Lerner points out, it is a "well-established principle that it is equal-status contact among persons of different races that reduces intergroup prejudice" ; Lerner, "Empire Strikes Back,"19. Admitting students under a racial double standard produces contact between students who arrive at college with *un*equal status.

132. Nathan Glazer, *We Are All Multiculturalists Now* (Cambridge, Mass.: Harvard University Press, 1997), 1–21.

133. Bowen and Bok, *Shape of the River*, 224, Table 8.1.

134. *Ibid.*

135. Ben Gose, "Most Students Oppose Racial Preferences in Admissions, Survey Finds," *Chronicle of Higher Education*, May 5, 2000, A52.

136. Bowen and Bok, *Shape of the River*, xxv.

137. Gose, "Most Students."

138. For a provocative elaboration of the point that "[e]verybody talks about diversity, but no one knows what it means," see Jim Chen, "Diversity in a Different Dimension: Evolutionary Theory and Affirmative Action's Destiny," *Ohio State Law Journal* 59 (1998): 811, 815, 821–29. In striking down a race-based admissions system at the Boston Latin School, the First Circuit criticized the highly abstract and generalized use of the concept of diversity by school officials, and concluded that the policy under attack was, "at bottom, a mechanism for racial balancing," which it concluded was "almost always constitutionally forbidden." See *Wessmann v. Gittens*, 160 F.3d 790, 799 (1st Cir. 1998). Bowen and Bok are as casual and vague as the representatives of the Boston School Committee were in asserting that the race-based policies they favor are essential to making schools properly diverse.

139. Bowen and Bok, *Shape of the River*, xxii–xxiii.

140. For instance, a remarkable four out of ten students in the Harvard class of 1986 were the offspring of physicians, attorneys, or college professors, three groups that made up just 1.7 percent of the labor force. A mere 5.5 percent had parents who were manual workers or farmers, roughly half of the U.S. population. The little that the vast majority of Harvard students know about "how the other half lives" comes from reading a book; Stephan Thernstrom, "Poor but Hopeful Scholars," in Bernard Bailyn et al. eds., *Glimpses of the Harvard Past* (Cambridge. Mass.: Harvard University Press, 1986), 115, 125.

141. Bowen and Bok, *Shape of the River*, 24, 286, n.12.

142. *Ibid.*, 41, Figure 2.11.

143. Figures for all the Ivy League schools, including the four out of eight that were not in the C&B sample (Brown, Cornell, Dartmouth, and Harvard), were

calculated from NCAA data; *1997 NCAA Division I Graduation-Rates Report*. We were unable to locate a similar report for 1989, but the 1997 figures cannot have been dramatically different.

144. Bowen and Bok, *Shape of the River*, 30, Figure 2.6.

145. For a review of the University of California (UC) admissions numbers immediately after the end of preferences and an analysis of the highly slanted press coverage of the story, see Stephan Thernstrom, "Farewell to Preferences?" *Public Interest* (Winter 1998).

146. Bowen and Bok, *Shape of the River*, 32–33.

147. Kenneth R. Weiss, "Fewer Blacks and Latinos Enroll at UC," *The Los Angeles Times*, May 21, 1998, A3.

148. Gail Heriot, "Equal Opportunity Works: The End of Racial Preferences in California Has Been an Unheralded Success," *Weekly Standard*, April 17, 2000, 19.

149. For evidence that this has become the case at the UC Riverside campus in the postpreferences era, see James Traub, "The Class of Prop. 209," *New York Times Magazine*, May 2, 1999, 44.

150. The figures are reported in Kenneth R. Weiss, "Asian Americans Lead in Entry to Top UC Campuses," *Los Angeles Times*, April 4, 2000, A3. It is possible, alas, that the rebound in the admission numbers for "underrepresented minorities" at the University of California means that admissions offers are evading the law and still using race in their decisions. For a disturbing report from the University of Washington, where administrators seem determined to frustrate the will of the voters as expressed in I-200, a version of Proposition 209 passed in 1998, see Siobhan Gorman, "After University Action," *National Journal*, April 8, 2000, 24–28. One inventive technique to award applicants bonus points for "cultural awareness," a subjective concept that in practice may simply be determined by the color of one's skin. From the facts given here, the University of Washington would seem highly vulnerable to a complaint that it continues to violate the Fourteenth Amendment rights of white and Asian applicants.

151. *1997 NCCA Division I Graduation Rate Report*, 66.

152. Stephan Thernstrom and Abigail Thernstrom, "The Consequences of Colorblindness," *The Wall Street Journal*, April 7, 1998, A18. We calculated dropout rates by race for freshmen entering a UC school from 1987 to 1990. Data were available for only four of the eight campuses (Berkeley, Irvine, UCLA, and Santa Barbara), and we assumed the mean for these four applied to the system as a whole. We then took the numbers admitted in the fall of 1998 and calculated how many could be expected to graduate if (1) the black graduation rate rose to equal that for whites, and (2) the black rate rose enough to cut the racial gap in half.

153. Reasons for optimism that the racial gap in graduation rates will be substantially narrowed as a result of the end of preferences may be found in recent experience at Berkeley. In the 1997 entering class, chosen with racial preferences, the median SAT score for black admits was 1130, 260 points below the white median. As a result of the abolition of racial double standards, the median black

score rose by 135 points, cutting the racial gap for 1998 freshmen in half. See Jack Citrin, Draft of Report on the New Policy, Appendix Tables 3A, 3B (unpublished University of California Faculty Senate draft report, 1999, on file with authors). For further discussion, see Jack Citrin, "Desperately Seeking Diversity," *Sacramento Bee*, March 28, 1999, H1. Cf. *Shape of the River*, 42, where it is estimated that the racial gap would shrink by a mere thirty-six points with race-neutral admissions at five schools. Bowen and Bok's hypothetical calculations to the contrary notwithstanding, the quality of the black students attending Berkeley improved dramatically when preferences were eliminated. This is also evident from the rise in high school GPAs of admitted blacks from 3.75 to 4.18, which narrowed the racial gap from .45 to .09, an 80 percent decline; see Citrin's Appendix, Tables 3A and 3B. The new admissions policy at Berkeley, it is important to note, did not entail admissions based strictly on academic criteria, which would inevitably shrink the SAT score gap even more. Factors like athletic talent and socioeconomic disadvantage were still taken into account.

154. Bowen and Bok, *Shape of the River*, 286.

155. This intellectual tradition is brilliantly analyzed in Andrew Kull, *The Color-Blind Constitution* (Cambridge, Mass.: Harvard University Press, 1992).

156. *Univ. of Cal. vs. Bakke*, 438 U.S. 265 (1978).

157. Synott, *Half-opened Door*, 58–80.

158. Bowen and Bok, *Shape of the River*, 36.

159. *Ibid.*, 36–37. The quoted words are by Thomas Kane, from whom the authors borrowed this analogy.

160. Calculated from NCAA, *1997 Graduation Rates Report*.

161. Thernstrom, "An End to Preferences?" 42.

162. It is interesting that the review in the liberal journal, *The American Prospect*, comments that "if blacks are admitted to Berkeley or UCLA at demonstrably higher rates than are Chinese applicants with higher scores, even the most eloquent defense of an institution's larger social obligation may sound like a hollow rationale for yet another form of Asian exclusion"; Schrag, "Muddy Waters," 88. We agree. But, unlike Schrag, we suggest that the moral argument applies equally to Stanford.

163. *Statistical Abstract of the US:1998*, 417.

164. Jeffrey Selingo, "What States Aren't Saying About the 'X Percent Solution,'" *Chronicle of Higher Education*, June 2, 2000, claims that aides to Governor Bush have admitted this.

165. One wishes it were not so, but all the evidence we have reviewed convinces us that Christopher Jencks is correct in concluding that "by the time students are old enough to apply to college, their minds have developed in particular ways; some neural paths have grown strong, others have atrophied. The mental differences among seventeen-year-olds do not completely determine their future, but neither are they easy to change"; Jencks and Phillips, *The Black-White Gap*, 73.

166. Roger Clegg, "Old Man Quota," in "The Empire Strikes Back," 30.

167. Bowen and Bok, *Shape of the River*, 287–89.

168. *Ibid.*, 288.

169. For a critical appraisal, see Abigail Thernstrom and Stephan Thernstrom, "Admissions Impossible: California without the SATs," *National Review*, March 19, 2001.

Dual Citizenship +
Multiple Loyalties =
One America?*

Stanley A. Renshon

In 1916, writing against what he saw as the excesses of the Americanization program for new immigrants, the journalist and cultural essayist Randolph Bourne called for a "Trans-National America." He envisioned the United States as a country populated by nationals and new immigrants with strong emotional ties to their countries of origin. In this new world, America would be united primarily by in the fact that we all were "international citizens."

In recent decades the number of countries allowing, and for many immigrant-sending countries, encouraging their nationals to hold multiple citizenships has exploded. Once relatively rare, there are a surprisingly large number of countries that now do so. No doubt others will soon be added to that list.

Bourne's vision (1916) seems on its way to being realized. Some now directly champion that vision (Aleinikoff 1998b; Spiro 1997). One advocate has called on dual or multiple citizenship to become a basic human right enforced by the United Nations General Assembly (McGarvey-Rosendahl 1985, 305, 321–25). The question I want to raise in this essay is whether Bourne's vision represents a dream to which we should give our support, or whether it is a muddled utopian fantasy with implications for this country Bourne, and his advocates, did not seriously think through.

At its most basic level dual citizenship[1] involves the simultaneous holding of more than one citizenship or nationality.[2] That is, a person can have all, or many, of the rights and responsibilities that adhere to a citizen in each of the several countries in which he or she is a citizen regardless of the length of time of his or her actual residence in a country, geographical proximity to the country, or the nature of his or her economic, cultural, or political ties.[3] My concern here, however, is not with dual citizenship as an international migration issue; rather, it is with its impact on American national identity and culture.

The United States does not formally recognize dual citizenship, but neither does it take any stand politically or legally against it (Kelly 1991–92). Congress has the constitutional power to regulate immigration, including allowing or disallowing multiple citizenship; however, to date it has chosen not to do so. One question I want to raise in this essay is whether it ought to do so.

The issues arising out of dual citizenship cannot be considered apart from patterns of immigration into the United States over the last forty years. The latest census figures show that the number of legal and illegal immigrants living in the United States has almost tripled since 1970, rising from 9.6 million to 28.4 million today (Escobar 1999; Rodriguez 2000; Camarota 2001). A substantial percentage of these immigrants arrive here from countries that allow, and in many cases for their own purposes encourage, their nationals to become dual citizens here.

The consequences of allowing or encouraging the acquisition of multiple citizenship by immigrants and citizens in the United States rarely has been discussed outside of a small group of law school professors and postmodern theorists, but they deserve to be. This narrow group generally has endorsed the desirability of allowing new immigrants and American citizens to pursue their associations with their "countries of origin." Some go farther and advocate the acquisition and consolidation of active attachments to other countries as a means of overcoming what they view as the parochialism of American national identity.

Yet the basis for either endorsing or advocating the development of multiple national attachments ordinarily is based on narrow legal analysis wherein anything permitted is acceptable, or on the advocates' highly abstract "postmodern" theoretical musings, wherein anything imaginable is suitable. The psychological implications and political consequences of having large groups of Americans holding multiple citizenship are rarely if ever seriously considered.

Yet such questions go to the very heart of what it means to be an American and a citizen. The answers to such questions also hold enormous implications for the integrity of American civic and cultural traditions. Is it possible to be fully engaged and knowledgeable citizens of several countries? Is it possible to follow two or more very different cultural traditions? Is it possible to have two possibly conflicting core identifications and attachments? Assuming such things are possible, are they desirable?

Before we can address these questions, there are several prior ones. How many countries allow their nationals to have multiple citizenship? Solid numbers are in short supply. Jorge Vargas (1996, 2) put the number at forty. One year later, a 1997 draft memorandum on dual citizenship prepared for the United States Commission on Immigration Reform (Morrison & Foerster LLP 1997, 9) said that "at least thirty-seven and possibly as many as forty-seven countries allow their nationals to possess dual nationality." Goldstein and Piazza's (1998) list of countries allowing multiple citizenship puts the number at fifty-five. Most other authors who have written on multiple citizenship mostly seem content to list a few countries allowing multiple citizenship, perhaps believing that the actual number of such countries has no bearing on their analyses or the appropriate responses for countries like the United States for whom this might be an issue.

How many Americans are eligible for, or claim, multiple citizenship status? We don't know. As *The Wall Street Journal* puts it (Zachary 1998), "no one knows just how many citizens claim a second nationality," or are entitled to do so. Why? According to Peter Spiro (1997, 1455, note 199), an enthusiastic advocate of multiple citizenship, "Statistical surveys of the number of dual nationals appear never to have been undertaken, nor have the United States or other governments sought to collect such information."[4] Yet he estimates that Mexico alone, which recently passed a law allowing its nationals dual citizenship rights, could create in the United States, "almost overnight a concentrated dual-national population numbering in the millions." How many millions? He doesn't say.

According to T. Alexander Aleinikoff (1998a, 27, italics mine), another advocate of multiple citizenship, "The U.S. Government does not record and has not estimated, the number of U.S. dual citizens, *but the total may be quite large.*" How large? He doesn't say, either.

One purpose of this paper is to provide some numerical specificity to vague or otherwise nonexistent estimates of the number of persons in the United States who are eligible for dual- or multiple-citizenship status. Numbers alone, of course, do not necessarily confer political or cultural significance; however, neither are they irrelevant to them. Vast numbers of citizens eligible for multiple citizenship are surely of more concern than small numbers.

In the analysis that follows, I first briefly discuss the concept of multiple citizenship. I then turn to an enumeration of those countries that allow it and examine them in the context of American immigration policy from 1986 to 1997. I then turn to a consideration of some implications of these figures for American politics and national identity.

What Is Dual Citizenship?

As noted, at its most basic level, dual or multiple citizenship involves the simultaneous holding of more than one citizenship or nationality. The idea seems counterintuitive. How could a person owe allegiance or fully adhere to the responsibilities of citizenship in several or more countries at the same time? In the United States, the legal answer is: easily.

The United States does not formally recognize dual citizenship, yet no American citizen can lose his or her citizenship by undertaking the responsibilities of citizenship in one or more countries. This is true even if those responsibilities include obtaining a second or even a third citizenship, swearing allegiance to a foreign state, voting in another country's election, serving in the armed forces (even in combat positions, and even if the state is a "hostile" one), running for office, and if successful, serving.[5] Informed constitutional judgment suggests Congress could legislatively address any of these, or other, issues arising out of these multiple, perhaps conflicting. responsibilities. [6] Yet, as noted, it has chosen not to do so.

A person in the United States may acquire multiple citizenship in any one of four ways (Aleinikoff 1998a, 26–27; O'Brien 1999, 575). He or she may be born in the United States to immigrant parents. All children born in the United States are U.S. citizens regardless of the status of their parents (*jus soli*). Second, a person may be born outside the United States to one parent who is a U.S. citizen and another who is not (*jus sanguinis*). A child born to an American citizen and British citizen in the United Kingdom, for example, would be a citizen of both countries. Third, the act of a person becoming a naturalized citizen in the United States is ignored by his or her country of origin.[7] This is true even if the country of naturalization requires, as the United States does, those naturalizing to "renounce" former citizenship/nationality ties. In the case of the United States, failure to take action consistent with the renunciation carries no penalties, and other countries can, and often do, simply ignore that oath of allegiance. Fourth, a person can become a naturalized citizen of the

United States and in doing so lose her citizenship in her country of origin, but can regain it at any time and still retain her U.S. citizenship.[8]

Dual or multiple *citizenship* is not the same as dual *nationality*. Citizenship is a political term. It draws its importance from political, economic, and social rights and obligations conferred on a person by virtue of having been born into, or having become a recognized or certified member of, a state.

Nationality, on the other hand, refers primarily to the attachments of members of a community to each other and to that community's ways of viewing the world,[9] practices, institutions, and allegiances. Common community identifications develop through several or more of the following elements: language, racial identifications, ethnicity, culture, geography, historical experience, and identification with common institutions, behavior, and worldview that orient people to understanding the world.

In many culturally homogenous countries nationality and citizenship coincide, yet they are not synonymous. Or, as has been noted in a Harvard Law School journal editorial (1997, 1817), "an individual's national identity is not necessarily the same as the passport she holds." This, of course, is precisely the problem.

Multiple Citizenship Countries: A Large and Fast-growing Group

People, even those who are attentive to public life and affairs, are genuinely surprised at the number of countries that allow and encourage multiple citizenship. It is a large number and it is growing, rapidly. In 1996, a survey by a Hispanic advocacy group studied seventeen Latin American countries; only seven of seventeen (41 percent) were listed as allowing some form of multiple citizenship. As of 2000, only four years later, fourteen out of seventeen Latin American countries in that survey (84 percent) allowed multiple citizenship, and another, Honduras, had introduced a bill to do so (de la Garza et al., 1996). (See Appendix A for a list of countries that allow or encourage multiple citizenship.)

Drawing on several helpful,[10] but sometimes inconsistent,[11] lists in conjunction with my own inquiries,[12] I have established that there are currently ninety-three countries that allow some form of multiple citizenship. It is important to underscore, however, that the specific rights and responsibilities that accrue to such citizens vary.

Some countries, such as Germany, allow their citizens to become dual citizens, but balk at allowing immigrants to do so.[13] New Zealand now permits dual nationality unless, in a specific instance, this "is not conducive to the public good." The French Civil Code formerly provided that any adult who voluntarily accepted another *nationality* would automatically forfeit French *citizenship*, but this provision was amended in 1973 so that now "any adult, habitually residing abroad, who voluntarily accepts another *nationality* will only lose the French *nationality* if he expressly so declares" (italics mine). Some countries like Algeria and France allow their nationals to chose in which country's armed forces they will serve. Others do not.[14] Irish citizens in Britain may vote and sit in Parliament. The Irish constitution was changed in 1984 to permit Britons living in the republic to vote in elections to the lower house of the Irish national parliament. Spain does not permit those who hold Latin American citizenships to vote or stand for election (Hammer 1985). Peru, Argentina, and Columbia allow absentee voting by their dual citizenship nationals. El Salvador, Panama, Uruguay, and the Dominican Republic do not (de la Garza 1996, 2–3; Jones-Correa 2000, 3, 5). A recent Mexican law creates dual citizenship (but not nationality) and regulates it. Holders of declaration of Mexican nationality IDs will not be able to vote or hold political office in Mexico, to serve in the Mexican armed forces, or to work aboard Mexican-flagged ships or airlines (Martin 2000; "Mexico" 2000).

This brief survey is not meant to be exhaustive. However, it is meant to underscore one important point: *Countries that allow multiple citizenship vary substantially in the specific ways and the extent to which they encourage or limit the responsibilities and advantages of their multicitizenship nationals.* It is possible to both permit and regulate dual citizenship. Most countries that allow it also restrict it, but not the United States.

It would be useful to have an up-to-date survey of the practices of all countries allowing multiple citizenship. Yet, if additional evidence is consistent with the limited survey above, the United States would surely be among the most, if not *the* most permissive, having no restrictions whatsoever in any of the wide range of practices that other countries regulate. This seems not to be so much a matter of conscious public or political choice as the result of one core Supreme Court case[15] that has made it virtually impossible to lose one's American citizenship coupled with the economically, politically, and culturally motivated acts of other countries behaving in their own self-interest.

Multiple Citizenship and American Immigration

Why should Americans care how many other countries allow their nationals to hold multiple citizenship, their motivations for doing so, or the specific ways in which they regulate, encourage, or limit specific responsibilities and entitlements? The answer to this question is complex and cannot be fully analyzed here. However, surely one central element of the answer has to do with recent patterns of American immigration.

The numbers noted at the beginning of this essay reflect the well-known sea change in the rates and nature of immigration to the United States following Congress's 1965 landmark changes in the country's immigration law. No single number, of course, can do justice to the complex array of changes this law has promoted. However, some perspective can be gained from the most recent U.S. Census Bureau figures.[16]

The latest official estimate (Rodriguez 2000; Camarota 2001) of the number of foreign-born persons, of whatever legal status, living in the United States is over twenty-eight million (28.4). This is the largest foreign-born population in our history and represents a 30 percent rise (6 million) over the 1990 figures. The number of immigrants for the last few years of the decade stretching from 1990, coupled with the total number of immigrants in the previous decade (1980–90), add up to the largest consecutive two-decade influx of immigrants in the country's history. Half of the foreign-born population is from Latin America, and more than a quarter (28 percent) of that number is from Mexico.

The Census Bureau estimates that the proportion of the foreign-born population is likely to increase in future years given that group's relative youth and high fertility rates. For example, the average foreign-born household had a larger number of children under eighteen than the native-born household (1.02 versus .067). Or, to put it another way, 60 percent of those with at least one foreign-born householder had one or more children under eighteen compared with 45 percent of native households. Foreign-born households were more likely to have two (44 versus 36 percent) or more (16 versus 9 percent) children than native-born households. Twenty-five percent of families with a foreign-born householder from Latin America had three or more children, and among married couples with householders from Mexico this figure is 79 percent. And, of course, illegal immigrants have children who are American citizens.

We now have reached almost the threshold necessary to begin answering the question, So what? However, before we do so, there is still one further relationship to explore: What is the relationship between the countries that provide the vast pool of immigrants to the United States and the multiple-citizenship status of those they send us? Some data are presented in Appendix B.

Appendix B presents a list of twenty selected countries sending high numbers of immigrants, gathered from the Immigration and Naturalization Service (INS) official figures for 1994–1998. Those countries that allow their nationals to hold multiple-citizenship status are highlighted in bold print. The data show that seventeen of these top twenty[17] countries (85 percent) allow some form of multiple citizenship. One of the remaining three, Korea, is actively considering adopting such legislation.

The numbers for specific years are even more graphic. In 1998, of the 443,058 immigrants admitted that year from the top twenty sending countries, 374, 531 (84.5 percent) were from countries allowing multiple citizenship. In 1997, of 552,556 immigrants from the top twenty sending countries, 493,493 (89.3 percent) were from countries allowing multiple citizenship. The figures for the years 1996, 1995, and 1994 are comparable, with countries allowing multiple citizenship accounting for 86.1 percent, 85.4 percent, and 84.8 percent, respectively, for each of these years.

Recall, too, that while seventeen of the top twenty countries sending immigrants are countries allowing multiple citizenship, that number (seventeen) represents only a small percentage of the total number (92, not including the United States) of such countries. And, of course, many of these remaining seventy-five (75) countries allowing multiple citizenship send the United States many thousands of immigrants. A more detailed analysis might well find that of all immigrants, numbers approaching or exceeding 90 percent come from countries allowing multiple citizenship.[18]

Another way to gauge the possible impact of dual citizenship in the United States is to examine the contribution that countries allowing multiple citizenship make to the United States immigration stream. The data are presented in Appendix C.

Appendix C presents data on immigration to the United States by nationals from all countries allowing dual/multiple citizenship for the three decades beginning in 1960 and then for every year beginning in 1991 and extending to 1997. Figures in bold underneath the dates represent the total level of legal immigration for that period. Figures in bold at the bottom represent the total contribution of countries allowing dual/multiple citizenship for that same period and their percentage of the total for that period. Given that data for some countries in some periods is not available (N/A), these figures underrepresent the actual numbers. Even so, they clearly show the extent to which immigrants to the United States are disproportionately from countries that allow or encourage dual/multiple citizenship and the retention of ties to their countries of birth/origin. Leaving aside the question of cohort replacement, of the almost twenty-two million immigrants legally admitted into this country between 1961 and 1997, over seventeen million, or slightly over 79 percent, are from countries allowing dual/multiple citizenship.

There are several ways in which to gain a somewhat fuller appreciation of these figures. For example, if you examine the countries of birth that contributed 500,000 or more persons to America's foreign-born population in both 1990 and 1997, ten of thirteen (76 percent) are countries encouraging dual/multiple citizenship. In six of these countries there has been a substantial and significant increase in the number of immigrants to the United States in the seven years between the two sets of figures. In 1990, the last enumerated census year, seven of the top ten countries of birth of the foreign-born population in the United States were countries encouraging dual citizenship.[19]

All these figures provide different ways of viewing a set of numbers that have been gathering size and importance since the sea change in American immigration law in 1965. These numbers have been accumulating by the tens of millions, yet they have largely done so without notice or analysis.

These numbers establish a basic and important fact: *American immigration policy is resulting in the admission of large numbers of persons from countries that have taken legislative steps (for economic, political, and cultural reasons) to maintain and foster their ties with countries from which they emigrated.* One may disagree about the importance or implications of these facts, but not with their presence.

Some Implications of Multiple Citizenship

These figures raise critical questions for the United States as a country. Here, I would like to address some of them, doing so in a way balanced somewhat between the determinedly enthusiastic embrace of massive dual-citizenship immigration as a matter of little consequence to us (Spiro 1997) and the premature, but not unrealistic, concern of our possible evolution into a country where separate psychological, cultural, and political loyalties trump a coherent national identity (Geyer 1966).

Theory vs. Advocacy

The current "discourse," to use a term favored by the trendy, on this issue has been decidedly narrow. Those with legal backgrounds have looked to the law to see if what they find desirable is legally possible. They have been joined by political theorists.

Generally, the political theorists are of two types. The first are those who emphasize America's liberal tradition and our continued failure to live up to it. They see an America indelibly stained by its treatment of American Indians, Americans with darker skins or accents, women, and anyone else who has a quarrel with America's distribution of wealth, influence, and public attention and their share of them. The response to any disparity for these theorists is more liberalism, which is to say, more emphasis on rights—group-based if necessary—and more emphasis on government guarantees of outcomes that such advocates favor. They prefer mandated measures to ensure that "recognition," to use Taylor's (1992) term, is not trumped by an unacceptable (to them) individualism that might lead to reserving the right to decide what will and will not be viewed as acceptable or desirable. They welcome multiple citizenship because it represents a long step in the direction of ensuring more democracy, defined as parity for diverse cultural traditions (Kymlicka 1995; Habermas 1992; Smith 1987). Whether there are any limits to the cultural and political accommodations that can be made by any culture that wishes to preserve its way of life is a question these theorists rarely seriously consider.

The second group of theorists includes the postmodernists. Their single, partially correct insight is that social organization is a byproduct of intent and is thus, to use their term, "constructed." From this they conclude that no social form has much intrinsic or functional value, except those they advocate. They have little, if any, regard for America's cultural and political traditions, which they see as inherently racist, xenophobic, and anachronistically nationalistic. Their remedy is to welcome, and when possible to further, the demise of American national culture and substitute "larger loyalties," which, in their view, are more "democratic" and conducive to strong "multicultural" identifications (Isbister 1996, 1998; Maharidge 1996). Needless to say, they welcome multiple citizenship because they believe that it weakens the ties to "hegemonic" capitalism of which the United States is their chief exemplar.

There is much to be said of the dangers of assuming that democracy unbalanced by a concern for the public culture and psychology that make it possible is a virtue, or that a preference for proven traditional cultural forms is a vice. One of the many ironies of these discussions is that those who would never dream of imposing America's "dominant" cultural values on any group they feel worthy of cultural self-determination seem incapable of applying the same standards to the culture that makes their own complaints on behalf of others possible.

Unlimited Identities?

The problems with the narrow substantive basis of most theoretical discussions of multiple citizenship, however, go beyond issues of reciprocity. Consider the question of multiple loyalties and national identity. Most advocates subscribe to the "Why not one more?" theory. We are reminded that we are, as in my own case, sons, husbands, and fathers.[20] We are labeled as Caucasian and Western. We are working class by background and (perhaps) upper middle class by socioeconomic status (SES) categories. We are Jewish and reformed, New Yorkers, Manhattanites, and Upper West Siders. We are professors, scholar/writers, psychologists, psychoanalysts, and neo-Freudians. We are moderate progressives economically, politically centrist, and culturally conservative. And we are American, Northerners, and Jewish-Americans.

Postmodern theorists see us as comprising a virtually unlimited and replaceable set of selves that can be enacted or abandoned at will (Gergen 1998). Liberal political theorists and their allies count up all the categories by which we may be understood and conclude that adding one more, say Mexican or Indian nationality, will make little, if any, difference (Martin 1999, 8–9).

The first basic assumption of these arguments is that core identity elements are infinitely malleable. They are not. The second is that all identifications can carry equal weight. They cannot.

Clinically, psychologically diffused, dysfunctionally organized, or inconsistent identities are a concern, not an ideal. Politically, therefore, they should not be an aspiration. Moreover, the fact that we can have many elements in our complex modern identities does not negate the need to integrate them into a coherent and functional package. It only makes that required task more difficult.

The "Why not one more?" theory fails to distinguish between the elements that form a central core of one's psychology and identity and those that are more peripheral. I am much more a father than a Caucasian, much more a political moderate and cultural conservative than an Upper West Sider. And I am definitely more of an American than most of the categories in my list.

Advocates of porous identities like Aleinikoff contend that multiple attachments do not produce "anomie or postmodern neurosis."[21] Indeed, he argues that, "on the contrary, it appears that human beings are rather adept at living in more than one world, bringing the insights of one to bear on the other, or compartmentalizing their lives into separate spheres." He then gives as evidence the case of friends of his who adopted a Russian baby, held a ceremony of a Jewish ritual circumcision, and at the same time had the baby naturalized as American citizen, at which ceremony the parents recited the oath of allegiance for him. This, in his view, "shows that the opposite of a single fixed identity is not necessarily a loss of bearing or radical personal conclusion. The two identities—Jew and U.S. citizen—are deeply significant to their relevant communities; but the assembled friends and family did not see a contradiction (or even a tension) between them."

Of course, they didn't. The parents were presumably native born, or had lived here long enough to be naturalized, Americans. The baby would therefore be raised by parents who were themselves a product of a lifetime, or many years, as Americans with all that entails. They would speak the same language, have the same cultural patterns and outlooks, and the baby would grow up with the connection to its new country as a very early and primary experience. What these two parents shared was binding, not contradictory or tension filled.

Holding multiple identifications, even those with deep significance, does not mean they must be, or are, equal. Consider that it is certainly permissible for our political leaders to have, and even to express, a commitment to their faith that has deep meaning to them. However, as discussions surrounding John F. Kennedy's Catholicism in 1960 and Joe Lieberman's Judaism in 2000 make clear, we also expect that their identity as, and commitment to, being an American will take precedence.

As a practical matter, however, why expect tension at all when the categories of religion and national identity essentially have become fused? As Herberg pointed out (1955) almost fifty years ago, the religion of America is Americanism. Or to put it another way, religion in the United States has become secularized and, to the extent that it has, Americanized. So there is very little tension present in contemporary American society, especially that part of it that is highly educated, affluent, and occupationally well placed, in being both an American and a Catholic or a Protestant or a Jew.

No sensible person argues that people can't function with multiple commitments. People are wife and mother, Catholic and professor, some child's parent and some parent's child. Most often in the United States, these commitments are tensionless. Even when they aren't, they rarely call into question fundamental values or ways of being in and seeing the world. Husbands and wives who are American and Jewish do not inhabit separate identity worlds; they share one.

In short, it is important to draw a distinction between core and less central elements of our identities. It is important to understand the hierarchical relationships that exist among these elements. It is absolutely essential to ask how culturally, psychologically, and cognitively compatible the various elements are with each other.

Before we can talk sensibly about whether it is truly possible to have two or more divergent core national identities, we had better be clear about what it takes to develop and maintain a coherent, integrated one. We had better be clear about whether, and how, elements of the identity that we acquire early shape the reception of those other important identity elements that are developed later. We had better be clear about the conditions in which various elements become harmonious or disruptive to an overall identity. And, above all, we had better be clear about how personal and national identity function to support the cultural and political arrangements that underlie this fabulous experiment, the United States.

Metaphors and Muddles

Such understanding might help us make less of a muddle of our metaphors. For example, critics of dual citizenship often compare it to bigamy.[22] However, in my view, that analogy is deficient. Marriage is a voluntary union between two adults, later in their lives searching for intimacy, companionship, and partnership. It is based on a combination of similarity, complementariness, practicality, and the hope for wish fulfillment.

Nationality, on the other hand, that combination of national identification, psychology, and outlook, begins with the earliest experiences of language, family, custom, and parental psychology. The word "outlook" is important in this list, because culture is deeply imbedded in not only *what* we think, but *how* we do so. Deep cultural frames are not interchangeable.

Furthermore, this early foundation ordinarily develops within a relatively consistent institutional, cultural, and psychological setting that is not freely chosen, nor easily abandoned.[23] In these and other ways, nationality and national identity are quite the opposite of marriage.

Another marriage metaphor that is often used compares dual citizenship to the relations to one's family and one's in-laws. Aleinikoff (1999, 39) and others who use this metaphor agree that conflicts can arise, but believe you can still be loyal to both. There is, of course, much that lies behind the word *can*, as in the phrase "can still be loyal." In some societies, the wish of the elders takes precedence over the wishes of the couple, if they differ. In our society, it is easier to be loyal to your spouse because the preferences of the couple are expected to outweigh the wishes of the parents. Yet there is a more basic question here.

What happens when both parties feel very strongly about an issue, a matter of principle for each? How does one resolve and maintain fidelity to dual loyalties in those circumstances? Not every issue between in-laws, or countries, will involve irreconcilable principles and policies. However, strong tensions and conflicts can arise out of differences that do not necessarily involve irreconcilable principles, even though these might well arise.

And what are the effects of siding with your family at the expense of your spouse—on the relationship between the husband and wife, and on the spouse whose views were trumped by the spouse's family? Translated into the concerns here, what is the effect of having groups of your dual citizens side with or give strong weight to the official views of their "country of origin" on them, the United States, and the country that asked for and received their agreement?

Nationality and national identity, therefore, seem closer to family than married life.[24] The bigamy metaphor asks whether it is possible to have equally full, deep, and enduring relationships with two spouses. I doubt it. However, if the family metaphor is more apt, it may be more accurate to begin with a basic fact and then ask some different questions.

That basic fact is the pattern of our post-1986 immigration, which is heavily weighted toward immigrants with non-Western cultural and political traditions. Given that fact, questions framed through the lens of the family metaphor would be: Is it possible to have two different sets of parents, with sets of different core psychologies, different sets of values, different sets of beliefs, different world views, and the information and experiences that support them all? I don't think so.

Is it possible to give equal weight to all these elements that help form one's central emotional attachments? No, not without an extremely shallow, fragile foundation for ones' identity. Such identities may develop what appears to be an elaborate superstructure, but lack the foundation to support it.

The idea that individuals can integrate multiple, conflicting basic orientations toward life may well prove a form of cultural conceit. It is apparently easier for some in the privileged elite to disregard the primary attachments that most citizens have to their own countries. In so doing they appear to have confused sophistication with a new form of modern rootlessness. Such people may go anywhere, but essentially belong nowhere.[25]

Dual Citizenship and American Democracy

This is the opposite of civic engagement. The American ideal of civic republicanism is, after all, the citizen, not the subject. Citizenship in a democracy, especially one that is itself facing complex, divisive issues arising from its increasing diversity, and which is located in a world in which the same is true, requires much of those who enjoy its benefits.

Advocates consistently minimize the difficulties of being fully engaged, knowledgeable, and effective citizens in one political system, much less two. What do citizens in this country need to understand and appreciate? It would be helpful to have some knowledge of the ways in which the ideals of personal, religious, political, and economic freedoms motivated those who founded this country and those who followed. It would be useful to be familiar with the courage, determination, self-reliance, optimism, and pragmatism that accompanied those motivations. It also would be necessary to have to some knowledge of the country's struggles always to realize these aspirations.

These are large matters, but necessary ones. They apply equally to present and prospective citizens. Yet we are failing badly in both groups on these matters. The "test" for citizenship requires knowledge of a number of disjointed facts requiring little, if any, knowledge of the traditions—political and psychological—that have shaped this country. Many thousands become citizens and require translations of ballots on which they cast their vote. It is hardly likely that these citizens have followed the complex pros and cons of these policy issues,[26] the hallmark of a truly informed citizen, since they don't understand well the language in which these debates are conducted. More likely, they gain their information from advocacy groups who probably have a very particular point of view, but one that certainly is not based on dispassionate presentation of the issues so that new voters can make up their own minds.

Some ask whether it is legitimate to hold immigrants to a standard unmet by citizens. Many studies underscore that question. A recent report by the American Council of Trustees and Alumni, a group that supports liberal arts education, recently asked a series of high-school-level multiple-choice questions to a randomly selected group of graduating seniors at the nation's most elite colleges, including Harvard, Princeton, and Brown. The results were dismal. Seventy-one percent of our nation's best students did not know the purpose of the Emancipation Proclamation. Seventy-eight percent were not able to identify the author of the phrase "of the people, for the people, by the people." Seventy percent could not link Lyndon Johnson with the passage of the historic Voting Rights Act. Yet 99 percent correctly identified Beavis and Butthead, and 98 percent could correctly identify Snoop Doggy Dog (Veale 2000).

There is a legitimate case to be made for asking those seeking citizenship to be conversant with the traditions and practices of the country to which they are asking entry. However, it could be argued that both immigrants and native-born citizens have much to learn about their country. It remains to be seen whether it is truly possible to be conversant with the traditions and policy debates of two countries. Evidence keeps mounting that doing so even in one country is a task beyond the reach of increasing numbers of American citizens.

That fact, however, does not argue for lower standards. On the contrary, the informed exercise of citizenship plays a central, critical role in this democracy. Therefore, it is extremely inconsistent for advocates to push more liberal dual-citizenship policies in the name of furthering democracy, while at the same time pushing for standards of knowledge and commitment that undermine it.

The dilemmas are well captured in the work of David A. Martin (1994), who first emphasized the importance of "common life," and later said he was persuaded to support dual citizenship, albeit subject to limits.[27] The dilemma is starkly framed by Martin's assertion (1999, 13) that

Democracy is built on citizen participation, and its ideal is meaningful participation—of an engaged and informed citizenry. This presupposes a certain level of devotion to the community enterprise, to approach public issues as a unified community, even while leaving much to individual choice in deciding on the aims the policy should pursue or on the specific policies to address specific public issues.

Yet, he goes on say (1999, 27) quite directly that

It must be conceded that the claims made, . . . [i]f pushed to their limits, would argue strongly against dual nationality in the first place. If focusing primary political activity in this fashion [by allowing the right to vote in only one place] carries such benefits for solidarity, democratic engagement, and civic virtue, how much more could these goods be expected to flow from channeling *exclusive* political activity? And the point is even stronger if the person, by surrendering, or being required to renounce all other national ties, has thereby forsworn use of the exit option when policies do not turn out as she favors.

Yes, precisely!

Dual citizenship advocates routinely tout the beneficial effects of dual citizens living here on democratizing the politics of their home countries. No data exists to support this contention. However, it is quite possible, for example, that leaders aspiring to power will promise reforms that benefit those dual citizens abroad who might support them. They in turn might well support those who favor a broadening of *their* rights—economic or political. This narrow form of interest-group politics surely is not what advocates have in mind when they discuss the virtues of multiple voting and allegiances. It seems clear, then, that the politics of dual citizens might well be self-interested without necessarily being more widely democratic.

The War of 1812 Redux?

Advocates of dual citizenship look to the past and reassure us that we are unlikely to go to war over dual citizenship, as we did with the British in 1812 (Spiro 1997, 1461–65). That conflict arose when the British, then following the "perpetual allegiance" theory of citizenship, forcibly tried to repatriate American citizens at sea.[28] Yes, it is true that we will not go to war with Britain over these kinds of matters. Neither will we use forceful coercion to require Israel to return one of its dual citizens who committed a murder in the United States and fled the country. It is a fact of contemporary international politics that democracies rarely go to war with each other (Russett 1993).

However, democracies do still have armed conflicts with nondemocracies. And as David Martin (1999, 8, note 23) points out, "If relaxed rules on dual nationality are adapted or expanded over the coming decades, persons with such a mix of citizenship (one democratic and one nondemocratic) will doubtlessly make up a significant percentage." Martin adds the "especially worrisome cloud" of the rise of ethnic tensions and identity politics that increase the structural fault lines in a large number of what he terms "polyglot nations," of which the United States is surely now one. Given these facts, the optimism of multiple-citizenship advocates that international conflict that has implications for dual citizens is an historical relic represents an act of will.

International military conflicts that engage or test the loyalties of dual citizens cannot therefore easily be ruled out. However, the more likely problem is not war, but cohesion—social, political, and psychological. Countries like the United States have become increasingly diverse because of changes in their immigration laws and there are some advantages to that. A country can be enriched by different points of view, traditions, and contributions. However, the expectations, both those that immigrants bring with them and those already present when they arrive, make an enormous difference.

The Domestic Context of Dual Citizenship: American National Culture in Transition

Any serious discussion of the implications of dual citizenship for the United States must take into account some fundamental facts of contemporary American cultural and political life. It must consider the extent to which the fundamental personal, institutional, and cultural understandings that have provided the *unum* for the *pluribus* increasingly have become matters of contention. There is little disagreement that American national culture and identity are changing (Smelser and Alexander 1999). The question, and it is a profound one, is whether it is doing so for better or worse.

That debate is usually, and I think too narrowly, framed in terms of common values. [29] A major problem with a focus on values is that they are too abstract. Who doesn't believe in democracy? Who is against opportunity? One is reminded of the classic study that found that almost every American supports free speech, until asked about the first specific application of the principle that was controversial (Prothro and Grigg 1960).

The consequences of conducting the analysis of contentious issues at the rarified level of highly abstract categories leads easily to conflicts over who is rightful heir to the values being discussed. So, for example, liberal political theorists, law school professors, and postmodernists take a permissive stance toward dual citizenship, arguing that their views represent the best realization of democratic values. Perhaps, but I'm doubtful.

Too abstract a level of analysis can also lead to a focus on artificial and shallow similarities. One article in Smelser and Alexander's recent book on diversity argues that both supporters and opponents of abortion really hold the same common values and beliefs. How is that possible? Well, according to Seidman (1999, 177), they don't disagree "on a women's right to have sex, not on the value of her life and the life of her children, and not on the broader social and sexual values such as the individual's right to be sexual, the linking of sex to affection or love or the importance of the family, or considerations of public or social welfare."

I'm certain those who support limits on abortion would be surprised to learn that they share the exact same reverence for human life as those who advocate abortion without limits. However, I'm very uncertain that most Americans, even those who believe "in a woman's right to have sex," would approve of their daughters doing so at any age, with any person or persons, and at the expense of a stable, loving, long-term relationship. In short, when they are not riddled with errors and nonsequiturs, such highly abstract commonalties do little to address or resolve the real issues involved.

Finally, one can find examples of those who struggle to stake out an Olympian middle ground, wishing to be on both sides of the issues at the same time. As a result, it is sometimes difficult to follow their arguments. Thus, in a chapter introducing their recent book, Smelser and Alexander[30] warn us that a glance at earlier periods of intense polarized conflict "highlights not only the uniqueness of contemporary cultural emphasis but also the unique polarizing nature of the rhetoric." Should Americans then worry? No, because "the contemporary sense of decline and anxiety about social cohesion is nothing new," and "the nation does not seem to be at a turning point."

The problem with this position, as one of the book's own contributors John Higham (1999) points out in connection with immigration, is that in many ways the contemporary circumstances of immigrant incorporation do not resemble the past and are much more worrisome. Neither is the fact that the country has not yet reached a turning point, if that is an accurate reason not to be concerned about the direction in which the country appears to be heading.

That there might indeed be something worth worrying about seems to be implied by the editors' (1999, 11) characterization of the country as having "deep structural strains and cultural polarization." However, they are reassured that "common values are still a social reality." What common values are these? Highly abstract ones, such as "belief in democracy" and "the value of American life."

The authors are further reassured that "expanding commercialized popular culture, reflected in everything from musical hits to sports stars to fast foods and afternoon talk shows, is a homogenizing cultural focus that pervades differences of religion, ethnicity and social class." Yet one contributor, Zelizer (1999, 198), notes, "In an age of diversity, it seems, commonality can only be found at the mall." However, she also argues that appearances are deceiving because homogenization is not incompatible with diversification. Even currency, that most universal of mediums, shows evidence of becoming segmented along ethnicity, race, class, sexual orientation, and gender lines. New monetary instruments like affinity cards are marketed as a form of multicultural money—the Rainbow card (for homosexuals), the Unity Visa Card (for Americans of African descent), and so on (Zelizer 1999, 197).

The problem here is that all these commercialized cultural markets don't imply unity within that diversity. It is not clear that just because different groups recognize and adapt specific designer labels their shared values are anything more than skin deep. Not recognizing this, it is easier to see evidence of our cohesion in a "shared culture and tradition—whether authentic or ersatz" (Alexander and Smelser 1999, 9). Yet, in coherent, integrated societies and cultures, the former experiences are more likely to be predominant.

Americans may agree at the stratospheric level that democracy is best. However, that hasn't exempted any of our major social, cultural, or political institutions or patterns of traditional practice from acute conflicts over the specific ways in which they are constituted and operate. That is, after all, the meaning of the phrase "culture wars" and the many basic institutional conflicts that term now includes.

Yes, it is true that if you examine public opinion polls on a variety of contentious issues, there *is* a consensual political center (DiMaggio, Evans, and Bryson 1996). Yet it is also true that in every major sphere of American life the basic agreements that allow these institutions and practices to be effective, integrated parts of social, cultural, and political life are permeated by conflict, often severe. The legitimacy of America's basic institutions and practices is no longer a matter of fact, but rather of debate.

Bourne Revisited

The recourse to "common values" as the glue that holds America together is directly contrary to the vision that Bourne enunciated of a "Transnational America." He thought hyphenated Americans would retain and develop their ties to their "countries of origin or home countries" and that would make each group more "valuable and interesting to each other." Moreover, these sustained and enhanced national-origin differences would spur the development of an "intellectual sympathy," which gets to the "heart of different cultural expressions," and enables each person in one group to feel "as they [the other group members] feel." That, in Bourne's view, would be the basis of the new cosmopolitan outlook, transnational identity, which he favored. Americans would be bound together by the sum of their differences, a remarkable psychological assertion, and such an "intellectual internationalism . . . will unite and not divide" (Bourne 1916).

Bourne's enthusiasm for his vision is understandable given that he wrote well before advances in the understanding of human psychology and cognition that might have caused him to question some of his premises. The same cannot be said for his contemporary champions (Aleinikoff, 1998a). No psychological theory of identity with which I am familiar argues that the more central and consolidated your own cultural identity becomes, the more open you are to holding other equally strongly held, and very different, identities at the same time.

That literature really is quite unequivocal. People who hold deep convictions—identities based on common values, cultures, psychologies, world views, and so on—are much more likely to take their identities as given, the ways things are and the way the ought to be. There is no evidence historically or empirically that taking your Japanese identity seriously makes you more openminded toward Africans, or that growing up with a strong identity as an Italian or Moroccan makes you better able to feel what it is like to be an Israeli. When cultural identities are "contested," a lack of sympathy and empathy can easily turn to hostility and hatred.

Finally, in a country whose citizens are drawn from every country in the world, is it realistic and not just fanciful to believe that Somalians will learn about Italians, who will in turn learn about Filipinos, who in turn will know about all the remaining peoples and cultures that make up this diverse country? Simply to state the point is to underscore its cognitive and practical absurdity. There are limits to the amount of information one can take in and make use of, even if one is inclined to, which is another large presumption of Bourne's theory. To add to this burden the view that it is possible to have the desire and capacity for empathy for all the different cultural and subcultural groups that now populate America is a form of intellectual malpractice.

The Domestic Context of Dual Citizenship: American Character in Transition?

Historically, there have been many answers to the question the Frenchman de Creveceour famously asked (1970 [1783], 43–44): "What, then, is the American, this new man?"[31] However, it seems clear that the origin of

American national culture can be traced to the twin motivations behind the establishment of the first colonies, and the psychology necessary to realize them. The twin motivations were *economic and social opportunity* on one hand and *personal and political freedom* on the other. The psychologies that made them possible were symbolized and reflected in the frontier, which required courage, independence, and self-reliance from those living there. Of course, the psychology of independence and self-reliance were, from the start, embedded in a setting of interpersonal, social, and community connections.[32]

Neither religious freedom nor economic opportunity were isolated, absolute values and motivations. Religious freedom was embedded in a community context. Moreover, these communities had to find ways to live with others whose beliefs differed. Communities that came together for economic opportunity coexisted with a strong belief in public social and political equality. No person was deemed better than any other, the ethic of "democratic egalitarianism" (Lipset 1963, 123). From its inception, then, one fundamental paradox of American national psychology was that people were expected both to fit in and stand out.

The tension between individualism and community is clearly evident by examining the modern evolution of American ambivalence toward achievement, belonging, and independence. These are well captured in Riesman's influential theory of "inner- and other-directedness" (Riesman, 1950). It is often not appreciated that Riesman's "other-directed" and "inner-directed" were two of three forms of *conformity*. In Riesman's theory, the "inner-directed" person simply has internalized general social norms in a society in which population and economic changes have made learning the details of social customs ("tradition-directed" psychologies) too complex and cumbersome to individually teach and maintain. Such persons, of course, could stand against elements of the community, but the point was that they often weren't required to do so.

Internalizing the generalized standards of a community worked well, but only if those standards were relatively stable. If not, the skill most needed, and rewarded, was the ability to ascertain just what standards were expected, and adapt accordingly. Riesman's postwar America was a society characterized by large-scale social and economic changes. It was also one in which these changes coincided with the development of large-scale social institutions in which efficient performance depended on teamwork.

In such circumstances, being "other-directed" was an economic asset, as well as a socially valued skill and personality trait.

It is not as great a psychological distance as it might seem at first from Riesman's other-directed character to Lasch's (1979) "culture of narcissism." In Riesman's "other-directed" character the extensive veneer of sociability becomes a well-refined tool for "making it." Achievement is still paramount, and competition continues unabated. However, now success is achieved in group settings, by fitting in, not by self-reliance. Autonomous thinking, or fidelity to an independent sense of personal values and ideals, is a minority position. It becomes a cause for others' concern, not admiration. Small wonder that Arthur Miller's Willy Loman proved a more accurate fictional representative of his time than Ann Ryan's Howard Roark.

The lack of any firmly established internal psychological compass makes people vulnerable to the temptations of increasing abundance and repeated messages that delayed consumption is unnecessary and perhaps even odd. In the past, Lasch noted, the American penchant for self-improvement had been associated with achieving something solid and lasting. However, in an age that promised "you could have it all," or advised you to "be all that you can be," and some professional psychologists touted "self-actualization" as the north star of psychological development, enticing images of endless and easy satisfaction trumped the hard work of building a satisfying life.[33] Consumption might well fuel an economy, but an increasing emphasis on "self-fulfillment"[34] could not quiet increasing feelings of emptiness, isolation, and dissatisfaction.

Lasch (1979) argued that American life was increasingly dominated by ambitiously aggressive and self-centered individuals. One might characterize it as a culture of selfish individualism. Riesman (1980) agreed, and, while finding evidence of narcissistic elements elsewhere in American history, nonetheless thought what was different now was the public acceptance and even "approval" of clearly "self-serving conduct." This is certainly one way to understand the general public acceptance of a president whose behavior brought about his impeachment but who did so in a time of increasing economic prosperity (Renshon 1998).

It is only a small step from this to what appears to have become the public's eleventh commandment (Wolfe, 1998), "Thou shall not judge." The "non-judgmentalism of middle class Americans" in matters of religion, family, and other personal values emerges as the major finding of Wolfe's in-depth interviews with Americans across the country.[35] Needless to say, a strong ethic of self-fulfillment coupled with the view that whatever I, or anyone else, does that doesn't directly harm anyone else is all right "often collides violently with traditional rules, creating a national battle of cultural norms" (Yankelovich 1981, 5).[36]

Dual Citizenship and Integration of Immigrants

Immigrants arriving into American culture arrive in circumstances where not only the basic legitimacy of the culture's institutions and practices are at issue. They arrive as well in a culture in which the basic psychology necessary to sustain the founding principles of freedom and opportunity are eroding. Strong, independent-minded convictions and the courage to maintain fidelity to them, independence and the ability to stand apart from others, if necessary, and self-reliance are becoming increasingly scarce. The pervasive complaint that one group or another has been victimized because of disparities runs counter to the historically and psychologically deeply embedded connection between the intensity, consistency, and quality of efforts to achieve one's ambitions and the possibilities of doing so. Demands for equality regardless of achievement and tolerance, regardless of behavior, are increasingly becoming the ethic by which Americans are being asked to live.

What are the implications of changes in American national culture and psychology for the very large number of dual-citizenship immigrants entering the country in these new circumstances? Two very basic consequences seem clear. First, the cultural stability of the receiving country makes a critical difference. Immigrants, whether from countries that allow or discourage multiple citizenship, enter into different cultural circumstances in countries in which the primary culture is stable and secure and those in which it is not. Conversely, multiple citizenship has different meanings and implications in these two different circumstances. It seems quite clear that immigrants entering into a country whose cultural assumptions are fluid and "contested" will find it harder to assimilate, even if the wish is to do so. And, in such a circumstance, it will be more likely for dual citizen immigrants to maintain former cultural/country attachments that put at risk development and consolidation of newer cultural/country identifications.

Second, a country in which the institutional operations and legitimacy of assimilation to its ways of life are under attack and weakened is different than one in which they are not. In the past, assimilation, with its implications that there is a legitimate and worthwhile national identity and immigrants choosing to come here should, in good faith, try to accommodate it, was both the expectation and the reality.[37] Today, neither is true. Assimilation is equated in some quarters with forced and unnecessary demands for conformity to a culture that has little legitimate basis for asking for it (Takaki 1993).

As a result, immigrants are more likely to maintain and further develop psychological attachments and loyalties to their "home" countries and their traditions, values, customs, ways of viewing the world, and the psychologies that these reflect. Technology and mobility aid these efforts. Whether one applauds or laments this development in the United States, it is important to keep this fact in view. Arriving into a solidly assimilationist, receiving culture is very different than entering into a porous and "contested" one.

The impact of the enormous numbers of multiple-citizenship immigrants coming into this country varies as a function of the context in which their older and newer attachments unfold. It is within the frames of these two critically important contextual elements that the entry of enormous numbers of immigrants from countries that allow and increasingly actively encourage the maintenance and deepening of ties to their "homeland" must be considered. Surely when over 85 percent of the very large number of immigrants that the United States admits each year are from such countries it is time to carefully consider the implications. When immigrants enter into a country in which the assumption that they should be motivated to adapt to the values and traditions of the country they have chosen is fiercely debated, it is time to pause and reflect. And when the question of assimilation becomes "To what?" and is increasingly difficult to answer, dual citizenship in America is indeed truly an issue of vast proportions and broad significance.

The United States is facing a virtually unprecedented set of circumstances with regard to multiple citizenship. It is a country whose culture and politics were forged around allegiance to a set of principles and prac-

tices contained within a specific territory, with a specific history and a focused though not unchanging identity: *America*. It was not organized
around a specific, ethnically based nationality, as were European countries,
but rather a more generalized one: *American*. You could come from any
geographical, ethnic, racial, or religious origin and still be welcome,
though not always unambivalently, to develop an American identity and
nationality.

That American nationality has distinctive elements. It has long been
associated with the American "creed," which is to say support for democracy and tolerance. Yet it is also a nationality that prefers, and works
to develop, a specific set of *psychologies*. Americans have traditionally preferred self-reliance to dependence, moderation to excess, optimism to fu-
tility, pragmatism to rhetoric, and reflection to impulsiveness, to name a
few of those elements.

Several of these are, of course, the core characteristics of the "Protestant Ethic." Yet critics like Aleinikoff (1999) are wrong in asserting that
concerns with assimilation mask a demand to conform to what he terms
"Anglo/White culture." The genius of American national culture and
identity is that over time they have become decoupled from ethnicity, separated from religion, and detached even from race. In all these aspects,
these elements of national psychology have repeatedly proved to be open
and inclusive, even if not always wholeheartedly.

Successive waves of immigrants—the Irish, Jews, blacks from Trinidad
or the Bahamas, educated Hispanics of all nationalities, South Asians, Chinese, and Japanese—were certainly not Protestant, definitely not Anglo, and
never considered "white." Yet all of these groups have found a successful
place in American society—not a place realized without difficulty, not a
place in which everyone is a success, but a place realized nonetheless.

Becoming an American, then, is not simply a matter of agreeing that
democracy is the best form of government. It is a commitment to a psychology and the way of life that flows from it. It ultimately entails an appreciation of, a commitment to, and at its best, yes, even a love and reverence for, all that it stands for and provides.

It is easy to see America instrumentally. It is a place of enormous personal freedom and great economic opportunities. America has always recognized that many arrive seeking those treasures that are in such short
supply in so many of the countries from which they come. The fear that
self-interest will come at the expense of a developing appreciation and

genuine emotional connection to the country has always been, I think, the subtext of attempts to ensure that new arrivals became "American."

That has been the tradeoff. America takes the chance that it can leverage self-interest and transform it to authentic commitment. Immigrants agree in coming here to reorient themselves toward their new lives and away from their old ones. This involves some basics—learning to be at home with English, understanding the institutions and practices that define American culture, and reflecting on the ways in which *their* search for freedom and opportunity fit in with the history, with all its vicissitudes, that has shaped the idea and promise of *America*.

It is only at that point that the transformation from self-interest to genuine emotional connection can be made. In the past, that implicit contract was buttressed by some practical facts. One might be an Italian, but the ability to read Italian newspapers and keep up with the news in your local village or city was limited and the chance to see your country of origin was a seminal life event.

Today that is far from the case. Jet travel and its accessibility to all but the most financially marginal have erased boundaries of time and geography. Internet access to newspapers and people has likewise eroded distances. Anxiety about finding psychological grounding in a culture that allows, perhaps even encourages, the diffusion of the traditional sources of individual identity leads people to seek it somewhere, anywhere. The unprecedented search for "roots" can best be understood in a society with anxieties about rootlessness.

Conclusion

America reached its present state of political, economic, and social development by providing enormous personal freedom and abundant economic opportunity. In doing so, it leveraged personal ambitions as a tool to transform individuals' social and economic circumstances. In the process, it helped develop and reinforce psychological elements that were consistent with personal success and civic prudence. An emphasis on consistency, hard work, delay of immediate gratification, prudence, pragmatism, and optimism were among them.

In return, it asked of immigrants that they learn the country's language, culture, and political practices. Thus oriented toward their new home, immigrants could become part of the fabric of American cultural and political life. Leaving a life behind, even one that one wanted to leave, was of course difficult. Yet generations of earlier immigrants thought the sacrifice worthwhile.

Dual citizenship and its associated bifurcation of attention and commitment change that traditional and successful recipe. Immigrants increasingly come from countries that encourage dual citizenship. Their purposes in doing so are primarily self-interested. They may be to ensure the continued flow of financially critical remittances from those working in the United States. Or, they may be to organize their nationals to further their home country's policy preferences, for example amnesty for those who enter the country illegally or the support of bilingual language policies that help to maintain and facilitate ties to the "home" country. Whatever the specific purposes, sending countries are increasingly mobilizing to retain immigrants' emotional attachment and to further develop commitment to the "home" country from which they emigrated.

This mobilization may take the form of lobbying in the immigrant's interest, for example "open borders," amnesties, and maintenance of native languages, all of which the sending countries have strong self-interest in supporting. It may take the form of making American citizens and resident aliens sources of financial support for political leaders or parties in the "home" country. Or it may take the form of systematic electronic efforts to keep such immigrants in touch with developments in their "countries of origin."

These developments set the stage for a direct conflict of interest among new immigrants and citizens, many of whom retain deep attachments to their home country. Given the geographical distribution of such immigrants, it is possible that whole states and certainly some localities will have a substantial portion of dual citizens with active and deep connections to their "countries of origin" being asked to put aside these experiences and connections in favor of American community interest. Whether that is possible as a matter of psychology or politics remains to be seen. I mean no implication that such immigrants will be disloyal. However, it is prudent to consider that in such circumstances they are likely to be conflicted.

This poses a dilemma for the United States. It has traditionally taken in immigrants with the assumption that they would eventually become anchored to American identity and nationality over time in a way that was not primarily instrumental. In the past this was a reasonable assumption. It no longer is.

Dual citizenship seems well suited to an age in which advocates, theorists, and politicians tell us there are no limits to what we should expect to have. Want the benefits of freedom and opportunity buttressed by a twenty-first-century infrastructure and unlimited access to consumer goods, but still want to maintain and further develop your emotional, economic, social, and political ties to your "home" country? No less an authority on self-interest without responsibility, former President Clinton found the idea of dual citizenship publicly appealing. And why not? To the immigrant it dramatically lowers the costs of immigration while raising its benefits.

Yet to a democracy, especially one facing issues of cultural coherence and solidarity, the costs of admitting and allowing large numbers of dual citizens are not so favorable. In a time characterized by enormous worry regarding the decline of social capital (Putnam 2000) and its implications for American civic life, the split attachments of large numbers of dual citizens is another source of deep concern. No country, and certainly no democracy, can afford to have large numbers of citizens with shallow national and civic attachments. No country facing divisive domestic issues arising out of its increasing diversity, as America does, benefits from large-scale immigration of those with multiple loyalties and attachments. And no country striving to reconnect its citizens to a coherent civic identity and culture can afford to encourage its citizens to look elsewhere for their most basic national attachments.

Appendix A

Countries/Territories Allowing Dual Citizenship in Some Form

1. Albania
2. Antigua & Barbuda
3. Argentina
4. Australia[38]
5. Bahamas
6. Balsarius
7. Bangladesh
8. Barbados
9. Belize
10. Benin
11. Bolivia
12. Brazil
13. Bulgaria
14. Burkina Faso
15. Cambodia
16. Canada
17. Cape Verde
18. Chile
19. Colombia
20. Costa Rica
21. Croatia
22. Cyprus
23. Cyprus (North)
24. Dominica
25. Dominican Republic
26. Ecuador
27. Egypt
28. El Salvador
20. Fiji
30. France
31. Germany [39]
32. Ghana
33. Greece
34. Grenada
35. Guatemala
36. Guyana
37. Haiti
38. Hungary
39. India
40. Iran
41. Ireland
42. Israel
43. Italy
44. Jamaica
45. Jordan
46. Latvia
47. Lebanon
48. Lesotho
49. Liechtenstein
50. Lithuania[40]
51. Macao (with Portugal)
52. Macedonia
53. Madagascar
54. Malta
55. Mexico
56. Montenegro (Yugoslavia)
57. Mongolia
58. Morocco
59. Netherlands[41]
60. New Zealand
61. Nicaragua
62. Nigeria
63. Northern Ireland
64. Panama
65. Pakistan
66. Paraguay
67. Peru
68. Pitcairn
69. Philippines
70. Poland
71. Portugal
72. Romania
73. Russia
74. Saint Kitts (Saint Christopher) & Nevis
75. Saint Lucia
76. Saint Vincent
77. Serbia (Yugoslavia)
78. Slovenia
79. South Africa
80. Spain
81. Sri Lanka
82. Sweden
83. Switzerland
84. Taiwan
85. Trinidad/Tobago
86. Thailand
87. Tibet
88. Turkey
89. United Kingdom
90. United States
91. Ukraine
92. Uruguay
93. Vietnam

Appendix B

Dual Citizenship (DC) Status of Top 20 Immigrant-Sending Countries: 1994–1998

Country of birth	Number/% 1998	Number/% 1997	Number/% 1996	Number/% 1995	Number/% 1994
1. Mexico	131,575(19.9)	146,865(18.4)	163,572(17.9)	89,932(12.5)	111,398(13.8)
2. China	36,884(5.6)	41,147(5.2)	41,728(4.6)	35,463(4.9)	53,985(6.7)
3. India	36,482(5.6)	38,071(4.8)	44,859(4.9)	34,748(4.8)	34,921(4.3)
4. Philippines	34,446(5.2)	49,117(6.2)	55,876(6.1)	50,984(7.1)	53,535(6.7)
5. Dominican Republic	20,387(3.1)	27,053(3.4)	39,604(4.3)	38,512(5.3)	51,189(6.4)
6. Vietnam	17,649(2.7)	38,519(4.8)	42,067(4.6)	41,752(5.8)	41,345(5.1)
7. Cuba	17,375(2.6)	33,587(4.2)	26,466(2.9)	17,937(2.5)	14,727(1.8)
8. Jamaica	15,146(2.3)	17,840(2.2)	19,089(2.1)	16,398(2.3)	14,349(1.8)
9. El Salvador	14,590(2.2)	17,969(2.3)	17,903(2.0)	11,744(1.6)	17,644(2.2)
10. S. Korea*	14,268(2.2)	14,329(1.8)	18,185(2.0)	16,047(2.2)	16,011(2.0)
11. Haiti	13,499(2.0)	15,057(1.9)	18,386(2.0)	14,021(1.9)	13,333(1.7)
12. Pakistan	13,094(2.0)	12,969(1.6)	12,519(1.4)	9,774(1.4)	8,698(1.1)
13. Colombia	11,836(1.8)	13,004(1.6)	14,283(1.6)	10,83 (1.5)	10,847(1.3)
14a. Russia	11,529(1.7)	16,632(2.1)	19,668(2.1)	14,560 (2.0)	15,249(1.9)
14b. Ukraine	NR	15,696(2.0)	21,079(2.3)	17,432(2.4)	21,010(2.6)
15. Canada	10,190(1.5)	11,609(1.5)	15,825(1.7)	12,932(1.8)	16,068(2.0)
16. Peru	10,154(1.5)	10,853(1.4)	12,871(1.4)	8,066(1.1)	9,177(1.1)
17. United Kingdom	9,011(1.4)	10,651(1.3)	13,624(1.5)	12,427(1.7)	16,326(2.0)
18. Bangladesh	8,621(1.3)	NR	NR	NR	NR
19. Poland	8,469(1.3)	12,038(1.5)	15,772(1.7)	13,824(1.9)	28,048(3.5)
20. Iran	7.883(1.2)	9,642(1.2)	11,084(1.2)	9,201(1.3)	11,422(1.4)
Total "Top 20" Immigration	443,058	552,556	624,460	476,592	559,282
DC "Top 20" Immigration	374,531	493,493	538,081	407,145	474,559
%	(84.5%)	(89.3%)	(86.1%)	(85.4%)	(84.8%)
Other** Immigration	217,419	245,822	291,440	243,869	245,134
Total Immigration	660,477	798,378	915,900	720,461	804,416

Key: Dual citizen countries in bold.

NR/not reported.

* Dual-citizenship legislation pending in legislature.

** Includes both dual and nondual-citizenship-allowing countries.

Appendix C

DC Countries Only—Listed in Alphabetical Order

1961–1997: Immigrants Admitted by Region and Country of Birth

Country	1961–1970 3,321,677	1971–1980 4,493,314	1981–1990 7,338,062	1991 1,827,167	1992 973,977	1993 904,292
1 Albania	N/A	N/A	N/A	6,713,934	682	1,400
2 Antigua & Barbuda	N/A	N/A	12,900	944	619	554
3 Argentina	42,100	25,100	25,700	3,889	3,877	2,824
4 Austria ·	N/A	N/A	N/A	589	701	549
5 Australia	9,900	14,300	13,900	1,678	2,238	2,320
6 Bahamas	N/A	N/A	7,300	1,062	641	686
7 Bangladesh	N/A	N/A	15,200	10,676	3,740	3,291
8 Barbados	9,400	20,900	17,400	1,460	1,091	1,184
9 Belize	N/A	N/A	18,100	2,377	1,020	1,035
10 Belarus	N/A	N/A	N/A	N/A	3,233	4,702
11 Benin	N/A	N/A	N/A	24	10	21
12 Bolivia	N/A	N/A	12,300	3,006	1,510	1,545
13 Brazil	20,500	13,700	23,700	8,133	4,755	4,604
14 Bulgaria	N/A	N/A	N/A	623	1,049	1,029
15 Burkina Faso	N/A	N/A	N/A	8	16	11
16 Cambodia	1,200	8,400	116,600	3,251	2,573	1,639
17 Canada	286,700	114,800	119,200	13,504	15,205	17,156
18 Cape Verde	N/A	N/A	N/A	973	757	936
19 Chile	11,500	17,600	23,400	2,842	1,937	11,778
20 Colombia	70,300	77,600	124,400	19,702	13,201	12,819
21 Costa Rica	17,400	12,100	15,500	2,341	1,480	1,368
22 Croatia	N/A	N/A	N/A	N/A	77	370
23 Cyprus	N/A	N/A	N/A	243	262	229
24 Cyprus (North)	N/A	N/A	N/A	N/A	N/A	N/A
25 Dominica	N/A	N/A	N/A	982	809	683
26 Dominican Republic	94,100	148,000	251,800	41,405	41,969	45,420
27 Ecuador	37,000	50,200	56,000	9,958	7,286	7,324
28 Egypt	17,200	25,500	31,400	5,602	3,576	3,556
29 El Salvador	15,000	34,400	214,600	47,351	26,191	26,818

Appendix C (continued)

DC Countries Only—Listed in Alphabetical Order

1961–1997: Immigrants Admitted by Region and Country of Birth

Country	1994 804,416	1995 720,461	1996 915,900	1997 798,378	TOTAL 22,997,644
Albania	1,489	1,420	4,007	4,375	6,727,307
Antigua & Barbuda	438	374	406	393	16,628
Argentina	2,318	1,762	2,456	1,964	111,990
Austria	499	518	554	487	3,897
Australia	2,049	1,751	1,950	1,630	51,716
Bahamas	589	585	768	641	12,272
Bangladesh	3,434	6,072	8,221	8,681	59,315
Barbados	897	734	1,043	829	54,938
Belize	772	644	786	664	25,398
Belarus	5,420	3,791	4,268	3,062	24,476
Benin	18	23	38	48	182
Bolivia	1,404	1,332	1,913	1,734	24,744
Brazil	4,491	4,558	5,891	4,583	94,915
Bulgaria	981	1,797	2,066	2,774	10,319
Burkina Faso	16	17	17	13	98
Cambodia	1,404	1,492	1,568	1,638	139,765
Canada	16,068	12,932	15,825	11,609	622,999
Cape Verde	810	968	1,012	920	6,376
Chile	1,640	1,534	1,706	1,443	75,380
Colombia	10,847	10,838	14,283	13,004	366,994
Costa Rica	1,205	1,062	1,504	1,330	55,290
Croatia	412	608	810	720	2,997
Cyprus	204	188	187	148	1,460
Cyprus (North)	N/A	N/A	N/A	N/A	0
Dominica	507	591	797	746	5,115
Dominican Republic	51,189	38,512	39,604	27,053	779,052
Ecuador	5,906	6,397	8,321	7,780	196,072
Egypt	3,392	5,648	6,186	5,031	107,091
El Salvador	17,644	11,744	17,903	17,969	429,620

Appendix C (continued)

DC Countries Only—Listed in Alphabetical Order

1961–1997: Immigrants Admitted by Region and Country of Birth

Country	1961–1970 3,221,677	1971–1980 4,493,314	1981–1990 7,338,062	1991 1,827,167	1992 973,977	1993 904,292
30 Fiji	N/A	N/A	N/A	1,349	807	854
31 France	34,300	17,800	23,100	2,450	3,288	2,864
32 Germany	200,000	66,000	70,100	6,509	9,888	7,312
33 Ghana	N/A	N/A	14,900	3,330	1,867	1,604
34 Greece	90,200	93,700	29,100	2,079	1,858	1,884
35 Grenada	N/A	N/A	10,600	979	848	827
36 Guatemala	15,400	25,600	87,900	25,527	10,521	11,870
37 Guyana	7,100	47,500	95,400	11,666	9,064	8,384
38 Haiti	37,500	58,700	140,200	47,527	11,002	10,094
39 Hungary	17,300	11,600	9,800	1,534	1,304	1,091
40 India	31,200	176,800	261,900	45,064	36,755	40,121
41 Iran	10,400	46,200	154,800	19,569	13,233	14,841
42 Ireland	42,400	14,100	32,800	4,767	12,226	13,590
43 Israel	12,900	26,600	36,300	4,181	5,104	4,494
44 Italy	206,700	130,100	32,900	2,619	2,592	2,487
45 Jamaica	71,000	142,000	213,800	23,828	18,915	17,241
46 Jordan	14,000	29,600	32,600	4,259	4,036	4,741
47 Latvia	N/A	N/A	N/A	86	419	668
48 Lebanon	7,500	33,800	41,600	6,009	5,838	5,465
49 Lesotho	N/A	N/A	N/A	4	15	5
50 Liechtenstein	N/A	N/A	N/A	3	1	3
51 Lithuania	N/A	N/A	N/A	157	353	529
52 Macao (w/ Portugal)	N/A	N/A	N/A	267	320	334
53 Macedonia	N/A	N/A	N/A	N/A	N/A	N/A
54 Madagascar	N/A	N/A	N/A	23	41	32
55 Malta	N/A	N/A	N/A	83	85	52
56 Mexico	443,300	637,200	1,653,300	946,167	213,802	126,561
57 Mongolia	N/A	N/A	N/A	2	6	8
58 Montenegro	N/A	N/A	N/A	N/A	N/A	N/A
59 Morocco	N/A	N/A	6,700	1,601	1,316	1,176
60 Netherlands	27,800	10,700	11,900	1,283	1,586	1,430
61 New Zealand	N/A	N/A	N/A	793	967	1,052
62 Nicaragua	10,100	13,000	44,100	17,842	8,949	7,086
63 Nigeria	1,500	8,800	35,300	7,912	4,551	4,448

Appendix C (continued)

DC Countries Only—Listed in Alphabetical Order

1961–1997: Immigrants Admitted by Region and Country of Birth

Country	1994 804,416	1995 720,461	1996 915,900	1997 798,378	TOTAL 21,997,644
Fiji	1,007	1,491	1,847	1,549	8,904
France	2,715	2,505	3,079	2,568	94,669
Germany	6,992	6,237	6,748	5,723	385,509
Ghana	1,458	3,152	6,606	5,105	38,022
Greece	1,440	1,309	1,452	1,049	224,071
Grenada	595	583	787	755	15,974
Guatemala	7,389	6,213	8,763	7,785	206,968
Guyana	7,662	7,362	9,489	7,257	210,884
Haiti	13,333	14,021	18,386	15,057	365,820
Hungary	880	900	1,183	949	46,541
India	34,921	34,748	44,859	38,071	744,439
Iran	11,422	9,201	11,084	9,642	300,392
Ireland	17,256	5,315	1,731	1,001	145,186
Israel	3,425	2,523	3,126	2,448	101,101
Italy	2,305	2,231	2,501	1,982	386,417
Jamaica	14,349	16,398	19,089	17,840	554,460
Jordan	3,990	3,649	4,445	4,171	105,491
Latvia	762	651	736	615	3,937
Lebanon	4,319	3,884	4,382	3,568	116,365
Lesotho	8	10	11	6	59
Liechtenstein	0	2	1	1	11
Lithuania	663	767	1,080	812	4,361
Macao (w/ Portugal)	287	373	453	277	2,311
Macedonia	367	666	863	783	2,679
Madagascar	27	42	43	33	241
Malta	75	72	52	54	473
Mexico	111,398	89,932	163,572	146,865	4,532,097
Mongolia	21	17	17	22	93
Montenegro	N/A	N/A	N/A	N/A	0
Morocco	1,074	1,726	1,783	2,359	17,735
Netherlands	1,239	1,196	1,423	1,059	59,616
New Zealand	18	727	800	655	5,912
Nicaragua	5,255	4,408	6,903	6,331	123,974
Nigeria	3,950	6,818	10,221	7,038	90,538

Appendix C (continued)

DC Countries Only—Listed in Alphabetical Order

1961–1997: Immigrants Admitted by Region and Country of Birth

Country	1961–1970 3,321,677	1971–1980 4,493,314	1981–1990 7,338,062	1991 1,827,167	1992 973,977	1993 904,29
64 Northern Ireland	N/A	N/A	N/A	N/A	N/A	N/A
65 Panama	18,400	22,700	29,000	4,204	2,845	2,679
66 Paraguay	N/A	N/A	N/A	538	514	668
67 Pakistan	4,900	31,200	61,300	20,355	10,214	8,927
68 Peru	18,600	29,100	64,400	16,237	9,868	10,447
69 Philippines	101,500	360,200	495,300	63,596	61,022	63,457
70 Pitcairn	N/A	N/A	N/A	N/A	N/A	N/A
71 Poland	73,300	43,600	97,400	19,199	25,504	27,846
72 Portugal	79,300	104,500	40,000	4,524	2,748	2,08
73 Romania	14,900	17,500	38,900	8,096	6,500	5,60
74 Russia/SU	15,700	43,200	84,000	56,980	8,857	12,07
75 Saint Kitts & Nevis	N/A	N/A	N/A	830	626	54
76 Saint Lucia	N/A	N/A	N/A	766	654	63
77 Saint Vincent	N/A	N/A	N/A	808	687	65
78 Serbia/ Yugoslavia	46,200	42,100	19,200	2,713	2,604	2,80
79 Slovenia	N/A	N/A	N/A	N/A	8	5
80 South Africa	4,500	11,500	15,700	1,854	2,516	2,19
81 Sri Lanka	N/A	N/A	N/A	1,377	1,081	1,10
82 Sweden	16,700	6,300	10,200	1,080	1,463	1,39
83 Switzerland	16,300	6,600	7,000	696	1,023	97
84 Taiwan	N/A	N/A	N/A	13,274	16,344	14,32
85 Thailand	5,000	44,100	64,400	7,397	7,090	6,65
86 Tibet	N/A	N/A	N/A	N/A	N/A	N/
87 Trinidad/ Tobago	24,600	61,800	39,500	8,407	7,008	6,5
88 Turkey	6,800	18,600	20,900	2,528	2,488	2,2
89 UK	230,500	123,500	142,100	13,903	19,973	18,7
90 Ukraine	N/A	N/A	N/A	N/A	14,383	18,3
91 Uruguay	N/A	N/A	8,300	1,161	716	5
92 Vietnam	4,600	179,700	401,400	55,307	77,735	59,6
Total	2,594,700	3,298,600	5,777,500	1,678,064	806,103	720,1
%DC	(80)	(73)	(78)	(91)	(82)	(7

1961–1997 %DC = Total DC (17,437,607) /immigration total (21,997,664) =

Appendix C (continued)

DC Countries Only—Listed in Alphabetical Order

1961–1997: Immigrants Admitted by Region and Country of Birth

Country	1994 804,416	1995 720,461	1996 915,900	1997 798,378	TOTAL 21,997,644
Northern					
Ireland	N/A	N/A	N/A	N/A	0
Panama	2,378	2,247	2,560	1,981	88,994
Paraguay	789	559	615	304	3,987
Pakistan	8,698	9,774	12,519	12,967	180,854
Peru	9,177	8,066	12,871	10,853	189,619
Philippines	53,535	50,984	55,876	49,117	1,354,587
Pitcairn	N/A	N/A	N/A	N/A	0
Poland	28,048	13,824	15,772	12,038	356,531
Portugal	2,169	2,615	2,984	1,665	242,586
Romania	3,444	4,871	5,801	5,545	111,158
Russia/SU	15,249	14,560	19,668	16,632	286,925
Saint Kitts					
& Nevis	370	360	357	377	3,464
Saint Lucia	449	403	582	531	4,019
Saint Vincent	524	349	606	581	4,212
Serbia/					
Yugoslavia	3,405	8,307	11,854	10,750	149,942
Slovenia	67	65	77	62	329
South Africa	2,144	2,560	2,966	2,093	48,030
Sri Lanka	989	960	1,277	1,128	7,921
Sweden	1,140	976	1,251	958	41,461
Switzerland	877	881	1,006	1,063	36,418
Taiwan	10,032	9,377	13,401	6,745	147,652
Thailand	5,489	5,136	4,310	3,094	152,670
Tibet	N/A	N/A	N/A	N/A	0
Trinidad/					
Tobago	6,292	5,424	7,344	6,409	173,361
Turkey	1,840	2,947	3,657	3,145	565,109
UK	16,326	12,427	13,624	10,651	601,787
Ukraine	21,010	17,432	21,079	15,696	107,916
Uruguay	516	414	540	429	12,644
Vietnam	41,345	41,752	42,067	38,519	942,039
Total	633,847	594,291	736,269	628,039	
%DC	(78)	(78)	(80)	(78)	

Notes

*This paper builds on Renshon (2000). I would like to thank Nathan Glazer, Eugene Goldstein, and Mark Krikorian for their helpful comments. I would also like to acknowledge the valuable assistance of Ms. Sandra Johnson.

1. Americans may be slightly more familiar with the term *dual citizenship*, which denotes holding official citizenship status in two separate countries. Yet the term *multiple citizenship* is the more accurate one since it covers the holding of two *or more* citizenships. No country that allows its nationals dual citizenship prohibits holding more than one other. Along similar lines, Jones-Correa (2000, 2, 32) notes that a number of South American countries (Argentina, Chile, Guatemala, Honduras, Nicaragua, and Paraguay) have dual-citizenship agreements with other Central American countries or with Spain, which itself is part of the European Union, whose common citizenship treaties are being implemented. These countries, in turn, have more robust dual-citizenship laws for their own citizens and foreign-born nationals. Dual and multiple citizenship(s) are therefore used interchangeably throughout this paper.

2. I take up the important distinctions between these two terms later in this essay.

3. There are variations among other countries in which specific citizenship rights are allowed and under what conditions. Some European countries—for example Sweden, Denmark, Norway, and Finland—grant foreign citizens voting rights in local and regional elections. Some Latin American countries that permit or encourage their nationals to gain second citizenships in the United States allow those citizens to vote in elections in their country of origin (e.g., Peru, El Salvador, Colombia); some (e.g., Honduras, Brazil, and Mexico) do not. See Hammar (1985); Rodolfo O. de la Garza et al. (1996, 2-3), and Jones-Correa (2000, 3, 5).

4. The Swedish researcher Tomas Hammer (1985, 445) reaches similar conclusions about Europe. He says, "The actual number of dual nationals is not known." Moreover, "even now when cases of dual nationality tend to become numerous, no statistics are kept anywhere in Europe."

5. While the Department of State now takes the position that acceptance of policy-level employment with a foreign government *will* be presumed to be a basis for denaturalization, a number of American dual citizens have held rather high positions without loss of citizenship. Raffi Hovannisian became foreign minister of Armenia, and stated publicly, "I certainly do not renounce my American citizenship," thus closing off a legal challenge to what he had done. Muhamed Sacirbey, foreign minister of Bosnia in 1995–96, is an American citizen and dual-national. The chief of the Estonian army in 1991–95 also was an American, Aleksander Einseln. Many Americans have served at the United Nations as ambassadors of their other country's citizenship (Franck 1996).

6. For example in 1986, following the Supreme Court's decision in *Afroyim v. Rusk* (387 U.S. 253), Congress repealed parts of the statutory provisions of Ameri-

can citizenship law by adding the key requirement that loss of citizenship could occur only on the citizen's "voluntarily performing any of the following acts with the intention of relinquishing United States nationality" (Act of Nov. 14, 1986, § 18, 100 Stat. 3655, 3658 [codified as amended in 8 U.S.C. § 1481 (1988)]). With that, the onus shifted to the government to demonstrate that a designated act had been performed both voluntarily and with the specific intent to renounce U.S. citizenship. See Franck (1996).

7. The reasons for ignoring these circumstances vary. A country simply may not perceive the practice as sufficiently important or widespread to merit attention or action. Or it may serve its own purposes—political, economic, or cultural—by ignoring other ties from which they benefit. The country may have legal prohibitions against the practice that are weakened by another of that country's political institutions. For example, as Franck points out, Australian law as legislated in 1948 appeared to withdraw citizenship from any Australian who "does any act or thing: (a) the sole or dominant purpose of which; and (b) the effect of which; is to acquire the nationality or citizenship of a foreign country." Yet a recent court case there held that this provision did not apply to an Australian of partly Swiss origin who applied to the Swiss government for recognition of her *jus sanguinis* status as a Swiss citizen. The case thereby opened the door to recognition of dual nationality since the court held that to lose Australian citizenship, the citizen's motive must have been to *acquire* Swiss citizenship, rather than to obtain recognition of an already existing status of foreign nationality. See Franck (1996).

8. For example, Jones-Correa (2000, 32) offers Bolivia, Honduras, and Venezuela as examples of Latin American countries that allow repatriation upon return. Goldstein and Piazza (1998, 1630) add Haiti to this list. This is, of course, a form of *de facto* dual citizenship. This form does not allow the exercising of formal political rights in the immigrant's country of origin, but to the extent that repatriation is the person's ultimate goal, it may very well affect attachments to a new country.

9. Nationality is often thought of as expressed primarily through emotional attachments, and these are important. Yet it would be a mistake to divorce a person's emotional attachments from the understandings and knowledge that both reflect and inform them.

10. These include: Capriotti & Associates, International Law, Portland, Ore. 97208–2792. <*http://www.capriotti.com*> (ND); Aleinikoff (1988a, 28–29); Goldstein and Piazza (1996, 517–21; 1998, 1613–17; Kalvaitis (1998, note 184); Kang (1998, 1); Kempster (1999, 8); Schuck (1998, 223); Spiro (1997) 1455, 1457–58); Vargas (1996, 50, note 198); Zappala and Castles (1999, 273); and Jones-Correa (2000, 3, 5).

11. Most discussions of dual citizenship do not attempt comprehensive listings of those countries that allow it. Even those that do provide such lists are not always accurate or in agreement. So for example, Goldstein and Piazza do not list Ireland (which does permit dual citizenship). More troublesome are

inconsistencies that arise from conflicts between what two or more different authors assert is erroneous information.

Thus, Goldstein and Piazza (1996) list the Philippines and India as nondual-citizenship countries, while Schuck (1997, 11; 1998, 222) says they are, for American-born children of Filipino and Indian nationals. Along similar lines, Jones-Correa (2000) lists Argentina as having limited dual citizenship (with other treaty countries), while Goldstein and Piazza (1998) make no such distinction. And finally, Goldstein and Piazza list the Netherlands as a nondual-citizenship country, while Schmitter-Heisler (1998) discusses the effects of the Dutch dual citizenship law passed in 1992. In all cases of differences, inquiries were made of the appropriate embassies. In the few cases where this did not produce clarification, preference was given to the views of authors with established records of scholarship.

12. The strategy employed for this study was to accept as accurate countries listed as allowing dual citizenship by reputable academic authorities in the study of immigration. Where a country was not listed as accepting multiple citizenship by previous studies, but which was important for our purposes in the analyses that follow, we e-mailed and called the embassies of those countries directly. After explaining our general interest in the subject and saying we would greatly appreciate their help we asked the following: (1) Whether your country now permits the children born of your nationals living abroad (for example, in the United States) to obtain or retain their citizenship in your country; and (2) Whether your country now permits adult nationals living abroad to retain their citizenship in your country if they also become a citizen of another country (for example, the United States).

13. This, and the examples that follow, are drawn from Franck (1996).

14. Hammer (1985, 446) notes that some dual nationals face the risk of having to serve in two different armed forces if they travel to the country in which they hold citizenship/nationality but did not serve. He further notes that others countries, like Turkey, mandate in the constitution that service in the army is a requirement for all Turks, period.

Later evidence, however, suggests Turkey may have modified its position on this somewhat. Miller reports that at a conference organized by the Alien Commission of the West Berlin Senate in 1989, the Turkish councilor in Berlin said that his government permitted Turkish males living in Germany to pay 10,000 deutsche marks over a ten-year period to reduce their active time of service in Turkey to two months. See Miller (1991, 948).

15. There are a number of cases relevant to the circumstances in which American citizens may give up or lose their citizenship: *Perkins v. Elg* (1939); *Kawakita v. US.* (1952); *Mandoli v. Acheson* (1952); *Perez v. Brownell* (1958); *Trop v. Dulles* (1958); *Schneider v. Rusk* (1964); *Afroyim v. Rusk* (1967); *Rogers v. Bellei* (1971); *Vance v. Terrazas* (1980); and *Miller v. Albright* (1998).

However, by far the most important case is *Afroyim v. Rusk*, 387 U.S. 253 (1967), decided by the U.S. Supreme Court on May 29, 1967. In that ruling, the Court

held that to sustain a finding of citizenship loss under the [then current] statement and the rules, there must be forthcoming persuasive evidence establishing
that the action taken by the citizen was accompanied by an *affirmative intention* to
transfer allegiance to the country of foreign nationality, abandon allegiance owed
the United States, or otherwise relinquish United States citizenship (emphasis
mine).

See Immigration and Naturalization Service, Interpretations of the Citizenship and Naturalization Law, 350.1 Expatriation in the absence of elective action
by persons acquiring dual nationality at birth prior to repeal of section 350.

What does "affirmation intention" mean? On 16 April, 1990, the State Department adopted a new set of guidelines for handling dual citizenship cases
which assumes that a U.S. citizen intends to retain his or her U.S. citizenship
even if he or she (1) is naturalized in a foreign country; (2) takes a routine oath
of allegiance to a foreign country; or (3) accepts foreign government employment that is of a "nonpolicy-level" nature.

So, taking an oath of allegiance to another country is no longer firm evidence
of intent to give up U.S. citizenship, even if that oath includes a renunciation of
U.S. citizenship. These assumptions do not apply to persons who (1) take a
"policy-level" position in a foreign country; (2) are convicted of treason against
the U.S.; or (3) engage in "conduct that is so inconsistent with retention of U.S.
citizenship that it compels a conclusion that [he] intended to relinquish U.S. citizenship." The third is unspecified and decided on a case-by-case basis.

16. U.S. Department of Commerce (1997, 8–49). Definitions of terms used
are found in Appendix A, 52–53.

17. See U.S. Department of Justice/Immigration and Naturalization Service
(1999a, 8; 1999b, 9). Both reports provide legal immigration figures for *selected*
countries for the years they cover. As a result, some additional information is
necessary to understand why the term "top twenty," while essentially accurate, is
in quotes. One anomaly is that neither of the two documents includes the countries making up the former Yugoslavia (Serbia and Montenegro, Croatia, Bosnia-
Herzegovina, Macedonia, and Slovenia, all multiple-citizenship-allowing countries) in their list of top immigrant-sending countries. Yet with 10,750 immigrants
in 1997 and 11,854 in 1996 coming from these countries in those two years, they
certainly sent more immigrations than several of the countries included in document's list of high-sending countries. For these reasons, the numbers and percentages of multiple-citizenship-country immigrants as a function of the total
number of listed "top twenty" countries tend to under report their magnitude.

One other anomaly of the table should be noted. The May 1999 report of
1995–98 immigration figures includes one country (Bangladesh) that is not included in the top-sending-country list in the January 1999 document reporting
the immigration figures for 1994–97. The reports follow each of the countries
listed back through several previous years. So the May 1999 report contains figures for Bangladesh for the years 1995–98, even though it is not listed as a top-
sending country in the earlier January 1999 report, which covered the years

1994–97. In that latter report, the Ukraine is listed as a top-immigrant-sending country and its immigrant-sending history is traced back from 1994–97. However, in that report Bangladesh is *not* listed. Otherwise the specific countries listed are the same.

To more accurately reflect the realities of the data on high ("top twenty") immigrant-sending countries, I have reported the Bangladesh data for 1998, but not for previous years when the numbers are well below those of the Ukraine, which is listed in that "top twenty" group in the January 1999 report.

18. As substantial or surprising as these figures may be, they do not tell the whole story of the number of multiple citizens arriving and living in the United States. To further deepen our understanding we would need to turn to two other categorical sources: illegal immigrants and immigrant fertility rates. The reason for this has to do both with the possibility that new or *de facto* amnesty for illegal aliens might add appreciably to these numbers and the fact that children of legal and illegal immigrants are automatically U.S. citizens.

19. The figures that follow are drawn from the U.S. Department of Commerce, Economics and Statistics Administration, U.S. Census, "Profile of the Foreign Born Population in the United States: 1997," *Current Populations Reports Special Studies* (P23-195): 8–49. Definitions of terms used are found in Appendix A, 12.

20. For an eloquent formulation of this view see Levinson (1986, 1463–70); see also Spiro (1997, 1473).

21. The quotes in this paragraph are drawn from Aleinikoff (1999).

22. See Geyer (1996, 68). David Martin (1999, 8, note 24) points out that the bigamy metaphor was made in the context of dual-citizenship debates in the early-nineteenth-century.

23. An example of the confusion that accompanies failures to think clearly about these distinctions can be seen in the recent article by David Martin. He begins his discussion of dual citizenship by informing the reader that he will use the terms *citizenship* and *nationality* interchangeably, and elsewhere refers to "mere" nationality. He terms the distinction between citizen(ship) and national(ity) a "technical one," which is "rarely important for my purposes." He then goes on to discuss the issue of multiple and conflicting loyalties in which, of course, the distinction between nationality and citizenship are central, not mere technicalities. See Martin (1999): 1, note 1, 8–11.

24. The metaphor linking family life and national identity suggests certain parallels. There are, of course, differences as well. The nation is not a parent. It does not have the primary responsibilities to nurture, guide, and socialize its citizens that are comparable to a parent's responsibility to raise a child.

On the other hand, the nation, like the family, is present from the child's earliest experiences. It is to be found in the parents' language, cultural practices, and national cultural identifications. It is also the consistent context in which the child's development unfolds, and it provides the institutions (e.g., schools, civic, and community organizations) and objects (flags, rituals like the pledge of allegiance) through which the child's personal and national identities become fused at an early age.

25. See for example the arguments of Michael Waltzer (1997, 87) who notes, "In immigrant societies people have begun to experience what we might think of as a life without clear boundaries and without secure or singular identities."

26. What David Martin (1999, 31) refers to as "simple voting" is in fact anything but simple. On the complexities of voting, see Stanley J. Kelley and T. Mirer (1974).

27. Martin (1999, 4–14) offers five elements favoring liberalization of dual nationality: increasing globalization, peace, the complex nature of loyalties, more effective human rights regimes, and expanding democratization. I cannot more fully analyze his arguments here; however, several of them—the complex nature of loyalties and expanding democratization—would not seem, on balance, to be strong arguments in favor of further liberalization.

28. On the role of dual nationals as an important ingredient of this conflict, see Spiro (1997, 1422–23; also Martin 1999, 20; and McGarvey-Rosendahl 1985, 310–21). The first part of Spiro's article, pages 1417–32, provides an excellent overview of the historical difficulties associated with the international diplomacy of dual citizenship.

29. Or as Alexander and Smelser (1999, 3) in their new book on American cultural discontent put it, "The core of the complaint concerns common values in American society. "

30. The quotes that follow are drawn from Alexander and Smelser (1999, 3, 8, 9, 11).

31. Historical views of American national identity coupled with a modern reformulation of the concept may be found in Renshon (2000, 285–310).

32. After all, Natty Bumpo (Hawkeye) had Uncas and his father Chingachgook, and even that icon of righteous individualism, the Lone Ranger, had Tonto.

33. The best book on the seductive psychology of the image and the public's role in encouraging it is still Boorstin (1992 [1933]).

34. Yankelovich's (1981, xix, 259–60) national opinion data on the growing emphasis on self-fulfillment in American culture led him to conclude "it was not a by-product of affluence, or a shift in the national character toward narcissism, [but rather] a search for a new American philosophy of life." Of course, "philosophies of life" are themselves reflections of values and psychology and, as noted, helped to facilitate the very psychologies that will buttress them.

Optimistically, he saw Americans growing "less self-absorbed and more prepared to take a first step toward an ethic of commitment." However, he also noted that the development of such an ethic would require direct support from "the larger society—political leadership, the mass media, institutional leadership (business, education, labor, artists and scientists, the intellectual community)," in short, for the most part all the groups caught up in the ethic of relentless self-interest. Small wonder that seventeen years later, Nicholas Lemann (1998,

38) writing in the *New York Times Magazine*, lamented a new consensus that "represents an embrace of . . . one-way libertarianism: the average citizen has no obligation to the country, but the government has a very serious obligation to that citizen."

35. There is an important distinction to be drawn between being slow to judgment and being averse to making judgments. Why Americans now seem more averse than slow is a question left unanswered by Wolfe (1998), but is nonetheless critical in understanding the public's response to the dilemmas of diversity being fought out around them.

36. For example, he reports that in the mid-1960s, 72 percent of college students agreed that "hard work always pays off." By the early 1970s, this figure had dropped to 40 percent. These findings were paralleled in adults for whom, between the late 1960s and the late 1970s, the percentage of adults agreeing with that aphorism fell from 58 to 43 percent. See Yankelovich (1981, 38–39, 163–218).

37. In an early work on American national character, the English psychoanalyst Geoffrey Gorer (1964, 25; see also Salins 1997) wrote:

> With few exceptions, the immigrants did not cross the ocean as colonists to reproduce the civilization of their homes on distant shores; with the geographical separation they were prepared to give up, as far as lay in their power, all their past: their language, and the thoughts which that language could express; the laws and allegiances they had been brought up to observe, the values and assured ways of life of their ancestors and former compatriots; even to a large extent their customary ways of eating, of dressing, of living.

This is the immersion into the "melting pot," which colors the myths of both assimilation's advocates and critics. The former see that process as natural and desirable, and the latter see it as little better than the cultural rape of immigrant identity. Yet both sides would do well to keep in mind Gorer's answer to his question of why early immigrants might not have wished to reproduce their homelands here. The answer was to be found in the fact that most immigrants had "escaped . . . from discriminatory laws, rigid hierarchical structures, compulsory military service and authoritarian limitation of the opportunities open to the enterprising and the goals to which they could aspire."

38. Zappala and Castles (1999, 273, note 137; see also Castles, 1997) quote the Australian Citizenship Act of 1948 as follows: "People must have deliberately sought and acquired the citizenship of another country in order to lose their Australian citizenship; if they acquire it automatically rather than by taking some action to acquire it they do not lose their Australian citizenship."

39. In July 1999, the Citizenship Law Reform Act was published in the German official gazette. This act went into force on January 1, 2000. Under the new law, German citizenship has always been and will continue to be passed on by

parents to the children. Any child of a German national (mother or father, married or not married) will be considered a German citizen by birth, whether born inside or outside Germany. The Reform Act introduces an aspect of "territorial acquisition": any child born inside Germany to parents of foreign nationality will acquire German nationality by birth if at least one parent has been lawfully residential in Germany for at least eight years and has for at least three years been the holder of a certain higher form of residence permit. This new provision will apply to most children of migrant workers who have been living in Germany for at least eight years. Those children, however, will grow up having to decide between keeping German citizenship and renouncing their other citizenship (i.e., that of their parents) or keeping the foreign nationality and losing the German nationality.

Under the earlier German citizenship law (which in this respect corresponds to that of many other countries, the United States included), German nationals lost their German citizenship if and when they acquired a foreign nationality upon their own application, i.e., by naturalization. It has always been possible in theory to be granted a waiver by German authorities for keeping German citizenship when acquiring a foreign nationality. Under the new law this waiver will be granted more easily. The relevant section of the act reads: "When deciding upon an application in accordance with sentence 1 (waiver), the public and private interests will have to be balanced. In the case of an applicant with residence abroad, it will have to be taken into consideration whether he/she can make the case for continuing links to Germany." That means, in effect, that in terms of the naturalization of foreigners as well as the acquisition of foreign citizenship by Germans, the threshold of tolerance of dual citizenship (which has never been a problem in the case of acquisition of several nationalities by birth) will be made much more flexible.

While there is a provision requiring renunciation, Stephan Senders says that in the past there has been no requirement to prove that it was done. He reports that according to unofficial government estimates 8 percent of naturalizing Turks retain their Turkish citizenship. Ethnic Germans who have other citizenships were allowed, even under the old law, to retain their German citizenship even when they were naturalized in other countries. A 1993 government study estimated that 1.2 million Germans legally held a second foreign citizenship (Senders 1996, 158–59). The fact that the United States makes no effort to follow through on the renunciation clause in its own oath of allegiance essentially renders any such provisions in the laws of other countries moot.

40. Kalvaitis (1998, 231, notes 184, 227) reads: "Members of the Latvian diaspora, however, are allowed to hold dual citizenship." See Law on Citizenship (Lat.), supra note 175, transitional provisions 1, 2. Footnote 227 reads: "Lithuania, however, allows members of its Western émigré community to hold dual nationality, despite the fact there is no established law to this fact."

41. See Schmitter-Heisler (1998, 103–04, note 14).

References

Aleinikoff, T. Alexander. "Between National and Post-National: Membership in the United States." *Michigan Journal of Race and Law* 241 (1999).

———. " Between Principles and Politics: The Direction of U.S. Citizenship Policy." Washington, D.C.: Carnegie Endowment for International Peace, 1998a.

———. "A Multicultural Nationalism?" *The American Prospect* (January/February, 1998b): 80–86.

Alexander, Jeffrey C., and Neil J. Smelser. "The Ideological Discourse of Cultural Discontent: Paradoxes, Realities, and Alternative Ways of Thinking." In *Diversity and Its Discontents: Cultural Conflict and Common Ground in Contemporary American Society*, ed. Neil J. Smelser and Jeffrey C. Alexander. Princeton, N.J.: Princeton University Press, 1999.

Boorstin, Daniel. *The Image*. New York: Vantage, 1992 [1933].

Bourne, Randolph S. "Trans-National America." In *War and the Intellectuals: Collected Essays, 1915–1919*, edited by Carl Resek. New York: Harper & Row, 1964, pp. 107–23. First published in *Atlantic Monthly*, July 1916.

Camarota, Steven A. "Immigrants in the United States—2000: A Snapshot of America's Foreign-Born Population." Washington, D.C.: Center for Immigrations Studies, 2001.

Capriotti & Associates. "International Law." Portland, Ore., April 16, 2000. <www.capriotti.com>

Castles, Stephen. "Multiculturalism Citizenship: A Response to the Dilemma of Globalisation and National Identity?" *Journal of Intercultural Studies* 18, no. 5 (1997).

de Creveceour, J. H. St. John. *Letters from an American Farmer*, ed. Susan Manning. New York: Oxford University Press, 1970 [1783], 43–44.

de la Garza, Rodolfo O., Miguel David Baranoa, Tomas Pachon, Emily Edmunds, Fernando Acosta-Rodriguez, and Michelle Morales. "Dual Citizenship, Domestic Politics, and Naturalization Rates of Latino Immigrants in the U.S." Policy Brief. Claremont, Calif.: The Tomas Rivera Center, June 1966.

DiMaggio, Paul, John Evans, and Bethany Bryson. "Have Americans' Social Attitudes Become More Polarized?" *American Journal of Sociology* 102 (1996): 444–96.

Editorial. "The Functionality of Citizenship." *Harvard Law Review* 110 (1997): 1814–31.

Escobar, G. "Immigrants' Ranks Tripled in 29 Years." *The Washington Post* (January 9, 1999): A1.

Franck, Thomas M. "Clan and Superclan: Law Identity and Community in Law and Practice." *The American Journal of International Law* 90, no. 359 (1996).

Gergen, Kenneth J. *The Saturated Self*. Cambridge, Mass.: Harvard University Press, 1998.

Geyer, Georgie Anne. *Americans No More: The Death of Citizenship.* New York: Atlantic Monthly Press, 1996.

Goldstein, Eugene, and Victoria Piazza. " Naturalization and Retention for Foreign Citizenship: A Survey." *Interpreter Releases* 73, no. 16 (1996): 517–21.

———. "Naturalization and Retention for Foreign Citizenship: A Survey." *Interpreter Releases* 75, no. 45 (1998), Appendix 1.

Gorer, Geoffrey. *The American People: A Study in National Character.* Revised Edition. New York: Norton, 1964.

Habermas, Jurgen. "Citizenship and National Identity: Some Reflections on the Future of Europe." *Praxis International* 17 (1992).

Hammer, Tomas. "Dual Citizenship and Political Integration." *International Migration Review* 19, no. 3 (1985): 438–50.

Herberg, Will. *Protestant, Catholic, Jew: An Essay in American Religious Sociology.* Garden City, N.Y.: Doubleday, 1955.

Higham, John. "Cultural Responses to Immigration." In *Diversity and Its Discontents: Cultural Conflict and Common Ground in Contemporary American Society,* ed. Neil J. Smelser and Jeffrey C. Alexander. Princeton, N.J.: Princeton University Press, 1999, 339–61.

Isbister, J. " Is America Too White?" In *What, Then, Is the American, This New Man?* compiled by E. Sandman. Washington, D.C.: Center of Immigration Studies, 1998, 25–32.

———. *The Immigration Debate: Remaking America.* New York: Kurnarian Press, 1996.

Jones-Correa, Micheal. "Under Two Flags: Dual Nationality in Latin America and Its Consequence for the United States." Working Papers in Latin America (no. 99/00-3). Cambridge, Mass.: The David Rockefeller Center for Latin American Studies, Harvard University, 2000.

Kalvaitis, Ruta M. "Citizenship and National Identity in the Baltic States." *Boston University International Law Journal* 16 (1998): 231.

Kang, K. Connie. "Dual U. S.–Korean Nationality Nears." *The Los Angles Times* (June 14, 1998).

Kelley, Stanley J., and T. Mirer. "The Simple Act of Voting." *The American Political Science Review* 68 (1974): 572–91.

Kelly, H. Ansgar. "Dual Nationality, The Myth of Election, and a Kinder, Gentler State Department." *University of Miami Inter-American Law Review* 23, no. 2 (1991–92): 421–64.

Kempster, Norman. "Crises in Yugoslavia; 3,000 to 4,000 U.S. Civilians Believed Stuck, Many of Those Living in the Two Republics Hold Dual Citizenship." *The Los Angeles Times* (April 3, 1999).

Kymlicka, William. *Multicultural Citizenship: A Liberal Theory of Minority Rights.* Oxford: Clarendon Press, 1995.

Lasch, Christopher. *The Culture of Narcissism: American Life in an Age of Diminishing Expectations.* New York: Basic Books, 1979.

Lemann, Nicholas. "The New American Consensus: Government of, by, and for the Comfortable." *New York Times Magazine* (November 1, 1998): 37–42, 68–70.

Levinson, Sanford. "Constructing Communities through Words That Bind: Reflections on Loyalty Oaths." *Michigan Law Review* 1440 (1986): 1463–70.

Lipset, Seymour Martin. *The First New Nation.* New York: Basic Books, 1963.

Maharidge, Dale. *The Coming White Minority: California's Eruptions and America's Future.* New York: Times Books, 1996.

Martin, David A. "New Rules on Dual Nationality for a Democratizing Globe: Between Rejection and Embrace." *Georgetown Immigration Law Review* 14 (1999): 1–34.

———. "The Civic Republican Ideal for Citizenship, and for Our Common Life." *Virginia Journal of International Law* 35 (1994): 301.

Martin, Philip. "U.S. and California Reactions to Dual Nationality and Absentee Voting." Foreign Ministry of Mexico. February 17, 2000.

McGarvey-Rosendahl, Patricia. " A New Approach to Dual Nationality." *Houston Journal of International Law* 8, no. 305 (1985): 305–26.

"Mexico: Dual Nationality," *Migration News* 7, no. 3 (March 2000) <http://migration.ucdavis.edu>.

Miller, Mark J. "Dual Citizenship: A European Norm?" *International Migration Review* 33, no. 4 (1991): 945–50.

Morrison & Foerster LLP. "Issues Raised by Dual Nationality and Certain Reform Proposals." Draft memorandum prepared for the U.S. Commission on Immigration Reform, July 13, 1997.

O'Brien, Jeffrey R. "U.S. Dual Citizenship Voting Rights: A Critical Examination of Aleinikoff's Proposal." *Georgetown Immigration Review* 13, no. 533 (1999): 573–95.

Prothro, James W., and C. M. Grigg. "Fundamental Principles of Democracy: Basis of Agreement and Disagreement." *Journal of Politics* 22 (1960): 276–94.

Putnam, Robert D. *Bowling Alone: The Collapse and Revival of American Community.* New York: Simon and Schuster, 2000.

Renshon, Stanley A. "American Identity and the Dilemmas of Cultural Diversity." In *Political Psychology: Cultural and Cross Cultural Foundations*, ed. Stanley A. Renshon and John Duckitt. London: Macmillan, 2000, 285–310.

———. *High Hopes: The Clinton Presidency and the Politics of Ambition.* New York: Routledge, 1998.

Riesman, David, with N. Glazer and R. Denny. *The Lonely Crowd: A Study of the Changing American Character.* New Haven, Conn.: Yale University Press, 1950.

———. Egocentrism: Is the American Character Changing?" *Encounter* 55 (August–September, 1980): 19–28.

Rodriguez, Cindy. "Latino Influx Boosts Number of U.S. Immigrants to All-time High." *Boston Globe* (September 12, 2000): A1.

Russett, Bruce. *Grasping the Democratic Peace: Principles for a Post-Cold War World.* Princeton, N.J.: Princeton University Press, 1993.

Salins, Peter D. *Assimilation American Style.* New York: Basic Books, 1997.

Schmitter-Heisler, Barbara. "Contexts of Immigrant Incorporation." In *Immigration, Citizenship, and Welfare in Germany and the United States: Welfare Policies and*

Immigrants' Citizenship, ed. Herman Kurthen, Jurgen Fijalkowski, and Gert. G. Wagner. Stanford, Conn.: JAI, 1998, 95–106.

Schuck, Peter M. *Citizens, Strangers, and In-Betweens: Essays on Immigration and Citizenship.* Boulder, Colo.: Westview Press, 1998.

———. "The Re-Evaluation of American Citizenship." *Georgetown Immigration Law Journal* 12, no. 1 (1997): 1–34.

Seidman, Steven. "Contesting the Moral Boundaries of Eros." In *Diversity and Its Discontents: Cultural Conflict and Common Ground in Contemporary American Society*, ed. Neil J. Smelser and Jeffrey C. Alexander. Princeton, N.J.: Princeton University Press, 1999, 177.

Senders, Stephan. "National Inclusion in Germany. *New German Critique* 67 (1996): 147–75.

Skerry, Peter. "Do We Really Want Immigrants to Assimilate?" *Society* (March/April, 2000): 57–62.

Smelser, Neil J., and Jeffrey C. Alexander, eds. *Diversity and Its Discontents: Cultural Conflict and Common Ground in Contemporary American Society.* Princeton, N.J.: Princeton University Press, 1999.

Smith, Rogers M. " The 'American Creed' and American Identity: The Limits of Liberal Citizenship in the United States." *Western Political Quarterly* 41 (1987): 225–51.

Spiro, Peter J. "Dual Nationality and the Meaning of Citizenship." *Emory Law Review* 46, no. 4 (1997): 1412–85.

Takaki, Ronald. *A Different Mirror: A History of Multicultural America.* Boston: Little Brown, 1993.

Taylor, Charles. *Multiculturalism and the Politics of Recognition.* Princeton, N.J.: Princeton University Press, 1992.

U.S. Department of Commerce, Economics and Statistics Administration, U.S. Census. "Profile of the Foreign Born Population in the United States: 1997." *Current Populations Reports Special Studies.* P23-195. Washington, D.C.: U.S. Government Printing Office, 1997.

U.S. Department of Justice/Immigration and Naturalization Service. "Annual Report: Legal Immigration, Fiscal Year, 1998," no. 2, May 1999b.

U.S. Department of Justice/Immigration and Naturalization Service. "Annual Report: Legal Immigration, Fiscal Year, 1997," no. 1, January 1999a.

Vargas, Jorge A. "Dual Nationality for Mexicans?" *Chicano-Latino Law Review* 18, no. 1 (1996): 1–58.

Veale, Scott. "History 101: Snoop Doggy Roosevelt." *The New York Times* (July 2, 2000): sec. wk. 7.

Walzer, Michael. *On Toleration.* New Haven, Conn.: Yale University Press, 1997.

Wolfe, Alan. *One Nation After All.* Chicago: University of Chicago Press, 1998.

Yankelovich, Daniel. *New Rules: Searching for Self-fulfillment in a World Turned Upside Down.* New York: Random House, 1981.

Zachary, G. Pascal. "Dual Citizenship Is a Double-Edge Sword." *The Wall Street Journal* (March 25, 1998): B1.

Zappala, Gianni, and Stephan Castles. "Citizenship and Immigration in Australia." *Georgetown Immigration Law Journal* 13, no. 273 (1999).

Zelizer, Viviana A. "Multiple Markets, Multiple Cultures." In *Diversity and Its Discontents: Cultural Conflict and Common Ground in Contemporary American Society*, ed. Neil J. Smelser and Jeffrey C. Alexander. Princeton, N.J.: Princeton University Press, 1999.

PART THREE

Reflections on American National Identity in an Age of Diversity

The End of American Identity?

Jack Citrin

Is a strong American national identity withering away? Cassandras dominate recent assessments, gloomily prophesying that disaffection and fragmentation are entrenched in American life. Robert Reich (*The Worth of Nations* 1992) worries about the erosion of social solidarity in the new global economy. Arthur Schlesinger Jr. warns of *The Disuniting of America* (1991) if multiculturalist incursions into public education go unchecked. Peter Brimelow prophesies that immigration policy is creating an *Alien Nation* (1995). On the left, Todd Gitlin argues that the rise of "identity politics" means *The Twilight of Common Dreams* (1995). On the right, Gerturde Himmelfarb describes America as *One Nation, Two Cultures* (1999) now that the cultural contradictions of capitalism identified long ago by Daniel Bell (1976) are dissipating as the antinomian ethos of dissent, self-expression, and relativism triumphs over the bourgeois standards of the Protestant ethic. Set against these laments, Alan Wolfe's *One Nation, After All* (1998) is the ode of a lonely Pollyanna.

In joining the debate over whether America is breaking apart, this essay considers the attitudes of ordinary citizens rather than the pronouncements of intellectuals, college administrators, or government officials. It summarizes public conceptions of national identity and assesses support for the ideal of *e pluribus unum* among the country's diverse ethnic groups. After a brief comment about globalization, the essay concentrates on multiculturalism's consequences for the future of American nationalism.

Globalization versus One America

Nationalism, in the sense of a "people's" right to self-determination, has global legitimacy as the basis for demarcating autonomous political communities. National identity denotes the criteria for belonging to a distinct "people," and history shows that the attributes used to decide who is in and who is out of "the circle of we" are varied, malleable, and contested. Nationalism can coexist with multiple loyalties, but holds that the sense of national identity should be the citizen's overriding group loyalty, superseding other foci of affiliation such as race, religion, language, gender, and occupation. Accordingly, nation-builders strive to create and sustain this hierarchy of identifications through public education and official ceremonies, among other means. The extent to which Americans continue to regard their national identity as fundamental and transcendent is the central empirical concern of this essay.

Globalization theorists regard nations and nationalism as products of modernization, integral parts of the syndrome of capitalism, industrialism, mass communications, and secularism that took hold in the last century. Now, they argue, technology is vanquishing the nation. The world is becoming more integrated and interdependent. In economics, the growing mobility of goods and capital erodes the sovereignty of even the United States, the richest and most powerful country (Friedman 1999). With the fraying of connections between citizenship and economic well-being, the nation-state's value diminishes, particularly for mobile professionals (Reich 1992). Ease of travel exposes people with different cultural backgrounds to each other, and the revolution in communications spreads habits of speech and consumption across geographic boundaries. Crossing borders is so easy that people readily can establish allegiances to more than one country. The cumulative impact of these developments, it is widely held, is to erode a nation's distinct identity and prepare the ground for the spread of a cosmopolitan global culture. For the globalizers, the American ideal of *e pluribus unum* is not unworthy, just obsolete. Because of the revolution in technology, the only relevant *unum* is the world market where, these twenty-first-century Marxist mutants believe, the universal fetishism of commodities ultimately trumps national differences in culture.

Philosophers seeking to breathe ethical life into this new stage of history call for a new political identity based on the commitment to universal human rights to replace bounded loyalties toward fellow nationals (Nussbaum 1996). But whatever the normative merits of global citizenship and a generalized love of humankind, the rootless cosmopolitanism of "one world, one family" seems too thin an emotional gruel to satisfy most people's need for a shared identity. As Anthony Smith remarks, "every time United States soldiers are killed or captured in a UN mission, every time trade negotiations threaten to favor America's competitors, the sense of a separate and unique American destiny still looms" (Smith 1995, 45).

Competing Conceptions of American Identity

As a nation of immigrants the United States has always faced the challenge of sustaining a national culture that serves as the basis for unity and social cohesion. Nativism is one ideological solution. The nativist response to a multiethnic society is to prescribe cultural conformity (Higham 1988). If there is to be immigration, the government should only admit people who already are familiar with the dominant national culture (Brimelow 1995). Once here, newcomers should undergo a program of "Americanization" that speeds the shedding of their native customs and imparts knowledge of the prevailing language, social habits, and political values. Nativism thus gives an ethnocentric cast to American national identity. For nativists, nationality does not simply trump ethnicity; rather government-sponsored acculturation fuses American identity with a particular ethnicity—variously labeled as Anglo-Saxon, European, and Western (Lind 1995). Nativism preaches the message of Ernest Gellner's theory of nationalism: in a multiethnic state, minority cultures must choose between assimilation and secession.

After World War II, a more inclusive, liberal conception of American identity replaced nativism as the dominant nationalist ideology. Liberal nationalism defines Americanism in civic, not ethnic, terms. Belonging is equated with common beliefs and customs rather than shared blood, so anyone, regardless of ancestry, can become American merely through adherence to the national creed of democracy, equality, and individualism. In principle, if not always in practice, liberal nationalism is inclusive. Since the newcomers inexorably blend into the American melting pot, there is no need for a program of indoctrination to cleanse them of their ethnic heritage. Indeed, the cultural mainstream itself is a continuously evolving hybrid as immigrants add new words, songs, and foods to the popular mix.

Liberal nationalists thus are optimistic about the ability of contemporary American society to absorb immigrants—whether they come from Latin America, Asia, or Europe. As long as there is a consensus on political principles, including the value of tolerance, and nationality takes priority over ethnicity, cultural diversity is not a threat. Some critics (Lind 1995), however, maintain that common political ideals are insufficient to forge one people out of culturally diverse groups. In Lind's view, Americanism means more than support for abstract political ideals that have only a symbolic meaning to many ordinary citizens. He argues that there is a shared American culture broader than Tocqueville's civil religion—a common vernacular, common holiday customs, common knowledge of sports. Adopting these folkways is part of the process of Americanization, but there is no ethnic barrier to joining the cultural melting pot. Moreover, Lind's fleshed-out version of American identity does not ask very much of immigrants and fits readily within the liberal framework.

Multiculturalism versus One America

Twenty-five years ago, Harold Isaacs (1975) observed that we are globalizing and fragmenting at the same time. He explained the seeming paradox of eroding national boundaries and proliferating identity movements within established states as evidence of man's essential tribalism (Isaacs 1975, 26). Large-scale immigration and economic interdependence unsettle nationalist sentiments, but the affirmation of more restricted group identities is a more likely reaction than the development of a supranational identity (Smith 1995). If this is true, then the politicization of ethnicity is relocating to subnational cultural groups, rather than dissolving into a global "humanity."

While globalization tears at attachment to the nation from the outside, multiculturalism gnaws from within. Multiculturalism *as a fact* merely denotes the presence of people of different ethnicities in a single polity. *As an ideology*, multiculturalism takes as axiomatic that the presence of people of varied ethnic origins within a single polity means that there exist diverse cultures, in the sense of distinct sets of beliefs, values, habits, and observances. Multiculturalism assumes that ethnic identity is essential to personal dignity and self-realization (Raz 1994). Accordingly, government should help preserve the minority cultures that would otherwise decline due to the power of the majority group.

In the current debate, there are both weak and strong versions of multiculturalism. Weak multiculturalists diverge from liberal nationalists mainly by emphasizing the virtue of cultural diversity and the need to empathize with minority groups. They maintain that today "we cannot simply expect newcomers to assimilate to our culture, but must accept that they will change it" (Aleinikoff 1998, 80). This vacuous statement has a déjà vu quality. Did not the Irish, Italian, and Jewish immigrants change American culture while simultaneously assimilating or blending in?

If the weak version of multiculturalism adds anything to the liberal nationalism, it is the demand for the government to actively promote recognition and appreciation of minority cultures. Weak multiculturalists thus support reforming the history curriculum, revising the literary canon, renaming streets, adding new "ethnic months" to focus attention on the achievements of minority cultures, elevating minority figures to the status of national heroes, and other devices to celebrate diversity. Tolerance, sensitivity, and openness are the watchwords of weak multiculturalism, an outlook that flirts with the idea of group rights without wholly embracing it.

Strong multiculturalism provides a clearer alternative to both nativist and liberal conceptions of American identity. Portraying the Enlightenment idea of universal values as hegemonic ethnocentrism, strong multiculturalists hold that differences among communities of descent are basic and persisting because, as Horace Kallen put it in the early twentieth century, "one cannot change one's grandfather." Since no culture is superior to any other, none should be privileged in a multiethnic society. The ideal of the melting pot thus is not only fraudulent, but also oppressive; a more appropriate image of the United States is a mosaic of differently colored tiles separated by impenetrable grout. With ethnicity as the foundation of one's political identity, strong multiculturalism conceives of the nation as a confederation of ethnic groups with equal rights. The principle of group rights, however, is advanced in order to advance the standing of "historically disadvantaged" minorities and leads to the justification of the "special" rights embedded in policies such as affirmative action and racial gerrymandering.

At the core of strong multiculturalism, then, is the conviction that group representation should govern the allocation of political, economic, and cultural resources. All public policies must be judged in terms of how they affect the balance of power among the carriers of different cultures; disparate impact is the ultimate sin. In the United States, the failure of the civil rights movement to overcome entrenched racial inequality fueled cultural nationalism in the black community during the late 1960s (Glazer 1997). Massive immigration then enlarged the groups with an interest in multiculturalism's program of redistribution. However, deciding which groups deserve official recognition and protection turns out to be a matter of politics more than anthropology. Today's multiculturalists lump together the "old ethnics" from Europe as whites and treat people of Japanese, Chinese, Korean, and Vietnamese origin as a homogeneous Asian ethnic category.

"Identity politics," the mobilization of people around group pride, is multiculturalism's political motif. Identity politics views oppression and historical calamity as the true warrant of a group's claim to recognition. Victimhood confers moral worthiness, unifying ethnic minorities, women, homosexuals, and the disabled. In this vein, Ronald Takaki (1993) argues that official discrimination has "racialized" Hispanics and Asians in America, making them, unlike European immigrants, into "people of color" who do not and should not assimilate. Of course, the economic success of recent Asian immigrants makes it difficult to use them as exemplars of discrimination and disadvantage. More generally, the manifest cultural and economic conflicts within the putative coalition of "wounded" identities diminish the prospect for a common "minority" politics going beyond criticism of dominant American institutions.

Multiculturalism devalues allegiance to a common national identity without furnishing an alternative basis for social solidarity among America's ethnic groups save the principle of mutual tolerance. But Susan Okin (1999) has pointed out that equal rights for all cultural groups may legitimate illiberal practices that violate the rights of individuals, particularly women. And if "live and let live" is the only prescribed attitude toward other groups, there is no civic obligation to assist the disadvantaged or sacrifice on behalf of the community as a whole.

Even writers sympathetic to multiculturalism recognize the problem. David Hollinger (1995) yearns for a "postethnic" America in which group identities would be fluid, "subject to voluntary revision through interaction with other kinds of people." People may opt to link their identity to their ethnic ancestry or not, as they please. And others will respect either choice, as well as the redefinition of group cultures through learning. After admitting the need for national solidarity in even this high-minded, new world of sympathy for and appreciation of other cultures, however, Hollinger fails to provide a concrete basis for a common identity. Like Michael Lind, he envisages interracial marriage, something that cannot be legislated, as perhaps the surest path to postethnicity. But the creation of a "racial" melting pot (Lind 1995, 298) would undermine the multiculturalist goal of preserving ethnic group differences. In fact, interracial and interethnic marriages have increased, leading to calls for new categories in the census. However, government policies tend to reify past distinctions rather than present realities, largely because of pressure from ethnic interest groups seeking to expand their share of government benefits, including seats in the legislature, that are allocated on the basis of the ethnic census.

Like Hollinger, T. Alexander Aleinikoff tries to formulate a nationalist ideology congenial to multiculturalism. This conception of American identity should "foster a nation at peace with its constituent groups and groups that identify with the nation" (Aleinikoff 1998, 86). Like liberal nationalists, Aleinikoff accepts that there must be a common allegiance to the nation, an identification with the whole beyond its ethnic parts. Group identities would persist in multicultural America, but they would be volitional and fluid. Significantly, though, the sense of national identity would be "paramount" (Aleinikoff 1998, 86).

The idea of a fluid group identity lacks sufficient concreteness to be useful. Perhaps the term means no more than the truism that context determines which of one's multiple and overlapping group memberships is salient. Take the question "where are you from?" Abroad, my answer is "America;" in Washington, "California;" in Los Angeles, "Berkeley." These shifting responses do not indicate that my cultural identity is fluid. I live where I live. Similarly, though I was born in Shanghai, I do not volitionally cross an ethnic group boundary when I eat at Mandarin Garden and order in Chinese. Indeed, if identities truly are a matter of choice, why insist on the priority of a common national identity?

Aleinikoff's invocation of a multicultural nationalism represents the triumph of hope over experience. He advocates a definition of American identity as subjective opinion, requiring only that immigrants identify themselves as Americans and be committed to this country's "continuing flourishing" (Aleinikoff 1998, 86). A search for common ground thus ends on a narrow strip of spongy feeling; we must be willing to accept others as Americans even if they have a divergent conception of the nation's identity. It is implausible that this minimal consensus on "live and let live" could create a shared patriotism strong enough to override group affiliations rooted in historical memory and current social interactions.

If the only obligations of citizenship are to recycle weekly, pay taxes yearly, and fill out census forms once a decade, there is little reason to worry about constructing a common national identity compatible with multiculturalism's preference for separate but equal group identities. The positive function of a strong group identity is to foster a willingness to aid fellow members of the group, to sacrifice for the collective benefit. A strong sense of *national* solidarity should improve relations among across ethnic groups and enhance feelings of mutuality. These sentiments should foster support for policies that assist those within the "circle of we." And the liberal and nativist conceptions of American identity are better equipped than multiculturalism to commit America's diverse ethnic groups to common undertakings. After all, why should one pay taxes to provide for people identifying themselves first and foremost as members of a distinct cultural group with fortified boundaries? In fact, a pervasive belief in One America might well benefit minority groups lacking the resources to develop the communal institutions for mutual aid implied by multiculturalist principles.

Variety, the saying goes, is the spice of life. Unquestioned acceptance of this proverb animates the current embrace of cultural diversity in the American establishment. Paeans to multiculturalism resound in government, in the corporate boardroom, and, above all, in elite universities, where top administrators rush to line up behind affirmative action, bilingual education, ethnic studies, and diversity training. They do so, however, without questioning the underlying assumption that numerous distinct cultures actually exist in the United States.

In a trenchant attack on this idea, Russell Jacoby (1999) underscores the homogenizing influence of advanced industrial society, a process that globalization is taking a step further. Whatever their ethnicity, he writes, all Americans tend to consume the same goods, watch the same shows, and pursue the same material goals. Marketers may highlight ethnic symbolism to develop niche products, but distinctive tastes in food, music, dance or clothing do not equal a difference in basic political identities. Even multiculturalists admit that among European immigrants assimilation has all but eliminated differences in language and customs. Few third-generation immigrants speak German, Italian, Norwegian, or Russian. There is clear evidence that the recent immigrants from Asia and Latin America are learning English and forgetting their native languages just as fast as their predecessors did. For example, a recent survey indicates that only 10 percent of the American-born children of Latino immigrants rely mainly on Spanish (Goldstein and Suro 2000). And, as already noted, intermarriage across ethnic lines also is rapidly increasing.

Moreover, recent studies confirm that the processes of structural and cultural assimilation are mutually reinforcing. Among Latino respondents in recent national surveys, the native-born, English speakers, those living in heterogeneous neighborhoods, and those with "Anglo" social contacts, are more likely to identify themselves with the larger society, more likely to feel positively about "Anglos," more likely to participate in politics, and more likely to believe that other immigrants also should assimilate (Welch and Sigelman 2000; Newton 2000). If these trends continue, the future portends cultural assimilation rather than balkanization in America.

The answer to the question "are there many different cultures in America?" depends, of course, on how one defines culture. If ethnic, class, or regional differences in beliefs and habits are the evidence for multiple cultures, then it is obvious that Americans of different background share many cultural practices while varying in others. My concern here is only with American political culture, and specifically with what data regarding public conceptions of national identity indicate about the existence of One America.

One America in Mass Opinion

From a psychological perspective, the concept of national identity is comprised of self-categorization, affect, and normative content (Citrin, Wong, and Duff 2001). The first step is to probe self-identification, although the subjective opinion of oneself as "American" is not always affirmed by others. (As multiculturalists complain, the daughter of Chinese immigrants may call herself an American, yet be told by fellow citizens that she lacks the criteria for membership in the national community.) The affective dimension of national identity refers to feelings of closeness to and pride in one's country and its collective symbols and should be assessed separately from self-categorization. The normative content of a national identity refers to ideas about what makes the nation distinctive—ideas about its members, its core values, the territory it ought to occupy, and the legitimacy of identification with subnational communities of descent.

Nativism, liberalism, and multiculturalism are alternative theories about the proper content of American national identity. Each proposes a different solution for how to balance national and ethnic identities, with conflicting implications for policymakers. For example, a nativist concern about cultural disunity suggests an immigration policy favoring the admission of English speakers of European origin. By contrast, multiculturalist anxieties about assimilation encourage bilingual education programs aimed at the maintenance of immigrant children's original language and culture.

Several recent national and local surveys assess the level of public support for these competing conceptions of American national identity (Citrin et al. 2001; Sears et al. 1999). The main body of evidence reported here comes from the 1994 and 1996 General Social Surveys (GSS) conducted by the National Opinion Research Center (Davis and Smith 1997). To provide more information about ethnic minorities, these data are buttressed by information from 1994 and 1995 surveys (LACSS) of Los Angeles County, an extraordinarily diverse community where the political salience of ethnicity is a constant.

Each public opinion poll is just a snapshot in time, and the level of support one records with the questions and response items employed. Still, the evidence that Americans in all ethnic groups share a strong sense of national identity is overwhelming. The 1994 GSS and the 1994 and 1995 Los Angeles surveys asked respondents "When you think of social and political issues, do you see yourself mainly as a member of a particular ethnic, racial, or nationality group, or do you think of yourself mainly as just an American?" The question calls for people to rank their national and ethnic identities and explicitly places the choice in a political context. The national and Los Angeles data are remarkably similar: although the tendency is strongest among whites, more than two-thirds of each ethnic group identifies as Americans (see Table 1).

The virtual unanimity among whites is consistent with the idea that the various groups of European immigrants indeed have "melted" (Alba 1990). The 1995 Los Angeles study included a follow-up question for respondents calling themselves "just an American," asking whether "it was truer to say you are *both* an American *and* a member of a particular ethnic group." Only 17 percent of whites, compared to 54 percent of blacks, 59 percent of Hispanics, and 59 percent of Asians, opted for a dual identity rather than an exclusively American self-definition. Strong multiculturalism's priority on ethnicity over nationality is a minority viewpoint concentrated among recent immigrants (Citrin, Wong, and Duff 2001), suggesting that a sense of national identity is the normal outcome of socialization in the United States. More generally, national and ethnic

Table 1. National and Ethnic Identification, by Ethnicity

	Whites (%)			Blacks (%)			Hispanics (%)			Asians (%)
	1994 LACS	1995 LACS	1994 GSS	1994 LACS	1995 LACS	1994 GSS	1994 LACS	1995 LACS	1994 GSS	1994–95 LACS
On social and political issues, do you think of yourself as:										
Just an American	93	94	96	68	70	66	72	67	80	71
Just an American, but also as a member of a group	–	16	–	–	55	–	–	56	–	59
Member of an ethnic/racial/ nationality group	4	5	3	30	30	29	26	29	17	27
On all, most, some, or just a few issues:										
Just an American on all/most issues	81	82	89	50	46	51	37	36	69	46
Member of ethnic/racial/ nationality group on all/ most issues	2	9	2	22	42	21	16	54	6	13

Sources: 1994 and 1995 Los Angeles County Social Surveys, 1994 General Social Survey. Entries for Asians pool the two Los Angeles County surveys. In all cases the basis for percentaging is the total number of respondents in the specified ethnic group interviewed in that survey, excluding only those failing to respond to the original question. Adapted from Sears et al. (1999, 54).

Table 2. American Patriotism, by Ethnicity

	Total %	Whites %	Blacks %	Hispanics %
Attachment				
Saying that being American is				
"most important thing in their life"	46	47	49	26
Saying that they feel "close" or				
"very close" to America	81	83	69	83
Agreeing that "I would rather be a				
citizen of America than any other country"	91	92	89	79
Pride				
Saying that they are "very" or "somewhat"				
proud of:				
The way American democracy works	83	85	77	81
American history	88	92	69	81
America's fair and equal treatment of all groups				
in society	57	60	42	51

Source: 1996 General Social Survey. Adapted from Citrin, Wong, and Duff (2001).

identities tend to be complementary rather than competing. Two-thirds of every ethnic group in the 1996 GSS national survey said they felt strongly attached to both the country as a whole and their own ethnic group, a pattern of allegiance that belies the image of a disunited country.

Feelings of pride in and belonging to America also are pervasive. When asked to rate the personal importance of being an American on a ten-point scale, an impressive 46 percent of the 1996 GSS sample said it was "the most important thing in their life," with most other respondents saying it was "important." In addition, 91 percent of the sample agreed that they would "rather be a citizen of American than of any other country," and 83 percent said they were proud of "the way democracy works in America" (see Table 2). Strong patriotic sentiments do not, however, mean that one believes the nation is perfect. Relatively fewer respondents (57 percent) expressed pride in "the country's record in treating all groups in society equally."

The nativist prediction that diversity erodes national unity assumes that minority groups are less committed to the idea of a common American

Table 3. Normative Conceptions of American Identity, by Ethnicity

Saying Very or Fairly Important for a "Truer American"	Total %	Whites %	Blacks %	Hispanics %
To have been born in America	69	67	82	42
To be a Christian	54	50	77	50
To have lived in America for most of one's life	73	71	84	77
To be able to speak English	93	94	91	85
To feel American	87	89	81	72
To have American citizenship	93	92	93	93

Source: 1996 General Social Survey. Adapted from Citrin, Wong, and Duff (2001).

identity. Multiculturalists agree that minorities are less likely than the dominant ethnic group to feel allegiance to the nation as a whole, but are unworried. In fact, ethnic differences in patriotism are slight (see Table 2). There is no disagreement between blacks and whites regarding the personal importance of American citizenship. Blacks (69 percent) were somewhat less likely than whites (83 percent) or Hispanics (83 percent) to say they feel "very close" or "close" to America, but again a large majority of all groups expressed a strong sense of attachment to the nation.

The opinions of Hispanics illustrate the natural tendency of more recent immigrants to retain psychic ties to their country of origin. In the 1996 GSS, Hispanic respondents were less likely than either blacks or whites to say that being an American was important to them and more willing to say that they would move to another country. Hispanic and Asian respondents in the Los Angeles surveys were less likely than whites to express pride in being an American, but this difference in opinion largely reflects the fact that many of them were recent arrivals who were not citizens. The Latino National Political Survey (de la Garza et al. 1996, 346) found that after controlling for one's length of residence in the United States, Mexican-Americans express patriotism at levels equal to Anglos. In sum, the pattern of ethnic group differences indicates that the development of strong feelings of patriotism remains an element in the normal process of assimilation of newcomers to America.

Ethnic differences do emerge when one moves from the support for national ideals and symbols to judgments about historical experience. Minorities largely agree with whites about the goal of achieving a common

Table 4. Support for Norms of Multiculturalism, by Ethnicity

	Whites (%)			Blacks (%)			Hispanics (%)			Asians (%)
	1994 LACS	1995 LACS	1994 GSS	1994 LACS	1995 LACS	1994 GSS	1994 LACS	1995 LACS	1994 GSS	1994–95 LACS
Should ethnic/racial groups:										
Maintain distinct cultures?	26	27	30	27	34	41	27	35	31	29
Blend in, as in a melting pot?	50	46	39	53	41	37	60	56	47	53
Is too much/too little attention given to racial/ethnic history?										
Too much	24	–	31	11	–	6	10	–	–	18
Too little	28	–	16	60	–	60	44	–	48	44
People should think of themselves as individual Americans, not as members of racial/ethnic/national groups (% disagree)	9	9	–	22	24	–	24	25	–	19
Should congressmen match constituent ethnicity? (% yes)	8	–	6	18	–	27	23	–	15	9
Should teachers match student ethnicity? (% yes)	6	–	6	13	–	18	10	–	18	11
Are people best represented politically by someone from their OWN ethnic group? (% yes)	35	–	33	41	–	43	37	–	47	43

Sources: 1994 and 1995 Los Angeles County Social Surveys, 1994 General Social Survey. Entries for Asians pool the two Los Angeles County surveys. In all cases the basis for percentaging is the total number of respondents in the specified ethnic group interviewed in that survey, excluding only those failing to respond to the original question. Adapted from Sears et al. (1999, 5).

identity, one nation out of many, but they also display a heightened sensitivity to their collective status and are much more likely to perceive discrimination against their ethnic group (Sears et al. 1999).

Questions about what makes one "truly an American" refer to normative conceptions of national identity. Each of the attributes listed in Table 3—American citizenship, feeling American, speaking English, being born in American, or being Christian—were deemed either very or fairly important by a largely majority of the public, indicating that most Americans believe that there is a distinct national identity (see Table 3). An earlier study of California opinion found that the norms of treating people of all backgrounds equally and trying to get ahead on one's own were the most widely cited attributes of Americanism (Citrin, Reingold, and Green 1990). The evidence from a national sample presented here similarly indicates that inclusive political criteria were chosen more often than the ethnocultural qualities embodied in nativist thinking.

True, almost everyone (93 percent) in the GSS sample agreed that speaking English was important for being a true American, but this is an achieved rather than an ascribed trait. In fact, recent immigrants are as likely as whites or blacks and the native-born to emphasize language as an important criterion of national identity (Citrin, Reingold, and Green 1990). The public clearly rejects the multiculturalist challenge to the symbolic hegemony of English in the United States; by a margin of 63 to 28 percent, respondents in the 1994 GSS favored a proposal to designate English as the country's official language. However, this preference for English is pragmatic, not harshly dogmatic. Just 37 percent agreed that election ballots in localities with large numbers of non–English speakers should be printed only in English. In addition, 68 percent gave generalized support to the idea of bilingual education provided that this policy aimed at speeding the acquisition of English rather than at maintaining immigrant children's original language.

Assimilation may be a dirty word in activist circles (Glazer 1994), but ordinary Americans continue to express faith in the idea of the melting pot. When respondents were asked whether the country's different ethnic groups "should blend into the larger society or maintain their distinct customs and traditions," blending in was the more prevalent answer among all ethnic groups in both the national and Los Angeles surveys (see Table 4). Opinion was not one-sided, however, and many people find it difficult to choose. An early 2000 national survey conducted by the Kaiser Family

Foundation and Harvard University asked separate questions about the importance of blending into the larger society and maintaining one's distinct ethnic culture. When respondents were not forced to choose, more than 80 percent of all ethnic groups said that both were important goals (Goldstein and Suro 2000). Most Americans apparently do not perceive an inherent conflict between assimilation into the mainstream and maintaining elements of one's ethnic heritage. If anything, they believe that the common national identity can accommodate cultural pluralism and only a minority (31 percent) of whites say that the history of ethnic minorities is getting too much attention in the public schools (see Table 4).

Whereas multiculturalists envisage a significant role for the state in validating and preserving cultural differences, only 4 percent of the 1994 GSS sample believed that "it is up to government to help racial and ethnic groups retain their original cultures." A large majority (82 percent) also rejected the notion of preferential treatment for immigrants, stating that "today's newcomers to America" should "work their way up without special favors from the government, just like the Italian, Irish, and Jews."

There is strong public opposition to the ideas of formalizing group representation and substituting ethnic preferences for individualistic norms (see Table 4). Not surprisingly, whites almost unanimously oppose this facet of multiculturalism's policy agenda; in both the national and Los Angeles surveys only 8 percent or fewer approved of tying the allocation of congressional seats or teaching positions to the relative size of various ethnic groups. But since ethnic minorities are the presumed beneficiaries of group representation, their general preference for a system of individually based rights is noteworthy. Despite the promise of more legislative seats for their members of their own group, three-fourths or more of the blacks, Hispanics, and Asians in both the national and Los Angeles surveys disapproved of making Congress mirror the ethnic composition of the general population. Similarly large majorities opposed communal representation among public school teachers.

Popular attitudes thus belie both the hopes of multiculturalism and the fears of nativism. Tocqueville's civil religion has impressive staying power. A majority of Americans oppose the articulation of ethnic identities in a form that challenges the older liberal ideal of a common civic identity. This preference for an inclusive nationalism coexists with the widespread acceptance of diversity in cultural practices, provided that the *unum* should retain priority over the *plures*. Significantly, attachment to the traditional liberal image of American identity is the dominant outlook of all ethnic groups. An ethnic divide in opinion does emerge on policy issues such as affirmative action or immigrant rights that visibly touch on group interests, but the pattern of cleavages varies from issue to issue. At the level of norms and symbols, however, One America retains its hold on the public mind.

Immigration and Assimilation

The passage of the Civil Rights Act in 1964 and the Immigration and Nationality Act of 1965 signaled the triumph of the liberal conception of American citizenship and prepared the ground for nativist and multiculturalist challenges. The interplay of rising ethnic consciousness and the influx of Hispanic and Asian immigrants once family reunification replaced national origins as the primary basis of immigration spurred demands for language rights that, in turn, sparked a reactive "Americanization" movement (Citrin et al. 1990).

The public's view is that "Americanness" requires knowledge of the country's common language and belief in its liberal democratic and egalitarian political principles. Policies that sustain faith in this political creed and deepen understanding of its implications for civic participation are worth undertaking. If this is all that Americanization means, then many native-born citizens as well as immigrants undoubtedly could benefit from the process.

Within the limits imposed by international commitments, a nation-state is free to choose how many immigrants to admit and on what terms. The United States abandoned a racist system of immigration, in part because we finally acknowledged that it was inconsistent with the liberal conception of national identity. However, the collective interest in economic progress and social peace remains a legitimate basis for deciding how to allocate scarce entry visas.

Most immigrants come to America to seek a better life for themselves or their families. Americans historically have expected newcomers to assimilate. Fitting in without much fuss becomes a rite of passage; you go along, then you get along, then you belong. Whereas nativists worry that today's immigrants are not assimilating, multiculturalists claim that new arrivals do not want to give up their traditional way of life and should not be coerced to do so. This essay argues that both positions are mistaken. There is abundant evidence that immigrants are assimilating—learning English, acquiring contemporary leisure habits, moving out of ethnic enclaves, intermarrying. The process is uneven, occurring at rates that vary with one's skills and cultural background, but assimilation is ongoing and quite rapid. Moreover, most immigrants do not need to be forced to accept a substantial dose of Americanization (Appiah 1998). They seem to understand that leaving home and adapting to a strange culture brings on feelings of longing and loss, but accept this as the price of helping their families. The surveys summarized above indicate that most ethnic minorities, including recent immigrants, accept the value of blending into the mainstream culture.

Over time, then, the current wave of immigrants seems likely to become "*desocialized* from their native group . . . even if the emotional significance of attachment to the group persists" (Glazer and Moynihan 1975, 8). Each succeeding generation is more likely to define itself as "just American" than as a particular ethnic group. The hyphenated identity itself is an accepted element of American political culture, a kind of stage in the assimilation process rather than a sign of alienation. The political implications of immigration depend on how people resolve a perceived conflict between their loyalty to both nation and ethnic group. In this regard, recent research about minority attitudes (Tyler et al. 1998) found that the "assimilated" (who had just an American self-identification) and "biculturalist" (who had both an American and ethnic self-identification) were equally likely to express trust in political institutions and to comply with government policy. Both groups were more likely than "separatists" (who had just an ethnic self-identification) to respond in these ways.

As Peter Skerry (2000) points out, however, in the short run assimilation generates social costs as well as benefits. Structural assimilation—increased contacts among ethnic groups in economic and social life—may lead to increased competition and conflict. When previously advantaged ethnic groups resist changes to group positions with discrimination and violence, minorities often react by asserting their distinctiveness and demanding recognition. Political assimilation would seem to make more likely this multiculturalist response to a persistent gap between egalitarian principles and social reality.

Assimilation to contemporary American habits and lifestyles also may do damage. Immigrants seem to be the main carriers of the Victorian morality admired by Gertrude Himmelfarb, living the Protestant ethic of frugality, hard work, and self-reliance and emphasizing responsibility to family, respect for authority, and rectitude in personal conduct (Goldstein and Suro 2000). If these values do fade with assimilation into American life, so too may the commitment to economic and educational achievement that contributes to society as a whole. As Skerry puts it, before endorsing assimilation, we should ask "assimilation to what?" Whatever the causes of moral decay in America, immigration is not to blame.

The Politics of Fragmentation

The consensual attachment to a common American identity in the general public is strangely discordant with the ethnic tensions evident in contemporary politics. Racial issues deeply divide the country's two main political parties. The allocation of political offices, government contracts, places in universities, time on television, and other benefits among ethnic groups is closely watched by activists and journalists. The slightest slur on a group's reputation or heritage usually evokes immediate outrage. The GSS and LACSS polls may fail to detect disagreement between whites and minority groups because they focus on support for abstract norms and symbols. The rhetorical salute to One America may mask ethnic conflict over distributive policies. As noted above, blacks and, to a lesser extent, other ethnic minorities are much more positive about national *ideals* than *realities*. The survey evidence indicates that ethnic differences in opinion are significant on issues such as affirmative action and government spending on blacks that clearly engage group interests.

Ethnic group cleavages on specific issues, however, do not contradict consensus on core values or the persistence of a common sense of national identity. In most political contexts, the dictates of national and ethnic identifications do not collide; the relevant question is how do people resolve the tension when it does arise. Japanese-Americans fought against Japan in World War II, indicating the priority of their national identity. Thankfully, there is no equivalent contemporary test to apply, but one doubts that ethnicity would trump nationality today either.

The gulf between elite advocacy of multiculturalism and stubborn mass support for assimilation to a common national identity also deserves attention. One possibility is that the gap will narrow as elite values permeate political discourse and are disseminated through mass communications and public education. There are signs that the youngest and best-educated cohorts are somewhat more sympathetic to multicuturalist orthodoxy, but these differences are not yet great and a majority of every age and education group still supports the liberal conception of American identity (Citrin et al. 2001; Sears et al. 1999).

Because of the continuing affective tie to the ethnic group among minorities, appeals to ethnicity can enlist mass support in the pursuit of individual or group interests. Activists have an instrumental motive for emphasizing ethnic identity and sustaining its emotional significance within their group. Indeed, the policies they pursue through mobilizing shared feelings of identification and resentment often deliver tangible benefits for relatively few and only symbolic gratification for the many (Horowitz 1985).

The articulation of group identities thus does not occur in a political vacuum. In the post–civil rights era in the United States, institutions and government programs have increased the incentives for minorities to identify in ethnic rather than economic or geographic terms. Though crafted in the name of enhancing the generally approved value of equal opportunity, these policies actually may encourage group conflict. For example, an electoral system of single-member constituencies combined with residential segregation on ethnic lines encourages candidates to appeal to voters by promising to serve "us," not "them." Legislation demanding racial gerrymandering institutionalizes the idea that ethnic polarization in voting is natural. By allocating scarce positions on ethnic lines, affirmative-action programs give people an interest in adopting and maintaining an ethnic identity. History shows that once one group is designated a protected category, others rush to achieve the advantage this status confers. Witness the successful effort of Indian businessmen in San Francisco to be classified as Asians rather than Caucasians and thus to benefit from the city's set-asides in public contracts.

Politics rather than culture is a force for fragmentation in American society. The university is a microcosm of what can occur. There the paraphernalia of multiculturalism—ethnic preferences in admissions, theme houses, speech codes, consciousness-raising classes—often create separate but equal racisms rather than enhancing racial equality. The assimilated minority student learns that she is inauthentic unless she redefines herself as an "ethnic." Of course, the mobilization of group consciousness among minorities can stimulate progress toward greater equality and social justice. But the enhanced expression of ethnic identification in one group tends to be emulated by others, thereby diffusing feelings of grievance and intensifying competition for scarce resources. That is, the tendency of one group to insist on its distinctiveness and the legitimacy of in-group favoritism leads those excluded or blamed to respond in kind. Multiculturalism's politics of difference is a redistributionist ploy, but one that may reduce the incentives for mutual cooperation and sacrifice that a sense of common identity can furnish.

One America remains a worthwhile ideal as long as it is an America worthy of respect. A common identity is a lubricant that helps a nation achieve collective goals. Liberal nationalism is a formula for fusing individual members of American society into a system that assures equality of status and a measure of commonality to all while, at the same time, allowing the maintenance of different cultural traditions. The enduring challenge to this vision of American identity is the failure to assimilate fully the first wave of immigrants, the involuntary arrivals from Africa. The persistence of racial discrimination and inequality is multiculturalism's strongest political asset. But if ethnic entitlements are to be swept away in the name of individual rights and a common American identity, we must make the changes and sacrifices necessary to close the racial divide.

References

Alba, R. D. 1990. *Ethnic Identity: The Transformation of White America.* New Haven, Conn.: Yale University Press.

Aleinikoff, T. A. 1998. "A Multicultural Nationalism?" *American Prospect* 36:80–87.

Appiah, K. A. 1998. "Citizenship in Theory and Practice: A Response to Charles Kessler." In *Immigration and Citizenship in the 21st Century,* ed. N. M. Pickus. New York: Rowman & Littlefield.

Bell, D. 1976. *The Cultural Contradictions of Capitalism.* New York: Basic Books.

Brimelow, P. 1995. *Alien Nation: Common Sense about America's Immigration Disaster.* New York: Random House.

Citrin, J., C. Wong, and B. Duff. 2001. "The Meaning of American National Identity: Patterns of Ethnic Conflict and Consensus." In *Group Identity, Group Conflict, and Conflict Resolution,* ed. R. Ashmore, L. Jussim, and D. Wilder. New York: Oxford University Press.

Citrin, J., D. Sears, C. Muste, and C. Wong. 2001. "Multiculturalism in American Public Opinion." *British Journal of Political Science* 31:247–75.

Citrin, J., B. Reingold, and D. P. Green. 1990. "American Identity and the Politics of Ethnic Change." *Journal of Politics* 52:1124–54.

Citrin, J., B. Reingold, E. Walters, and D. P. Green. 1990. "The Official English Movement and the Symbolic Politics of Language in the United States." *Western Political Quarterly* 43:535–60.

Davis, J., and T. Smith. 1997. *The General Social Survey Codebook*. Chicago: National Opinion Research Center.

de la Garza, R. O., A. Falcon, and C. Garcia. 1996. "Will the Real Americans Please Stand Up: Anglo and Mexican-American Support of Core American Political Values." *American Journal of Political Science* 40:335–51.

Friedman, T. L. 1999. *The Lexus and the Olive Tree*. New York: Farrar, Straus, Giroux.

Gitlin, T. 1995. *The Twilight of Common Dreams*. New York: Henry Holt & Co.

Glazer, N. 1997. *We Are All Multiculturalists Now*. Cambridge, Mass.: Harvard University Press.

Glazer, N., and D. Moynihan. 1975. *Ethnicity: Theory and Experience*. Cambridge, Mass.: Harvard University Press.

Goldstein, A., and R. Suro. 2000. "Latinos in America: A Journey in Stages." *The Washington Post* (16 January, 2000).

Higham, J. 1988. *Strangers in the Land: Patterns of American Nativism, 1860–1925*. 2nd ed. New Brunswick, N.J.: Rutgers University Press.

Himmelfarb, G. 1999. *One Nation, Two Cultures*. New York: Knopf.

Hollinger, D. 1995. *Postethnic America*. New York: Basic Books.

Horowitz, D. 1985. *Ethnic Groups in Conflict*. Berkeley: University of California Press.

Isaacs, H. 1975. *Idols of the Tribe*. Cambridge, Mass.: Harvard University Press.

Jacoby, R. 1999. *The End of Utopia: Politics and Culture in an Age of Apathy*. New York: Basic Books.

Lind, M. 1995. *The New Nationalism and the Fourth American Revolution*. New York: The Free Press.

Newton, L. 2000. "Why Some Latinos Supported Proposition 187: Testing Economic Threat and Cultural Identity Hypotheses." *Social Science Quarterly* 81:180–93.

Nussbaum, M. C. 1996. *For Love of Country: Debating the Limits of Patriotism*. Boston: Beacon Press.

Okin, S.M. 1999. *Is Multiculturalism Bad for Women?* Princeton, N.J.: Princeton University Press.

Raz, J. 1994. "Multiculturalism: A Liberal Perspective." *Dissent* 41:67–79.

Reich, R. B. 1992. *The Work of Nations: Preparing Ourselves for 21st Century Capitalism*. New York: Vintage Books.

Sears, D., J. Citrin, S. Cheleden, and C. Van Laar. 1999. "Cultural Diversity and Multicultural Politics: Is Ethnic Balkanization Psychologically Inevitable?" In *Cultural Divides: The Social Psychology of Cultural Contact*, ed. D. Prentice and D. Miller. New York: Russell Sage.

Schlesinger, A. M., Jr. 1991. *The Disuniting of America: Reflections on a Multicultural Society.* New York: Norton.

Skerry, P. 2000. "Do We Really Want Immigrants to Assimilate?" *Society* 37 (3): 58–62.

Smith, Anthony. 1995. *Nations and Nationalism in a Global Era.* Cambridge, U.K.: Polity Press.

Takaki, R. T. 1993. *A Different Mirror: A History of Multicultural America.* Boston: Little, Brown & Co.

Tyler, T., E. A. Lind, K. Ohbuchi, and I. Sugawara. 1998. "Conflict with Outsiders: Disputing within and across Cultural Boundaries." *Personality and Social Psychology Bulletin* 24:137–47.

Welch, S. and L. Sigelman. 2000. "Getting to Know You? Latino-Anglo Social Contact." *Social Science Quarterly* 81:67–83.

Wolfe, A. 1998. *One Nation, After All.* New York: Viking.

TEN

American National Identity in a Postnational Age

Jim Sleeper

That American nationalism eludes not only its critics on the left but also its champions on the right became startlingly clear during the 2000 presidential primaries, when Conservative Republican leaders long associated with flag-waving patriotism scrambled to discredit an American war hero who charged that their own global capitalist "iron triangle" of big money, bad lobbyists, and undemocratic legislation has debased the country for which he fought. Liberals and even some leftists, meanwhile, found themselves casting shy, admiring glances at John McCain's insurgency: on National Public Radio, former Clinton labor secretary Robert Reich marveled that McCain had electrified apathetic citizens who value their patriotism enough not to want it left to Pat Buchanan. In Seattle, World Trade Organization protesters discovered that Third World regimes (some of which their elders had romanticized) were blocking environmental and worker protections that are found, *mirabile dictu,* in *American* laws. "Our country has many things well worth protecting, and most . . . are social inventions, not individual factories," commented Robert Kuttner, editor of the left-liberal *American Prospect.* "If this idea makes me a protectionist, I wear the made-in-U.S.A. label with pride" (Kuttner 2000, E-7).

These aren't stadium shouts of "U.S.A.!," nor is there racism or imperialism in such stirrings of national pride. McCain tapped what the German philosopher Jurgen Habermas admiringly called the "constitutional patriotism" of Americans who joined the civil rights and antiwar movements to oppose the government on behalf of a civic nation beyond celebrations of "blood and soil," beyond ideological crusades against communism, and even, sometimes, beyond the capitalist pursuit of profit (Habermas 1998, 21). More recently, the American philosopher Richard

Rorty has unnerved some fellow leftists by arguing, in *Achieving Our Country*, that national pride is as vital to struggles for social justice as individual self-respect is, but that the left has abdicated its responsibility to keep American pride on the sound footing set by Eugene V. Debs, A. Philip Randolph, and others who were anything but conservatives (Rorty 1998, 3, 33, 51).

What more propitious moment for an ideologically conciliatory reengagement with American identity and citizenship? Surveying the ruins of the past century's world-saving schemes, Rorty, Michael Lind (in *The Next American Nation*), the political scientist Benjamin Barber (in *Jihad vs. McWorld*), the sociologist Seymour Martin Lipset (in *American Exceptionalism*), and others find the United States pretty exceptional, after all. Not that the country is divinely blessed or racially superior; rather, it's a unique experiment in civic nationalism and a test of the democratic prospect in a postnational dispensation.

The European Union is such an experiment, too, but the American experiment may be the more fateful. First, this country was founded self-consciously, in liberal Enlightenment terms that, for all their violations, have proven more resilient than mystical invocations of white supremacy or other ethnic destiny. Second, the United States has been peopled differently than almost anywhere else—often unjustly, but mostly with a voluntarism too fluid and diverse to be comprehended by old world solidarities or Ford Foundation ethnic corralling under the banner of "diversity." Anomalies like these have made the American nation, for better or worse, the progenitor of the very globalism and cosmopolitanism that have nudged even the EU into being. The United States is deeply, vastly flawed, but not, I think, in quite the ways many of us on the left assumed: riddled with injustices and contradictions though it is, the country's liberal-democratic-capitalist regime has proved too protean, supple, and absorptive to sustain indictments that turn mainly on race, class, and gender. There are other, even deeper problems inherent in social atomization and consequent cultural absurdities that cross racial and sexual lines. These are driven by a "culture" of consumer marketing ever more relentless and intimately intrusive—and ever less racist and sexist. Surely, new and daunting tests of American national and civic culture lie before us.

My argument is that in order to meet those tests, we will have to reckon with American national identity more fully, and less dismissively and destructively. And to do that, we need to rescue the very notion of national identity from two extreme misconceptions that have palsied our political imaginations and our politics itself.

The first is a widespread misunderstanding of the political scientist and historian Benedict Anderson's characterization of nations as "imagined communities," nourished by sacred myths that commingle blood and soil in a kind of mystical bond. We see that sort of nationalism everywhere, writhing and dying—or, more accurately, inflicting death on millions—in the Balkans, the Middle East, central Africa, and elsewhere. We see it stirring in Austria and even in the United States, where it surfaces in revivals of a white-supremacist manifest destiny and of other, seemingly more benign but, in my view, insidiously destructive notions of non-white racial destiny that sometimes collect under rubrics of multiculturalism and diversity.

But our understanding of national identity has been prejudiced or tainted by more than such eruptions and insurgencies of imagined communities of racialist and ethnic belonging. We need to rescue the notion of national identity as well from what I call the "imagined vacuities" of a late-academic, professedly postnationalist, cosmopolitan discourse that considers all nationalism atavistic and outmoded. We should keep a guarded respect for the kind of nationalism manifested in Danish voters' decision of September 2000 not to merge their currency with the Euro. That particular hesitation before the prospect of full European integration was not mainly an eruption of "blood and soil" nationalism but a well-advised hesitation, based in an understanding that something important would be lost in too headlong a rush into the arms (the tentacles?) of global, transnational capitalism.

The Danish, British, and other rebuffs to full European integration suggest that although both Marxists and global capitalists consider nationalism to have been discredited morally and outmoded economically, we still need nations anthropologically and, in the deepest sense, politically, in ways we had better understand. Even if we can agree that human dignity and rights are universal, we can no more rely on a world government or the "global village" than we can on subnational ethnic or racial groups to nourish a predisposition to respect individual rights or a political consensus to defend them juridically.

Some people's inclination to dismiss nations as defenders of human rights is partly a legacy of Marxism, which held—citing plenty of compelling evidence—that nation-states are little more than shills or shells for warring capitalist elites. Leftists of my anti–Vietnam War generation, enraged at the American capitalist imperium, seldom acknowledged or understood national identity's richer, vitally necessary layers of cultural resonance and nurture—a necessity I will illustrate in a moment. There was something verging on hypocrisy in the few exceptions we made to our contempt for nationalism: people who wanted nations to disappear in the West celebrated the nationalist, often xenophobic passions and claims of Third World regimes and "people's liberation" movements, as well as of Native Americans and other "Indians" (whom some "postnationalists" now laud as "First Nations," without any apparent sense of self-contradiction). It was as if nationalism was good for Vietnam's National Liberation Front or for East Timor or China, but not for Polish Solidarity, and certainly not for the United States, where national pride was little more than a vessel of racism, imperialism, and exploitation.

Such notions linger. A lot of scholarly writing about nationalism is oddly silent about the United States, perhaps because it is too vast, variegated, and dynamic to be subsumed under either mystical invocations of ancient peoplehood or under ideologies of economic and social class that present themselves as functional accounts of nation-building. When this country figures at all in discussions of nationalism, it is as a grudgingly acknowledged anomaly, to be set aside for another discussion, or as an overarching and somewhat sinister imperium that asphyxiates noble solidarities of all kinds, nationalist or otherwise. Americans themselves have been little more helpful in characterizing their nation than have observers from abroad, at least after Tocqueville. Few Americans seem disposed or able to envision a national identity, progressive in the spirit of Abraham Lincoln and Walt Whitman or of Herbert Croly and Randolph Bourne, that is transcendent of the racism and imperialism to which it is so often reduced. It is as if we have forgotten how to talk about citizenship as Progressives did—not as an exclusive and exploitive or cooptive club but as a democratic project that can nourish a sometimes-glorious but, more often, prosaic benevolence across lines of race, sex, and even class.

A deeper, more respectful reckoning with such undramatic American civic and constitutional strengths would indeed challenge some of the racial and religious identities and social pillars to which we defer now so elaborately, and not just to repent or compensate the country's exclusionary past. A colder-eyed reckoning might actually ennoble instead of trivialize such identities, as liberal multiculturalism tends to do, or oppress them, as some kinds of assimilationism tend to do. The new American-ism I envision would open territory somewhere between the old nationalism's "imagined communities" of blood and soil and the late academy's "imagined vacuities" of postnationalist, anti-American dis-course—legacies of American racism and the Vietnam War more than of global forces that have supposedly discredited national pride.

There is no reason to argue that we can or should dispense with imag-ined communities whose basis is civic, not racial. However much global forces have sidelined nations economically and sometimes juridically, we do still need them politically, in the Aristotelian sense: just as each of us individual bearers of universal, Kantian rights has to uphold them within our idiosyncratic personal bodies and biographies, so must groups of in-dividuals sustain rights within shared structures and storylines, in soci-eties where each of us has a voice and a sense of belonging and we must sometimes be nudged, by laws, to respect. Since men aren't angels, as Madison famously warned, they need legal and civic structures to vindi-cate their rights and train the young in the arts and graces of public trust (Madison 1961, 322).

Only civic nationalism can do that for populations as diverse as America's, and such civic or republican nationalism must be clearly dis-tinguished from the older, *jus sanguinis* nationalism that sacralizes blood ties through myths of ancient descent that are seldom empirically true. Even though racial and ethnic subcultures may nurture certain important social values and dispositions, the "blood" nationalism of such subcul-tures can't vindicate the spirit or the reality of liberty and equality for individuals from diverse populations. Nor can worldwide consortia and treaties sustain good societies. But the next American nation, if it could reaffirm its best and highest strengths and rebuild citizenship around them, might advance justice beyond its own borders, without imperialism or exploitation. It could be the bearer, sometimes almost despite itself, of a "progressive" spirit invoked variously by Whitman, Bourne, Rorty, Lind, Lipset, and others. The country is willy-nilly a microcosm of enough of the world to be a crucial model, even if not at all the "city on a hill" of the Puritan imagination.

But the American civic project is imperiled now, perhaps more than ever, by an unrestrained Lockean ethic of work and property that, how-ever well it served society in a Christian, quasi-Calvinist harness (on which even Adam Smith and John Locke relied), has broken from that covenant and is running wild in a consumer market that is more intimately and deeply (if more subtly) destructive of dignity than any secular, economic force the world has known. It has Americans seesawing between an empty moralism and an emptier materialism. It measures out American individualism increasingly by the slender power it gives individuals to make personal choices in markets that stimulate them ever more intrusively, as atomized consumers. That drains other associations, forcing us to privatize our pleasures and socialize our pains, as Robert Reich has put it (Reich 1987). An older, republican American ethos that Daniel Aaron characterized as "ethical and pragmatic, disciplined and free" (Aaron 1988, 37) is giving way to an ethos more antisocial, apolitical, infantilizing, and absurd—an anomic social decay that masquerades as liberation.

That's not an American exceptionalism to cheer about. Then again, in this nation of brave departures, clean breaks, and fresh starts, we're almost accustomed to concocting identities more or less *ex nihilo,* in a society we've often thought was disintegrating but which turned out only to be reconfiguring itself along somewhat better moral as well as material lines. If we can manage that again, so much the worse for the hand-wringing moralists, angry ideologues, rational-choice "methodologues" among us, and for detractors abroad.

Admittedly, that's a big "if."

An Encounter with Civic Nationalism

Let me begin with what might strike some as anything but an expression of American pride, drawn from my own first direct encounter with civic nationalism more than thirty years ago—an experience of the sort John McCain appreciates now but has said he didn't at the time. One gray, wintry morning early in 1968, I was plodding across Yale University's Beinecke Plaza, a typical junior on my way to class, when I passed a group of undergraduates gathered silently around three seniors and the university chaplain, William Sloane Coffin Jr. One of the seniors was speaking barely audibly, not only because of the gusting wind but because he was trying to find his voice against fear. "The government claims we're criminals," he said, as I leaned in to listen, "but *we* say it is the government that is criminal in waging this war." He and the others were handing Coffin draft cards just like the ones the rest of us carried in our wallets. They were declaring that they would refuse conscription into the Vietnam War upon graduation three months hence, when their student deferments would end.

Coffin, who would send the cards to the Selective Service System, was there to bear witness to—and, in a way that I think is important in American civic terms, to *bless*—a courage few of us fully understood. "Believe me," he said, smiling, a strand of his graying hair aloft in the wind, "I know what it's like to wake up in the morning feeling like a sensitive grain of wheat lookin' at a millstone." It was a kind of Calvinist humor, jaunty in its defiance of "the powers that be" on behalf of a higher power; and something in us grasped at that little ray of hope, because we were scared. For all we knew, these guys were about to be arrested and taken to jail; and many of us who weren't sure yet whether we were on their side felt morally arrested by their bravery.

I think that we were scared in another way, as well: what these seniors were doing turned upside down any connection we felt to the Second World War experiences of our fathers, whom Steven Spielberg has since brought back, after a fashion, in *Saving Private Ryan,* and whom McCain evokes well, even as a Vietnam veteran. Not far from where we stood that day, the names of thousands of Yale men who had perished in wars were inscribed on the ghostly marble walls of the university's Woolsey Hall memorial, next to sculpted Periclean citizen-warriors and apothegms such as, "Courage Disdains Fame and Wins It." Now the draft resisters were challenging us to join them in disdaining fame, but with scant prospect of winning even the posthumous honor the memorial bestowed on those of the age that is past.

There was no escaping these contradictory, wrenching feelings. Most of us felt no such conflict in supporting, from a safe distance, the same period's civil rights activists in the South. The state governments there might be criminal, but, by the time we were aware of that, the federal government stood with the civil rights movement in ways that strengthened our own moral self-satisfaction in backing it, too. Here on Beinecke Plaza, that same federal government was being condemned and a summons to defy it was being served, in effect, to each of us draft-age men. And yet something in the resisters' and Coffin's bearing and speech made them seem as heroically "American" as would Private Ryan and Colonel McCain—and as free of anti-Americanism as Rosa Parks had been in refusing to move to the back of the bus in Montgomery. Parks's protest was tendered with such dignity, crediting even racist whites with some integrity, even while exposing their shortcomings, that she helped to redeem even a racist society, reconstituting what was best in it rather than simply trashing or deconstructing it as inherently, eternally damned.

Now, too, on Beinecke Plaza, the students' performance of civil disobedience was an act of national reconstitution. Jacques Derrida has used variations of the words "performative" and "constative" with some irony to challenge romantic ideas about the signing of the Declaration of Independence: since the "We" who held certain truths self-evident was constituted collectively only by a handful of privileged white men's performance in signing the document, he says, any suggestion that a larger "We" actually declared independence is a fiction, perhaps an elite sleight of hand (Derrida 1986, 7–12). But Derrida is noting only a truism inherent in all leadership and therefore in many moments in politics. It's not clear whether he fully appreciates the public alchemy of grave personal risk that made credible the American founders' performance and, later, the best labor and civil rights activists' and war resisters' performance.

With Coffin's help, the Yale students, too, were *performing* in public a real risking of their lives, fortunes, and sacred honor to resist the United States government in the name of the American *nation*. So doing, they were *reconstituting*, or at least revivifying, that nation. It was as if American civil society had arisen from a long slumber and was breathing and walking on its own, remoralizing the state and the law; as we watched, the silent, wild confusion we were feeling gave way to something like awe.

We have all had more than enough nostalgia from aging veterans of 1960s protests, paeans to the heroism of a generation that, in truth, wasn't all that noble. In the 1968 elections more than half of voters under thirty voted for Richard Nixon and George Wallace against Hubert Humphrey. Some people argue, Michael Lind among them, that the Vietnam War was justified morally, even if it was conducted badly (Lind 1999). Still others insist that even those who actually resisted the war weren't so moral about it; some may have made a virtue out of little more than an elitist, moralist revulsion at getting their hands dirty in an ugly business. Had not universal conscription hung over our heads, few of us would have challenged the war so frontally; when the draft was replaced by a lottery, the antiwar movement subsided. In this view, ours really wasn't a high civic nationalism on the move, and even the indisputably noble in it was puny beside the evil in America—the racism that some insist is endemic in our national structure and narratives; the militarism; the greed and concentrations of economic power that generate exploitative, transnational entities and policies.

Yet somehow the antiwar movement did rouse or shame enough Americans to make Lyndon Johnson decline to seek reelection and to drive John Kerry, a Yalie who'd fought in Vietnam and is now a senator from Massachusetts, to lead other vets in throwing combat medals back at the Capitol and in storming Senate hearing rooms to confront those who'd sent them. "This war broke my American heart," wrote Carl Oglesby, a literary tribune of the antiwar movement; his heart was "American" because he took seriously the old socialist activist Norman Thomas's admonition not to burn the flag but to wash it. The best of the civil rights and labor movements did that. They envisioned the reconstitution of a democratic people with a particular history and culture through an ongoing, reflexive transformation and experimentation. One of John Kerry's closest friends in later years was John McCain: two men who would have been at each other's throats in 1975 understood that constitutional patriotism can take many forms, and that even lethal disagreements can share in the honor of a commitment to human dignity that transcends narrow self-interest or group interest.

To put it another way, like that quintessentially American music, jazz, American national identity is a rolling synthesis of forces it generates yet doesn't wholly control. We should be impatient with people who can't get past indictments of it. We should match our revulsion at an Oliver North or a Pat Buchanan with our mistrust of those, much closer to the left, who default on the national pride Thomas evoked and, in so doing, let North and Buchanan set the terms of national belonging. "The great glory of American democracy is the right to protest for right," said Martin Luther King Jr. in a speech inaugurating the Montgomery bus boycott Parks had sparked. (King 1991, 48–51). That is what made Habermas marvel at the "constitutional patriotism" of ordinary Americans, who drew their strength to resist the state not from fantasies of racial and ethnic destiny but from their love of an experiment that tests, as Lincoln put it, whether republics that rely on higher principles, and on freedom that is based ultimately and irreducibly on personal responsibility and civic virtues, can long endure.

Lest these arguments be tainted by nostalgia for the movements of the 1960s, let me propose that prolife activists—those who remain true to their belief that life is a continuous, sacred current whose beginning and end shouldn't be set only by the personal decisions of individuals exercising their "rights"—may be constitutional patriots, too, if they peacefully contest opponents' demand that government should suborn and even fund what they think is murder. We may disdain such activists—or others who would curb the First Amendment rights of entertainment conglomerates like Time-Warner—as heartily as cultural conservatives disdained those of us who opposed the Vietnam War or the false racial comity of the old South. But the test should be whether we and they are loyal, as both Kerry and McCain now understand themselves to have been, to a larger framework within which such disagreements can be reckoned with, contained, and kept from spilling over into violence.

At least we now appreciate a constitutional framework's avoidance of gratuitous violence somewhat better than we used to. Good evidence of this is that several young journalists out of Harvard, such as Michael Ignatieff, Philip Gourevich, and David Rieff, have produced ideologically unsparing accounts of genocidal wars in African and other Third World nations, some of which were fatuously indulged by writers and activists of my own generation simply because they were anti-American. It is almost as if the recent spate of reporting on genocide were a semiconscious corrective of an older cohort's unwarranted romanticism. Not only isn't the United States, even at its militaristic worst, as bad as these disintegrating societies; the country's liberal-democratic-capitalist regime overcomes even the milder litany of complaints that it is unrelentingly racist and sexist. Is gayness inherently "progressive" because American capitalism depends on patriarchal, macho, homophobic strictures? Tell that to *The New York Times* and its advertisers, which are capitalist corporations, last time I checked, and which are driving a change. Does American capitalism depend any longer on racism? Are we sure? Why were the biggest defenders of affirmative action during the Washington State referendum of 1998 the Boeing, Microsoft, and Starbuck's corporations? Perhaps there is something wrong with an identity politics that only revivifies old group reactions to oppressions it should be trying to transcend.

Surely he or she is truly an American who thinks it a privilege and moral obligation to embrace a "to-die-for" identity that can rise above blood and skin and sexuality, and even beyond salvific ideologies and utopias, secular and religious. It entails a commitment to Lincoln's vision. But how do we fashion such an identity? One needn't be a communitarian to see that a civic culture is fragile and that its dispositions to engage in reasoned discourse, tolerance, self-discipline, respect for rights, and, finally, noble protest don't come from just anywhere. They require nurture and upkeep, energetic pedagogy, citizenship building, and constant public discourse—homely truths and habits that too many of us no longer have at hand. My notion of civic nationalism as the best, even the only, venue for such a project is contested by cosmopolitans who claim to be "above" nationalism, as well as by champions of "blood and soil" solidarities and other subnational groups that claim to be grounded from "below" the nation-state. Let us look more closely at each of these in turn.

Who Needs Nations?

One reason Americans have trouble talking about nationalism is that we take too much for granted the durability of the civil rights protected by our nation-state and its liberal democratic civic culture. We take them so much for granted that sometimes we imagine that they can be assured better by something broader and more cosmopolitan than the national civic culture itself. The political philosopher Martha Nussbaum, for instance, warns that an "emphasis on patriotic pride is both morally dangerous and ultimately subversive of some of the worthy . . . moral ideals of justice and equality" (Nussbaum 1996, 4). In liberal-universalist terms, she's right: we can't draw territorial lines around one populace and say that only there will we grant and protect the human dignity and opportunities we claim are universal rights. Liberal universalists can also cite structural constraints on nationalism: in the nineteenth century, American nationhood was strengthened by the "breakthrough" economic entities and technologies of the industrial age—railroads, telegraphs, and mass newspapers, for example—that brought the continent together and spawned not only national capitalist entities like Standard Oil but corresponding nationalist political movements, like Progressivism, to temper the abuses. Today, however, in this view, national identity has been weakened, even outmoded, by more recent breakthroughs—multinational corporations, mobile labor markets, cheap airline flights, the Internet. These scramble some old lines of color and even class, both between nations and within them, changing settlement and work patterns and making possible new kinds of "imagined community" where ideas, information, and experience are exchanged at the speed of light. From the cosmopolitan point of view, it is only in reaction to such seismic, kaleidoscopic shifts that some nationalist passions still ignite—defensively, belatedly, and destructively—flushes on the cheek of a dying age.

But what seems philosophically, economically, or technologically outmoded can remain anthropologically imperative. Although it's hard philosophically to reconcile a commitment to liberal-universal rights with drawing and enforcing national boundaries around solidarity and equality, it's just as hard to reconcile philosophizing about what may be good, true, and right for all times and places with how people actually live and move in the world. By universalist logic, no one should have celebrated the British "hand-over" of Hong Kong to China, which, celebrating its own nationalist consolidation against British "colonialism," posed a very serious threat to such democratic and human rights as the Western imperialists had in fact introduced into a culture with scant experience of them.

Such ironies should confound assumptions that nationalism and human rights are always at odds. Sometimes they need each other. Rorty, Habermas, and Seyla Benhabib remind us, in their different ways, of a cautionary analogy I posed here at the outset: Although as individuals every one of us bears a universal, Kantian dignity, each of us must give that dignity expression in an idiosyncratic physical body and mind whose hopes, fears, loves, and bruises give each of us a distinctive biography (Benhabib 1999, 5), And yet these personal odysseys have meaning and prospects only as they find acknowledgment in cultural and political vessels—that is, in *social* bodies without whose languages, rites, symbols, and institutions no individual's "body" could be human at all. Sustaining social bodies takes hard work. Aristotle said that humans are the noblest of animals under law, the most depraved of animals when they abandon politics in the broad sense. "We are not *born* equal," as Hannah Arendt put it; "we *become* equal as members of a group on the strength of our decision to guarantee ourselves mutually equal rights" through politics, by recognizing one another as consociates when we agree to enter into civic society and to induct the young into it (Arendt 1968, 177–78). It does take a village to raise a child.

But why does it take a nation? Only a nation can be large and diverse enough, and at the same time specific enough, to sustain a liberal civic polity—not a narrowly ethnic or sectarian community—in which people tie group narratives to institutional structures that vindicate universal, individual rights. Again I ask, who or what else besides nations can give or withhold the right to have rights? Not the Pope. Not the world communist movement. Not the United Nations. Not the World Trade Organization. Here the cosmopolitan critique of nationalism "from above" runs aground: nations remain what the Latin economist Hernando de Soto calls "the skin of the poor" because they alone nourish collective narratives and discourse that sustain a jurisprudence with the legitimized coercive power to protect people's rights (Carey 1999). David Hume, although he was not a liberal, posed the problem well by writing that "the general interest of mankind is better promoted" when "every man consults the good of his own community" than it is "by any loose indeterminate views to the good of a species, whence no beneficial action could ever result for want of a duly limited object on which they could exert themselves (Hume 1966, section V, part II). And Kant foresaw in world government a "soulless despotism."

Religious and Marxist attempts to soar on grand humanist rhetoric about individual dignity to transnational utopias have soured too often into inquisitions and gulags because they didn't comprehend Hume's and constitutional patriotism's way of attaching homely, communal sentiments to liberal, universal truths. American civic culture does that. At its best, it comprehends the legal scholar Frank Michelman's observation that "the right to have rights depends upon the receipt of social recognition and acceptance . . . that is, on one's juridical status within some particular, concrete community" (Michelman 1996, 200–204). Civic nationalism may not be a philosophical solution to the dilemmas of securing human rights, but it is the only institutional solution anyone can rely on.

It isn't only certain varieties of Marxism and religion that violate this understanding. The right to have rights can't be upheld by transnational corporations or by the Internet (or by movements linked through the Internet), either. Not only that: The evidence so far is that global capitalism generates an overclass that is no longer bound in any enforceable way to nurturing, political communities of workers. When transnational managerial elites in effect secede from national social responsibilities, the world their investments are creating loses its capacity or desire to vindicate the right to have rights—to help people judge and act as free persons.

So we end up needing nationalism to serve humanist universalism. When Hume's "limited objects on which [citizens] can exert themselves" and the political consensus and trust that surround such communities thin out or fail, some people do seek succor in separate racial or religious camps or in a proliferation of personal memoirs and private adventures that try to reinvent plausible social constructs; here the opposition to nationalism "from below," in subcultural or personal secessions, reveals its own limitations. Too often such communities and identities, some virtually concocted by their own would-be elites, abandon the universal for dreams of racial and other exotic destinies that exclude more people than civic nationalism ever could—and that, not incidentally, subordinate, to ethnic or religious demagoguery, the personal autonomy of those they do claim to empower. And most subnational groups have proved hopeless as defenders of human rights, except episodically and tactically, on the way to new "nationalist" formations.

It isn't often emotionally satisfying to ponder how to balance "rights" and equality through civic nationalism, but only prosaic national, institutional protections of rights can sustain the personal freedom and equal dignity most of us seek. No one should claim that civic nationalism can flourish without subcultural wellsprings, religious faith, or world-embracing visions of social justice. The point is that those things need social and juridical vessels that actually work, just as even cosmopolitan individuals need nurture in physical bodies that work.

A bitter irony in store for those who ignore this lesson is that their purported cosmopolitanism can become a Trojan horse for elites whom no one has ratified. That was the warning implicit in the Danish vote against adopting the Euro, and if it is not heeded, precipitous globalism can prompt darker, reactive retribalizations that are worse than civic nationalism. Joseph Bove, the French farmer who tore the roof off a McDonald's restaurant under construction in his native Provence to protest U.S. taxes on the Roquefort cheese he produces, came to the World Trade Organization demonstration in Seattle not so much because he cared about living wages and environmental standards, especially in the Third World, but because he wanted to defend his own economic and cultural ways. Fair enough, perhaps: his rhetoric soon transcended his narrower interests. But the French protest against crass American commercialization, justified though it certainly was, wasn't the moral or political equal of young American and Canadian protesters' insistence on anti–child labor laws and minimum wages for people in poor countries they'd never visited and in which they had no obvious material stake. *That* kind of protest was a true extrapolation of civic nationalism, in the spirit I first encountered in college.

Against this example, Nussbaum's caution that nationalist sentiments can end up subverting humanist values and can even curdle into racism and militarism is a truism, little more helpful than a warning that individual self-respect and pride can turn into self-aggrandizement through force and fraud. Of course, they can. But both personal and national aggression must be channeled and socialized; they can't be wished away by people who pronounce them dangerous. We don't decline to ride horses because they are strong and can throw us; we break them in. That's what civilization requires. Why are there contact sports? It's not clear whether Nussbaum has any idea. Yet it's when we fail to engage and elevate the prideful aggressions that drive nations that we get *The Fight Club*, the Nation of Islam, white militias, and urban gangs—filled with young men hungry for nobler rites of passage toward arts and graces of public trust, amid broader horizons.

What's So Unusual about the American Nation?

When we think about rites of passage, it's worthwhile to think of American civic nationalism as a citizenship-building project whose genius has been to temper the universal with the parochial *without succumbing to the tribal.* The nation was founded with that balancing act in mind. Even while climbing only slowly out of history's muck and slime and the country's own internal contradictions and hypocrisies, the United States has done quite a lot to enlarge and defend the right to have rights, even in Mississippi, even at Yale's Beinecke Plaza. Cultural identities reflect the human need to generate collective narratives, memories, rites of passage, and bonds of affection, and to find one's individual self within such narratives. If the larger society isn't providing them, subgroups of all kinds will try. But not all such subgroups sustain liberal principles. Groups based in "blood and soil" seldom do. Only a democratic national community can harness communal needs to universal values. It's when it doesn't that a Louis Farrakhan or Aryan militias emerge.

It is disturbing, therefore, that many Americans now accept as beyond question the notion that there is a substantial correlation between culture and color. They do so not out of conviction as often as because such assumptions seem to be in the air they breathe and the water they drink. In discussions of campus "diversity" programs, I often give students pause by asking a young champion of "diversity" to "tell me three specific things you'd like me to presume that I know about you if I know only your race or ethnicity." Most people find such a question difficult because, when push comes to shove, they value their ethnic affinities far less than they do freedom to choose their interests and memberships and even to leave behind racial or ethnic labeling. The point is not that there aren't cultural differences deserving respect but that they shouldn't be concocted or promulgated to command respect. If true diversity depends on respect for a range of differences that is broader and deeper than colors on a racial spectrum, such respect requires that we accent and enrich the broader and deeper commonalities that sustain the disposition to respect one another across lines of race and ethnicity. Precisely because the country *is* so diverse racially, ethnically, sexually, and religiously—complex beyond any coding of it, as the census is discovering—we should all be working overtime to identify common bonds and nurture them in rites of passage that give us the civic leadership we need. The point is not that racial narratives should disappear, but they shouldn't become the central organizing principles of civic or political life.

When they do become central, some people respond to color-coded cultural, institutional, and governmental signals by making careers out of cashing in on ethnic identity, not just in preferments or subsidies, but moralistically, as if hoping to reap a kind of cachet. There is a bitter irony in this: just as the women's movement has been breaking down assumptions about sexual differences—so that knowing only a person's sex entitles one less often to presume anything about that person's inclinations or capacities—"diversity" advocates are "discovering" one new racial difference after another. It's as if, when postmodernists and queer theorists who favor gender bending turn to race, they become racial *conservatives* by trying to *conserve* and enhance racial differences.

In urban centers, such line drawing can become poisonous, as in the jury deliberations in New York City's infamous "Central Park Jogger" case a decade ago. A young white woman had been raped and bludgeoned by several young black and Hispanic men. Racial demagogues and even some academic racialists were portraying the defendants as victims of a lynching, although they were manifestly guilty, some having confessed tearfully on videotape upon realizing what they had done. At one point in the deliberations, according to some reports, a Puerto Rican juror slammed his fist on the table, glared at two black jurors across the room, and said, "All right, all right; I'll vote to convict Ramon Santana if you'll vote to convict the black guys" (Sleeper 1998, 39). If such an attempt to broker justice racially was actually made by this juror, thinking himself the delegate of a race as he weighed individuals' guilt or innocence, we should have no difficulty in calling his thinking "un-American." Failure to retake that phrase from those who used it to redbait Communists in the 1950s would cheat universalism as much as patriotism.

The jogger case incident shows negatively why emphasizing ascriptive identities to expose abuses can end up reinforcing the abuses as well as the identities. It's one thing to show that false claims of comity and transcendence have suppressed truths about exclusion and oppression; it's another to leave people thinking there's been nothing *but* oppression. We'd be better off acknowledging that even if white racism could be dispelled, even if every broken heart could be mended and every theft of opportunity redressed, people would find other ways to divide and oppress, for ultimately the evil is not racism but the fear of freedom behind it that American rites of passage should teach us to face down and transcend.

Imagine if such rites of passage yielded movie producers who'd cast a Puerto Rican Jimmy Stewart in the role of a juror who persuades fellow jurors to abandon racial brokering for justice in tense deliberations during a jogger trial. We need leadership brave and savvy enough to point beyond identities that are negative, identities that shout, "I am excluded; therefore I am," or, "I am transgressive! Therefore I am." Some may ask whether we'd have anything of any value left to share if ethnic affinities lost all weight in our social equations and race receded in importance to the equivalent of differences in hair or eye color among whites. The answer, as Ellison said, is that "blood and skin do not think;" human beings are so much more protean, so much more creative than race doctors would have us believe.

As Randolph Bourne put it—and this was in 1916—"Only America, by reason of the unique liberty of opportunity and traditional isolation for which she seems to stand, can lead in this cosmopolitan enterprise. Only the American—and in this category I include the migratory alien who has lived with us and caught the pioneer spirit and sense of new social vistas—has the chance to become that citizen of the world. America is coming to be, not a nationality but a transnationality, a weaving back and forth, with the other lands, of many threads of all sizes and colors. Any movement which attempts to thwart this weaving, or to dye the fabric in any one color, or to disentangle the threads of the strands, is false to this cosmopolitan vision" (Bourne 1992, 262).

Bourne had a friend, Mary Antin, a Russian-Jewish immigrant whose memoir of becoming an American, *The Promised Land*, is too often misremembered as a tract for assimilation. In fact, it was both a poignant reflection on parochialism and a testament to the nation that had made her a citizen of the world. Reflecting in 1941, in her last published essay, on the European Jews' debacle, Antin wrote, "Not to dissociate myself from the Jewish lot, but to establish the more unassailable bond, I here declare that the point where I come to life as a member of modern society, where my fullest sense of responsibility is kindled, is deep below the ache and horror of the Jewish dilemma, at the juncture of social forces where I see the persecution or belittlement of a group—*any* group, whether of race, creed or color—as an attack on democracy" (Antin 1997, 1).

That is the fruit of the schoolgirl's paeans to George Washington; those who would dismiss Antin as a flag-waving patriot miss the truth that American patriotism was her stairway to liberal universalism; it may be a measure of liberal deformity today that we do not appreciate her message for what it was. Who, indeed, helps to express and uphold Bourne's and Antin's vision now? They and other turn-of-the-century Progressives were part of an open elite of public intellectuals, artists, and activists who rewove the national tapestry by posing Bourne's challenges. I think that he would condemn now, as "false to this cosmopolitan vision," not only white supremacists and Anglo-Saxon assimilationists but separatists of any color or kind who would try to "disentangle the threads of the strands."

In 1993, when I was a political columnist for the New York *Daily News*, I questioned Mayor David Dinkins's resort to the metaphor of the city as "a gorgeous mosaic" of racial, ethnic, religious, and sexual groups. I noted that while a mosaic's pattern can be beautiful, each of its tiles is rigid, fixed in place, unable to change its color or shape. Not only doesn't a mosaic describe the malleability of most groups or their individual members in a city as fluid as New York; even if we accept the metaphor, and everyone is a tile, who is the glue, the bonding agent, looking out for the whole? Or, for that matter, who is the solvent, the acid that sometimes undoes the glue and helps new patterns, new wholes, to form?

The question seemed beyond the mayor's reckonings, but in a democracy the answer should be that each of us sometimes devotes himself or herself to being glue or solvent, to standing for the whole. There is a special role for intellectuals, artists, political activists, and leaders of all kinds in stimulating new configurations. There are, of course, false prophets, demagogues, hustlers of one group identity or another, ethno-centric and political hacks, not to mention self-appointed revolutionary or "nationalist" elites that become oppressors of imagined communities or proletariats, which often prove reluctant to follow them very far. Mo-saics can congeal around such duplicitous and warring elites only when people are corralled and kept apart by their leaders.

In more promising American terms, each of us might be raised in a particular racial or ethnic subculture, but each of us could graduate from it at times (or forever, if we want to), to participate in a larger civic cul-ture that is "thick" enough to live in, on its own affectional, race-transcending terms. Again, it isn't that religious or racial narratives should disappear; it's that they can't become the central organizing principles of a democratic civic or public life, and that someone has to nourish this common culture, or we are all lost.

If our ethnocentrism has shown some capacity to correct itself, it has done so for at least one reason too few of the cosmopolitan progressives among us seem to grasp: One of this country's deepest and still strongest religious traditions acknowledges a contradiction in the heart of liberal universalism by portraying knowledge, through the Garden of Eden myth, as an apprehension of the world haunted by a serpent and a corruptible couple of humans. That understanding and the epistemological humility it ought to protect gives liberalism a modest advantage: it acknowledges the imperfectibility of politics within which personal freedom takes root.

Americans have done this in a unique way that deepened faith with-out clinging to doctrine or ecclesiastical rule—indeed, often by defying them. When Coffin quipped that he felt like a sensitive grain of wheat looking at a millstone, he reminded us students that the resisters were drawing on something that passes rational understanding: Coffin's own conservative, very American Calvinist theology, with its emphasis on per-sonal communion with God outside of ecclesiastical frames, strengthened his stand against the dominant temporal powers (Oppenheimer 1996). By separating church from state, the founders managed brilliantly to expand both civil and religious liberty; freedom from state coercion necessitated and strengthened voluntarist religious impulses like Coffin's, which in turn suffused the legal system with a moral depth it wouldn't otherwise have had. By keeping American understandings of personal dignity and liberty free of doctrinal or priestly—and therefore corruptible—frames, separation of church and state reinforced presumptions of natural rights while rejecting arbitrary claims of divine right in politics.

Arguably, in consequence, "Only America has united nationality and universality, civic and spiritual selfhood, secular and redemptive history, the country's past and paradise to be, in a single synthetic ideal," as Sacvan Bercovitch puts it (Bercovitch 1993). *The country rests on an expectation of faith without an imposition of doctrine.* Rorty speaks similarly of American civic culture's need to save its religious impulses and capacity for awe without institutionalizing the infantile needs for security he associates with established religions (Rorty 1998, 15–21). But this is a balance too many liberals have lost, and the price they pay for ignoring questions of faith is that fundamentalists rush in where liberals fear to tread.

One might also believe that America is "exceptional," not in being divinely blessed but in being the anomalous bearer of so many prospects. Precisely because the United States is the progenitor of many of the seismic economic, technological, demographic, and cultural shifts I've mentioned, and because it has been struggling with some of the consequences for more than two hundred years, mightn't this country actually stimulate new configurations of human dignity, or serve as a training ground for expressions of them that transcend its origins?

Americans take their peculiar nation-state so much for granted that we don't think about what its absence would do to "the right to have rights." Secure in our regime, we still take eighteenth-century assumptions about natural rights almost for granted, and that is both a strength and a weakness. To the extent that we don't realize how bad things could get, we tend to think that any gap between assertion and implementation is an abyss that must be crossed. The strength in this is that it makes us sally forth in crusades as constitutional patriots in the ways Habermas admired—in civil rights, ecology movements, antisweatshop movements, in the best of the WTO protests, even in the leavening electoral ventures of John McCain, Bill Bradley, and Ralph Nader. The weakness is that when such efforts post only limited gains, or when new abysses open as quickly as we have crossed the old, some moralists and idealists fall into despair.

We are better off on those relatively rare occasions when civic nationalism wells up significantly from society's margins, as it did in the civil rights movement, when ordinary people struggled to secure recognition and decency as well as opportunities and advantages. Herbert Croly posed that part of the challenge in nationalist, not Marxist terms: "So long as the great majority of the poor in any country are inert and are laboring without any hope in this world, the whole associated life of that community rests on an equivocal foundation. Its moral and social order is tied to an economic system that starves and mutilates the great majority of the population, and under such conditions its religion necessarily becomes a spiritual drug, administered for the purpose of subduing the popular discontent and relieving the popular misery" (Croly 1964 [1909], 22).

Rorty, quoting Croly, says the left wrongly considers nationalism itself such a spiritual drug. It can be, just as personal pride can be self-deluding. But many in the academy are captive to such cautions about national sentiment, and they wonder why their politics has no traction off campus. "Americanization" should denote an ambitious project to build the sort of citizenship the late Congresswoman Barbara Jordan invoked when she chaired the U.S. Commission on Immigration Reform in 1995. Calling for new programs to Americanize immigrants, she noted that "Americanization earned a bad reputation when it was stolen by racists and xenophobes in the 1920s, . . . but it is our word and we are taking it back" (Pickus 1998, xvii). We need to nourish the nation on behalf of something transnational that comes not only from a Barbara Jordan, Norman Thomas, Rosa Parks, or Yalies on Beinecke Plaza, but from many, many others.

An Open Elite and a New Challenge

American constitutional patriotism and the identity that grows from it rests on a civic-democratic project requiring an open elite of democratic leaders—people skilled, like Coffin or Parks and others I've cited, in the arts and graces of intergroup communication and of standing for the whole. Such an elite is "open" to anyone willing to undergo its arduous rites of passage, as Rosa Parks did, as those Yale seniors on Beinecke Plaza did. An open elite doesn't admit everyone; it uses vigorous public discourse and judgment by acknowledged leaders to stimulate and certify people of all types and stations who've shown intelligent passion to nourish the whole, to relieve cruelty and humiliation, to strengthen others' dignity and skills.

Rosa Parks, for example, was a seamstress in a department store, but she was also the secretary of her NAACP chapter; she had been trained to do what she did on that Montgomery bus and was prepared—as much as any powerless, private black person in the South could have been at that time—for the vilification and violence that would come with taking her case to court and to the streets. Membership in America's open elite can and sometimes must be like that. Compared to Parks, the war resisters at Beinecke Plaza couldn't have been more privileged, and, of course, they were white, while the war they were trying to stop was being fought by an American army disproportionately nonwhite. Yet they risked everything they had to stop it. The point of both the resisters' and Parks's stories is that an open elite isn't grounded or justified in racial or class ties.

I've said that American national identity tries to balance the universal with the parochial without succumbing to the tribal, and that it relies on faith even while assuring freedom from doctrinal or ecclesiastical coercion. But we are losing these balances, and I want to close on that note of concern.

In *The Protestant Ethic and the Spirit of Capitalism,* Max Weber described how that ethic, based in both individual liberty and responsibility, in both materialism and delayed gratification, unleashed but also tempered entrepreneurial capitalism and also tempered it (Weber 1958). Arguably, only within the tensions of such a paradox can a "democratic" nation hope to balance personal freedom and social obligation in ways that advance both liberty and equality. But such advances today are imperiled by a post-Lockean ethic of work and property that, however well it functioned in quasi-Calvinist harness, has burst from its original social covenants into a consumer marketing that is relentlessly, intimately intrusive and deeply degrading.

Ironically, but happily enough, consumer marketing has decoupled blackness a little from class and from sex, confounding "liberationist" leftists and cultural conservatives alike. Until relatively recently, white segregationists of the South conflated blackness with sexual license and moral decay, which they said caused black poverty. In reaction, many liberal whites and blacks embraced romantic racialist notions that ended up recycling the old segregationist assumptions: like the by now emblematic "radical chic" partygoers at Leonard Bernstein's cocktail reception for Black Panther thugs in his Manhattan aerie, too many liberals and radicals transmuted an exotic blackness and sexual license into an imagined source of their own "liberation" from their middle-class restraints and anomie, if not of the poor's liberation from poverty.

But capitalism, "the system," as we called it then, has proved more supple and absorptive than even its strongest defenders anticipated. Groping with racial challenges the left and liberals helped to pose, it has shuffled the racial deck enough so that color doesn't correlate so clearly with class or with sexual liberation—at least not as we look ahead down most economic and cultural trend lines. Reports of racism's demise are greatly exaggerated, yet "race is over," as Stanley Crouch puts it, because, whether in segregationists' or cultural radicals' hands, it offers little leverage against new entertainments that demoralize and divert *black and white together* from the civic and economic work we need to do. When people as unlike one another as C. Dolores Tucker and William Bennett join hands against Time-Warner to protest mindlessly violent and degrading entertainment; when more complacent blacks and whites can sit together in television-studio audiences clamoring for rituals of degradation that titillate their most intimate impulses, race *has* lost its traction both for and against threats to civic comity that run as deeply through American life as racism itself.

Consider, too, the newly emblematic "white-on-white" tragedies in the Colombine High School massacre in Colorado and its analogues, which have decoupled race from youth violence in the American mind. Think, as well, of the "Bill and Monica" and even the "Clarence and Anita" shows—real-life soap operas that advance the disassociation of race from sexual license. So thoroughly, indeed, has consumer capitalism shuffled our libidinal as well as racial decks that it is even comfortable peddling sexual degradation. Those Calvin Klein-*cum*-kiddie porn ads that showed up a few years ago on the sides of public buses in New York City had been put there by private investors in free markets, not by people pursuing leftist or liberal agendas; it was nonmarket, civic forces that removed them.

Chilling commercial insinuations of sadistic violence, sexual torpor, and cynicism into our daily lives deepen despair and inequity, not by dividing people along racial or sexual lines, and not by uniting them against spiritual and cultural exploitation, but by atomizing the social alienation. In effect, they induce or sometimes intimidate weak individuals of all colors and sexual orientations to drop out of public discourse, one by one, deflating politics, which is our only recourse to "the right to have rights."

We have no more helpful a vocabulary to describe this kind of decay in our public life than most Americans had to describe racism in, say, 1940. The old passion plays against racism and sexism no longer work because "the system" they used to condemn doesn't need so much of the racism and sexism that powered the sacrifices of white, male managers. No longer can even queer theorists imagine gayness as inherently "progressive" or even transgressive, let alone subversive of a putatively "patriarchal," homophobic capitalism; any reader of *The New York Times* news columns and advertisements knows that much of today's capitalism *embraces* gayness in its typically vapid, commercializing way. (Conservative defenders of "bourgeois" values such as Irving Kristol and Norman Podhoretz who oppose the new sexual pluralism will have to break with corporate capitalism in order to sustain their beliefs. But if they did that, they'd lose a lot of their influence. So trust them to finesse their discomfort.)

Yet the moral challenge is real, and not only for partisan cultural conservatives. The best labor, civil rights, and other social movements should be worried, too, by the capitalization of sexuality and even of racial identity in niche marketing. Once, progressives could appeal to consensual moral and civic narratives that were already dear to most of the larger society: The narrative dramatized by the civil rights movement, for example—a twentieth-century rendering of the Exodus myth on the evening news—linked the passions of the aggrieved to myths and principles that were very widely shared, or at least professed. The protesters revivified a common moral and civic language; they didn't drain it in mocking, bitter defiance. They understood that when one group's idea of oppression is another's idea of justice, only civic and legal processes rooted in common beliefs can keep otherwise irreconcilable camps from spiraling off into a violence that terminates civic life. No matter how justified the most exemplary protesters felt in recoiling from racism into separatism and violence, they didn't withdraw from civil society or assault it by taking the law into their own hands; they didn't lie to the public or vilify it or speak in a mystical tongue others couldn't understand.

A society that loses shared beliefs and a common language and the little daily expressions of trust that grow from them degenerates into a slippery web of contracts and rights that can't be moved morally. It sinks into anomic litigation and the huckstering of political cardsharps. It snuffs out civic virtue to buy a false peace through brokering in racial or market terms, eclipsing principle and courage in personal and political exchanges. It drifts witlessly, from alarm to alarm.

Yet both liberals and conservatives have forgotten these truths. Neither camp seems to have anticipated that while negative liberties of "free

markets" and "free speech" are indispensable in loosening oppressive strictures, they don't by themselves actually liberate anyone. It's not enough to
break sexual and other taboos to lift what Herbert Marcuse called "surplus repressions" if we leave unchallenged stark inequalities or, amid relative prosperity, the alienation and melancholy shadowing the unchecked
commodification of our talents and desires (Marcuse 1966, 274). No wonder some flee commercial pseudoliberations for the succor of racial and
sexual camps, where mythic roots beckon but identities are often more
concocted than nourished. The chief peril to American civic health isn't
the left's utopian/totalitarian impulses or the right's libertarian/fascist
vagaries but the "bread and circus" decadence that is reminiscent more
of the late Roman Empire than of the Soviet Union or Nazi Germany
and that is coming our way via the tube, the Internet, the casino, the sex
shop, and the psychiatric clinic, where even irreducibly moral crises are
medicated away. It is driven less by the left than by the quarterly bottom
line and by the marketing division. The next American civil rights movement, alongside drives to organize the unorganized, will have to repeal the
"civil rights" of conglomerates that do what they want in our public and
even private lives yet restrict our speech and actions in their own corporate realms.

This imbalance between expressive and associative power now hobbles
our discourse. It won't be addressed by ideological leftists or rightists or
by the terminal cynicism that has drawn so many from the civic center.
The rewards of deconstructing civic nationalism in those ways are passing, not because our sins are gone but because we are already well convicted of them and need now to reenvision and build.

Wistful in our diffuse, new disaffection, Paul Simon sang in "An
American Tune,"

We come on the ship they call the Mayflower
We come on the ship that sailed the moon
We come in the age's most uncertain hour
And sing an American tune.
But it's all right, it's all right,
You can't be forever blessed.

No, you can't. But decency needs a home. It won't be sustained by tan-
gled abstractions about rights or by rubrics that countenance a corpo-

rate "free speech" driven by prurience, sadism, or greed. Nor can civil society be saved by those too wracked by guilt to love their country. "America is the greatest of opportunities and the worst of influences," wrote George Santayana in *The Last Puritan;* "Our effort must be to resist the influence and improve the opportunity" (Santayana 1995). We can only hope that young readers will find the strength and savvy to do that in civic rites of passage that forge such power and wisdom.

References

Aaron, Daniel. *American Notes.* Boston: Northeastern University Press, 1988, 37.

Antin, Mary. "Introduction." *The Promised Land.* New York: Penguin, 1997, l.

Arendt, Hannah. *The Origins of Totalitarianism.* New York: Harcourt, Brace, Jovanovich 1968 [1951]), 177–78.

Barber, Benjamin, and Andrea Schulz, ed. *Jihad vs. McWorld: How Globalism and Tribalism Are Reshaping the World.* New York: Ballantine Books, 1996.

Benhabib, Seyla. "Hannah Arendt and 'The Right to Have Rights.'" *Hannah Arendt Newsletter* (December 1999), 5.

Bercovitch, Sacvan. *The Rites of Assent: Transformations in the Symbolic Construction of America.* New York: Routledge, 1993.

Bourne, Randolph. "Trans-National America." In *Randolph Bourne: The Radical Will: Selected Writings, 1911–1918,* ed. Olaf Hansen, with a preface by Christopher Lasch. Berkeley: University of California Press, 1992, 262.

Carey, James. Columbia School of Journalism, in a letter to the author containing quote from Hernan de Soto, Latin American economist, 11 March 1999.

Croly, Herbert. *The Promise of American Life.* New York: Capricorn Books, 1964 [1909], 22.

Derrida, Jacques. "Declarations of Independence." *New Political Science* 986 (Summer 1986): 7–12.

Habermas, Jurgen. "The European Nation-State: On the Past and Future of Sovereignty and Citizenship." In *The Inclusion of the Other: Studies in Political Theory,* ed. Ciaran Cronin and Pablo De Greiff. Cambridge, Mass.: MIT Press, 1998.

Hume, David. *An Enquiry Concerning the Principles of Morals,* [1777]. Open Court Publishing Co., 1966, 60.

Jordan, Barbara. "The Americanization Ideal." *The New York Times,* 11 September 1995. Quoted in Noah M. J. Pickus, *Immigration and Citizenship in the 21st Century* (Lanham, Md.: Rowman and Littlefield, 1998), xvii.

King, Martin Luther, Jr. "Speech at the Holt Street Baptist Church" (December 5, 1955). In *Eyes on the Prize: Civil Rights Reader,* ed. David J. Garrow. New York: Penguin, 1991, 48–51.

Kuttner, Robert. "Debate on Trade with China Misses the Point." *The Boston Globe* (14 May 2000): E-7.

Lind, Michael. *The Next American Nation: The New Nationalism and the Fourth American Revolution.* New York: The Free Press, 1995.

———. *Vietnam the Necessary War: A Reinterpretation of America's Most Disastrous Military Conflict.* New York: The Free Press, 1999.

Lipset, Seymour Martin. *American Exceptionalism: A Double-Edged Sword.* New York: W.W. Norton & Co., 1997.

Lipset, Seymour Martin, and Gary Marks. *It Didn't Happen Here: Why Socialism Failed in the United States.* New York: W. W. Norton & Co., 2000.

Madison, James. "No. 51." *The Federalist Papers.* New York: Mentor Books, New American Library, 1961, 322.

Marcuse, Herbert. *Eros and Civilization.* Boston: Beacon Press, 1966, 238–74.

Michelman, Frank. "Parsing 'A Right to Have Rights.'" *Constellations: An International Journal of Critical and Democratic Theory* 3, no. 2 (October 1996): 200–204.

Nussbaum, Martha. "Patriotism and Cosmopolitanism." In *For the Love of Country: Debating the Limits of Patriotism,* ed. Joshua Cohen. Boston: Beacon Press, 1996, 4.

Oppenheimer, Mark. *A Conservative Radical: William Sloane Coffin's Sermon Theology.* Unpublished manuscript, Senior Essay, Yale College, 1996.

Reich, Robert. *Tales of a New America.* New York: Times Books, 1987.

Rorty, Richard. *Achieving Our Country: Leftist Thought in Twentieth-Century America.* Cambridge, Mass.: Harvard University Press, 1998, 3, 33, 51.

Santayana, George. *The Last Puritan: A Memoir in the Form of a Novel.* Cambridge, Mass.: MIT Press, 1995.

Sleeper, Jim. *Liberal Racism.* New York: Penguin, 1998, 39.

Weber, Max. *The Protestant Ethic and the Spirit of Capitalism.* New York: Charles Scribner's Sons, 1958.

Wills, Gary. *Inventing America: Jefferson's Declaration of Independence.* New York: Vintage Books, 1979, 288.

ELEVEN

How to Achieve One America

Class, Race, and the Future of Politics

Richard D. Kahlenberg

In chapter 4 of this book on the "promise and disappointment" of President Clinton's Initiative on Race, I argued that Clinton was poised to offer a "third way" on affirmative action and race relations but never bit the bullet, opting instead for continued reliance on race-specific measures. I also argued that timid conservative policies leave large economic gaps between racial groups that continue to impede the goal of One America.

If the Clinton and conservative approaches are both lacking, what is the most promising route to One America? In order to achieve the end, public policies need to do three things: they need to promote integration by race and class, so we do not continue to grow apart; they need to reduce reliance on the use of race per se in order both to sustain legal challenge and to minimize the balkanizing side effects of such policies; and they need to be perceived as generally fair and just in order to draw strong support and minimize resentment. Need-based programs work best to fulfill these goals. What follows are two major public policy ideas that serve as examples of ways to achieve integration and One America without the divisive reliance on race: integrating public schools by economic status, and need-based affirmative action.

Economic School Integration

In seeking to forge One America, the logical starting place is the public schools. Public primary and secondary education has historically played a very important role in providing the glue that holds together the people of the United States. As the U.S. increasingly draws its population from every corner of the world, the role the public schools play in keeping the country from balkanizing becomes more and more important.

In particular today, education must also be about creating Americans. We are now experiencing levels of immigration unknown since the late nineteenth century (Ascher, Fruchter, and Berne 1996, 99). The question becomes, as Arthur Schlesinger Jr. asks in *The Disuniting of America*: "What happens when people of different ethnic origins, speaking different languages and professing different religions, settle in the same geographic locality and live under the same political sovereignty?" His answer: "Unless a common purpose binds them together, tribal hostilities will drive them apart" (Schlensinger 1991, 10). The public schools have always been understood to be a key source of that common purpose and unity. Public education, wrote Justice Felix Frankfurter in 1948, is "the most powerful agency for promoting cohesion among heterogeneous democratic people ... at once the symbol of our democracy and the most pervasive means for promoting our common destiny" (*McCollom v. Board of Education* 1948, 216, 231).

The goal of political assimilation is widely shared by Americans of all ethnic backgrounds. A 1998 survey conducted by Public Agenda found that 80 percent of Americans in all racial groups said it was "absolutely essential" for schools to teach students that "whatever their ethnic or racial background, they are all part of one nation." The survey found that Americans also want students to learn "the common history and ideas that tie all Americans together" (Broder 1998).

If schools educate well-off and poor, or majority and minority students, separately, they are unlikely to promote the national interest in political and economic assimilation. Teachers can stand in front of the classroom and tell students that all are equal under the law, but the message may fall flat in schools where all students are white and middle class or all students poor and of color. The nineteenth-century educator Horace Mann noted that if the children of laborers attended different schools from the children of doctors and lawyers, the "children of the less favored class" would be degraded by "the consciousness that they are attending a school unworthy of the patronage of those whom they have been led to regard as the better part of the community" (Clark 1996).

Ethnically separate schools, likewise, can produce black students who think that most whites are members of the KKK or are conspiring to infect black babies with AIDS, or white students who fear black people because their only exposure comes from the nightly news crime report. Such is not a unified nation. In 1996, the Connecticut Supreme Court noted in a school desegregation case, "If children of different races and economic and social groups have no opportunity to know each other and to live together in school, they cannot be expected to gain the understanding and mutual respect necessary for the cohesion of society" (*Sheff v. O'Neill* 1996, 1285). In a 1974 school desegregation case, Justice Thurgood Marshall declared, "unless our children begin to learn together, there is little hope that our people will ever learn to live together" (*Milliken v. Bradley* 1974, 783). The academic studies support this claim. African-American students who attend integrated schools are more likely to attend integrated (rather than all-black) colleges, to live in integrated neighborhoods, and have interracial friendships as adults (Braddock, Crain, and McPartland 1984, 260; Bok 1996, 185; Liebman 1990, 1626–27; and Denton 1996, 822–23).

Today, efforts at school desegregation under *Brown v. Board of Education* are winding down, and now even the voluntary use of race to create diversity in schools is being questioned by the courts. In 1999, Gary Orfield of the Harvard Desegregation Project reported that the percentage of black students attending predominantly minority schools had increased from 62.9 percent in 1980–81, to 68.8 percent in 1996–97 (Orfield and Yun 1999, 13 [Table 9]).

A new national public policy to explicitly promote economic integration of schools is the single most effective educational strategy for fostering greater national unity. As efforts to desegregate schools by race are curtailed by the courts, integration by socioeconomic status provides a way to indirectly promote racial school integration without running afoul of the Constitution. (While racial classifications are generally disfavored and require a compelling justification, considering socioeconomic status in student assignment is perfectly legal.) Today, 25 percent of schools have a student population in which a majority of students are low income, meaning they are eligible for free or reduced-price lunch because their family incomes are below 185 percent of the poverty line. Students in those schools should be integrated through public school choice programs with students in the other 75 percent of schools so that 100 percent of schools have a majority of students who are "middle class" (defined as too well off to be eligible for free or reduced-price lunch).

Economic school integration may be justified primarily as a way of giving all students a fair chance to attend good schools that will raise their achievement and attainment (Kahlenberg 2001). But economic integration will also foster One America by producing a good measure of racial integration without relying on race per se. If there is a strong overlap between race and poverty in the United States, there is an even stronger correlation between race and concentrated poverty. While only 5 percent of predominantly white schools have high poverty rates, more than 80 percent of predominantly African-American and Latino schools are high poverty (Orfield, Bachmeier, and Eitle 1997, 2). In fact, schools with 90 to 100 percent black and Hispanic representation are fourteen times more likely to have a majority of students eligible for free or reduced-price lunch than schools that are 90 percent or more white (Orfield and Eaton, 1996, 55).

White middle-class families want more integration and diversity in their schools, but they also want a middle-class tone. Ensuring that all schools are majority middle class can give the suburban parents the diversity they seek without the overwhelming behavioral problems associated with majority poor schools.

Class-Based Affirmative Action in College

On the issue of affirmative action, likewise, there is a strong case to be made that preferential policies based on class rather than race would promote One America more effectively than current race-based policies.

Class-based preferences will achieve a fair amount of racial integration. In large measure because of our history of discrimination, people of color are disproportionately poor, and so they will disproportionately benefit from class-based preferences. At UCLA Law School, for example, administrators provided a leg up to students who overcame obstacles, using an objective six-part definition of economic disadvantage. The school looked at an applicant's family income, mother's education, father's education, proportion of single-parent households in an applicant's neighborhood, proportion of families receiving welfare, and proportion of adults who had not graduated from high school.

This economic preference produced an enrollment of blacks, Latinos, and Native Americans five times what it would have been in the absence of preferences. According to data from UCLA Professor Richard Sander, racial preferences yielded a class that was 25.1 percent black, Latino, and Native American; tests and grade scores would have yielded a class with 2.3 percent representation of these groups, and class-based affirmative action yielded a class right in the middle: 13.1 percent. The "racial dividend" of such class-based affirmative action programs is only likely to increase in the future. According to a recent RAND study, by the year 2015, Latinos and African Americans will constitute 78 percent of those students having no parent with a high school diploma (National Task Force 1999, 11).

Moreover, a university like UCLA could easily take further steps to improve the fairness of this program by including additional factors of economic disadvantage, steps that will also have the effect of raising the racial yield. Adding family wealth and family structure to the mix, for example, is justified on the merits because growing up in a family with a small or negative net worth and being raised by a single parent represent disadvantages above and beyond growing up in a family with low income. Including these factors will also boost racial diversity. Black income is 60 percent of white income, but black net worth is just 9 percent of white net worth. Whites with incomes of $7,500 to $15,000 have a higher net worth on average than blacks with incomes of $45,000 to $60,000 (Kahlenberg 1996, 168; 1998, 27). Likewise, of children under the age of eighteen, whites are more than twice as likely to live with both parents (76 percent versus 33 percent) (Kahlenberg 1996, 169; 1998, 27). Finally, UCLA provided a much smaller socioeconomic preference than the university previously had been giving for race. Providing instead a comparably sized economic preference is fully justified and would further increase the racial yield (Kahlenberg 1998, 28).

At the same time, class-based preferences are race blind and appeal more to universal values of fairness than to diversity and representation. If one evaluates two applicants, one poor and black and the other middle class and white, most Americans would agree that the poor African-American applicant deserves a leg up. But if the reverse is true, and a poor white applicant is up against a privileged black applicant, as a matter of fairness most Americans believe class should predominate. The reason: racism is not the only source of inequality—in addition to discrimination, there is deprivation.

Today, a child born into the top 10 percent by income is twenty-seven times as likely to end up as an adult in the top 10 percent as a child born into the bottom 10 percent [Kahlenberg 1996, 89 (citing numerous studies)]. In all, about 70 percent of Americans stay in the same socioeconomic class to which they were born, and the children of poorly educated parents make up just 2 percent of the professional and managerial class in this country (Harwood, 1998). In *The Shape of the River*, William Bowen and Derek Bok found that the bottom 28 percent economically have only a 3-percent representation at the elite universities they studied. This degree of underrepresentation today is *greater* than the underrepresentation of African Americans would be if race-based affirmative action were *ended* (African Americans, 13 percent of the population, would have about a 3-percent representation in the absence of racial preferences) (Bowen and Bok 1998, 39 and 341). As Martin Luther King Jr. noted in 1964: "It is a simple matter of justice that America, in dealing creatively with the task of raising the Negro from backwardness, should also be rescuing a large stratum of the forgotten white poor" (King 1964, 138).

One America and Political Leadership

Pursuing the need-based policies that offer the best promise for One America will require a special kind of political leadership. The leadership need not be suicidal: quite the opposite, polls show that need-based policies are far more popular than race-based policies. In the December 1997 *The New York Times* poll, Americans rejected preferences for blacks by 52 to 35 percent, but supported replacing these measures with a "preference" for "people from poor families" by 53 to 37 percent (Verhovek 1997, A34). Helping economically needy individuals is much more powerful politically than policies that divide by race. Dick Morris's endorsement of need-based affirmative action should by itself make clear the cold political viability of this program.

The leadership instead requires that political figures confront two influential interest groups—the civil rights and feminist communities—whose positions are normally quite valid, but whose narrow self-interest doesn't always meet up with the general interest. The group best equipped to broaden the progressive concern to include economic need is America's leading class-based interest group: organized labor. Historically, labor has sought (imperfectly) to back multiracial approaches that benefit working-class people generally. Where racial preferences have spawned division, class-based affirmative action would unite members of various races, and remind the ranks of labor who their true friends are.

With the notable exception of the late Albert Shanker, however, labor has done very little to support the class-based alternative to racial preferences. In an earlier era, labor might have represented working Americans in the Clinton administration debate, and would have championed broad-based help for the disadvantaged, since racial polarization always gives labor's opponents the upper hand. Class-based affirmative action is a natural for the labor movement.

This country has not seen a genuine need-based coalition in a long time, but our best leaders have always tried. In November 1967, King began to plan the Poor People's Campaign, and announced, "Gentlemen, we are going to take this movement and we are going to reach out to the poor people in all directions in this country. We're going into the Southwest after the Indians, into the West after the Chicanos, into Appalachia after the poor whites, and into the ghettoes after Negroes and Puerto Ricans. And we're going to bring them together and enlarge this campaign into something bigger than just a civil rights movement for Negroes" (Kahlenberg 1996, xiii). In 1968, likewise, Robert F. Kennedy told journalist Jack Newfield in 1968, "You know, I've come to the conclusion that poverty is closer to the root of the problem than color. . . . We have to convince the Negroes and the poor whites that they have common interests" (Newfield 1969, 287).

The case for the primacy of class is even stronger today than when Kennedy and King lived because we now have a whole post–civil rights generation who feels much less personal responsibility over race. Of course, the dramatic change in the legal landscape also cries out for a nonracial approach.

Bill Clinton appeared at one point to be poised to take up the King–Kennedy torch. Had he pursued the class-based approach, he could have answered the two great criticisms of the Clinton race initiative. He would have held out the promise for genuine racial conciliation by providing a solution that appeals to the majority of the population that opposes racial preferences and he would have answered the criticism that the initiative was all talk and no action by providing a new set of bold policy initiatives. Now that task will fall to someone else.

References

Advisory Board of the President's Initiative on Race. 1998. *One America in the 21st Century: Forging a New Future.* Washington, D.C: U.S. Government Printing Office (18 September, 1998).

Ascher, Carol, Norm Fruchter, and Robert Berne. 1996. *Hard Lessons: Public Schools and Privatization.* New York: Twentieth Century Fund.

Bok, Derek. 1996. *The State of the Nation.* Cambridge, Mass.: Harvard University Press.

Bowen, William G., and Derek Bok. 1998. *The Shape of the River: Long-Term Consequences of Considering Race in College and University Admissions.* Princeton, N.J.: Princeton University Press.

Braddock, Jomills, Robert Crain, and James McPartland. 1984. "A Long Term View of School Desegregation." *Phi Delta Kappan* (December 1984): 259.

Broder, David. 1998. "The Unity among Us." *The Washington Post* (25 November 1998): A21 (reporting findings of Public Agenda report).

Clark, Charles S. 1996. "Public, but Not Common, Schools." *St. Petersburg Times* (18 August 1996): 1D (reprinted from CQ Researcher, quoting Mann).

Denton, Nancy A. 1996. "The Persistence of Segregation." *Minnesota Law Review* 80 (April 1996): 795ff.

Harwood, Richard. 1998. "Classrooms and Class." *The Washington Post* (20 April 1998): A19.

Kahlenberg, Richard D. 1996. *The Remedy: Class, Race, and Affirmative Action.* New York: Basic Books.

————. 1997. *The Remedy: Class, Race, and Affirmative Action* (including a new preface to the paperback edition). New York: Basic Books.

————. 1998. "In Search of Fairness: A Better Way." *The Washington Monthly* (June 1998): 26–30.

————. 2001. *All Together Now: Creating Middle-Class Schools through Public School Choice.* Washington, D.C.: Brookings Institution Press.

King, Martin Luther, Jr. 1964. *Why We Can't Wait.* New York: New American Library.

Klinkner, Philip. 1998. "The 'Racial Realism' Hoax." *The Nation* (14 December 1998): 34.

Klinkner, Philip, and Rogers Smith. 1999. *The Unsteady March: The Rise and Decline of Racial Equality in America.* Chicago: University of Chicago Press.

Liebman, James S. 1990. "Desegregating Politics: 'All-Out' School Desegregation Explained." *Columbia Law Review* 90 (October 1990): 1463ff.

Lind, Michael. 1998. "The Beige and the Black." *New York Times Magazine* (16 August 1998): 38.

McCollom v. Board of Education. 1948. 333 U.S. 203 (1948) (Frankfurter, J. concurring).

Milliken v. Bradley. 1974. 418 U.S. 717 (1974) (Marshall, J., dissenting).

National Task Force on Minority High Achievement. 1999. *Reaching the Top.* New York: The College Board.

Newfield, Jack. 1969. *Robert Kennedy: A Memoir.* New York: Bantam Books.

Orfield, Gary, Mark Bachmeier, and Tamela Eitle. 1997. *Deepening Segregation in American Public Schools.* Cambridge, Mass.: Harvard Project on School Desegregation (5 April 1997).

Orfield, Gary, and Susan Eaton. 1996. *Dismantling Desegregation: The Quiet Reversal of Brown v. Board of Education.* New York: The New Press.

Orfield, Gary, and John Yun. 1999. *Resegregation in American Schools.* Cambridge, Mass.: Harvard Project on School Desegregation (June 1999).

Packer, George. 1999. "Trickle Down Civil Rights." *New York Times Magazine* (12 December 1999): 75–79.

Patterson, Orlando. 1999. "What to Do When Busing Becomes Irrelevant." *The New York Times* (18 July 1999): 17.

———. 2000. "Race Over." *The New Republic* (10 January 2000): 6.

"Race Sensitive Admissions in Higher Education: Commentary on How the Supreme Court Is Likely to Rule." 2000. *Journal of Blacks in Higher Education* (Winter 1999/2000): 97–100.

Schlesinger, Arthur M., Jr. 1991. *The Disuniting of America: Reflections on a Multicultural Society.* New York: W. W. Norton.

Sheff v. O'Neill. 1996. 678 A.2d 1267 (Conn. 1996).

Sniderman, Paul M., and Edward G. Carmines. 1997. *Reaching beyond Race.* Cambridge, Mass.: Harvard University Press.

Steinhorn, Leonard, and Barbara Diggs-Brown. 1999. *By the Color of Our Skin: The Illusion of Integration and the Reality of Race.* New York: Dutton.

Stephanopoulos, George. 1999. *All Too Human: A Political Education.* New York: Little, Brown and Co.

Verhovek, Sam Howe. 1997. "In Poll, Americans Reject Means but Not Ends of Racial Diversity." *The New York Times* (14 December 1997): A1.

PART FOUR

Political Leadership and the Dilemmas of Diversity Reconsidered

Leadership Capital and the Politics of Courage

The President's Initiative on Race

Stanley A. Renshon

As America begins a new millennium, one of the most important domestic questions facing its citizens is whether their political leaders are up to the difficult task of governing a truly diverse but divided nation. Hopefully the answer to that question would be yes. Yet, realistically, the evidence to date would lead one to answer maybe.

However, before we reach any conclusion regarding our leaders and the leadership they provide, we might first begin with some basic questions. Is successful leadership different in divided societies than in harmonious ones? It would seem the obvious answer to that question is yes. Yet, how is it different? And in what ways does division call on different skills and capacities on the part of society's leaders? Must they have less, or different kinds, of ambition? Must they be increasingly empathetic to the many and varied calls for "recognition" (Taylor 1992) that come from advocates of our increasingly diverse population? Are minimalist small-gauge policies an inevitable byproduct of our failure to reach or build on common understandings?

To address these questions we must begin with a paradox. America is, and is not, a deeply divided society. Americans agree on most contentious issues that divide them. Whether it is bilingual education, same-sex marriage, affirmative action, abortion, the importance of American identity in any national self-definition, or so on, the evidence from repeated polling is clear. There is a clear, decisive, and reliable political center on each and all of these issues (DiMaggio et al. 1996; Citrin, Reingold, and Green 1990; see also Wolfe 1996, 1998). Yet these issues have roiled American public life for several decades now and show no signs of abating. How are we to explain this anomaly? And, equally important, what, if anything, can be done about it?

I frame the explanation of this paradox through the lens of *leaderless politics*. This I define as a failure of personal or political courage, conviction, or both. When this happens, leaders are unable or unwilling to resist the demands of the loudest public voices or to counter them with their own steady and thoughtful appraisals. As a result, political leaders are neither willing to invest their accumulated leadership capital nor, therefore, capable of replenishing its supply. This is, of course, one particularly modern but not widely recognized definition of leadership failure.

In this essay I begin with the political contradictions of contemporary American politics. I then ask what role leadership capital and the politics of courage play in governing divided societies. I examine several contemporary circumstances that help us to distinguish between the appearance of courage and its more uncommon actual appearance.

A New Beginning or a Troubled Continuation?

America begins a new millennium blessed and troubled as never before. There is unprecedented economic prosperity at home and no immediate or catastrophic military involvements on the near horizon. Instead of worrying about staggering federal deficits, both presidential candidates in 2000 debated what to do with equally large projected surpluses. And Al Gore and George W. Bush argued that prosperity alone can't sustain the civic order. Their caveats to what seems like the best of times reflected a deep unease among the American public about the state of our national life.

The numbers of crimes committed, babies born out of wedlock, marriages that end in divorce, students performing below par, declining trust in major institutions including government, declining interest in social and political participation—these and other indicators all suggest a country whose robust economic performance has outpaced the quality of its cultural, social, and political life.

Some see great hope in the fact that some of these trends for crime and out-of-wedlock births are declining (Easterbrook 1999; Morin 1999). However, others note that the current figures do not approach the low levels evident in the 1950s, and make use of a baseline that inflates the change,[1] and fail to include relevant information like the fact that crime rates may be falling, but only 45 percent of crime is reported (Sleven 2000). This may be one reason why the American public, in spite of these improved figures, still substantially believes the country is heading in the wrong direction and is worried about its future. A *Wall Street Journal*/NBC News poll (1999) found that 67 percent of its respondents thought social and moral values were stronger when they were growing up and 66 percent thought that standards of acceptable and unacceptable behavior were lower today than in recent years. A report by the Pew Research Center (1999) found that "Misgivings about America today are focused on the moral climate with people from all walks of life looking skeptically on the ways in which the country has changed both culturally and spiritually."[2]

Why? Politically, the left, right, and center are united in believing that the culprit is our obsession with ourselves and our success. On the right, Bork (1997) believes we neglect our culture and worship narcissism at the expense of our values. On the left, Wachtel (1994) believes America neglects its poor and worships affluence at the expense of its communities. And, from the center, Elshtain (2000) criticizes the "commodification" of our most intimate relationships, as well as our more public ones

These critics echo Daniel Bell's (1976) critical insight that one danger of successful capitalism is that it might achieve success at the cost of the foundations that support it. He worried that narrow ambitions for markets and profits, without due attention to values, could undermine the moral and cultural basis of the society. He did not foresee the extent to which political leaders torn between their need for funds to realize their ambitions and the need to respond to public concerns in order to gain office would be tempted to sacrifice the former for the latter. He did not foresee the extent to which leaders' ambitions might weaken their commitment to making hard public policy choices. Neither did he see that many leaders faced with a choice between alienating key supporters and responding to heartfelt public concerns might prefer the appearance of courageous leadership to its practice.

Thus, one presidential candidate in the 2000 election, Al Gore, decried a federal report (Stern 2000) documenting the targeting of violent material to underage children and promised "harsh regulation if the industry does not shape up in six months" (quoted in Allen and Nakashima 2000). A few days later, he was at a lavish Hollywood-sponsored fundraiser at New York's Radio City Music Hall that raised 6.5 million dollars for his party. A few days after that, at a Beverly Hills dinner that raised

4.2 million dollars for his campaign, Mr. Gore promised to "nudge" (a Yiddish word that means mildly suggest) but never to have the government regulate the industry (Allen 2000; Seelye 2000).

Bell's important insight about the cultural contradictions of capitalism, however, represents one aspect of our contemporary dilemma. The ferocious engine of successful capitalism now has an equal and parallel engine of social and political change: the ferocious engine of rights-based advocacy democracy.

Political Leadership and the Political Contradictions of Democracy

Over thirty years ago, Theodore Lowi published his landmark book *The End of Liberalism*. His title was a statement, not a question. In it, Lowi (1969, 214) confidently subtitled one of his chapters "The End of the Welfare State." With the benefit of hindsight we now know that the anomalies he pointed out in "New Welfare" and other policies of interest-group liberalism did not result in its demise but, paradoxically, in its expansion.

Lowi's oversight was to assume that, because Americans were growing weary of the welfare state, that weariness extended to government itself. Republicans made the same mistake when they took over Congress in 1994. "New Democrats" like Bill Clinton and Al Gore learned that committing the government to large numbers of small, but expandable, new programs is one way around the public's reluctance to support traditional large-scale government efforts.

Berry's (1999) study of liberal interest-group lobbies in Washington shows that, contrary to conventional wisdom, such groups have flourished. He investigated major congressional proposals in 1963, 1979, and 1991—205 in all. And he found that the liberal lobby groups increasingly win their battles.

Ralph Nader, the Green Party presidential candidate, based his candidacy on the premise that Republicans and Democrats are so intent on coddling corporations that once-powerful liberal advocates now go unheard. Yet, as Sebastian Mallaby (2000, 19) points out:

> Nader's claim is wrong not just in portraying liberal activists as marginal. His claim that they have been marginalized by indifferent politicians is almost completely backward. The truth is that Republicans and Democrats

disagree on a lot of things, but advocacy groups often prevent them from making their differences count.

Mallaby notes that liberal advocacy groups have grown bigger and there are more of them. They have also expanded their staffs while becoming richer. Public Citizen, for example, has a staff of seventy-five, up from about fifty-five two decades ago. The World Wildlife Fund, started in the 1960s, is negotiating to buy a gleaming office building in Washington, complete with a tree-filled atrium.

Not surprisingly, these professional outfits are good at getting their message out. Their techniques? Ones that are basic, yet infrequently associated with liberal groups—money, professional staff and organization, and substantially funded "research" designed to support their group's position. Other resources they employ are found on both sides of the ideological spectrum—direct mail, passionate and not wholly accurate messages stigmatizing the opposition, and so on (Hunter 1991, 135–70). However, liberal groups have been invaluably aided in one critical way that their conservative group counterparts have not: the tacit, and sometimes more explicit, support of their worldview allies, the press.

This is not a complaint about a media conspiracy. It is a fact supported by empirical research. A 1995 poll of Washington reporters (*cf.* Samuelson 1999) found that only 2 percent of media professionals rated themselves "conservative," while 89 percent had voted for Clinton in 1992 (against 43 percent of the popular vote). Only 4 percent were Republicans (50 percent were Democrats, 37 percent "independents"). The result is not a conscious effort to advance an agenda; it is more of a shared perspective that comes from shared beliefs. Journalists often see "the story" in the same way as liberal lobbyists. Business is regarded as greedy, self-interested, and undemocratic. Conservative groups are "out of touch" or socially dangerous. By contrast, liberal lobbies are public-spirited "watchdogs."[3]

The causes are many. There are the hardy perennial issues: affirmative action, abortion rights, immigration, English as the primary language, same-sex marriage, and educational standards. But there are also dozens more that pop up periodically like bottles in a storm-tossed sea: the treatment of serious crimes committed by juveniles as adult offenses, the number of Americans of African descent working as clerks for Supreme Court justices or receiving Oscars for their acting efforts, the unfairness of "zero tolerance" policies adapted to forestall charges of disparate treatment, the building of more jails, and literally *any* disparity whatsoever, regardless of cause, between any groups that can be used to lay a claim for more attention and recognition.

As a result, basic questions that Americans thought were generally, though never fully, satisfactorily answered are now reopened. What's fair? How should we define and implement "opportunity"? How much should merit count? What does, and should, it mean to be an "American"? What is government's legitimate role in shaping, or if necessary bending, cultural traditions in light of these controversies? Given the deep cultural and political significance of these questions it is small wonder that Hunter (1991) subtitled his book on the culture wars *The Struggle to Define America*.[4]

The goals sound principled: ever more justice, fairness, equality, tolerance, basic human rights, democracy, equality, legitimacy, freedom, and respect for everyone and every conceivable claim.

Who could be against more democracy? Who could oppose tolerance? What's wrong with having more democracy? Nothing, so long as it is coupled with respect for obligation. Democracy without responsibility is a form of government-sanctioned narcissism. What's wrong with more tolerance? Not anything, so long as it is balanced by a sense of cultural and personal values that frame boundaries. Tolerance without limits reflects an abdication of civic judgment. What's wrong with more fairness? Nothing, so long as the government does not get into the business of enforcing one group's idea of what this means. Fairness is a conceptual framework for approaching questions of equality, not answering them.

Bell's insight about capitalism parallels the concerns of those who wrote the Constitution. Unrestrained capitalism not only led to aggregations of capital that distorted the democratic political process, but it also undermined the very culture that supported both. The Constitution's authors had similar concerns about democracy. They too feared accumulations, but of political power. As a result, we operate under a system of checks and balances. They too were caught between the need to both expand and constrain democracy. As a result, we are a republic. They too worried about finding a proper balance between individual rights and the rules necessary to sustain a viable constitutional government. As a result, we have a Bill of Rights, a specific listing of the powers reserved respectively to the federal and state governments and the people, and the establishment of an independent judiciary to adjudicate among them.

The political contradictions of democracy are found in the fact that unrestrained excesses of democratic virtues run the risk of compromising the political foundations from which they draw their legitimacy and gain a respectful hearing. More justice, more fairness, more equality, more redefinitions of wants into rights, more equality, more freedom, and more unconditional respect for every conceivable preference do not automatically result in a better democracy.

Champions of each of these expansions address their demands, not to other citizens but to those in a position to make them civic practice: political leaders. This places our leaders in a difficult position. They are charged with the responsibility to see beyond a particular's group self-interest, but also govern in a system constructed to make them responsive to it. The ability to reframe group demands, and if necessary deflect, defer, or moderate them is a core responsibility of leaders in any democracy, but especially one in which the basic frameworks of its culture are matters of fierce debate. However, there are others, as well.

Leadership Capital and Governing in Divided Societies

Social capital is the latest conceptual attempt to account for democracy's persistence and, when it occurs, its success. Unlike civic culture arguments, social capital theory locates the foundations of democracy neither primarily in citizens' beliefs, nor in their institutions, but rather in the *relationships* of each to the other. Constitutions may provide a framework and institutions a setting, but it is the engagement of citizens in the view of social capitalists that provides the building blocks of successful democracy.

Clearly social capital is important to democratic political life. However, it is a good idea to ask whether citizens don't also have important relationships with those whom they select to represent and govern them. It seems clear that they do. I frame this relationship through the term *leadership capital* (Renshon 2000). It is central to successful democracies and especially critical to those that are divided.

What is leadership capital? It consists of the competence, integrity, and capacities for leadership of those given discretion to make society's consequential decisions. Leadership capital, like social capital, can be accumulated or depleted. However, the source of the accumulation or depletion of leadership capital is found in the behavior of leaders themselves.

Leadership capital reflects a leader's character, capacities, and performance. Character refers to the core elements of a leader's (or really, anyone's) interior psychology. It is the building block of personality (although not synonymous with it) and the foundation in which leadership capacities are embedded. Elsewhere (Renshon 1998b), I have developed a formulation of character for use in leadership analysis that relies on three essential elements; ambition, character integrity, and relatedness. Ambition refers to what it denotes, while character integrity reflects a person's fidelity to a consolidated set of ideals and values. Relatedness refers the person's basic stance toward others, whether, beneath whatever skill of social facilitation he presents, he tends to move psychologically toward, against, away, or apart from others.

What does it take to lead in a divided society? Certainly it takes the strong ambition to gain office. Ambition is leadership's fuel. That's so because it provides the motivation for political efforts, whether that be gaining office, formulating policies, or providing the leadership to enact them. The skills that support these ambitions, whether intellectual, characterological, or interpersonal, help determine whether the match between capacities and ambitions results in a surplus or a deficit. Of course, any surplus generated by a good match between a leader's ambitions and skills is very much a matter of public interest.

Yet ambition that is disconnected from consolidated values and ideals is a hazard, not an advantage. A leader who allows his ambitions to trump his expressed values runs many risks. If his intimate personal wishes trump his public responsibilities, as President Clinton's did, a leader runs the risk of public disgust, loss of time to spend elsewhere, and a sense of betrayal for those who hoped he would use his time in more important pursuits. If an ambition for large-scale policy monuments trumps a promise to govern as a fiscally and programmatically prudent "New Democrat," not only may the leader's programs be defeated (health care) and the leader be punished at the ballot box (as in the 1994 congressional elections), but also he may add to the public's sense that he is one more leader who has not followed through on his public word.

Leadership capital is not solely a matter of one president's performance. Consider the decline of public confidence in government. In 1958, at the end of the Eisenhower administration, almost 75 percent of the American public thought you could trust the government in Washington to do what is right "just about always," or "most of the time." By 1998, those figures had been exactly reversed, with 75 percent of the public believing you could not trust Washington to do what is right "just about always," or "most of the time." The number of people who thought the government looked out for the interests of the common person rather than itself took a parallel nosedive from 70 percent in 1958 to 20 percent in 1994 (Wayne et al. 1999, 219).

What do these numbers have to do with leadership capital? Just this: a recent Pew Center analysis (1999, emphasis mine) of the causes of the decline of trust in government concluded:

> Discontent with political leaders and lack of faith in the political system are principal factors that stand behind public distrust of government. *Much of that criticism involves the honesty and ethics of government leaders.*

In other words, it is the action of leaders themselves, their integrity and morality, that affect the degree of the public's trust (see also Nye, Zelikow, and King 1997; Charles 1997). The public's expectations about the integrity of its leaders affects, of course, the range and nature of what specific leaders can hope to accomplish.

Leadership Capital and the Politics of Courage

What personal and political capacities are important for leaders in such circumstances? If ambition is the fuel of performance, character integrity is its anchor. Character integrity is not only an anchor, but also a reflection of a clear link between who the leader presents himself to be and who he is. Character integrity not only anchors ambition, it also establishes authenticity.

It is also a resource for a leader in working through the difficult process of deciding and governing. It provides an anchor in a sea of ambiguity and uncertainty. It can sustain a leader's capacity to stay with a problem as well as provide a frame from which to view not only what is politically expedient, but also what is personally acceptable. And it can reinforce a leader's personal confidence and sense of personal integrity, themselves important elements of leadership capital and, as well, solace in a sometimes difficult and unforgiving political world.

But character integrity does more than buttress a leader in the difficult position of making judgments and trying to carry them through. It provides the public with a sense of reassurance that they have given their legitimacy to someone honest enough to deserve it. And it serves as the basis for extending to the leader the benefits of trust: time in which to complete his work, the benefit of the doubt in conflicted circumstances, and the capacity to tolerate setbacks. In short, character integrity, a key component of leadership capital, affects public trust, a key element of social capital.

Yet, as important as convictions are, fidelity to them is what makes character integrity an anchor, not a slogan. We see character integrity not in easy choices, but in hard ones. We see it not when the leader disagrees with his opponents, but when he disagrees with his supporters. And we see it when he is willing to incur some costs, politically, not when he tries to satisfy everyone with a combination of rhetorical flash and policy dissembling. In short, in order for political leaders to have the courage of their convictions, they must first have both.

I term failures in having either convictions or the courage of them, coupled with strong ambition, *leaderless politics*. The rise of leaders anxious for office and lacking either the skills to realize their ambitions or strong principled convictions, coupled with the courage to follow them, leads to a mismatch between ambitions and performance. Leaders often aspire to more than they are able to do or willing to publicly explain. As a result, there is a mismatch between what leaders wish to accomplish, what they know about the paths they've chosen, and what they help the public to understand.

One of the characteristics of contemporary American politics is that both real convictions and the courage to enact them have been in short supply. And they have been for some time. Presidents and candidates have tried to negotiate these treacherous currents for a decade, primarily by trying to finesse rather than engage them. The rise of "New Democrats" and "compassionate conservatives" are either artful mixes of political categories designed to escape hard choice, or a truly new categorical blend designed to build on a real vision with its own hard choices. There is no way to settle which it is *a priori*. The truth is to be found in the details of the choices that leaders make or don't make, the issues that they raise or avoid, and the honesty with which they lay out their views, do their best to explain them, and let the political chips then fall as they may.

In the sections that follow, I examine these issues through the lens of President Clinton's Initiative on Race. I note some of the issues that arose as that effort unfolded that compromised its integrity and effectiveness.

I conclude with some observations on courage and leadership capital and its implications for One America.

Dissipating Leadership Capital: The President's Initiative on Race [5]

Frank talk about America's racial and ethnic divisions has been noticeably absent in contemporary politics (Sleeper 1990). Harsh accusations have not (Sleeper 1997). Therefore, the President's Initiative on Race, to which the administration gave the hopeful name "One America," appeared to reflect considerable courage on Mr. Clinton's part.

If there was anyone who might have been able to initiate and sustain a frank dialogue, it was the president. Observers from many points on the political spectrum saw Mr. Clinton as uniquely suited to bridge American's racial and ethnic gaps (however, for a contrary view see Kelly 1997). Peter Baker (1998, 10) of *The Washington Post* wrote, "Few doubt the president's sincerity about race, and indeed it is one subject on which he is consistently credited for possessing deep, heartfelt beliefs." The liberal columnist Nicholas Lemann (1997, A17) noted, "the traditional test of racial communication for white politicians is whether they can win an enthusiastic reception from a black audience." Mr. Clinton, he said, "does that almost effortlessly." Ward Connerly, head of the organization that supported Proposition 209 in California, which ended racial preferences, said after his Christmas Eve meeting with the president that Clinton "understands race like no other President, living or dead" (quoted in Bennet 1997b, A1). And, as Michael Frisby (1997b, A1) pointed out in a front-page story in *The Wall Street Journal*, "not since Lyndon Johnson had an American president devoted such energy to race relations. So for many blacks, particularly outside politics, Mr. Clinton can do no wrong."

On the divisive issue of race, Mr. Clinton had clearly accumulated substantial leadership capital. Whether and how he would use it was a central question. What is clear is that Mr. Clinton understood the stakes. As he had when he ran for president in 1992, Mr. Clinton showed an accurate understanding of what the country needed and the nature of its basic public dilemma.[6] In a talk with reporters he said:

> It is really potentially a great thing for America that we are becoming so multi-ethnic. . . . But it's also potentially a powder keg of problems and

heart break and division and loss. And how we handle it will determine, really . . . that single question may be the biggest determination of what we look like fifty years from now . . . and what the children of that age will have to look forward to. (Clinton 1997a, 509)

So, Mr. Clinton understood the potentially explosive issues that faced this country. Yet there was a critical question that accompanied that understanding. Did color-conscious policies allow America to get "beyond race"? Or did government-sponsored designations of "protected" groups singled out for special and better treatment actually fuel feelings of resentment and entitlement on one side, and just plain resentment on the other?

Mr. Clinton was well positioned to have a frank and helpful conversation. Yet he never honestly or effectively engaged that critical question. That is one reason among several that few would wind up characterizing his initiative as a major contribution to either the country's engagement of these difficult issues or to President Clinton's legacy. In retrospect, it seems clear that the president failed to use his leadership capital on an issue of single personal interest to him and of vast importance for the country. The question before us is is: why?

The Great National Conversation Begins

The original impetus for the initiative came from Jesse Jackson, members of the "black" congressional caucus, and similarly minded advocates (Holmes 1995). After a march on Washington in October of 1995 by the controversial Muslim leader Louis Farrakhan, they pressed the president to create a presidential commission to address what they saw as the continuing, harrowing plight of African Americans in this country. Several months later President Clinton ordered his staff to find ways for him to "play a prominent role . . . in improving American race relations, a goal that he is trying to make a focus or legacy of his second term" (Bennet 1997b, A4). John Harris (1996, A12) reported at the time that the president was considering a list of "14 pillars" of policy including renewing cities, crime, entitlement reform, and others.

In December of 1997, *The New York Times* (Bennet 1997a, A22) reported that, "After months of White House debate over how to improve race relations and add heft to President Clinton's second term, Mr. Clinton has decided to hold town meetings and other events on race around the country, appoint a high powered panel, and write a report next year summarizing his findings." Then, at the University of California, San Diego commencement address in June of 1997, President Clinton (1997b) announced what he called a year-long national discussion, "a great and unprecedented conversation about race," that would "transform the problem of prejudice into the promise of unity." The President's Initiative on Race was born.

Some questioned whether such a discussion was needed. In their view, the discussion had already been in progress for some time, in many forums—political, legal, and cultural (Baker 1997). Some saw it as part of discussion that had been part of our national life almost from the beginning. Others thought this conversation had been going on at least since the Eisenhower presidency and certainly by the time of Lyndon Johnson's Great Society initiatives. Others, like Roger Wilkins, longtime civil rights leader, wondered why it had the taken the president so long to focus his administration on these issues. He was quoted (in Fletcher and Balz 1997) as saying, "This man has been president for 4 1/2 years, and now he is trying to make civil right part of his legacy? Isn't that kind of late?"

Even those who supported the proposal questioned whether public, televised forums with hand-picked participants were the best, or most useful, venues for conducting such discussions. Orlando Patterson (1997, 1) wrote, "If what the president proposes is yet another inquiry into America's 'racial dilemma,' his well-meaning initiative is likely to do more harm than good; but if what he has in mind is a debate about how we talk about and evaluate 'race,' it might do some good."

Framing the Issue

In spite of these doubts, Mr. Clinton pressed ahead, convinced, he said, that the country needed such an airing of its conflicts. In his commencement speech introducing the commission he said (1997b, 881):

> What do I hope we will really achieve as a country. If we do nothing more than talk, it will be interesting, but not enough. If we do nothing more than propose disconnected acts of policies, it will be helpful but it won't be enough. But if 10 years from now, people can look back and see that this year of honest dialogue lifted and concerted action helped to lift the heavy burden from our children's future we will have given a precious gift to America.

These are grand, almost heroic visions, and no one with deeply felt commitments to this country and its ideals could disagree with the sentiments or the hopes the president expressed. The question was, as always with any political leader, to what extent and in what ways would these ideals be translated into civic accomplishment. More concretely, President Clinton said (1997b, 881) he wanted this panel to

> . . . help educate Americans about the facts surrounding issues of race, to promote a dialogue in every community of the land, to confront and work through these issues, and recruit and encourage leadership at all levels to help breach racial divides, and to find, develop, and recommend how to implement concrete solutions to our problems—solutions that will involve all of us in government, business, communities, and as individual citizens.

Here, too, the president's stated goals[7] were worthy and desirable. Yet here, too, the question must remain before us: how were these noble goals to be reached? Were the methods selected to accomplish them consistent with their purpose? Of course, before it is possible to assess whether and in what ways the president (and his commission) achieved the goals he set, another matter must be addressed: what, exactly, the issue was that Mr. Clinton wished to address. The answer was far from obvious.

At a press conference on April 11, shortly before he introduced his commission, Mr. Clinton (1997b, 509, emphasis mine) had this to say about framing the issues:

> . . . and particularly I feel on this whole issue of how we deal with diversity. It's something . . . that's dominated my whole life because I grew up as a southerner. But it's a very different issue now. *It's more than black Americans and white Americans.* The majority of students in the Los Angeles County schools are Hispanic. And there are four school districts in America—four—where there are children who have more than a hundred different racial, ethnic, or linguistic backgrounds. So this is a big deal. And every issue we debate whether it's affirmative action or immigration or things that seem peripherally involved in this need to be viewed through the prism of how we can preserve One America. . . .

At that press conference, the president was saying directly that the issues arising out of America's unprecedented diversity transcend black-white issues. He said the same thing while introducing the commission and the national dialogue. "To be sure there is old unfinished business between black and white Americans, *but the classic American dilemma has now become many dilemmas of race and ethnicity*" (Clinton 1997b, 878, emphasis mine). So, it did not seem farfetched to expect the president to push for framing the commission's work through the lens of increasing ethnic and racial diversity rather than through the narrower lens of "black-white relationships." He did not.

One board member, Angela E. Oh, an American of Asian decent and an attorney, urged her colleagues on the panel to "move beyond the 'black-white' paradigm" (quoted in Baker 1997, A4). However, she was overruled by the commission's chairman, Professor John Hope Franklin, an African-American scholar of American race relations.

Shortly thereafter in an interview with a correspondent from Black Entertainment Television the following exchange took place (Clinton 1997e, 1185):

> *Mr. Smiley:* In the first meeting of your race commission, a small dispute erupted in that the commission chairman, Dr. John Hope Franklin and commissioner Angela Oh, a Korean-American commissioner from Los Angles, had a dispute about the focus, what the mission, the work of the commission ought to be. Dr. Franklin believes that the focus and the mission ought to be around the "black-white" conflict, which he sees as the nucleus of every other race problem this country has endured and continues to endure. . . . Commissioner Oh suggests that the work of the commission really ought to be about multiracialism and multiculturalism.
>
> As the leader, as the president who put this commission together, what kind of leadership are you going to provide? How are you going to get them on the right track? If the commission can't have a clear-stated mandate, how do we talk about it as a country?
>
> *The President:* First, I agree with John Hope Franklin that if you don't understand the black-white conflict, you can never understand how race works in America. If you don't know the history and if you don't know what the facts are now, you can never understand the rest.

Thus, from its inception, the president's initiative was misframed by primarily focusing on "black-white" issues rather than the larger issues of many races and multiple ethnicities. Not surprising, other ethnic and racial groups felt they were being excluded. Native Americans disrupted one meeting and were quickly rewarded with special meetings called to address their issues. Elaine Chao, a senior fellow at the Heritage Foundation and an invitee to the president's pre–Christmas Eve White House meeting with right-of-center critics, pointed out (in Clinton 1997f, 2090) that the debate had almost entirely left out Asian Americans. Hispanics were upset about their lack of representation and an Hispanic athlete was quickly added to the list of participants discussing why there were not more managers and owners of professional sports teams by Americans of African descent, and whether black athletes should have white business managers (Baker and Fletcher 1998, A2).

This was a major, but not the only, problem. The initiative was slow to get started (Baker 1998). Although long in the planning and announced in June, the executive director of the initiative, Judith Winston, was not hired until August. At first, the White House had no research or senior staff assigned to the effort. After several months spent to not much effect, Mr. Clinton assigned Chief of Staff Erskine Bowles to bring some focus to the commission.

The lack of advance planning that would have allowed the commission to get off to a fast start was important given that it was scheduled to last only one year. In that time it had a lot to accomplish, to understate the case. Mr. Clinton's somewhat loose approach, the details of presidential follow-through, were by this time well known. However, his failure to make an exception in the case of a major initiative that he said was of crucial importance to the country tended to send a mixed message.

Mr. Clinton was aware of the problem. In early September, he said that he was "going to try over the next few weeks to increase my public involvement in this racial dialogue that I called for . . ." (1997g, 1307). Two weeks later, he was gently trying to nudge his commission toward a more active stance. Appearing at their first public meeting, the president (1997h, 1462) gave members several ideas for going forward before saying "finally, and in the end, we have got to decide what we are going to do."

The causes of the commission's diffused focus were numerous. Critics from both the left and right criticized both the slow start and the lack of focus (Holmes 1997e, A17). Others noted that Mr. Clinton himself had not given the panel any clear direction (Holmes 1997d, A23). However, a more accurate description would be to say that Mr. Clinton had given them too ambitious an agenda rather than an unclear one.

Early on, one White House aide said, the commission was still differing over what they were trying to solve, racism or poverty. That aide was also quoted as saying, "There is no consensus that the issue is fundamentally about race, or about equality of opportunity and education" (quoted in Holmes and Bennet 1998, A1; see also Blow 1998). Some aides felt the initiative should suggest specific remedies, and others believed the goal was to spur talk about race. The president urged his aides to do both (Holmes and Bennet 1998). At the same time (January 1999), civil rights leaders had urged the president to narrow the initiative's focus, yet that conversation itself revealed just how fluidly the commission viewed its own mandate.

There were other substantive divisions in the commission as well. How much could "white racism" be held responsible for the contemporary plight of some groups of Americans of African descent? How much responsibility did individuals share for their circumstances? Had there been significant progress, or was there still very far to go in making any?

Divided views permeated not only the commission members, but also White House staff members. Holmes and Bennet (1998, A1) reported that:

> On the Saturday after Labor Day, members of the Advisory Commission Staff met with more than 20 aides from the White House . . . hoping to get a clearer idea of what they would do.
>
> Instead, much of the time was taken up by minority members of the White House Staff talking about personal experiences with racism. We got a recantation of why it was important to have the initiative, rather than what the initiative was supposed to accomplish, said one participant.

There were also issues of budget and cost connected with any major new initiatives, and issues of political support (Branegan 1999, 73). Finally, there had been the issue of how closely the president ought to be identified with his initiative, lest the members compromise the president politically by introducing controversial suggestions. One set of such suggestions appeared early on in the form of suggestions that the president apologize to the African-American community for slavery and that he consider sponsoring reparations.[8] As a result of these problems, the initiative that had made headlines when it was introduced "promptly dropped off the radar screen and ran into trouble" (Frisby 1997a, A24).

As late as December of 1977, six months after the initiative had been formally announced, the impression of disarray persisted. At first, in the privacy of a one-on-one interview with a reporter for the Knight-Ridder news service, the president acknowledged that the initiative had gotten off to a slow start and that he was partially responsible (Clinton 1997i, 1943–44). However, several weeks later at his national televised news conference on December 16, the following testy exchange occurred on the issue (1997k, 2053–54):

> *Q:* Mr. President, reports from the front lines of your race initiative suggest that the initiative is in chaos, it is confused. The Akron town meeting was little more than Presidential *Oprah.* Some people involved are beginning to—
>
> *The President:* That may be your editorial comment. That's not my report. I've received scores of letters, including letters from ordinary people, who said that they loved it, and they thought it was important. So, if that's your opinion, state it your opinion, but—
>
> *Q:* It's an opinion, sir, that I'm hearing from others who are beginning to question whether simply talking—
>
> *The President:* Who are they? Name one. Just one. Give me a name. All this "others" stuff—you know, it's confusing to the American people when they hear all these anonymous sources flying around.
>
> *Q:* I don't want to get them fired by you, sir, so, [laughter] but they are people who are involved in the process, who are beginning to question whether simply talking is enough.

Almost one month to the day after that exchange, the commission's chairman Dr. Franklin (Clinton 1998b, 54) was urged by the president to strongly publicize actions and events relating to the race initiative "because that had not attracted much media attention, thus far." And Mr. Clinton was promising, in response to a reporter's question (1998a, 25–26), to "do more and more visible things."

"The Great National Conversation": Honesty and Its Barrier

If framing the issues was a core requirement for the commission's success, the nature of the conversation was critical. An "honest dialogue" was central to the president's presentation of the initiative's purpose. It was also central to his more concrete goals of educating "Americans about the facts surrounding issues of race, to promote a dialogue in every community of the land to confront and work through these issues" (1997b, 881). There obviously could be no working through of these difficult issues without the honest and respectful engagement of differences.

The president himself emphasized this point, saying "*We must begin with a candid conversation* on the state of race relations today and the implications of Americans of so many different races living together and working together. . . . *We must be honest with each other.* . . ." Later, in the same address, he noted, "Honest dialogue will not be easy at first. We'll all have to get past defensiveness and fear and political correctness and other barriers to honesty" (Clinton 1997b, 880, 881).

Elsewhere he said (Clinton 1997f, 1302) that his race initiative was meant, "above all, to bring together Americans of different backgrounds together to face one another honestly across the lines that divide us." Commenting on the first meeting of his advisory board, the president (1997d, 1094) said it was full of "lively debate and honest disagreement . . . I like that. We should discover quickly that people who are honestly committed to advancing this dialogue will have honest differences and that they ought to be aired."

The president's concerns were well founded. Arthur Levin (1999, 7), president of Columbia University, reports that in group interviews on twenty-eight college and university campuses, conducted by a team of which he was a member between 1992 and 1997, "students were more willing to talk about intimate details of their sex lives than to discuss race relations on campus. . . . The usual response in heterogeneous focus groups was silence; their body language changed, smiles vanished, and students stared at the table rather than talking to each other. What followed was either a long, painful conversation with many pauses or an attempt to gloss over the topic."

That discussions of race are more sensitive than those regarding sex is not wholly surprising. In many ways, explicit public images have become commonplace and, as a result, sex has become deprivatized. That fact does not explain, however, why race has replaced sex as a taboo subject.

One piece of evidence on the subject comes from a national survey study conducted by *Public Agenda* (1998a, 1998b) on views among Americans of African and Caucasian descent on a range of difficult school issues. That survey was supplemented by eight focus groups in different parts of the country to give nuance and depth to the survey instruments.[9] Of relevance to us here is the question asked of all 1,600 respondents: is it hard for whites to talk honestly about problems in the black community because they are afraid that someone will accuse them of being racist?

Seventy-two percent of the white respondents agreed with that statement (1998b, 17). Very interestingly, 73 percent of the black parents also agreed with them! The same surprising convergence showed up when another question that bears on this matter also was asked: are blacks sometimes too quick to believe negative things happen to them because of their race? Seventy-nine percent of the white respondents agreed with that statement. However, so did 75 percent of the black respondents (1998b, 17).

Clearly, though, Caucasians feel more at risk and their discomfort is validated by those who would have little reason to misrepresent the truth for them. The study noted (1998a, 23) that "to whites, discussions about race carry considerable risk—they may say the wrong thing, be misunderstood, or worse, be accused of racism—so a more common response is to keep quiet or tread carefully." When asked why the conversation about race was uncomfortable, one respondent said, "Anytime you talk about black and white, there will be trouble." Another said," Whites have to walk on eggshells [when discussing race]."

This study was not alone in its findings of what it called "reluctant discussion." The study (1998a, 21–22) noted:

> Focus groups conducted for this and previous Public Agenda projects show that white parents are very reluctant to talk about education in racial terms, even in groups with no African Americans present. White parents in every part of the country and from every income and educational level would circle warily around the issue for a half an hour or more, resisting discussions about categories of people.... [T]he reluctance was especially strong when the subject was academic underachievement among African-American students. When the moderator persisted, the discomfort was clear and the reluctance to engage palpable.

"The Great National Conversation": Dialogue or Monologue?

Randall Kennedy wrote that the country had not yet had, and needed, an examination of racial issues that would clarify what we know and where we do or do not agree. Yet he (1997, C1) added:

The peril is that Clinton and his aides will squelch the possibilities for an informative, intense and surprising discussion and instead sponsor a series of scripted, pseudo-events devoid of the candor and contentious frankness required for any serious attempt to grapple with the race question. Given that an honest, respectful discussion was the foundation of all Mr. Clinton said he hoped to accomplish, it is a legitimate question to ask how, as the leader in charge, he handled it.

One place to begin looking is the composition of the commission itself. Its members were certainly distinguished enough and they were ethnically and racially diverse.[10] However, they seemed to be less diverse in their political views on the issues that they were examining. One board member, former New Jersey Governor Thomas Kean, commented (in Clinton 1997l, 2093) later that he, too, believed, "that the board had been too narrow." The decision not to include any persons with views from the moderate/conservative side of the political spectrum as commission members was obvious by their absence.

The "national conversation" was meant to bring all sides together to discuss the issues that divided them. Yet critics noted that from the start those with moderate, right-of-center, or conservative views were absent from the debate (Holmes 1997e, A17). This was a central criticism of the commission from its inception.

Early initiative events were marked by platitudes and the avoidance of anything that might give offense. Bland but carefully chosen personal narratives meant to highlight experiences that might lead to a consensus about what "needs to be done" predominated. So an adolescent minority youth related an experience of taking his mother's check to the bank and being asked for identification. This, he submitted, was an example of the special burdens placed on those like himself. No one, including the president who served as moderator, pointed out that trying to cash a check made out to someone else at a bank where you are not personally known might lead to questions for anyone. One news reporter characterized the public meetings as "a hodgepodge of personal anecdotes and grievances that did little to steer the conversation towards broad-based conclusions or recommendations" (Babington 1999, 29).[11]

At the first "town hall" meeting held in connection with the president's initiative on September 27, 1997, the subject was race and the public schools. It "produced near unanimity of opinion among those gathered . . . and those who took part by satellite in 20 other cities" (Holmes 1997c, A28). The report continued (italics mine) that participants "agreed that public schools had a responsibility to foster understanding [and]. . . they argued for more money for public education and called for training to make teachers more sensitive to students of different backgrounds. They supported bilingual education and denounced attacks on affirmative action. *But because the gathering lacked the dissenting voices, no questions were raised about whether school diversity should be the goal of blacks and other minorities and no arguments were made for such issues as English-only classes or school vouchers.*" One participant (quoted in Holmes 1997c, A28) said, "We seem to be preaching to the choir."

The criticism that the President's Initiative on Race lacked a diversity of views *within* the commission broadened to concerns that the national public dialogue itself suffered from the same problems. Secretary of Transportation Rodney Slater, an African American, took part in racial dialogue that "pointedly excluded whites" (Hunt 1997, A23). However, that criticism came into sharper focus at the November meeting of the committee at the University of Maryland discussing how to achieve diversity on college campuses. The chair of the committee, Dr. Franklin, said he saw no need to invite persons with different points of view about the value of diversity. In particular, he said he saw no reason to invite Ward Connerly, who led the fight against preferences at the University of California, to the meeting. Why? Because, he said (quoted in Holmes 1997f, A24; see also Holmes and Bennet 1998),

> "the people whom we did invite had something special to say about how to make universities more diverse than they are. The people in California that advocate Proposition 209, for example, are not addressing the subject of how to make the university more diverse. Consequently, I'm not sure what Mr. Connerly could contribute to this discussion."

The subject in Professor Franklin's mind was *how* to create more diversity, not whether there might be some serious issues associated with such efforts that ought to be examined. An administration official, asked if he was disappointed about the makeup of the discussion, replied, "We believe we had a good group of people for what we were trying to achieve, to teach about the value of diversity." Mr. Connerly, for his part, said that he "found it astounding that the President's race panel believes that it can have a national dialogue that we have been discussing in America for four years now, without involving those of us who represent a point of view that is shared by probably 60 percent of the people in the nation." A *New York Times* editorial (1997a, A34) pointed out,

> "Many Americans were skeptical when Bill Clinton called for a 'national dialogue on race,' but then delegated responsibility to a panel that has been slow to get started. The skepticism deepened this week when the panel held a hearing on diversity but declined to hear the opponents of affirmative action. This does not make for much of a dialogue."

Speaker of the House Newt Gingrich was sharply critical of the composition of the board for not including dissenting views. He asked (Holmes 1997g, A30), "When did your call for a dialogue become a monologue? Is your panel interested in educating our citizens or indoctrinating them?" This angered White House officials who noted that the board's chairman, Dr. Franklin, had written to Mr. Gingrich on July 7, seeking his advice and suggestions. They said he never responded. Mr. Gingrich then produced a copy of a detailed letter that had been sent to all the commission members dated September 29, 1997, suggesting a ten-point program to help close the racial divide (Holmes 1997g, A30).

The initiative began to look more and more like a poorly managed soliloquy than a real dialogue. The commission's executive director denied that the board had deliberately eschewed the views of conservatives, however she acknowledged there was a "perception" that it was not seeking a variety of views (quoted in Holmes 1997f, A24).

Yes or No? Yes or No!

In response, the president decided to engage the commission's critics, but he did so in a way that appeared to undercut his aim of a frank dialogue. The president announced that he would meet with critics of his racial policies (Holmes 1997d, A23) at the White House. That meeting, it turned out, was held on the last Friday evening before Christmas, when it would receive almost no public attention (Bennet 1997a, A1; Clinton 1997l, 2085–93; "Excerpts" 1997, A24; see also Begard 1997). Only one member of the president's commission, Governor Kean, was present.

In the meantime, the president invited one prominent critic of his racial preference programs, Dr. Abigail Thernstrom, to the nationally televised town meeting scheduled for Akron, Ohio. The president said that the decision to include a critic was made before the controversy surrounded Dr. Franklin's pointed exclusion of critics, but that a particular person had not been selected before the announcement (Holmes 1997h, A29). The Akron town meeting, with one notable exception, was much like other such forums. The one exception to polite, serial monologue was the exchange between the president and Dr. Thernstrom. At 6 foot 3 inches tall, towering over the petite and seated Dr. Thernstrom, the president (1997j, 1968) asked:

> *The President:* Abigail, do you favor the United States army abolishing the affirmative-action program that produced General Colin Powell: yes or no? Yes or no? (Applause). I get asked all these hard questions all the time. I want to do it.
>
> *Ms. Thernstrom:* I do not think that it is racial preference that made Colin Powell—
>
> *The President:* He thinks he was helped by it.
>
> *Ms. Thernstrom:* The overwhelming majority of Americans want American citizens to be treated as individuals. And we've heard the voices here of—
>
> *The President:* Should we abolish the army's affirmative-action program: yes or no?
>
> *Ms. Thernstrom:* We should. The army does one thing very, very right: it prepares kids. It takes kids before the army and it prepares them to compete equally. That's what you're talking about when you are talking about American education. Let us have real equality of education. These preferences disguise the problem. The real problem is the racial skills gap, and we ignore it when we—
>
> *The President:* Well, then, the real problem may be the criteria for how we admit people to college, too, how we do it.

This small exchange was much larger in what it revealed, both about the dialogue and the president's approach to using his leadership capital. Certainly, a president who had spent so much time touting the virtues of an honest dialogue and noting how difficult it would be to achieve it did nothing to help that cause in the exchange. Neither could his heckling tone and style—repeating "yes or no," "yes or no" several times—give others with somewhat different views the reassurance they might need to speak honestly. Nor, it turned out, was this a spontaneous exchange. The day after the debate, it emerged that "Mr. Clinton had been urged by aides to provoke such an exchange . . ." (Bennet 1997a, A1). As Hanna Rosin commented (1997, 28), "it was the meeting's only tense moment, but all it really showed was how willing the president was to score points at the expense of real debate."

Moreover, as almost every commentary on the exchange pointed out, the president's question could hardly be answered by either a yes or a no (Greenfield 1997, 84; Rosin 1997, 28; Hunt 1997, A23; Review and Outlook 1997, A18; Thernstrom 1997, 35; Editorial 1997b, A30). Thernstrom (1997, 35) pointed out that the army had an equal opportunity program, not a preference program, a point backed up by *The New York Times* (Bennet 1997b, A30) and *The Wall Street Journal* (Review and Outlook 1997, A18). In his own book, Colin Powell (1999, emphasis mine), writes that

> [e]qual rights and opportunity mean just that. They do not mean preferential treatment. Preferences, no matter how well intentioned breed resentment among the non-preferred. . . . The present debate has . . . a lot to do with deficiencies. If affirmative action means programs that provide real opportunity, then I am all for it. If it leads to preferential treatment or helps those who no longer need help, I am opposed. *I benefitted from equal opportunity and affirmative action in the army, but I was not shown preference.*

Some found the exchange not only flawed in execution, and as a matter of fact, but disquieting in its assumptions as well. Rosin (1997, 28) pointed out that "the president's suggestion that Powell was 'produced' by affirmative action was simplistic and very nearly offensive." The respected columnist Meg Greenfield (1997, 84) wrote,

> "Bill Clinton, who understands these things better than that exchange would show, knows that affirmative action does not 'produce' anyone. Given at least a fighting chance, people produce themselves. Colin Powell produced Colin Powell. His story and his views would be an excellent starting point for a revised national argument."

The Akron meeting drew its model from the "The Coming Together Project" that had been established in Akron after the Rodney King incident in Los Angeles (Holmes 1997i, A26).[12] Meant to foster racial dialogue, it may have complicated Mr. Clinton's efforts. There were moments when Mr. Clinton (1997j, 1962) seemed to show a measure of impatience with the kind of touchy-feely efforts that bring people together, but do not necessary result in social change. After two ministers joked and talked about their mutual efforts the president said that he would

> "be the cynic now just for purposes of argument. I'll say, okay this is really nice. You've got two churches, and you pray on Sunday and everyone is nice to each other. . . .We do all that kind of stuff, he said. How is it changing these people's lives? How is it changing the life in Akron? How does it result in less discrimination in the workplace? Or in the school, or people helping each other to succeed in school or at work. Can you give us any examples about what it's done other than make people feel good for an hour on Sunday or some other church event?"

In the end, as one observer (Lee 1997, w5) noted of the Akron meeting, "It may have been honest, but it wasn't dialogue. Like much of America's discussion of race, it was a serial monologue, an airing of grievances and personal perspectives. Two Hispanic women complained about being compared to the sort of character played by Rosy Perez. A biracial student said people perceive only half of who he is . . . it limped politely along to the end: a jumble of policy prescriptions and anecdotes."

The President's Initiative: A Postscript

After fifteen months of hearings, on September 18, 1998, the commission presented its report to the president. *The New York Times* headlined its coverage with the title: "Clinton Panel on Race Urges Variety of Modest Measures" (Holmes 1998b, A1). The commission had compiled suggestions that had been made during the hearings, yet "many of the suggestions were endorsements of policy positions—like money for school construction projects in minority areas, that the Administration has already made" (Holmes 1998b, A1). Its boldest, though not necessarily groundbreaking, proposal was for the president to establish a permanent Presidential Council on Race. This idea was later abandoned.

Instead, the president downgraded this recommendation and decided instead to establish an Office of Race Relations within the White House (Ross 1999). One official (quoted in Ross 1999) said the fact that the president chose to set up an office on a smaller scale did not mean the effort was being given a lower priority. Yet a further indication of its status was the appointment of a deputy director of outreach to fill the position. The office setup was similar to the White House Office for Women's Initiatives and Outreach, which Clinton established in 1995 to ensure smoother handling of women's concerns. In short, the president's grand plan for a national dialogue on race had devolved into a White House interest-group outreach effort.

Asked in March 1999 when he expected to complete his report to the nation on his race initiative, Mr. Clinton replied (1999, 480; see also Babington 1999; Baker 1998; Clinton 2000, 2224): "I hope it will be ready sometime in the next couple of months." As of May 2001, the country still awaited the president's major statement, in book form, of his summing up of the initiative's efforts and its implications for One America.

President Clinton's Other Race Initiatives

It seems clear that the president's ambitious hopes for his race initiative went unrealized. The question is: why? Were his ambitions for the initiative too large? Perhaps, yet the importance of the subject would seem to suggest that it is better to fail nobly than never to attempt the difficult.

Was the matter too difficult to publicly engage? Surely, the matter is sensitive. Yet the national conversation on race produced moments of real clarity. This happened in the town meeting on bridging the racial divide in primary and secondary schools held in Annadale, Virginia. Here, knowledgeable and articulate individuals with diverse views discussed their positions on one issue (vouchers) or a focused set of issues (standards), with the result that the issues were laid out squarely for all to engage (Holmes 1997j, A24). It also happened, in a decidedly less public way, in the Christmas Eve White House meeting with critics of the president's racial policies.

So, discussion that informed and honestly laid out the bases of the different views on a focused set of questions or problems could have been one of the initiative's valuable contributions. Yet it wasn't. Part of the problem lay in the premature and shallow consensus the initiative often produced because of the way it had been structured.

Those problems started with the lack of true diversity on the board the president appointed. It had not one person who disagreed with his basic policies. As a result, the mindset was precast and the result was that the commission set out with a set of like-minded truths, not open-minded questions. It seems clear, too, that the televised forums of average citizens sharing their very subjective experiences, each of those unique, can take public clarity and understanding of the complicated issues involved only so far. These experiences did provide important lessons, as I will argue at the conclusion of this essay, but not in the way they were put to the initiative's use. As they were presented, they represented diverse experiential elements that were difficult to use in accumulating either increased understanding or common ground.

Certainly, little evidence emerged that these disparate personal stories were very useful for those in attendance, those who watched, or those who thought about these matters on a more regular basis. Moreover, there was never any sense of how the public forums, with their less focused remarks that had difficulty adding up top a true dialogue, could be integrated with the more focused professional presentations that, at their best, did clarify and sometimes even refine. Could all the different conversations, some televised and some not, over more than a year, in different localities, by different kinds of people, some on national TV, some on local TV, some on sports cable networks (Clinton 1998d, 642–48), some on PBS, on a wide range of topics, ever become a real national conversation about so diverse and sensitive a set of issues as are contained in the word "race"?

I think not. The attempt to reach into different venues has some initial appeal. Yet it ran the risk of giving the public a very thin slice of the overall conversation. One lesson of the race initiative may be that in a highly differentiated "public education market," sustained and focused efforts may be more successful than varied and diffuse ones. Yet, in some ways, this observation misses a core reason why the initiative floundered— and that is the ways in which the president chose to carry out his initiative.

Honesty and Race: The President's Leadership as a Model

The president, as noted, had substantial leadership capital on the race issue. Certainly any fair reading of his more substantive discussions on the issue with his conservative critics (1997l, 2085–93); Jim Lehrer of PBS (1998c, 104–15); or his analysis of the issues in bilingual education (1998b, 56) would show a man well versed in the details of the various issues involved in the debates. However, it would also show a president equally adept at agreeing with every side of any issue, at least while he was talking with the group with whom he expressed agreement.

Consider the debate about whether the race initiative should focus on black-white relations, or more specifically on the larger issues of diversity raised by immigration and mixed-race/mixed-ethnic identities. One of the commission's members, Angela Oh, had opted for the latter, but had been overruled by the chairman, Dr. Franklin, long-steeped in the former. Asked about it at a news conference, Mr. Clinton sided with Dr. Franklin. However, consider the following exchange between the president and Richard Rodriguez of the Pacific News Service on the McNeil-Lehrer show (1998e, 1336):

> *Mr. Rodriguez* [paraphrased by transcriber]: Mr. Rodriguez asserted his belief that race issues in the country have become more complicated and that the national discussion unified under "One America: The President's Initiative on Race," and its chair John Hope Franklin, has not kept pace with that complexity.
> *The President:* Well, I basically agree with you about that.

One wonders why, if the president agreed with that sentiment, he did not do more to help frame the discussion in those terms either through the composition of the board or its focus. Or consider the question of class versus race in the dilemmas that the commission addressed. The dialogue is between the president and Cynthia Tucker (1998e, 1337), a reporter for the *Atlanta Constitution*.

> *Ms. Tucker* [paraphrased by transcriber]: Ms. Tucker suggested that what many consider racial differences are actually class differences, that disproportionately poor blacks resent whites, and that working-class whites with stagnant or declining incomes blame whites, blacks, and immigrants . . .
> *The President:* There's no doubt about that.

So, it is about class, not race. Well, not quite. Consider the exchange that followed (1998e, 1337) with Kay James, Dean of the School of Government, Regent University:

> *Mr. Lehrer:* Cynthia, is the unfinished business still black and white?
> *Ms. James* [paraphrased by transcriber]: Ms. James answered that no matter how middle class a person becomes, if that person is black, he or she will experience discrimination. She suggested that topics of poverty and

class are worthy topics, but they should not take precedence over discussions of racism in America.

The President: Well, obviously I agree with that, or I wouldn't have set up this
initiative.

Here the president agreed that racism is so ingrained in American life
that even middle-class blacks will experience discrimination and that it is
the racism of this country that led him to set up the initiative. This is an
extraordinary statement. Did the president truly believe that all or most
middle-class blacks experience discrimination? Did he really believe that
it is America's continuing racism that is the basic reason why the country
needs a national conversation on race?

Even in these more substantive and focused settings, the president
seemed to exempt himself from his call for honest discussion. Earlier in
January 1998, the president and Mr. Lehrer (1998c, 112) had this exchange
on blunt talk and race:

Mr. Lehrer: Why are you having trouble getting some blunt talk started on
this?

The President: I don't know—we finally got some blunt talk on affirmative
action. And there were some pretty compelling stories told in Phoenix
the other day. But I would like to see some blunt talk.

Mr. Lehrer: On affirmative action?

The President: Well, we had some blunt talk on affirmative action.

This exchange took place after the president's widely discussed demand for a "yes or no" answer from Abigail Thernstrom to a complicated
affirmative-action question in his Akron national forum. It is certainly possible that the Akron exchange provided pause, not an invitation, to those
who might wish to voice a view at variance with those embodied in the
framework of most of the public forums.

Mr. Clinton seemed to lay great stress on the "compelling stories" (of
discrimination) told at the Phoenix public form. Yet, given this emphasis,
his response to another such story, from Elaine Chao, former head of
United Way, during the later Lehrer PBS special (1998e, 1338) was extremely odd. This exchange occurred just after the one noted above between the president and Cynthia James on racism in America:

Mr. Lehrer: Elaine Chao, where do the Asian Americans—what kinds of obstacles do they start out with compared to white Americans, or Native Americans or black Americans, whatever?

Ms. Chao [paraphrased by transcriber]: Ms. Chao noted the increased strain
in relations between races due to feelings of unequal treatment and the
Asian-American community's underrepresentation in the minority
figures.

The President: Give us an example.

Ms. Chao [paraphrased by transcriber]: Ms. Chao noted the story of an
Asian-American single mother in San Francisco whose son was denied
admission into a school, despite high test scores, because it already had
'too many' Asian Americans."

The President: Let's go back to what Kay said. What do you think the roots
of racism are?

Apparently, some stories are more compelling than others.

Critics like Roger Wilkins had criticized the president for his late start
in beginning this initiative. However, a late start is not the same as a bad
idea. Others noted that the race initiative was part of an effort by the president to burnish his legacy and reputation. While that doubtlessly played
a role, it is not in itself a valid criticism of the effort. A portion of self-
interest and public interest is certainly compatible in a political leader.

The larger problem was that the president was not forthright about
some very divisive racial issues that led to the initiative being needed and
a good idea. Consider the case of affirmative action. Perhaps nowhere was
the president's tendency to be on many sides of an issue more evident, and
less straightforward, than in his remarks on affirmative action.

What is very striking in reading through the president's views on these
issues is how extreme some of them are. Why was the president in favor of
affirmative action? Because, he said (1997b, 879), "It has given a whole generation of professionals in fields that used to be exclusive clubs, where people
like me got the benefit of 100% affirmative action." Translation: any white
could get into any school or profession simply because they were white.

Or consider the president's undeniably correct assertion that many affirmative-action students "work hard, they achieve, they go out and serve
the communities that need them for their expertise and role models."
However, he continues (1997b, 879) we must "not close the door on

them." Does that mean that if the relatively few schools that have high standards for admission take only those who qualify without race-related criterion, including minorities, others will be denied a place in a college or university?

Even worse, the president (1997b, 880) added, is that "minority enrollments in law school and other graduate programs are plummeting for the first time in decades. Soon, the same will likely happen in undergraduate education. We must not resegregate higher education." So, if the non–affirmative-action minority students get into undergraduate and graduate schools, does that mean the affirmative-action minority students will be able to do neither? Of course not: the overwhelming evidence is that there is ample room in American undergraduate and graduate programs of all types for students who wish to pursue their interests. The specter of resegregation is a strong symbol to raise. Modifying affirmative action is hardly a parallel to the Jim Crow laws that governed the southern racial caste system.

Mr. Clinton was certain (1997b, 880) that "the vast majority" of those who voted against preferences in California, "did it with the conviction that discrimination and isolation were no longer barriers to achievement." Or, perhaps, they were concerned about the ways in which racial preferences appeared to trump considerations of merit. Or perhaps they felt uncomfortable with giving some groups preferences, which had an adverse effect on other, noncovered groups.[13]

The president was not beyond introducing more sinister motives to those who didn't agree with his views. Asked about the vote to stop granting racial preferences in California higher education, the president replied (1997d, 1097), "I don't know why the people who promoted this in California think it's a good idea to have a segregated set of professional schools." Oddly enough, the president was aware of all these points. And, he was also aware that many of the criticisms made of affirmative action by its critics were right. At the outreach program the president held with critics of his policies, he listened to them the whole evening and then recounted his own efforts as governor to develop and enforce standards. He then said to his critics (1997l, 2092, emphasis mine), "*I basically think all that stuff you said was right.*" Earlier (1997l, 2088, emphasis mine), he had told them in response to a number of points they had raised, "But let me just say, first of all, *I think what you generally just said is absolutely right.*"

Was this an example of the president's well-known tendency (Renshon 1998b, 114–15, 315–16) to strongly agree with an opponent's position while he or she is present? Perhaps. However, the president was too well versed and intelligent to know that his critic's argument were not without substantial substantive merit. No, the answer lies elsewhere. Why does he say he supports these views given that he disagrees with his critics? His answer (1997l, 2092):

> "The reason I have consistently supported affirmative-action programs— [is that] I am sick and tired of people telling me that poor minority kids who live in desperate circumstances, that they can't make it. . . . I think we should give them a hand up to make it. The reason I have supported affirmative-action programs is . . . I don't want to see all these kids be sacrificed to a principle that I agree with, because the practice of life could not be fixed in time to give them a chance."

This was a noble sentiment, but it actually contradicts something the president had said a little earlier. Responding to a number of points made by his critics, the president said (1997l, 2088) that the major problem with his administration's economic affirmative-action plan was that it was hard for those businesses to "graduate out" from dependence on government preferences. A second problem he saw was that it did not "reach the vast majority of the people who have a problem because it doesn't reach down into basically the isolated urban areas with people in the economic underclass." These are exactly the same arguments made by critics of preferences policies in higher education.

Elsewhere (1998e, 1340) the president gave a different basic reason:

> The reason I've supported affirmative action . . . is that I think number one test scores, and all those so-called objective measures are somewhat ambiguous, and they're not perfect measures of peoples' capacity to grow. But secondly, and even more importantly, I think our society has a vested interest in having people from diverse backgrounds.

The president introduced (1997b, 879) his plan for a nationwide, honest conversation about race with a criticism of those "who would argue that scores on standardized tests should be the sole measure of qualification for admissions to colleges and universities." Few argue that; but on the usefulness of such tests, the president had this to say (1997l, 2091) in his conversations with his critics about test scores: "As a matter of fact, the test scores were . . . they have been a pretty good rough indicator."

Diversity is a laudable goal. It also has some advantages. However, the Supreme Court has ruled that it cannot be used as the basis for preferential public policies.

The president (1997b, 880) called on opponents of affirmative action to "come up with an alternative. I would embrace it if I could find a better way." In a later set of remarks he raised the bar considerably. On affirmative action he said (1997c, 889, emphasis mine),

> "Look if I didn't think we needed it, I'd be happy to shed it. If someone could offer me a credible alternative, and then test it for a year or so, and proved that it worked, I'd be happy to shed it." This would seem to be a formula for keeping the status quo.

Other Presidential Race Initiatives

A president's credibility and leadership capital not only rests on what he says, but also on what he does. The Nixon administration's suggestion that reporters watch what they do, not what they say, is the perfect example of negative leadership capital.

Yet, Mr. Clinton's words, too, must be considered in the context of his actions. I do not want to take up the argument here that the president's credibility in matters pertaining to his relationship with Ms. Lewinsky created a pall on his policy credibility, although I think that accurate. What I wish to consider here is the president's policy, integrity, and truthfulness. In these respects, not only were the president's words contradictory, but his actions also tended to be at variance with his stated beliefs.

The president (1997a, 509) noted that divisive issues like affirmative action, "need to be viewed through the prism of how we can preserve One America." He gave an impassioned plea for the need to "mend, not end" affirmative action. He realized, he said, that affirmative action had not "been perfect" (1997b, 879) but pointed to his efforts to fix it.

One of these steps was taken after the Supreme Court limited the use of preference programs unless a demonstrated history of past discrimination could be sustained. The president began a program to open minority set-aside contractual bidding to qualified disadvantaged "white-owned" business (Holmes 1997a, A1; see also Editorial 1997, 11). How did "whites" qualify? They had to have a net personal worth of less than $250,000, excluding their homes, and had to *prove* that they have been victims of chronic discrimination to qualify as "economically disadvantaged" for purposes of Section 8A small business awards based on affirmative action. I emphasize the word *prove* because other already "protected groups" are presumed to have met these criteria regardless of their personal experiences or economic circumstances.

Consider the administration's program to revise the rules that funneled billions of dollars in federal contracts to "small disadvantaged businesses." The proposed revisions would rely on a sector-by-sector analysis of the "available minority firms" ("capacity") in relation to the amount of dollars given to those firms ("utilization"). If there are more such firms than dollars given, those firms will be given bidding preferences (Broder 1997, A1).

The fallacy of this approach was quickly pointed out by critics of such policies (Sullivan and Clegg 1998, A13). First, the approach assumes that any disparity is the result of discrimination. It may well be a result of other factors—for example, undercapitalization or thin experience. Second, it assumes that the only way to fight discrimination is by adding in preferences.

Critics point to other problems as well. Among the other issues they note are these: (1) the program aggregates all racial and ethnic minorities and assumes if one is discriminated against, they all must be; (2) availability is treated differently for whites and blacks, since the former must have already bid on a project to be included in the "capacity" part, and the former need not; (3) the rules ignore subcontracting, a prime means of participation for new companies, which many minority firms do, though the Supreme Court ruled this kind of information must be taken into account when seeking evidence of discrimination; (4) the rules assume that all members of minorities are socially disadvantaged regardless of education, income, family background, and so on; (5) the system aims for racial balance, not the end of discrimination; and (6) the program awards preferences no matter how slight the disparity.

The president aptly warned Americans that our growing diversity is "potentially a powder keg of problems, and heartbreak and division and loss." He concluded (1997a, 509) that "how we handle it [our diversity] will determine, really—that single question may be the biggest determinant of what we will look like 50 years from now and what our position will be in the world." Three months later the Clinton administration decided against adding a "multiracial" category to the 2000 Census (Office of Management and Budget 1997). In doing so, the administration preserved, untouched for another decade at least, increasingly divisive single race/ethnicity categories. In the process, it took a step away from helping to nurture a "group that is quintessential American" and emphasizing the melting pot quality of the population rather than the distinctions (Eddings 1997): the very outcome that the president had said he championed.

President Clinton's legitimacy as a national leader of a frank dialogue was further compromised by the almost dizzying succession of his positions on the *Taxman* affirmative-action case settled by affirmation-action advocates before the Supreme Court could render its decision. He holds the unique and, from the perspective of principle and candor, dubious distinction of heading the only administration ever to submit three distinct briefs to the Supreme Court, each taking a decidedly different position.

Ms. Taxman, who is white, brought suit against the board of education that fired her to maintain diversity. President Bush originally entered the case on the side of Ms. Taxman's position. When he became president, Mr. Clinton reversed that position and had the Justice Department enter on the side of the board and against Ms. Taxman.

Then, after two lower courts decided in favor of Ms. Taxman, the administration changed course again, this time submitting a brief urging the Supreme Court not to hear the case because its circumstances made it unusual and a poor vehicle for fashioning an important decision in this area. The Court decided to take the case anyway and the Clinton administration then submitted its third brief in the same case, this time on Ms. Taxman's side, but with a twist.

The administration then argued that only in case of a proven history of discrimination could the desire to increase diversity be a legitimate standard to use, but it also argued that the standard might be used in the absence of such a proven history when there was a tangible purpose for doing so, like a police or corrections department that might wish more diversity to better accomplish its mission. Eventually, the case was settled out of court by affirmative-action advocates funding the settlement with Ms. Taxman.

The President's Initiative on Race suggests that a symbolic focus on hard issues is no substitute for real and honest engagement. Lofty aspirations don't automatically translate into leadership capital. Instead, the example suggests that it is in the *how*, not necessarily the *what*, that leadership capital is accumulated.

President Clinton's multiple, conflicting, and seemingly strategic positions in this case made it hard to know just which conviction he was demonstrating the courage of given that there were three different ones from which to choose.

One America: In Retrospect

The President's Initiative on Race was an idea with a laudable purpose. It is questionable whether it might have succeeded in the form it took, even without the flaws in framing and process that became clear as it unfolded. Certainly, the many problems of the initiative were compounded by the president's failure to be honest with the public about what he truly believed.

If he understood the flaws in affirmative-action programs, why not tell the public so that the debate could begin from a different starting point? By not doing so, and being inconsistent, and sometimes evasive, his conversation began and stayed at the same level of impasse as advocates and foes debated if there were problems, and if so, what they were.

If he understood that the issues facing America were more than "black-white" relations, why not say so and move the debate on to those more immediate, pressing, and relevant issues? By not doing so directly and *consistently*, the president allowed those issues to be muddled, not clarified. As a result, the conversation never reached the level of clarity that was one of its main goals.

If the president really wanted an honest dialogue, why didn't he model it with his own appointments to the board and his own treatment of his opponents? Did confronting Abigail Thernstom on national television with his "yes or no" demands of a single answer to a complex question model the respect for opposing views that he said he wanted? Did it give others who had different views than those expressed the sense that it was safe to dissent?

There is one other fact that needs to be mentioned here and that is the president's impeachment. I am not referring to his relationship to Ms. Lewinsky, but rather to the fact that the report from his commission was given to the president almost at the same time that his four-hour, videotaped grand jury testimony about lying under oath in the Monica Lewinsky case was aired to the nation. That same day, more than 3,000 pages of documentation from the independent council's investigation were released by Congress (Simpson, Taylor, and Rogers 1998, A3).

The president's initiative was unfolding as, behind the scenes, the president was fully engaged in saving his presidency. And one of the linchpins of his effort was the overwhelming support he received from Americans of African descent (Sack 1998, A1). The figures are startling. In February 1997 as the events leading to his impeachment were unfolding, 93 percent of African Americans approved of the president's job performance, while 63 percent of whites did. Ninety-one percent of African Americans had a favorable view of Mr. Clinton; 52 percent of whites did. Only 5 percent of African Americans thought the president was to blame for his problems, while 85 percent said his enemies were at fault. The respective figures for whites were 38 percent and 51 percent. And finally, and perhaps most puzzling, 80 percent of African Americans thought the president had the "moral values that most Americans try to live by," while only 34 of whites thought so.

I am not imputing cynicism to the president, but I think it fair to say that President Clinton always had a very high level of self-interest. Even under normal circumstances, there have been many questions raised about his tendency to put his own self-interest before the public's, or to mask the former by appeals to the latter. It is certainly understandable that in fighting for his political life, he would be even more tempted to put his own interests before those of having a successful commission. It would be a great deal to ask of any leader, and perhaps particularly Mr. Clinton, to put the work of the commission, however laudable, ahead of his political survival.

One America = The Voices of Individualism?

Paradoxically, there were some important things to be learned from the public forums that were derided as "Oprah-like." The Akron meeting is a good case in point. Woven throughout the tales and complaints of unfair treatment was another story, equally compelling and perhaps more in keeping with the traditions of the country.

Vanessa Cordero (Clinton 1997j, 1964–65) asked the group to remember that "this is not black and white in America . . . it's hurt me all these years that I've been in the United States, since 1957, that all I hear is black issues and white issues." Another young lady had a similar concern. Referring to the segregation she witnessed on her college campus, she asked, "White people hang out here and black people hang out there. And as a Hispanic and coming from a Mexican background, where does that put me? I'm neither one."

McHoughton Chambers (Clinton 1997j, 1964), the biracial child of a mixed marriage, struggled to find his identity. He expressed his concern that people only see half of who he is, and that they often neglect to see the other side of his biracial makeup. Another student, Erika Sanders (Clinton 1997j, 1963), eloquently evoked (emphasis mine) her experiences as a black student in an all-white school:

> "I feel like I live in two different worlds. When I go to school, sometimes *I feel the burden to speak for all of black America.* And slowly, *I'm helping my class-mates to realize that I'm not all of black America, I'm Erika.*"

Anna Arroyo (Clinton 1997j, 1964) recalled her experience as a Puerto Rican in a college course on Latin America. She related that her class-mates thought that, because of her origin, she should be able to speak authoritatively on all Latin cultures. However,

> "What people don't understand is that I'm not Peruvian; I'm not Mexican. I don't understand their culture. I'm Puerto Rican and all I know is Puerto Rico."

What do all these narratives have in common? They share something extremely basic, yet very profound. The speakers all asked, each in their own way, to be taken as the unique persons that they are. They did not ask to be representatives of groups. Ms. Sanders does not want to have to speak for all African Americans; she would much prefer that her friends get to know her as who she is: Erika. Ms. Arroyo does not wish to be known by the fact that she is Hispanic, but rather by her *particular experiences and identification.* Mr. Chambers does not wish to be known for one-half of his biracial identity, whichever half is emphasized. He wants to be known as who he is: both.

Perhaps paradoxically, it seems that the road to One America lies through the path of individualism.

Notes

1. Morin (1999, 34) makes use of data collected from the National Commission on Civic Renewal (NCCR) and notes that some changes since 1994 "have been nothing short of astonishing." He goes on to note that between 1994 and 1997, the number of people who said they trusted government increased from 29 to 38 percent. Left unnoted is that fact that in 1956, that number was 78 percent.

Moreover, even the rise in trust in government is somewhat paradoxical given that the proportion of Americans who voted, surely one measure of their trust in government, fell from 46.9 percent in 1992 to 42.6 percent in 1996 and 1998.

The data from which Morin draws his optimism are themselves only marginally so. First, the report uses 1974 as the baseline, which it sets equal to zero, and which it then uses to compare the years that follow. This does result in modest improvements.

However, it is highly questionable whether 1974 is the appropriate baseline, since it is a post-1960s measurement start and that period was the most volatile for all the items the scales measures. Not surprisingly, the study quietly notes (NCCR 1999, 11) that "our best estimate shows that INCH (Index of National Civic Health) was far higher in previous decades." The study further notes (1999, 7) that over the last three years, "the largest improvements have come in the areas of trust and personal security."

In other words, the items that measure sense of security and trust have modestly increased (are they related?), but the other items that go into the composite index have not. Moreover, the results are still well below the levels of all those items in 1984 and those of course are well below the levels of those items in 1974 and certainly well below the levels during the 1950s.

The complete report may be found at *http://www.puaf.umd.edu/civicrenewal/*.

2. The complete report is available at *http://www.people-press.org/mill1rpt*.

3. A lead story in *The New York Times*, for example, indicated that business dominated Congress's last session ("Congress Leaves Business Lobbies Almost All Smiles"). Actually, the story showed that business groups won a few modest victories and played defense on the minimum wage and other issues.

4. For doubts about the "culture war" hypothesis see Wilson (1995) and Williams (1997). The titles of their books reflect both their premises and conclusions. Hunter's response to some of these critics of his "culture war" thesis can found in a later paper (Hunter 1996).

5. The case material and analysis in this section draws on a variety of data, including event transcripts, news accounts, survey data, and the words of the principles themselves. For a detailed consideration of the advantages and imitations of each kind of data and their usefulness in a composite analysis, see Renshon (1998a, 405–08).

6. Elsewhere, I (Renshon 1998b, 3–33) have described the basic public dilemma as a fundamental unresolved question concerning public psychology and gov-

ernance facing the president on taking office. It is not a specific question about public policy, but rather the public's psychological connections to its institutions, leaders, and political process. This unresolved public concern underlies and frames more specific policy debates.

7. White House material accompanying the initiative lists a fifth purpose, "to articulate the President's vision of a just, unified America." See "Background and Points of Progress" (Washington, D.C., no date, 2).

8. The questions had come up in various forums, but were put to the president directly in an interview (1997e, 1187–88) in the initiative's early days:

> *Mr. Smiley:* Your challenge to America to have a conversation about race has certainly spun of a number of conversations, including conversations about slavery and reparations. And I'm wondering, since you've had more time to reflect, [if] you think an apology to African Americans is warranted. And specifically, what do you think of the at least having a commission to study the feasibility of reparations, regardless to what (sic) your opinion is?
>
> *The President:* Well, I don't believe that—what I think I should do now is let the advisory board do its work and see what they have to say about the apology issue and all the related issues.

9. I am indebted to Dr. William Friedman of *Public Agenda* for making these data available.

10. They included former governors Thomas Kean of New Jersey (Republican) and William Winter of Mississippi (Democrat); Linda Chavez Thompson of the AFL-CIO; the Reverend Suzan D. Johnson Cook, a minister from the Bronx, New York; Angela Oh, a Los Angeles attorney and community leader; Robert Thompson, CEO of Nissan, U.S.A.; and the chair Professor John Hope Franklin of Duke University.

In the descriptions of the panel members and some excerpts from their remarks during the first meeting (Holmes 1997b, A1), it is clear that there is very little divergence in basic views among the board members.

11. In fact this proved to be truer of the community meetings than it was of meetings that focused on particular issues, like health or poverty. Yet, even in the latter, those invited to speak were skewed in the direction of the commission's basic assumptions and preferences regarding the issues.

On the difference between community-based meetings and those with more specialized audiences, compare the community meeting that took place in Phoenix on the morning of January 14, 1998, with the more focused meeting on race in the workplace that took place that afternoon. Transcripts of those meetings (November 1, 2000) and the other public meetings of the race initiative can be found online at *http://www.whitehouse.gov/Initiatives/OneAmerica/ america.html*.

12. A somewhat sobering, some would say chilling, observation about the program can be found in Rosin (1997, 29). She reports that the program was

coercive and measured "change in results in a desired direction." What is the desired direction? Rosin writes, "One question measured support for affirmative action. If, by the end of the program you showed stronger support, that meant you had changed in the desirable direction. If by the end of the program you showed less support for affirmative action, but loved your fellow man even more, well, that just didn't count as a better attitude."

13. The president made the same kind of characterization of those who opposed bilingual education in California. Speaking of that referendum, he said, "Now, . . . the initial polling . . . is deeply troubling to defenders of bilingual education because the initial polling has 70 percent of Hispanic voters voting for the initiative. Now, what does that mean? That doesn't mean they necessarily understand the implications of this initiative and that they want to vote for it" (1998b, 56).

References

Allen, Mike. "Democrats Stroke Hollywood at Dinner." *The Washington Post* (September 20, 2000): A19.

Allen, Mike, and Ellen Nakashima. "Clinton, Gore Hit Hollywood Marketing." *The Washington Post* (September 12, 2000): A1.

Babington, Charles. "A Grand Plan Loses Steam." *The Washington Post Weekly Edition* (June 28, 1999): 29.

Baker, Peter. "An Initiative That's Going Nowhere Fast." *The Washington Post Weekly Edition* (October 13, 1998): 10.

———. "A Splinter on the Race Advisory Board." *The Washington Post* (July 15, 1997): A4.

———. "We've Got to Talk." *The New York Times* (June 17, 1997): A21.

Baker, Peter, and Michael A. Fletcher. "Clinton's Town Hall Taking Discussion of Race into Sports Arena." *The Washington Post* (April 14, 1998): A2.

Begard, Paul. "Clinton Sets Up Session on Race with Critics." *The Washington Times* (December 11, 1997): A1.

Bell, Daniel. *The Cultural Contradictions of Capitalism.* Basic Books: New York, 1976.

Bennet, James. "Clinton, at Meeting on Race, Struggles to Sharpen Debate." *The New York Times* (December 4, 1997a): A1.

———. "Clinton Debates Conservatives on Racial Issues." *The New York Times* (December 20, 1997b): A1.

Berry, Jeffrey M. *The New Liberalism: The Rising Power of Citizen Groups.* Washington, D.C.: The Brookings Institution, 1999.

Blow, Richard. "Race Wars at the White House." *George* (March 1998).

Bork, Robert. *Slouching Towards Gomorrah.* New York: HarperCollins, 1997.

Branegan, Jay. "Bill's Block." *Time* (December 13, 1999): 73.

Broder, John M. "U.S. Readies Rules Over Preferences Aiding Minorities." *The New York Times* (May 6, 1997): A1.

Charles, Mark. "Americans Remain Wary of Washington." *The Wall Street Journal* (December 23, 1997): A14.

Citrin, Jack, Beth Reingold, and Donald P. Green. "American Identity and the Politics of Ethnic Change." *Journal of Politics* 52, no. 4 (1990): 1124–54.

Clinton, William J. "Remarks and Question and Answer Session with the American Society of Newspaper Editors" (April 11, 1997). *Weekly Compilation of Presidential Documents* 14, April, 33:15, 1997a, 501–10.

———. "Remarks at the University of California at San Diego Commencement Ceremony" (June 14, 1997). *Weekly Compilation of Presidential Documents* 23, June, 33:25, 1997b, 876–82.

———. "Remarks at a Democratic National Committee Dinner" (June 16, 1997). *Weekly Compilation of Presidential Documents* 23, June, 33:25, 1997c, 883–94.

———. "Remarks and Question and Answer Session with the National Association of Black Journalists in Chicago, Illinois" (July 17, 1997). *Weekly Compilation of Presidential Documents* 21, July, 33:29, 1997d, 1092–1101.

———. "Interview with Tavis Smiley of Black Entertainment Television" (August 4, 1997). *Weekly Compilation of Presidential Documents* 11, August, 33:32, 1997e, 1184—89.

———. "Remarks at American University" (September 9, 1997). *Weekly Compilation of Presidential Documents* 15, September, 33:37, 1997f, 1296–1308.

———. "Remarks at a Democratic Business Council Dinner" (September 9, 1997). *Weekly Compilation of Presidential Documents* 15, September, 33:37, 1997g, 1304–08.

———. "Remarks Prior to a Meeting with the President's Advisory Board on Race" (September 30, 1997). *Weekly Compilation of Presidential Documents* 6, October, 33:40, 1997h, 1462–63.

———. "Interview With Jodi Enda of Knight-Ridder Newspapers" (December 1, 1997). *Weekly Compilation of Presidential Documents* 8, December, 33:49, 1997i, 1943–48.

———. "Remarks in a Roundtable Discussion on Race in Akron" (December 3, 1997). *Weekly Compilation of Presidential Documents* 8, December, 33:49, 1997j, 1959–69.

———. "The President's News Conference" (December 16, 1997). *Weekly Compilation of Presidential Documents* 22, December, 33:51, 1997k, 2049–69.

———. "Remarks in an Outreach Meeting with Conservatives on the Race Initiative" (December 19, 1997). *Weekly Compilation of Presidential Documents* 22, December, 33:51, 1997l, 2085–93.

———. "Remarks and a Question and Answer Session at a Democratic National Committee Dinner" (January 8, 1998). *Weekly Compilation of Presidential Documents* 12, January, 34:2, 1998a, 21–27.

———. "Remarks on an Outreach Meeting on the Race Initiative" (January 12, 1998). *Weekly Compilation of Presidential Documents* 19, January, 34:3, 1998b, 50–57.

———. "Interview with Jim Lehrer of the PBS 'News Hour'" (January 21,

1998). *Weekly Compilation of Presidential Documents* 26, January, 34:4, 1998c, 104–115.

———. "Remarks at the ESPN Townhall Meeting on Race Relations in Houston" (April 1, 1998). *Weekly Compilation of Presidential Documents* 20, April, 34:16, 1998d, 642–48.

———. "Remarks in the 'Presidential Dialogue on Race' on PBS" (July 13, 1998). *Weekly Compilation of Presidential Documents* 8, July, 34:28, 1998e, 1336–44.

———. "The President's News Conference" (March 26, 1999). *Weekly Compilation of Presidential Documents* 19, March, 35:12, 1999, 471–84.

———. "Remarks on Departure for Dallas, Texas, and an Exchange with Reporters" (September 27, 2000). *Weekly Compilation of Presidential Documents* 2, October, 36:39, 2000, 222–25.

DiMaggio, Paul, John Evans, and Bethany Bryson. "Have American Social Attitudes Become More Polarized?" *American Journal of Sociology* 102, no. 3 (1996): 444–96.

Easterbrook, Greg. "America the O.K.," *The New Republic* (January 4 and 11, 1999): 19–25.

Eddings, Jerelyn. "Counting a 'New' Type of American: The Dicey Politics of Creating a Multiracial Category in the Census." *U.S. News and World Report* (July 14, 1997): 22–23.

Editorial. "Stifling the Race Debate." *The New York Times* (November 21, 1997a): A34.

Editorial. "Talking about Race in Akron." *The New York Times* (December 5, 1997b): A30.

Editorial. "Whitewash." *The New Republic* (September 22, 1997): 11.

Elshtain, Jean B. *Who Are We? Critical Reflections and Hopeful Possibilities.* Grand Rapids, Mich.: William D. Eerdmans, 2000.

"Excerpts from Round Table with Opponents of Racial Preferences." *The New York Times* (December 22, 1997): A24.

Fletcher, Michael A., and Dan Baltz. "Race Relations Initiative May Pose Risks for Clinton." *The Washington Post* (June 12, 1997): A1.

Frisby, Michael K. "White House Reworks Troubled Race Initiative as President Heads for a Town Meeting in Ohio." *The Wall Street Journal* (December 3, 1997a): A24.

———. "Race Course: Clinton Stays Popular with Blacks in Spite of Fraying of Safety Net." *Wall Street Journal* (June 13, 1997b): A1.

Greenfield, Meg. "The Colin Powell Test." *Newsweek* (December 15, 1997): 84.

Harris, John. "What's a President to Do?" *The Washington Post* (September 15, 1996): A12.

Holmes, Steven A. "After March, Lawmakers Seek Commission on Race Relations." *The New York Times* (October 18, 1995): A1.

———. "U.S. Acts to Open Minority Program to White Bidders." *New York Times* (August 15, 1997a): A1.

————. "Scholar Takes on His Toughest Study of Race." *The New York Times* (September 28, 1997b): A1.

————. "Talks about Race Get an Early Start." *The New York Times* (September 28, 1997c): A28.

————. "President Nudges His Race Panel to Take Action." *The New York Times* (October 1, 1997d): A23.

————. "Critics Say Clinton Panel about Race Lacks Focus." *The New York Times* (October 12, 1997e): A17.

————. "Race Panel Excludes Critics of Affirmative Action Plans." *The New York Times* (November 19, 1997f): A24.

————. "Clinton Panel on Race Relations Is Itself Biased, Gingrich Says." *The New York Times* (November 21, 1997g): A30.

————. "Policy Opponent to Join Clinton at Race Forum." *The New York Times* (November 27, 1997h): A29.

————. "In Akron, Dialogue But Few Changes." *The New York Times* (December 4, 1997i): A26.

————. "Conservatives' Voices Enter Clinton's Dialogue on Race." *The New York Times* (December 17, 1997j): A24.

————. "Clinton to Meet Conservatives." *The New York Times* (December 11, 1997k): A23.

————. "Race Advisory Panel Gives Report to Clinton." *The New York Times* (September 19, 1998a): A1.

————. "Clinton Panel on Race Urges Variety of Modest Measures." *The New York Times* (September 18, 1998b): A1.

Holmes, Steven A., and James Bennet. "A Renewed Sense of Purpose for Clinton's Panel on Race." *The New York Times* (January 14, 1998): A1.

Hunt, Albert R. "The Race Initiative: Tough but Worth the Effort." *The Wall Street Journal* (December 11, 1997): A23.

Hunter, James Davidson. *Culture Wars: The Struggle to Define America.* New York: Basic Books, 1991.

————. "Reflections on the Culture Wars Hypothesis." In *The American Culture Wars: Current Contests and Future Prospects,* ed. James L. Nolan, Jr. (Charlottesville: University of Virginia Press, 1996), 243–56.

Kelly, Michael. "The Great Divider." *The New Republic.* no. 6 (July 7, 1997): 41–42.

Kennedy, Randall. "Clinton Must Resist Impulse to Control the Race Debate." *The Washington Post* (June 15, 1997): C1.

Lee, Felicia R. "The Honest Dialogue That Is Neither." *The New York Times* (December 7, 1997): W 5.

Lemann, Nicholas. "Clinton the Great Communicator." *The New York Times* (January 20, 1997): A17.

Levin, Arthur. "President's Essay." In *Teacher's College Annual Report: Diversity* (1999): 1–13.

Lowi, Theodore J. *The End of Liberalism: Ideology, Policy, and the Crisis of Public Authority*. New York: Norton, 1969.

Mallaby, Sebastian. "Victim of His Success." *The Washington Post* (September 18, 2000): A19.

Morin, Richard. "Back to the Sixties." *The Washington Post Weekly Edition* (August 23, 1999): A34.

National Commission on Civic Renewal. "The Index of National Civic Health." College Park, Md., 1999, 1–17.

Neal, Terry M., and Ceci Connolly. "Hollywood Draws Cash For Gore, Ire in GOP." *The Washington Post* (September 14, 2000): A1.

Nye, Joseph F., Jr., Philip D. Zelikow, and David C. King, eds. *Why People Don't Trust Government*. Cambridge, Mass.: Harvard University Press, 1997.

Office of Management and Budget. 1997. "Recommendations from the Interagency Committee for the Review of the Racial and Ethnic Standards to the Office of Management and Budget Concerning Changes to the Standards for the Classification of Federal Data on Race and Ethnicity; Notice." *Federal Register*. Vol. 62, no. 131 (July 9, 1997): 36873–946.

Patterson, Orlando. *The Order of Integration*. Washington, D.C.: Civitas, 1997.

Pew Research Center for the People and the Press. "Technology Triumphs, Morality Falters" (July 13, 1999).

———. "Deconstructing Distrust: How Americans View Government" (March 10, 1988).

Powell, Colin. *My American Journey*. New York: Random House, 1999.

Public Agenda. "Time to Move On: African-American and White Parents Set an Agenda for Public Schools." New York, 1998a, 1–51.

———. "Time to Move On: Technical Appendix." New York, 1998b, 1–48.

Renshon, Stanley A. *The Psychological Assessment of Presidential Candidates*. New York: Routledge, 1998a.

———. *High Hopes: The Clinton Presidency and the Politics of Ambition*. New York: Routledge, 1998b.

———. "Political Leadership as Social Capital: Governing in a Divided National Culture." *Political Psychology* 21, no. 1 (2000): 199–236.

Review and Outlook. "Yes or No, Mr. President?" *The Wall Street Journal* (December 5, 1997): A18.

Rosin, Hanna. "Small Talk." *New York*. (December 15, 1997): 28–29.

Ross, Sonya. "President to Establish Race Office." *Associated Press* (February 4, 1999).

Sack, Kevin. "Blacks Stand by a President Who 'Has Been There for Us.'" *The New York Times* (September 19, 1998): A1.

———. "Gore Takes Tough Stand on Violent Entertainment." *The New York Times* (September 11, 2000): A1.

Samuelson, Robert J. "Stealth Power Brokers." *The Washington Post* (December 8, 1999): A33.

Seelye, Katherine Q. "Before a Hollywood Crowd, Democrats Lower the Volume." *The New York Times* (September 20, 2000): A1.

Simpson, Glenn R., Jeffrey Taylor, and David Rogers. "New Evidence Complicates Clinton Case." *The Wall Street Journal* (September 23, 1998): A3.

Sleeper, Jim. *The Closest of Strangers: Liberalism and the Politics of Race in New York.* New York: Norton, 1990.

———. *Liberal Racism.* New York: Penguin, 1997.

Sleven, Peter. "Violent Crime Down 10% in 1999." *The Washington Post* (August 28, 2000): A2.

Stern, Christopher. "FTC Finds Hollywood Aims Violence at Kids." *The Washington Post* (September 11, 2000): A1.

Sullivan, John, and Roger Clegg. "More Preferences for Minority Business." *The Wall Street Journal* (August 24, 1998): A13.

Taylor, Charles. *Multiculturalism and the "Politics of Recognition."* Princeton, N.J.: Princeton University Press, 1992.

Thernstrom, Abigail. "Going Toe to Toe with Bill." *Newsweek* (December 15, 1997): 35.

Wachtel, Paul. *The Poverty of Affluence.* New York: Basic Books, 1994.

Wayne, Steven, G. C. MacKenzie, D. M. O'Brien, and R. L. Cole. *The Politics of American Government.* New York: St. Martins, 1999.

Williams, Rhys H., ed. *Culture Wars in American Politics: Critical Reviews of a Popular Myth.* New York: Aldine De Gruyter, 1997.

Wilson, John K. *The Myth of Political Correctness: The Conservative Attack on Higher Education.* Durham, N.C.: Duke University Press, 1995.

Wolfe, Alan. *Marginalized in the Middle.* Chicago: University of Chicago Press, 1996.

———. *One Nation, After All.* Chicago: University of Chicago Press, 1998.

Wysocki, Bernard, Jr. "Americans Decry Moral Decline." *The Wall Street Journal* (June 24, 1999): A9.

Contributors

Jack Citrin is Professor of Political Science at the University of California, Berkeley. He received his B.A. and M.A. degrees from McGill University and his Ph.D. from the University of California, Berkeley, in 1970. His research centers on the dynamics of political culture in advanced industrial democracies and he has written widely on political trust and legitimacy, the tax revolt, and, most recently, on American national identity. He is the author of *The Politics of Disaffection among British and American Youth* (1976) and *Tax Revolt: Something for Nothing in California* (1985). His current project, in collaboration with David O. Sears, is the forthcoming book *The Politics of Multiculturalism: Challenge to American Identity*.

Richard D. Kahlenberg is a Senior Fellow at The Century Foundation (formerly the Twentieth Century Fund), where he writes about education, equal opportunity, and civil rights. He graduated magna cum laude from Harvard College in 1985 and cum laude from Harvard Law School in 1989. He is the author of *Broken Contract: A Memoir of Harvard Law School* (Hill and Wang, 1992), *The Remedy: Class, Race and Affirmative Action* (Basic Books, 1996), and *All Together Now: Creating Middle Class Schools through Public School Choice* (Brookings Institution, 2001). He is also the editor of *A Nation at Risk: Preserving Public Education as an Engine for Social Mobility* (Century Foundation, 2000). Mr. Kahlenberg's analyses have been published in *The New York Times*, *The Washington Post*, *The Wall Street Journal*, and *The New Republic*. He has been a guest on ABC's *Nightline*, CNN, C-SPAN, MSNBC's *InterNight with Katie Couric*, and National Public Radio.

Richard J. Payne is Distinguished Professor of Political Science at the Illinois State University Department of Political Science and a Distinguished Ph.D. alumnus of Howard University. He was a Visiting Scholar at the Center for International Affairs at Harvard University, a Fulbright Scholar, a Ford Foundation Fellow, and a member of the Council of the American Political Science Association. He is the author of six books, including *Getting Beyond Race: The Changing American Culture* (1998) and *The Clash with Distant Cultures: Values, Interests, and Force in American Foreign Policy* (1995). His articles have appeared in *The Journal of Politics*, *The Journal of Developing Areas*, and other publications.

Noah M. J. Pickus is Assistant Professor in the Terry Sanford Institute of Public Policy and the Department of Political Science at Duke University. He received his Ph.D. in Politics from Princeton University. His publications include essays on American political thought, immigration and citizenship, religion and politics, and ethics and public policy. He is the primary author of *Becoming American/America Becoming: The Final Report of the Duke Workshop on Immigration and Citizenship* (1998) and the editor of *Immigration and Citizenship in the Twenty-First Century* (1998). He has advised Pricewaterhouse Coopers on its redesign of the naturalization process and has served as a Program Consultant for the A. Philip Randolph Education Fund. He is completing a book on immigration and citizenship in American history.

Stanley A. Renshon is Professor of Political Science at The City University of New York and a certified psychoanalyst. He has authored over sixty articles and seven books, including *Psychological Needs and Political Behavior; Handbook of Political Socialization: Theory and Research; The Political Psychology of the Gulf War: Leaders, Publics, and the Process of Conflict; The Clinton Presidency: Campaigning, Governing, and the Psychology of Leadership; The Psychological Assessment of Presidential Candidates;* and *Political Psychology: Cultural and Cross-Cultural Foundations.* His psychological biography of William J. Clinton, *High Hopes: The Clinton Presidency and the Politics of Ambition* (Routledge 1998), won the Richard E. Neustadt Award for the best book on the presidency and the National Association for the Advancement of Psychoanalysis Gravida Award for the best psychoanalytic biography.

Russell L. Riley is Assistant Professor and Research Fellow with the White Burkett Miller Center of Public Affairs at the University of Virginia. He currently helps direct the Center's oral history project of the American presidency. He has taught at Georgetown University and the University of Pennsylvania, and has served as academic program director with the Salzburg Seminar in American Studies in Austria. He is the author of *The Presidency and the Politics of Racial Inequality: Nation-Keeping from 1831–1965* (Columbia University Press, 1999) and also has published essays on presidential leadership, American political parties, and race. Before turning to the academy, Riley was actively involved in politics in Alabama, serving as the chief legislative assistant to the lieutenant governor from 1979 to 1983. He received a gubernatorial appointment to the Alabama Environmental Management Commission in 1982, and served on that policymaking and oversight body for three years.

John David Skrentny received a Ph.D. in Sociology from Harvard University in 1994 and is Associate Professor of Sociology at the University of California, San Diego. His book, *The Ironies of Affirmative Action: Politics, Culture, and Justice in America* (University of Chicago Press, 1996), examines the origins and politics of this controversial policy. He also edited a volume, *Color Lines: Affirmative Action, Immigration, and Civil Rights Options for America* (University of Chicago Press, 2001), which explores the impact of the new immigration on civil rights policies and affirmative action in the United States and abroad. Skrentny has published several articles on a variety of topics, including the administrative politics of civil rights, women's rights, the impact of the cold war on the civil rights movement, welfare reform in the states, and crossnational variations in concern for the environment. He is currently finishing a book manuscript on the "minority rights revolution" of the 1965–75 period.

Jim Sleeper, a writer on American racial politics and civic culture, is the author of *The Closest of Strangers* (Norton, 1990) and *Liberal Racism* (Penguin, 1998). His reportage has appeared in *Harper's, The New Yorker, The Washington Monthly*, and newspapers and other publications, and he is an occasional commentator on National Public Radio's "All Things Considered." In the mid-1990s he chronicled the waning of "rainbow" electoral politics in New York and other cities as a columnist for the New York *Daily News* and a contributor to *The New Republic*. A native of Springfield, Massachusetts, and a 1969 graduate of Yale College, Sleeper received his doctorate in education from Harvard and has taught seminars on new conceptions of American national identity and on journalism and politics at Yale. He is currently at work on a book about the recent evolution and prospects of American national identity.

Abigail Thernstrom received her Ph.D. in Political Science from Harvard University in 1975 and is now a Senior Fellow at the Manhattan Institute, a member of the United States Commission on Civil Rights, and a member of the Massachusetts State Board of Education. She is the author of *Whose Votes Count: Affirmative Action and Minority Voting Rights* (Harvard University Press, 1987), which was a Twentieth Century Fund study and won four major awards. She is, more recently, the coauthor of the widely acclaimed and debated study *America in Black and White: One Nation Indivisible* (Simon and Schuster, 1997). She is a frequent contributor to a number of national newspapers and journals of political analyses, including *The New Republic, Commentary, The New York Times*, and *The Wall Street Journal*. She was one of three authors invited to participate in President Bill Clinton's first "town meeting" on race, where she engaged in a spirited personal debate with the president that made front-page news.

Stephan Thernstrom is the Winthrop Professor of History at Harvard University. He is the editor of *The Harvard Encyclopedia of American Ethnic Groups* (Harvard/Belknap Press, 1980); *Poverty and Progress: Social Mobility in a Nineteenth Century City* (Harvard University Press, 1964); *History of the American People, Vol. I: to 1877* (Harcourt Brace, 1984); and *History of the American People, Vol. II: Since 1865* (Harcourt Brace, 1984). He also is the author of *The Other Bostonians: Poverty and Progress in an American Metropolis* (Harvard University Press, 1973), which won the Bancroft Prize. Most recently he is the coauthor, along with his wife, Abigail, of *America in Black and White: One Nation Indivisible* (Simon and Schuster, 1997). He has written widely on affirmative action, race relations, and ethnicity in America for major national newspapers and journals of opinion.

Index